JOHN 1–10

WISDOM COMMENTARY

Volume 44A

John 1–10

Mary L. Coloe, PBVM

Mary Ann Beavis
Volume Editor

Barbara E. Reid, OP
General Editor

A Michael Glazier Book

LITURGICAL PRESS
Collegeville, Minnesota

www.litpress.org

A Michael Glazier Book published by Liturgical Press

1   2   3   4   5   6   7   8   9

Library of Congress Cataloging-in-Publication Data

Names: Coloe, Mary L., 1949– author. | Beavis, Mary Ann, editor. | Reid, Barbara E., editor.
Title: John / Mary L. Coloe, PBVM ; Mary Ann Beavis, volume editor ; Barbara E. Reid, OP, general editor.
Description: Collegeville, Minnesota : Liturgical Press, [2021] | Series: Wisdom commentary ; volume 44A-44B | "A Michael Glazier book." | Includes bibliographical references and index. | Contents: John 1-10 — John 11-21. | Summary: "This commentary on the Gospel of John provides a feminist interpretation of Scripture in serious, scholarly engagement with the whole text, not only those texts that explicitly mention women. It addresses not only issues of gender but also those of power, authority, ethnicity, racism, and classism"— Provided by publisher.
Identifiers: LCCN 2021003113 (print) | LCCN 2021003114 (ebook) | ISBN 9780814681688 (hardcover) | ISBN 9780814688144 (hardcover) | ISBN 9780814681930 (epub) | ISBN 9780814681930 (mobi) | ISBN 9780814681930 (pdf) | ISBN 9780814688397 (epub) | ISBN 9780814688397 (mobi) | ISBN 9780814688397 (pdf)
Subjects: LCSH: Bible. John—Commentaries. | Bible. John—Feminist criticism.
Classification: LCC BS2615.53 .C65 2021 (print) | LCC BS2615.53 (ebook) | DDC 226.5/07—dc23
LC record available at https://lccn.loc.gov/2021003113
LC ebook record available at https://lccn.loc.gov/2021003114

With gratitude for the Wisdom people
who have been my
teachers, mentors, and friends.

ὑμᾶς δὲ εἴρηκα φίλους

Sandra M. Schneiders, IHM; Francis J. Moloney, SDB;
Dorothy A. Lee; and Brendan Byrne, SJ.

Contents

Abbreviations

AB	Anchor Bible
ABD	*Anchor Bible Dictionary.* Edited by David Noel Freedman. 6 vols. New York: Doubleday, 1992.
ABR	*Australian Biblical Review*
ABRL	Anchor Bible Reference Library
AGJU	Arbeitum zur Geschichte des antiken Judentums und des Urchristentums
AJEC	Ancient Judaism and Early Christianity
AnBib	Analecta Biblica
ATANT	Abhandlungen zur Theologie des Alten und Neuen Testaments
BAIAS	*Bulletin of the Anglo-Israel Archeological Society*
BBR	*Bulletin for Biblical Research*
BDAG	Bauer, Walter, William F. Arndt, F. Wilbur Gringrich, and Frederick W. Danker. *Greek-English Lexicon of the New Testament and Other Early Christian Literature.* 3rd ed. Chicago: University of Chicago Press, 2000.
BETL	Bibliotheca Ephemeridum Theologicarum Lovaniensium
Bib	*Biblica*
BibInt	Biblical Interpretation Series
BibSem	The Biblical Seminar

BJS	Brown Judaic Studies
BMSEC	Baylor–Mohr Siebeck Studies in Early Christianity
BNTC	Black's New Testament Commentary
BSac	*Bibliotheca Sacra*
BT	*The Bible Translator*
BTB	*Biblical Theology Bulletin*
CBET	Contributions to Biblical Exegesis and Theology
CBQ	*Catholic Biblical Quarterly*
CBQMS	Catholic Biblical Quarterly Monograph Series
CNT	Commentaire du Nouveau Testament
CurBR	*Currents in Biblical Research*
DCLS	Deuterocanonical and Cognate Literature Studies
DisBT	Discovering Biblical Texts
ECF	Early Christian Fathers
EDNT	*Exegetical Dictionary of the New Testament.* Edited by Horst Balz and Gerhard Schneider, ET. 3 vols. Grand Rapids, MI: Eerdmans, 1990-1993.
EJL	Early Judaism and Its Literature
EstBíb	*Estudios bíblicos*
ETL	*Ephemerides Theologicae Lovanienses*
ExpTim	*Expository Times*
FBBS	Facet Books, Biblical Studies
FCB	Feminist Companion to the Bible
FCNTECW	Feminist Companion to the New Testament and Early Christian Writings
FF	Foundations and Facets
FRLANT	Forschungen zur Religion und Literatur des Alten und Neuen Testaments
GBS	Guides to Biblical Scholarship
HR	*History of Religions*
HTCNT	Herder's Theological Commentary on the New Testament

HTR	*Harvard Theological Review*
HUCA	*Hebrew Union College Annual*
JAAR	*Journal of the American Academy of Religion*
IDB	*The Interpreter's Dictionary of the Bible*. Edited by George A. Buttrick. 4 vols. New York: Abingdon, 1962.
IEJ	*Israel Exploration Journal*
IFT	Introductions in Feminist Theology
Int	*Interpretation*
JBL	*Journal of Biblical Literature*
JBQ	*Jewish Bible Quarterly*
JCTCRS	Jewish and Christian Texts in Contexts and Related Studies
JFSR	*Journal of Feminist Studies in Religion*
JNES	*Journal of Near Eastern Studies*
JPS	Jewish Publication Society
JSHJ	*Journal for the Study of the Historical Jesus*
JSJ	*Journal for the Study of Judaism in the Persian, Hellenistic, and Roman Periods*
JSJS	Supplement to the Journal for the Study of Judaism
JSNT	*Journal for the Study of the New Testament*
JSNTSup	Journal for the Study of the New Testament Supplement Series
JSOT	*Journal for the Study of the Old Testament*
JSOTSup	Journal for the Study of the Old Testament Supplement Series
LBS	Linguistic Biblical Studies
LNTS	Library of New Testament Studies
LTP	*Laval théologique et Philosophique*
LXX	Septuagint
MT	Masoretic Text
NCB	New Century Bible
NEA	*Near Eastern Archaeology*

NIB	New Interpreter's Bible
NICNT	New International Commentary on the New Testament
NIDB	*New Interpreter's Dictionary of the Bible*. Edited by Katharine Doob Sakenfeld. 5 vols. Nashville, TN: Abingdon, 2006-2009.
NovT	*Novum Testamentum*
NovTSup	Supplements to Novum Testamentum
NT	New Testament
NTL	New Testament Library
NTS	*New Testament Studies*
OBT	Overtures to Biblical Theology
OT	Old Testament
OTM	Old Testament Message
PL	Patrologia Latina
PrTMS	Princeton Theological Monograph Series
QD	Quaestiones Disputatae
RB	*Revue biblique*
RBS	Resources for Biblical Study
RelStTh	*Religious Studies and Theology*
SBFA	Studium Biblicum Franciscanum Analecta
SBL	Society of Biblical Literature
SBLDS	Society of Biblical Literature Dissertation Series
SBLMS	Society of Biblical Literature Monograph Series
SBLRBS	Society of Biblical Literature Resources for Biblical Study
SBLSymS	Society of Biblical Literature Symposium Series
SemeiaSt	Semeia Studies
SNTSMS	Society for New Testament Studies Monograph Series
SNTW	Studies of the New Testament and Its World
SP	Sacra Pagina
StBibLit	Studies in Biblical Literature
SubBi	Subsidia Biblica

SymS   Symposium Series

TBN   Themes in Biblical Narrative

TDNT   *Theological Dictionary of the New Testament.* Edited by
            Gerhard Kittel and Gerhard Friedrich. Translated by
            Geoffrey W. Bromiley. 10 vols. Grand Rapids, MI:
            Eerdmans, 1964-76.

ThTo   *Theology Today*

TynBul   *Tyndale Bulletin*

VE   *Vox Evangelica*

WBC   Word Biblical Commentary

WCS   Wisdom Commentary Series

WGRW   Writings of the Greco-Roman World

WUNT   Wissenschaftliche Untersuchungen zum Neuen
            Testament

ZNW   *Zeitschrift für die neutestamentliche Wissenschaft und die
            Kunde der älteren Kirche*

Contributors

Mary Ann Beavis is an editor of the Wisdom Commentary series, and coauthor of two volumes in the series: *Hebrews* and *2 Thessalonians*. Mary Ann has master's degrees in religious studies and theology from the University of Manitoba and the University of Notre Dame and a PhD in New Testament studies from Cambridge University (UK). She is professor emerita of religion and culture at St. Thomas More College, University of Saskatchewan (Saskatoon, Canada). She is the author of several single-author and edited books as well as many peer-reviewed journal articles, book chapters, and book reviews. She is the founding editor of the *Journal of Religion and Popular Culture*.

Rekha M. Chennattu is professor of biblical studies with a licentiate in Scripture from the Pontifical Biblical Institute, Rome, and a PhD in biblical studies from The Catholic University of America, Washington, DC. She has published *Johannine Discipleship as a Covenant Relationship* (Hendrickson, 2006). Rekha is a Member of the Federation of Asian Bishops Conference–Office of Theological Concerns (FABC-OTC) and is currently the superior general of the congregation of the Religious of the Assumption, Paris, France.

Margaret Daly-Denton is the author of three books: *David in the Fourth Gospel: The Johannine Reception of the Psalms* (Leiden: Brill, 2000), *Psalm-Shaped Prayerfulness: A Guide to the Christian Reception of the Psalms* (Dublin: Columba, 2010; Collegeville, MN: Liturgical Press, 2011), and *John: An Earth Bible Commentary; Supposing Him to Be the Gardener* (London:

Bloomsbury T&T Clark, 2017). Now retired from teaching at Trinity College Dublin, she has recently produced for the (Anglican/Episcopal) Church of Ireland *Caring for the Garden of the Earth*, an eco-hermeneutical Bible study guide.

Dorothy Lee is Stewart Research Professor of New Testament at Trinity College Theological School, Melbourne, a college of the University of Divinity. She has written extensively on symbolism in John's Gospel and has recently published *The Ministry of Women in the New Testament: Reclaiming the Biblical Vision for Church Leadership* (Grand Rapids: Baker Academic, 2021). She is also an Anglican priest.

Barbara E. Reid, OP, is general editor of the Wisdom Commentary series and coauthor of the volume on *Luke*. Barbara is a Dominican sister of Grand Rapids, Michigan. She holds a PhD in biblical studies from The Catholic University of America and is the first woman elected to be president of the Catholic Theological Union, Chicago. Her most recent publications are *Luke 1–9*, coauthored with Shelly Matthews, in the Wisdom Commentary series (Liturgical Press, 2021), *Wisdom's Feast: An Invitation to Feminist Interpretation of the Scriptures* (Eerdmans, 2016), and *Abiding Word: Sunday Reflections on Years A, B, C* (3 vols.; 2011, 2012, 2013). She served as vice president and academic dean at CTU from 2009 to 2018 and as president of the Catholic Biblical Association in 2014–2015.

Kathleen P. Rushton, RSM, of Otautahi Christchurch, Aotearoa New Zealand, is an independent scholar who seeks to interpret biblical texts so as to call forth spirituality to respond to both the cry of the earth and the cry of the poor. She holds a PhD from Griffith University, Brisbane. Her publications include *The Cry of the Earth and the Cry of the Poor: Hearing Justice in John's Gospel* (SCM Press, 2020).

Sandra Marie Schneiders, IHM, is professor emerita of New Testament and spirituality, with a doctorate in sacred theology from the Gregorian University, Rome (1975). Sandra is internationally recognized for her work in biblical hermeneutics, the Gospel of John, and Christian spirituality. She has been president of the Catholic Biblical Association of America (2010) and the Society for the Study of Christian Spirituality (1992). She has served on the editorial boards of numerous biblical and theological journals across the globe.

Elizabeth Schrader is a doctoral candidate in early Christianity at Duke University's Graduate Program in Religion. She holds an MA and an STM from the General Theological Seminary of the Episcopal Church. Her text-critical article "Was Martha of Bethany Added to the Fourth Gospel in the Second Century?" was published in the July 2017 issue of *Harvard Theological Review*.

Ruth Sheridan is an Australian independent scholar researching the Gospel of John. She has published *Retelling Scripture: 'The Jews' and the Scriptural Citations in John 1.19–12.15* (Leiden: Brill, 2012) and *The Figure of Abraham in John 8: Text and Intertext* (London: T&T Clark/Bloomsbury, 2020).

Foreword

"Come Eat of My Bread . . . and Walk in the Ways of Wisdom"

Elisabeth Schüssler Fiorenza
Harvard University Divinity School

Jewish feminist writer Asphodel Long has likened the Bible to a magnificent garden of brilliant plants, some flowering, some fruiting, some in seed, some in bud, shaded by trees of age old, luxurious growth. Yet in the very soil which gives it life the poison has been inserted. . . . This poison is that of misogyny, the hatred of women, half the human race.[1]

To see Scripture as such a beautiful garden containing poisonous ivy requires that one identify and name this poison and place on all biblical texts the label "Caution! Could be dangerous to your health and survival!" As critical feminist interpretation for well-being this Wisdom Commentary seeks to elaborate the beauty and fecundity of this

---

1. Asphodel Long, *In a Chariot Drawn by Lions: The Search for the Female in the Deity* (London: Women's Press, 1992), 195.

Scripture-garden and at the same time points to the harm it can do when one submits to its world of vision. Thus, feminist biblical interpretation engages two seemingly contradictory insights: The Bible is written in kyriocentric (i.e., lord/master/father/husband-elite male) language, originated in the patri-kyriarchal cultures of antiquity, and has functioned to inculcate misogynist mind-sets and oppressive values. At the same time it also asserts that the Bible as Sacred Scripture has functioned to inspire and authorize wo/men[2] in our struggles against dehumanizing oppression. The hermeneutical lens of wisdom/Wisdom empowers the commentary writers to do so.

In biblical as well as in contemporary religious discourse the word *wisdom* has a double meaning: It can either refer to the quality of life and of people and/or it can refer to a figuration of the Divine. Wisdom in both senses of the word is not a prerogative of the biblical traditions but is found in the imagination and writings of all known religions. Wisdom is transcultural, international, and interreligious. Wisdom is practical knowledge gained through experience and daily living as well as through the study of creation and human nature. Both word meanings, that of capability (wisdom) and that of female personification (Wisdom), are crucial for this Wisdom Commentary series that seeks to enable biblical readers to become critical subjects of interpretation.

Wisdom is a state of the human mind and spirit characterized by deep understanding and profound insight. It is elaborated as a quality possessed by the sages but also treasured as folk wisdom and wit. Wisdom is the power of discernment, deeper understanding, and creativity; it is the ability to move and to dance, to make the connections, to savor life, and to learn from experience. Wisdom is intelligence shaped by experience and sharpened by critical analysis. It is the ability to make sound choices and incisive decisions. Its root meaning comes to the fore in its Latin form *sapientia*, which is derived from the verb *sapere*, to taste and to savor something. Hence, this series of commentaries invites readers to taste, to evaluate, and to imagine. In the figure of *Chokmah-Sophia-Sapientia-Wisdom*, ancient Jewish scriptures seek to hold together belief in the "one" G*d[3] of Israel with both masculine and feminine language and metaphors of the Divine.

---

2. I use wo/man, s/he, fe/male and not the grammatical standard "man" as inclusive terms and make this visible by adding /.

3. I use the * asterisk in order to alert readers to a problem to explore and think about.

In distinction to traditional Scripture reading, which is often individualistic and privatized, the practice and space of Wisdom commentary is public. Wisdom's spiraling presence (*Shekhinah*) is global, embracing all creation. Her voice is a public, radical democratic voice rather than a "feminine," privatized one. To become one of Her justice-seeking friends, one needs to imagine the work of this feminist commentary series as the spiraling circle dance of wisdom/Wisdom,[4] as a Spirit/spiritual intellectual movement in the open space of wisdom/Wisdom who calls readers to critically analyze, debate, and reimagine biblical texts and their commentaries as wisdom/Wisdom texts inspired by visions of justice and well-being for everyone and everything. Wisdom-Sophia-imagination engenders a different understanding of Jesus and the movement around him. It understands him as the child and prophet of Divine Wisdom and as Wisdom herself instead of imagining him as ruling King and Lord who has only subalterns but not friends. To approach the N*T[5] and the whole Bible as Wisdom's invitation of cosmic dimensions means to acknowledge its multivalence and its openness to change. As bread—not stone.

In short, this commentary series is inspired by the feminist vision of the open cosmic house of Divine Wisdom-Sophia as it is found in biblical Wisdom literatures, which include the N*T:

> Wisdom has built Her house
> She has set up Her seven pillars . . .
> She has mixed Her wine,
> She also has set Her table.
> She has sent out Her wo/men ministers
> to call from the highest places in the town . . .
> "Come eat of my bread
> and drink of the wine I have mixed.
> Leave immaturity, and live,
> And walk in the way of Wisdom." (Prov 9:1-3, 5-6)

4. I have elaborated such a Wisdom dance in terms of biblical hermeneutics in my book *Wisdom Ways: Introducing Feminist Biblical Interpretation* (Maryknoll, NY: Orbis Books, 2001). Its seven steps are a hermeneutics of experience, of domination, of suspicion, of evaluation, of remembering or historical reconstruction, of imagination, and of transformation. However, such Wisdom strategies of meaning making are not restricted to the Bible. Rather, I have used them in workshops in Brazil and Ecuador to explore the workings of power, Condomblé, Christology, imagining a the*logical wo/men's center, or engaging the national icon of Mary.

5. See the discussion about nomenclature of the two testaments in the General Editor's introduction, page xxxix.

Editor's Introduction to Wisdom Commentary

"She Is a Breath of the Power of God" (Wis 7:25)

Barbara E. Reid, OP

General Editor

Wisdom Commentary is the first series to offer detailed feminist interpretation of every book of the Bible. The fruit of collaborative work by an ecumenical and interreligious team of scholars, the volumes provide serious, scholarly engagement with the whole biblical text, not only those texts that explicitly mention women. The series is intended for clergy, teachers, ministers, and all serious students of the Bible. Designed to be both accessible and informed by the various approaches of biblical scholarship, it pays particular attention to the world in front of the text, that is, how the text is heard and appropriated. At the same time, this series aims to be faithful to the ancient text and its earliest audiences; thus the volumes also explicate the worlds behind the text and within it. While issues of gender are primary in this project, the volumes also address the intersecting issues of power, authority, ethnicity, race, class, and religious belief and practice. The fifty-eight volumes include the books regarded as canonical by Jews (i.e., the Tanakh); Protestants (the "Hebrew Bible" and the New Testament); and Roman Catholic, Anglican, and Eastern

Orthodox Communions (i.e., Tobit, Judith, 1 and 2 Maccabees, Wisdom of Solomon, Sirach/Ecclesiasticus, Baruch, including the Letter of Jeremiah, the additions to Esther, and Susanna and Bel and the Dragon in Daniel).

A Symphony of Diverse Voices

Included in the Wisdom Commentary series are voices from scholars of many different religious traditions, of diverse ages, differing sexual identities, and varying cultural, racial, ethnic, and social contexts. Some have been pioneers in feminist biblical interpretation; others are newer contributors from a younger generation. A further distinctive feature of this series is that each volume incorporates voices other than that of the lead author(s). These voices appear alongside the commentary of the lead author(s), in the grayscale inserts. At times, a contributor may offer an alternative interpretation or a critique of the position taken by the lead author(s). At other times, they may offer a complementary interpretation from a different cultural context or subject position. Occasionally, portions of previously published material bring in other views. The diverse voices are not intended to be contestants in a debate or a cacophony of discordant notes. The multiple voices reflect that there is no single definitive feminist interpretation of a text. In addition, they show the importance of subject position in the process of interpretation. In this regard, the Wisdom Commentary series takes inspiration from the Talmud and from *The Torah: A Women's Commentary* (ed. Tamara Cohn Eskenazi and Andrea L. Weiss; New York: URJ Press and Women of Reform Judaism, The Federation of Temple Sisterhoods, 2008), in which many voices, even conflicting ones, are included and not harmonized.

Contributors include biblical scholars, theologians, and readers of Scripture from outside the scholarly and religious guilds. At times, their comments pertain to a particular text. In some instances they address a theme or topic that arises from the text.

Another feature that highlights the collaborative nature of feminist biblical interpretation is that a number of the volumes have two lead authors who have worked in tandem from the inception of the project and whose voices interweave throughout the commentary.

Woman Wisdom

The title, Wisdom Commentary, reflects both the importance to feminists of the figure of Woman Wisdom in the Scriptures and the distinct wisdom that feminist women and men bring to the interpretive process. In the Scriptures, Woman Wisdom appears as "a breath of the power of God, and a pure emanation of the glory of the Almighty" (Wis 7:25), who was present and active in fashioning all that exists (Prov 8:22-31; Wis 8:6). She is a spirit who pervades and penetrates all things (Wis 7:22-23), and she provides guidance and nourishment at her all-inclusive table (Prov 9:1-5). In both postexilic biblical and nonbiblical Jewish sources, Woman Wisdom is often equated with Torah, e.g., Sirach 24:23-34; Baruch 3:9–4:4; 38:2; 46:4-5; 2 Baruch 48:33, 36; 4 Ezra 5:9-10; 13:55; 14:40; 1 Enoch 42.

The New Testament frequently portrays Jesus as Wisdom incarnate. He invites his followers, "take my yoke upon you and learn from me" (Matt 11:29), just as Ben Sira advises, "put your neck under her [Wisdom's] yoke and let your souls receive instruction" (Sir 51:26). Just as Wisdom experiences rejection (Prov 1:23-25; Sir 15:7-8; Wis 10:3; Bar 3:12), so too does Jesus (Mark 8:31; John 1:10-11). Only some accept his invitation to his all-inclusive banquet (Matt 22:1-14; Luke 14:15-24; compare Prov 1:20-21; 9:3-5). Yet, "wisdom is vindicated by her deeds" (Matt 11:19, speaking of Jesus and John the Baptist; in the Lukan parallel at 7:35 they are called "wisdom's children"). There are numerous parallels between what is said of Wisdom and of the *Logos* in the Prologue of the Fourth Gospel (John 1:1-18). These are only a few of many examples. This female embodiment of divine presence and power is an apt image to guide the work of this series.

Feminism

There are many different understandings of the term "feminism." The various meanings, aims, and methods have developed exponentially in recent decades. Feminism is a perspective and a movement that springs from a recognition of inequities toward women, and it advocates for changes in whatever structures prevent full flourishing of human beings and all creation. Three waves of feminism in the United States are commonly recognized. The first, arising in the mid-nineteenth century and lasting into the early twentieth, was sparked by women's efforts to be involved in the public sphere and to win the right to vote. In the 1960s and 1970s, the second wave focused on civil rights and equality for women. With the third wave, from the 1980s forward, came global feminism and the emphasis on the contextual nature of interpretation. Now a fourth wave may be emerging, with a stronger emphasis on the intersectionality of women's concerns with those of other marginalized groups and the increased use of the internet as a platform for discussion and activism.[1] As feminism has matured, it has recognized that inequities based on gender are interwoven with power imbalances based on race, class, ethnicity, religion, sexual identity, physical ability, and a host of other social markers.

Feminist Women and Men

Men as well as nonbinary people who choose to identify with and partner with feminist women in the work of deconstructing systems of domination and building structures of equality are rightly regarded as feminists. Some men readily identify with experiences of women who are discriminated against on the basis of sex/gender, having themselves had comparable experiences; others who may not have faced direct discrimination or stereotyping recognize that inequity and problematic characterization still occur, and they seek correction. This series is pleased to include feminist men both as lead authors and as contributing voices.

Feminist Biblical Interpretation

Women interpreting the Bible from the lenses of their own experience is nothing new. Throughout the ages women have recounted the biblical stories, teaching them to their children and others, all the while interpreting them afresh for their time and circumstances.[2] Following is a very brief sketch of select foremothers who laid the groundwork for contemporary feminist biblical interpretation.

One of the earliest known Christian women who challenged patriarchal interpretations of Scripture was a consecrated virgin named Helie, who lived in the second century CE. When she refused to marry, her

---

1. See Martha Rampton, "Four Waves of Feminism" (October 25, 2015), at http://www.pacificu.edu/about-us/news-events/four-waves-feminism; and Ealasaid Munro, "Feminism: A Fourth Wave?," https://www.psa.ac.uk/insight-plus/feminism-fourth-wave.

2. For fuller treatments of this history, see chap. 7, "One Thousand Years of Feminist Bible Criticism," in Gerda Lerner, *Creation of Feminist Consciousness: From the Middle Ages to Eighteen-Seventy* (New York: Oxford University Press, 1993), 138–66; Susanne Scholz, "From the 'Woman's Bible' to the 'Women's Bible,' The History of Feminist Approaches to the Hebrew Bible," in *Introducing the Women's Hebrew Bible*, IFT 13 (New York: T&T Clark, 2007), 12–32; Marion Ann Taylor and Agnes Choi, eds., *Handbook of Women Biblical Interpreters: A Historical and Biographical Guide* (Grand Rapids: Baker Academic, 2012).

parents brought her before a judge, who quoted to her Paul's admonition, "It is better to marry than to be aflame with passion" (1 Cor 7:9). In response, Helie first acknowledges that this is what Scripture says, but then she retorts, "but not for everyone, that is, not for holy virgins."[3] She is one of the first to question the notion that a text has one meaning that is applicable in all situations.

A Jewish woman who also lived in the second century CE, Beruriah, is said to have had "profound knowledge of biblical exegesis and outstanding intelligence."[4] One story preserved in the Talmud (b. Ber. 10a) tells of how she challenged her husband, Rabbi Meir, when he prayed for the destruction of a sinner. Proffering an alternate interpretation, she argued that Psalm 104:35 advocated praying for the destruction of sin, not the sinner.

In medieval times the first written commentaries on Scripture from a critical feminist point of view emerge. While others may have been produced and passed on orally, they are for the most part lost to us now. Among the earliest preserved feminist writings are those of Hildegard of Bingen (1098–1179), German writer, mystic, and abbess of a Benedictine monastery. She reinterpreted the Genesis narratives in a way that presented women and men as complementary and interdependent. She frequently wrote about the Divine as feminine.[5] Along with other women mystics of the time, such as Julian of Norwich (1342–ca. 1416), she spoke authoritatively from her personal experiences of God's revelation in prayer.

In this era, women were also among the scribes who copied biblical manuscripts. Notable among them is Paula Dei Mansi of Verona, from a distinguished family of Jewish scribes. In 1288, she translated from Hebrew into Italian a collection of Bible commentaries written by her father and added her own explanations.[6]

Another pioneer, Christine de Pizan (1365–ca. 1430), was a French court writer and prolific poet. She used allegory and common sense

3. Madrid, Escorial MS, a II 9, f. 90 v., as cited in Lerner, *Feminist Consciousness*, 140.

4. See Judith R. Baskin, "Women and Post-Biblical Commentary," in *The Torah: A Women's Commentary*, ed. Tamara Cohn Eskenazi and Andrea L. Weiss (New York: URJ Press and Women of Reform Judaism, The Federation of Temple Sisterhoods, 2008), xlix–lv, at lii.

5. Hildegard of Bingen, *De Operatione Dei*, 1.4.100; PL 197:885bc, as cited in Lerner, *Feminist Consciousness*, 142–43. See also Barbara Newman, *Sister of Wisdom: St. Hildegard's Theology of the Feminine* (Berkeley: University of California Press, 1987).

6. Emily Taitz, Sondra Henry, Cheryl Tallan, eds., *JPS Guide to Jewish Women 600 B.C.E.–1900 C.E.* (Philadelphia: JPS, 2003), 110–11.

to subvert misogynist readings of Scripture and celebrated the accomplishments of female biblical figures to argue for women's active roles in building society.[7]

By the seventeenth century, there were women who asserted that the biblical text needs to be understood and interpreted in its historical context. For example, Rachel Speght (1597–ca. 1630), a Calvinist English poet, elaborates on the historical situation in first-century Corinth that prompted Paul to say, "It is well for a man not to touch a woman" (1 Cor 7:1). Her aim was to show that the biblical texts should not be applied in a literal fashion to all times and circumstances. Similarly, Margaret Fell (1614–1702), one of the founders of the Religious Society of Friends (Quakers) in Britain, addressed the Pauline prohibitions against women speaking in church by insisting that they do not have universal validity. Rather, they need to be understood in their historical context, as addressed to a local church in particular time-bound circumstances.[8]

Along with analyzing the historical context of the biblical writings, women in the eighteenth and nineteenth centuries began to attend to misogynistic interpretations based on faulty translations. One of the first to do so was British feminist Mary Astell (1666–1731).[9] In the United States, the Grimké sisters, Sarah (1792–1873) and Angelina (1805–1879), Quaker women from a slaveholding family in South Carolina, learned biblical Greek and Hebrew so that they could interpret the Bible for themselves. They were prompted to do so after men sought to silence them from speaking out against slavery and for women's rights by claiming that the Bible (e.g., 1 Cor 14:34) prevented women from speaking in public.[10] Another prominent abolitionist, Isabella Baumfree, was a former slave who adopted the name Sojourner Truth (ca. 1797–1883) and quoted the Bible liberally in her speeches[11] and in so doing challenged cultural assumptions and biblical interpretations that undergird gender inequities.

---

7. See further Taylor and Choi, *Handbook of Women Biblical Interpreters*, 127–32.

8. Her major work, *Women's Speaking Justified, Proved and Allowed by the Scriptures*, published in London in 1667, gave a systematic feminist reading of all biblical texts pertaining to women.

9. Mary Astell, *Some Reflections upon Marriage* (New York: Source Book Press, 1970, reprint of the 1730 edition; earliest edition of this work is 1700), 103–4.

10. See further Sarah Grimké, *Letters on the Equality of the Sexes and the Condition of Woman* (Boston: Isaac Knapp, 1838).

11. See, for example, her most famous speech, "Ain't I a Woman?," delivered in 1851 at the Ohio Women's Rights Convention in Akron, OH; http://www.fordham .edu/halsall/mod/sojtruth-woman.asp.

Another monumental work that emerged in nineteenth-century England was that of Jewish theologian Grace Aguilar (1816–1847), *The Women of Israel*,[12] published in 1845. Aguilar's approach was to make connections between the biblical women and contemporary Jewish women's concerns. She aimed to counter the widespread notion that women were degraded in Jewish law and that only in Christianity were women's dignity and value upheld. Her intent was to help Jewish women find strength and encouragement by seeing the evidence of God's compassionate love in the history of every woman in the Bible. While not a full commentary on the Bible, Aguilar's work stands out for its comprehensive treatment of every female biblical character, including even the most obscure references.[13]

The first person to produce a full-blown feminist commentary on the Bible was Elizabeth Cady Stanton (1815–1902). A leading proponent in the United States for women's right to vote, she found that whenever women tried to make inroads into politics, education, or the work world, the Bible was quoted against them. Along with a team of like-minded women, she produced her own commentary on every text of the Bible that concerned women. Her pioneering two-volume project, *The Woman's Bible*, published in 1895 and 1898, urges women to recognize that texts that degrade women come from the men who wrote the texts, not from God, and to use their common sense to rethink what has been presented to them as sacred.

Nearly a century later, *The Women's Bible Commentary*, edited by Carol A. Newsom and Sharon H. Ringe (Louisville: Westminster John Knox, 1992), appeared. This one-volume commentary features North American feminist scholarship on each book of the Protestant canon. Like Cady Stanton's commentary, it does not contain comments on every section of the biblical text but only on those passages deemed relevant to women. It was revised and expanded in 1998 to include the Apocrypha/Deuterocanonical books, and the contributors to this new volume reflect the global face of contemporary feminist scholarship. The revisions made in the third edition, which appeared in 2012, represent the profound advances in feminist biblical scholarship and include newer voices. In both the second and third editions, *The* has been dropped from the title.

---

12. The full title is *The Women of Israel or Characters and Sketches from the Holy Scriptures and Jewish History Illustrative of the Past History, Present Duty, and Future Destiny of the Hebrew Females, as Based on the Word of God.*

13. See further Eskenazi and Weiss, *The Torah: A Women's Commentary*, xxxviii; Taylor and Choi, *Handbook of Women Biblical Interpreters*, 31–37.

Also appearing at the centennial of Cady Stanton's *The Woman's Bible* were two volumes edited by Elisabeth Schüssler Fiorenza with the assistance of Shelly Matthews. The first, *Searching the Scriptures: A Feminist Introduction* (New York: Crossroad, 1993), charts a comprehensive approach to feminist interpretation from ecumenical, interreligious, and multicultural perspectives. The second volume, published in 1994, provides critical feminist commentary on each book of the New Testament as well as on three books of Jewish Pseudepigrapha and eleven other early Christian writings.

In Europe, similar endeavors have been undertaken, such as the one-volume *Kompendium Feministische Bibelauslegung*, edited by Luise Schottroff and Marie-Theres Wacker (Gütersloh: Gütersloher Verlagshaus, 2007), featuring German feminist biblical interpretation of each book of the Bible, along with apocryphal books, and several extrabiblical writings. This work, now in its third edition, has recently been translated into English.[14] A multivolume project, *The Bible and Women: An Encyclopaedia of Exegesis and Cultural History*, edited by Irmtraud Fischer, Adriana Valerio, Mercedes Navarro Puerto, Christiana de Groot, and Mary Ann Beavis, is currently in production. This project presents a history of the reception of the Bible as embedded in Western cultural history and focuses particularly on gender-relevant biblical themes, biblical female characters, and women recipients of the Bible. The volumes are published in English, Spanish, Italian, and German.[15]

Another groundbreaking work is the collection The Feminist Companion to the Bible Series, edited by Athalya Brenner (Sheffield: Sheffield Academic, 1993–2015), which comprises twenty volumes of commen-

14. *Feminist Biblical Interpretation: A Compendium of Critical Commentary on the Books of the Bible and Related Literature*, trans. Lisa E. Dahill, Everett R. Kalin, Nancy Lukens, Linda M. Maloney, Barbara Rumscheidt, Martin Rumscheidt, and Tina Steiner (Grand Rapids: Eerdmans, 2012). Another notable collection is the three volumes edited by Susanne Scholz, *Feminist Interpretation of the Hebrew Bible in Retrospect*, Recent Research in Biblical Studies 7, 8, 9 (Sheffield: Sheffield Phoenix, 2013, 2014, 2016).

15. The first volume, on the Torah, appeared in Spanish in 2009, in German and Italian in 2010, and in English in 2011 (Atlanta: Society of Biblical Literature). Five more volumes are now available: *Feminist Biblical Studies in the Twentieth Century*, ed. Elisabeth Schüssler Fiorenza (2014); *The Writings and Later Wisdom Books*, ed. Christl M. Maier and Nuria Calduch-Benages (2014); *Gospels: Narrative and History*, ed. Mercedes Navarro Puerto and Marinella Perroni; Amy-Jill Levine (English ed.), The Bible and Women: An Encyclopedia of Exegesis and Cultural History, New Testament 2.1 (Atlanta: SBL Press, 2015); *The High Middle Ages*, ed. Kari Elisabeth Børresen and Adriana Valerio (2015); and *Early Jewish Writings*, ed. Eileen Schuller and Marie-Theres Wacker (2017). For further information, see http://www.bibleandwomen.org.

taries on the Old Testament. The parallel series, Feminist Companion to the New Testament and Early Christian Writings, edited by Amy-Jill Levine with Marianne Blickenstaff and Maria Mayo Robbins (Sheffield: Sheffield Academic, 2001–2009), contains thirteen volumes with one more planned. These two series are not full commentaries on the biblical books but comprise collected essays on discrete biblical texts.

Works by individual feminist biblical scholars in all parts of the world abound, and they are now too numerous to list in this introduction. Feminist biblical interpretation has reached a level of maturity that now makes possible a commentary series on every book of the Bible. In recent decades, women have had greater access to formal theological education, have been able to learn critical analytical tools, have put their own interpretations into writing, and have developed new methods of biblical interpretation. Until recent decades the work of feminist biblical interpreters was largely unknown, both to other women and to their brothers in the synagogue, church, and academy. Feminists now have taken their place in the professional world of biblical scholars, where they build on the work of their foremothers and connect with one another across the globe in ways not previously possible. In a few short decades, feminist biblical criticism has become an integral part of the academy.

Methodologies

Feminist biblical scholars use a variety of methods and often employ a number of them together.[16] In the Wisdom Commentary series, the authors will explain their understanding of feminism and the feminist reading strategies used in their commentary. Each volume treats the biblical text in blocks of material, not an analysis verse by verse. The entire text is considered, not only those passages that feature female characters or that speak specifically about women. When women are not apparent in the narrative, feminist lenses are used to analyze the dynamics in the text between male characters, the models of power, binary ways of thinking, and the dynamics of imperialism. Attention is given to how the whole text functions and how it was and is heard, both in its original context and today. Issues of particular concern to women—e.g., poverty, food, health, the environment, water—come to the fore.

---

16. See the seventeen essays in Caroline Vander Stichele and Todd Penner, eds., *Her Master's Tools? Feminist and Postcolonial Engagements of Historical-Critical Discourse* (Atlanta: Society of Biblical Literature, 2005), which show the complementarity of various approaches.

One of the approaches used by early feminists and still popular today is to lift up the overlooked and forgotten stories of women in the Bible. Studies of women in each of the Testaments have been done, and there are also studies on women in particular biblical books.[17] Feminists recognize that the examples of biblical characters can be both empowering and problematic. The point of the feminist enterprise is not to serve as an apologetic for women; it is rather, in part, to recover women's history and literary roles in all their complexity and to learn from that recovery.

Retrieving the submerged history of biblical women is a crucial step for constructing the story of the past so as to lead to liberative possibilities for the present and future. There are, however, some pitfalls to this approach. Sometimes depictions of biblical women have been naïve and romantic. Some commentators exalt the virtues of both biblical and contemporary women and paint women as superior to men. Such reverse discrimination inhibits movement toward equality for all. In addition, some feminists challenge the idea that one can "pluck positive images out of an admittedly androcentric text, separating literary characterizations from the androcentric interests they were created to serve."[18] Still other feminists find these images to have enormous value.

One other danger with seeking the submerged history of women is the tendency for Christian feminists to paint Jesus and even Paul as liberators of women in a way that demonizes Judaism.[19] Wisdom Commentary

---

17. See, e.g., Alice Bach, ed., *Women in the Hebrew Bible: A Reader* (New York: Routledge, 1999); Tikva Frymer-Kensky, *Reading the Women of the Bible* (New York: Schocken Books, 2002); Carol Meyers, Toni Craven, and Ross Shepard Kraemer, eds., *Women in Scripture* (Grand Rapids: Eerdmans, 2001); Irene Nowell, *Women in the Old Testament* (Collegeville, MN: Liturgical Press, 1997); Katharine Doob Sakenfeld, *Just Wives? Stories of Power and Survival in the Old Testament and Today* (Louisville: Westminster John Knox, 2003); Mary Ann Getty-Sullivan, *Women in the New Testament* (Collegeville, MN: Liturgical Press, 2001); Bonnie Thurston, *Women in the New Testament: Questions and Commentary*, Companions to the New Testament (New York: Crossroad, 1998).

18. J. Cheryl Exum, "Second Thoughts about Secondary Characters: Women in Exodus 1.8–2.10," in *A Feminist Companion to Exodus to Deuteronomy*, FCB 6, ed. Athalya Brenner (Sheffield: Sheffield Academic, 1994), 75–97, at 76.

19. See Judith Plaskow, "Anti-Judaism in Feminist Christian Interpretation," in *Searching the Scriptures, vol. 1: A Feminist Introduction*, ed. Elisabeth Schüssler Fiorenza with Shelly Matthews (New York: Crossroad, 1993), 1:117–29; Amy-Jill Levine, "The New Testament and Anti-Judaism," in *The Misunderstood Jew: The Church and the Scandal of the Jewish Jesus* (San Francisco: HarperSanFrancisco, 2006), 87–117.

aims to enhance understanding of Jesus as well as Paul as Jews of their day and to forge solidarity among Jewish and Christian feminists.[20]

Feminist scholars who use historical-critical methods analyze the world behind the text; they seek to understand the historical context from which the text emerged and the circumstances of the communities to whom it was addressed. In bringing feminist lenses to this approach, the aim is not to impose modern expectations on ancient cultures but to unmask the ways that ideologically problematic mind-sets that produced the ancient texts are still promulgated through the text. Feminist biblical scholars aim not only to deconstruct but also to reclaim and reconstruct biblical history as women's history, in which women were central and active agents in creating religious heritage.[21] A further step is to construct meaning for contemporary women and men in a liberative movement toward transformation of social, political, economic, and religious structures.[22] In recent years, some feminists have embraced new historicism, which accents the creative role of the interpreter in any construction of history and exposes the power struggles to which the text witnesses.[23]

Literary critics analyze the world of the text: its form, language patterns, and rhetorical function.[24] They do not attempt to separate layers

---

20. For an overview of the work of Jewish feminists see Mara H. Benjamin, "Tracing the Contours of a Half Century of Jewish Feminist Theology," *JFSR* 36 (2020): 11–31.

21. See, for example, Phyllis A. Bird, *Missing Persons and Mistaken Identities: Women and Gender in Ancient Israel* (Minneapolis: Fortress, 1997); Elisabeth Schüssler Fiorenza, *In Memory of Her: A Feminist Theological Reconstruction of Christian Origins* (New York: Crossroad, 1983); Ross Shepard Kraemer and Mary Rose D'Angelo, eds., *Women and Christian Origins* (New York: Oxford University Press, 1999).

22. See, e.g., Sandra M. Schneiders, *The Revelatory Text: Interpreting the New Testament as Sacred Scripture*, rev. ed. (Collegeville, MN: Liturgical Press, 1999), whose aim is to engage in biblical interpretation not only for intellectual enlightenment but, even more important, for personal and communal transformation. Elisabeth Schüssler Fiorenza (*Wisdom Ways: Introducing Feminist Biblical Interpretation* [Maryknoll, NY: Orbis Books, 2001]) envisions the work of feminist biblical interpretation as a dance of Wisdom that consists of seven steps that interweave in spiral movements toward liberation, the final one being transformative action for change.

23. See Gina Hens-Piazza, *The New Historicism*, GBS, Old Testament Series (Minneapolis: Fortress, 2002).

24. Phyllis Trible was among the first to employ this method with texts from Genesis and Ruth in her groundbreaking book *God and the Rhetoric of Sexuality*, OBT (Philadelphia: Fortress, 1978). Another pioneer in feminist literary criticism is Mieke Bal (*Lethal Love: Feminist Literary Readings of Biblical Love Stories* [Bloomington: Indiana University Press, 1987]). For surveys of recent developments in literary methods, see Terry Eagleton, *Literary Theory: An Introduction*, 3rd ed. (Minneapolis: University

of tradition and redaction but focus on the text holistically, as it is in its present form. They examine how meaning is created in the interaction between the text and its reader in multiple contexts. Within the arena of literary approaches are reader-oriented approaches, narrative, rhetorical, structuralist, post-structuralist, deconstructive, ideological, autobiographical, and performance criticism.[25] Narrative critics study the interrelation among author, text, and audience through investigation of settings, both spatial and temporal; characters; plot; and narrative techniques (e.g., irony, parody, intertextual allusions). Reader-response critics attend to the impact that the text has on the reader or hearer. They recognize that when a text is detrimental toward women there is the choice either to affirm the text or to read against the grain toward a liberative end. Rhetorical criticism analyzes the style of argumentation and attends to how the author is attempting to shape the thinking or actions of the hearer. Structuralist critics analyze the complex patterns of binary oppositions in the text to derive its meaning.[26] Post-structuralist approaches challenge the notion that there are fixed meanings to any biblical text or that there is one universal truth. They engage in close readings of the text and often engage in intertextual analysis.[27] Within this approach is deconstructionist criticism, which views the text as a site of conflict, with competing narratives. The interpreter aims to expose the fault lines and overturn and reconfigure binaries by elevating the underling of a pair and foregrounding it.[28] Feminists also use other post-

---

of Minnesota Press, 2008); Janice Capel Anderson and Stephen D. Moore, eds., *Mark and Method: New Approaches in Biblical Studies*, 2nd ed. (Minneapolis: Fortress, 2008); Michal Beth Dinkler, *Literary Theory and the New Testament*, AYBRL (New Haven: Yale University Press, 2019).

25. See, e.g., J. Cheryl Exum and David J. A. Clines, eds., *The New Literary Criticism and the Hebrew Bible* (Valley Forge, PA: Trinity Press International, 1993); Edgar V. McKnight and Elizabeth Struthers Malbon, eds., *The New Literary Criticism and the New Testament* (Valley Forge, PA: Trinity Press International, 1994).

26. See, e.g., David Jobling, *The Sense of Biblical Narrative: Three Structural Analyses in the Old Testament*, JSOTSup 7 (Sheffield: University of Sheffield Press, 1978).

27. See, e.g., Stephen D. Moore, *Poststructuralism and the New Testament: Derrida and Foucault at the Foot of the Cross* (Minneapolis: Fortress, 1994); *The Bible in Theory: Critical and Postcritical Essays* (Atlanta: Society of Biblical Literature, 2010); Yvonne Sherwood, *A Biblical Text and Its Afterlives: The Survival of Jonah in Western Culture* (Cambridge: Cambridge University Press, 2000).

28. David Penchansky, "Deconstruction," in *The Oxford Encyclopedia of Biblical Interpretation*, ed. Steven McKenzie (New York: Oxford University Press, 2013), 196–205. See, for example, Danna Nolan Fewell and David M. Gunn, *Gender, Power, and Promise:*

modern approaches, such as ideological and autobiographical criticism. The former analyzes the system of ideas that underlies the power and values concealed in the text as well as that of the interpreter.[29] The latter involves deliberate self-disclosure while reading the text as a critical exegete.[30] Performance criticism attends to how the text was passed on orally, usually in communal settings, and to the verbal and nonverbal interactions between the performer and the audience.[31]

From the beginning, feminists have understood that interpreting the Bible is an act of power. In recent decades, feminist biblical scholars have developed hermeneutical theories of the ethics and politics of biblical interpretation to challenge the claims to value neutrality of most academic biblical scholarship. Feminist biblical scholars have also turned their attention to how some biblical writings were shaped by the power of empire and how this still shapes readers' self-understandings today. They have developed hermeneutical approaches that reveal, critique, and evaluate the interactions depicted in the text against the context of empire, and they consider implications for contemporary contexts.[32] Feminists also analyze the dynamics of colonization and the mentalities of colonized peoples in the exercise of biblical interpretation. As Kwok Pui-lan explains, "A postcolonial feminist interpretation of the Bible needs to investigate the deployment of gender in the narration of identity, the negotiation of power differentials between the colonizers and the colonized, and the reinforcement of patriarchal control over spheres

---

The Subject of the Bible's First Story (Nashville: Abingdon, 1993); David Rutledge, *Reading Marginally: Feminism, Deconstruction and the Bible*, BibInt 21 (Leiden: Brill, 1996).

29. See David Jobling and Tina Pippin, eds., *Semeia 59: Ideological Criticism of Biblical Texts* (Atlanta: Scholars Press, 1992); Terry Eagleton, *Ideology: An Introduction* (London: Verso, 2007).

30. See, e.g., Ingrid Rosa Kitzberger, ed., *Autobiographical Biblical Interpretation: Between Text and Self* (Leiden: Deo, 2002); P. J. W. Schutte, "When *They, We,* and the Passive Become *I*—Introducing Autobiographical Biblical Criticism," *HTS Teologiese Studies / Theological Studies* 61 (2005): 401–16.

31. See, e.g., Holly E. Hearon and Philip Ruge-Jones, eds., *The Bible in Ancient and Modern Media: Story and Performance* (Eugene, OR: Cascade, 2009).

32. E.g., Gale Yee, ed., *Judges and Method: New Approaches in Biblical Studies* (Minneapolis: Fortress, 1995); Warren Carter, *The Gospel of Matthew in Its Roman Imperial Context* (London: T&T Clark, 2005); *The Roman Empire and the New Testament: An Essential Guide* (Nashville: Abingdon, 2006); Elisabeth Schüssler Fiorenza, *The Power of the Word: Scripture and the Rhetoric of Empire* (Minneapolis: Fortress, 2007); Judith E. McKinlay, *Reframing Her: Biblical Women in Postcolonial Focus* (Sheffield: Sheffield Phoenix, 2004).

where these elites could exercise control."[33] Methods and models from sociology and cultural anthropology are used by feminists to investigate women's everyday lives, their experiences of marriage, childrearing, labor, money, illness, etc.[34]

As feminists have examined the construction of gender from varying cultural perspectives, they have become ever more cognizant that the way gender roles are defined within differing cultures varies radically. As Mary Ann Tolbert observes, "Attempts to isolate some universal role that cross-culturally defines 'woman' have run into contradictory evidence at every turn."[35] Some women have coined new terms to highlight the particularities of their socio-cultural context. Many African American feminists, for example, call themselves *womanists* to draw attention to the double oppression of racism and sexism they experience.[36] Similarly, many US Hispanic feminists speak of themselves as *mujeristas* (*mujer* is Spanish for "woman").[37] Others prefer to be called "Latina feminists."[38] As a gender-neutral or nonbinary alternative, many today use Latinx. *Mujeristas*, Latina and Latinx feminists emphasize that the context for their theologizing is *mestizaje* and *mulatez* (racial and cultural mixture), done *en*

---

33. Kwok Pui-lan, *Postcolonial Imagination and Feminist Theology* (Louisville: Westminster John Knox, 2005), 9. See also Musa W. Dube, ed., *Postcolonial Feminist Interpretation of the Bible* (St. Louis: Chalice, 2000); Cristl M. Maier and Carolyn J. Sharp, *Prophecy and Power: Jeremiah in Feminist and Postcolonial Perspective* (London: Bloomsbury, 2013); L. Juliana Claassens and Carolyn J. Sharp, eds., *Feminist Frameworks and the Bible: Power, Ambiguity, and Intersectionality*, LHBOTS 630 (London: Bloomsbury T&T Clark, 2017).

34. See, for example, Carol Meyers, *Discovering Eve: Ancient Israelite Women in Context* (New York: Oxford University Press, 1991); Luise Schottroff, *Lydia's Impatient Sisters: A Feminist Social History of Early Christianity*, trans. Barbara and Martin Rumscheidt (Louisville: Westminster John Knox, 1995); Susan Niditch, *"My Brother Esau Is a Hairy Man": Hair and Identity in Ancient Israel* (Oxford: Oxford University Press, 2008).

35. Mary Ann Tolbert, "Social, Sociological, and Anthropological Methods," in *Searching the Scriptures*, 1:255–71, at 265.

36. Alice Walker coined the term (*In Search of Our Mothers' Gardens: Womanist Prose* [New York: Harcourt Brace Jovanovich, 1967, 1983]). See also Katie G. Cannon, "The Emergence of Black Feminist Consciousness," in *Feminist Interpretation of the Bible*, ed. Letty M. Russell (Philadelphia: Westminster, 1985), 30–40; Renita Weems, *Just a Sister Away: A Womanist Vision of Women's Relationships in the Bible* (San Diego: Lura Media, 1988); Nyasha Junior, *An Introduction to Womanist Biblical Interpretation* (Louisville: Westminster John Knox, 2015).

37. Ada María Isasi-Díaz (*Mujerista Theology: A Theology for the Twenty-First Century* [Maryknoll, NY: Orbis Books, 1996]) is credited with coining the term.

38. E.g., María Pilar Aquino, Daisy L. Machado, and Jeanette Rodríguez, eds., *A Reader in Latina Feminist Theology* (Austin: University of Texas Press, 2002).

conjunto (in community), with *lo cotidiano* (everyday lived experience) of Latina women as starting points for theological reflection and the encounter with the divine. Intercultural analysis has become an indispensable tool for working toward justice for women at the global level.[39]

Some feminists are among those who have developed lesbian, gay, bisexual, and transgender (LGBT) interpretation. This approach focuses on issues of sexual identity and uses various reading strategies. Some point out the ways in which categories that emerged in recent centuries are applied anachronistically to biblical texts to make modern-day judgments. Others show how the Bible is silent on contemporary issues about sexual identity. Still others examine same-sex relationships in the Bible by figures such as Ruth and Naomi or David and Jonathan. In recent years, queer theory has emerged; it emphasizes the blurriness of boundaries not just of sexual identity but also of gender roles. Queer critics often focus on texts in which figures transgress what is traditionally considered proper gender behavior.[40]

Feminists have also been engaged in studying the reception history of the text[41] and have engaged in studies in the emerging fields of disability theory and of children in the Bible.[42]

---

39. See, e.g., María Pilar Aquino and María José Rosado-Nunes, eds., *Feminist Intercultural Theology: Latina Explorations for a Just World*, Studies in Latino/a Catholicism (Maryknoll, NY: Orbis Books, 2007). See also Michelle A. Gonzalez, "Latina Feminist Theology: Past, Present, and Future," *JFSR* 25 (2009): 150–55. See also Elisabeth Schüssler Fiorenza, ed., *Feminist Biblical Studies in the Twentieth Century: Scholarship and Movement*, The Bible and Women 9.1 (Atlanta: Society of Biblical Literature, 2014), who charts feminist studies around the globe as well as emerging feminist methodologies.

40. See, e.g., Bernadette J. Brooten, *Love Between Women: Early Christian Responses to Female Homoeroticism* (Chicago: University of Chicago Press, 1996); Mary Rose D'Angelo, "Women Partners in the New Testament," *JFSR* 6 (1990): 65–86; Deirdre J. Good, "Reading Strategies for Biblical Passages on Same-Sex Relations," *Theology and Sexuality* 7 (1997): 70–82; Deryn Guest, *When Deborah Met Jael: Lesbian Feminist Hermeneutics* (London: SCM, 2011); Teresa Hornsby and Ken Stone, eds., *Bible Trouble: Queer Readings at the Boundaries of Biblical Scholarship* (Atlanta: Society of Biblical Literature, 2011); Joseph A. Marchal, "Queer Studies and Critical Masculinity Studies in Feminist Biblical Studies," in *Feminist Biblical Studies in the Twentieth Century: Scholarship and Movement*, ed. Elisabeth Schüssler Fiorenza, The Bible and Women 9.1 (Atlanta: Society of Biblical Literature, 2014), 261–80.

41. See Sharon H. Ringe, "A History of Interpretation," in *Women's Bible Commentary*, 5; Marion Ann Taylor and Agnes Choi, eds., *Handbook of Women Biblical Interpreters: A Historical and Biographical Guide* (Grand Rapids: Baker Academic, 2012); Yvonne Sherwood, "Introduction," in *The Bible and Feminism: Remapping the Field* (New York: Oxford University Press, 2017).

42. See for example Sarah J. Melcher, Mikeal C. Parsons, and Amos Yong, eds., *The Bible and Disability: A Commentary*, Studies in Religion, Theology and Disability

Feminists also recognize that the struggle for women's equality and dignity is intimately connected with the struggle for respect for Earth and for the whole of the cosmos. Ecofeminists interpret Scripture in ways that highlight the link between human domination of nature and male subjugation of women. They show how anthropocentric ways of interpreting the Bible have overlooked or dismissed Earth and Earth community. They invite readers to identify not only with human characters in the biblical narrative but also with other Earth creatures and domains of nature, especially those that are the object of injustice. Some use creative imagination to retrieve the interests of Earth implicit in the narrative and enable Earth to speak.[43]

Biblical Authority

By the late nineteenth century, some feminists, such as Elizabeth Cady Stanton, began to question openly whether the Bible could continue to be regarded as authoritative for women. They viewed the Bible itself as the source of women's oppression, and some rejected its sacred origin and saving claims. Some decided that the Bible and the religious traditions that enshrine it are too thoroughly saturated with androcentrism and patriarchy to be redeemable.[44]

In the Wisdom Commentary series, questions such as these may be raised, but the aim of this series is not to lead readers to reject the authority of the biblical text. Rather, the aim is to promote better understanding of the contexts from which the text arose and of the rhetorical effects it has on people in contemporary contexts. Such understanding can lead to a deepening of faith, with the Bible serving as an aid to bring flourishing of life.

Language for God

Because of the ways in which the term "God" has been used to symbolize the divine in predominantly male, patriarchal, and monarchical

---

(Waco, TX: Baylor University Press, 2017), and Sharon Betsworth, *Children in Early Christian Narratives* (New York: Bloomsbury T&T Clark, 2015).

43. E.g., Norman C. Habel and Peter Trudinger, *Exploring Ecological Hermeneutics*, SymS 46 (Atlanta: Society of Biblical Literature, 2008); Mary Judith Ress, *Ecofeminism in Latin America*, Women from the Margins (Maryknoll, NY: Orbis Books, 2006).

44. E.g., Mary Daly, *Beyond God the Father: A Philosophy of Women's Liberation* (Boston: Beacon, 1973).

modes, feminists have designed new ways of speaking of the divine. Some have called attention to the inadequacy of the term *God* by trying to visually destabilize our ways of thinking and speaking of the divine. Rosemary Radford Ruether proposed *God/ess*, as an unpronounceable term pointing to the unnameable understanding of the divine that transcends patriarchal limitations.[45] Some have followed traditional Jewish practice, writing *G-d*. Elisabeth Schüssler Fiorenza has adopted *G*d*.[46] Others draw on the biblical tradition to mine female and non-gender-specific metaphors and symbols.[47] In Wisdom Commentary, there is not one standard way of expressing the divine; each author will use her or his preferred ways. The one exception is that when the tetragrammaton, YHWH, the name revealed to Moses in Exodus 3:14, is used, it will be without vowels, respecting the Jewish custom of avoiding pronouncing the divine name out of reverence.

Nomenclature for the Two Testaments

In recent decades, some biblical scholars have begun to call the two Testaments of the Bible by names other than the traditional nomenclature: Old and New Testament. Some regard "Old" as derogatory, implying that it is no longer relevant or that it has been superseded. Consequently, terms like Hebrew Bible, First Testament, and Jewish Scriptures and, correspondingly, Christian Scriptures or Second Testament have come into use. There are a number of difficulties with these designations. The term "Hebrew Bible" does not take into account that parts of the Old Testament are written not in Hebrew but in Aramaic.[48] Moreover, for Roman Catholics and Eastern Orthodox believers, the Old Testament includes books written in Greek—the Deuterocanonical books,

---

45. Rosemary Radford Ruether, *Sexism and God-Talk: Toward a Feminist Theology* (Boston: Beacon, 1993).

46. Elisabeth Schüssler Fiorenza, *Jesus: Miriam's Child, Sophia's Prophet; Critical Issues in Feminist Christology* (New York: Continuum, 1994), 191 n. 3.

47. E.g., Sallie McFague, *Models of God: Theology for an Ecological, Nuclear Age* (Philadelphia: Fortress, 1987); Catherine Mowry LaCugna, *God for Us: The Trinity and Christian Life* (San Francisco: Harper Collins, 1991); Elizabeth A. Johnson, *She Who Is: The Mystery of God in Feminist Theological Discourse* (New York: Crossroad, 1992). See further Elizabeth A. Johnson, "God," in *Dictionary of Feminist Theologies*, ed. Letty M. Russell and J. Shannon Clarkson (Louisville: Westminster John Knox, 1996), 128–30.

48. Gen 31:47; Jer 10:11; Ezra 4:7–6:18; 7:12-26; Dan 2:4–7:28.

considered Apocrypha by Protestants.[49] The term "Jewish Scriptures" is inadequate because these books are also sacred to Christians. Conversely, "Christian Scriptures" is not an accurate designation for the New Testament, since the Old Testament is also part of the Christian Scriptures. Using "First and Second Testament" also has difficulties, in that it can imply a hierarchy and a value judgment.[50] Jews generally use the term Tanakh, an acronym for Torah (Pentateuch), Nevi'im (Prophets), and Ketuvim (Writings).

In Wisdom Commentary, if authors choose to use a designation other than Tanakh, Old Testament, and New Testament, they will explain how they mean the term.

Translation

Modern feminist scholars recognize the complexities connected with biblical translation, as they have delved into questions about philosophy of language, how meanings are produced, and how they are culturally situated. Today it is evident that simply translating into gender-neutral formulations cannot address all the challenges presented by androcentric texts. Efforts at feminist translation must also deal with issues around authority and canonicity.[51]

Because of these complexities, the editors of the Wisdom Commentary series have chosen to use an existing translation, the New Revised Standard Version (NRSV), which is provided for easy reference at the top of each page of commentary. The NRSV was produced by a team of ecumenical and interreligious scholars, is a fairly literal translation, and uses inclusive language for human beings. Brief discussions about problematic translations appear in the inserts labeled "Translation Matters." When more detailed discussions are available, these will be indicated in footnotes. In the commentary, wherever Hebrew or Greek words are used, English translation is provided. In cases where a wordplay is involved, transliteration is provided to enable understanding.

---

49. Representing the *via media* between Catholic and reformed, Anglicans generally consider the Apocrypha to be profitable, if not canonical, and utilize select Wisdom texts liturgically.

50. See Levine, *The Misunderstood Jew*, 193–99.

51. Elizabeth Castelli, "*Les Belles Infidèles*/Fidelity or Feminism? The Meanings of Feminist Biblical Translation," in *Searching the Scriptures*, 1:189–204, here 190.

Art and Poetry

Artistic expression in poetry, music, sculpture, painting, and various other modes is very important to feminist interpretation. Where possible, art and poetry are included in the print volumes of the series. In a number of instances, these are original works created for this project. Regrettably, copyright and production costs prohibit the inclusion of color photographs and other artistic work.

Glossary

Because there are a number of excellent readily available resources that provide definitions and concise explanations of terms used in feminist theological and biblical studies, this series will not include a glossary. We refer you to works such as *Dictionary of Feminist Theologies*, edited by Letty M. Russell and J. Shannon Clarkson (Louisville: Westminster John Knox, 1996), and volume 1 of *Searching the Scriptures*, edited by Elisabeth Schüssler Fiorenza with the assistance of Shelly Matthews (New York: Crossroad, 1993). Individual authors in the Wisdom Commentary series will define the way they are using terms that may be unfamiliar.

A Concluding Word

In just a few short decades, feminist biblical studies has grown exponentially, both in the methods that have been developed and in the number of scholars who have embraced it. We realize that this series is limited and will soon need to be revised and updated. It is our hope that Wisdom Commentary, by making the best of current feminist biblical scholarship available in an accessible format to ministers, preachers, teachers, scholars, and students, will aid all readers in their advancement toward God's vision of dignity, equality, and justice for all.

Acknowledgments

There are a great many people who have made this series possible: first, Peter Dwyer, director of Liturgical Press, and Hans Christoffersen, publisher of the academic market at Liturgical Press, who have believed in this project and have shepherded it since it was conceived in 2008. Editorial consultants Athalya Brenner-Idan and Elisabeth Schüssler Fiorenza have not only been an inspiration with their pioneering work but have encouraged us all along the way with their personal involvement. Volume editors Mary Ann Beavis, Carol J. Dempsey, Gina Hens-Piazza, Amy-Jill Levine, Linda M. Maloney, Song-Mi Suzie Park, Ahida Pilarski, Sarah Tanzer, and Lauress Wilkins Lawrence have lent their extraordinary wisdom to the shaping of the series, have used their extensive networks of relationships to secure authors and contributors, and have worked tirelessly to guide their work to completion. Four others who have contributed greatly to the shaping of the project are Linda M. Day, Mignon Jacobs, Seung Ai Yang, and Barbara E. Bowe of blessed memory (d. 2010). Editorial and research assistant Susan M. Hickman provided invaluable support with administrative details and arrangements. I am grateful to Brian Eisenschenk and Christine Henderson who assisted Susan Hickman with the Wiki. I am especially thankful to Lauren L. Murphy and Justin Howell for their work in copyediting; and to the staff at Liturgical Press, especially Colleen Stiller, production manager; Stephanie Lancour, production editor; Julie Surma, desktop publisher; Angie Steffens, production coordinator; and Tara Durheim, marketing director.

Author's Preface

The Gospel of John is a narrative; it tells a story, with a narrator, a plot, and characters, who serve to express the particular point of view of the author. Because this is an ancient story, told to an audience from a different time, culture, and religious perception to most modern readers, there will be aspects of the story that are puzzling. The author makes use of the Scriptures of Israel available in Hebrew, Greek, and Aramaic, sometimes making this explicit but more frequently through an allusion that the original audience would have been expected to know. As well as the written Scriptures, the author works within the theological thinking of late Second Temple Judaism, again, with the expectation that the original audience would be familiar with that thought-world. An audience reading this story today needs a guide to make explicit what that first audience could be presumed to know and understand. It is my task in this commentary to be that guide.

My goal is to provide a coherent and intelligible reading of the entire Gospel narrative, while providing some discussion of particularly complex sections by engaging with the views of a range of scholars, even though it will not provide a detailed analysis of all verses or detailed arguments in favor of a particular reading. Footnotes and references to previous studies will provide the reader with further treatment of these matters; in particular I will often reference my own work where readers will find more substantial arguments for a particular interpretation.

My prior studies of this Gospel have led me to see some major themes that recur across the entire narrative and drive the narrative to give expression to a single, theological interpretation of Jesus, in his life, ministry, death, and resurrection. Jesus's identity as the "bridegroom" and "temple" are themes introduced in the opening chapters and continue to impact the narrative through to the final chapter. Jesus's ministry, as ushering in a new creation and drawing believers into a new relationship with God, is likewise introduced in the prologue (John 1:1-18) and then realized in a very different telling of the passion. The interplay of these themes and symbols give this Gospel its artistic richness and enduring appreciation as "a spiritual Gospel."

Every book emerges from within a community, and this book is no exception. Sandra Schneiders, Frank Moloney, Brendan Byrne, and Dorothy Lee had a significant impact on my undergraduate studies of the Fourth Gospel, and it is a joy to me that they continue to be my friends and occasional table companions. Many other scholars have shaped my views, and within this volume I am pleased to include a number of contributing voices. Ruth Sheridan was my first doctoral student from whom I learned greater sensitivity to the issue of "the Jews" in John. Rekha Chennattu from India joined me in editing a volume of essays to honor our common doctoral supervisor, Frank Moloney. Kath Rushton from New Zealand and Margaret Daly-Denton from Ireland have made excellent contributions to Johannine scholarship from the perspective of Earth. Elizabeth Schrader has frequently presented at the SBL, and her research on "Mary," the sister of Lazarus, challenges most, if not all, commentators. I am humbled and delighted that all these women agreed to contribute their voices to mine to make this commentary richer. Finally, Barbara Reid and Mary Ann Beavis, as well as being contributing voices, have also offered much encouragement, wisdom, and suggestions as this commentary made its way into print. Their wide knowledge of feminist interpretation enriched my perspective enormously. Without this community of scholars, this volume could never have been birthed. Thank you.

At Liturgical Press I have received painstaking editorial suggestions and corrections from Lauren L. Murphy and Stephanie Lancour, and the layout is the work of Julie Surma. Their work polishes the "rough diamond" of my text to make it a fitting addition to this Wisdom Commentary series. Thank you for your detailed attention.

I offer this commentary to you, the readers, as one way, my way, of reading and valuing this ancient text.

Author's Introduction

When Europeans arrived in Australia, they looked on the continent as *terra nullius*—ridding the land of one hundred thousand years of habitation, culture, agriculture, song, art, technology, and ecofriendly living. The aborigines were considered nonpeople and until 1967 were not even counted in the census of Australian people. Their existence was numbered with the stock, if they worked on cattle or sheep stations; otherwise they went unrecorded. The dark-skinned first people of this ancient land were made invisible and nonexistent by European eyes.

Women can resonate with this. The experience of many women requires the suffix "less"—powerless, voiceless, moneyless, stateless, homeless. On the world stage women seem to be constantly in the shadows of written his-tory, watching on as if nonexistent. Their lives and experience are not worth recording. Within the limits of an ancient text that emerged from within a patriarchal social context, I wish to invite women take their place within the Johannine narrative. Some women appear as full characters and have primary roles, such as the mother of Jesus, the woman of Samaria, Martha and Mary of Bethany, and Mary Magdalene. Others seem to be lost in the crowd or submerged within the group of disciples. But this Gospel, more than any other New Testament book, requires that all characters—women, men, Jews, Gentiles—all participate equally in the divinization of creation when the "Word became flesh" (1:14). The fundamental theology of the text is that all creation is open to be the tabernacling presence of God. The commentary is written from this presumption.

Methodologically, the analysis will involve two deliberate strategies. The first recognizes that the Gospel draws on the OT[1] figure of Wisdom (Gk: *Sophia*) in its portrayal of Jesus. Although Wisdom is not named, her place with God at the dawn of creation (Prov 8:22), her journey to tabernacle with humankind (Sir 24:8-12), her seeking disciples and making them "friends of God and prophets" (Wis 7:27) resonate with the Johannine text. Jesus gives flesh and bones to Wisdom's pilgrimage and task (John 1:14). Each chapter will begin with a brief text from the Wisdom literature so that her presence does not go unrecognized.

The word "wisdom" is feminine in both Hebrew (*Ḥokmah*) and Greek (*Sophia*). This means that in the commentary it is appropriate to speak of Sophia and then to use feminine pronouns such as "she" or "her." While any language to speak of God is metaphorical, how we use language does shape our thinking and ideas. When so much of the Christian discourse has used only male imagery and then consistently spoken of God and prayed using the pronoun "he," to bring the grammatically feminine language into theology both challenges the absolute imaging of a male God and offers a corrective.

More important than the grammar is the genre of the wisdom literature. When Sophia announces her presence, she does not make a declaration couched in metaphysical propositions; she sings herself into creation.

> [23]Ages ago I was set up,
>   at the first, before the beginning of the earth.
> [24]When there were no depths I was brought forth,
>   when there were no springs abounding with water.
> [25]Before the mountains had been shaped,
>   before the hills, I was brought forth. (Prov 8:23-25)

Sophia inhabits the places of women, and she acts as women do in setting her table and offering an invitation to her neighbors (Prov 9:1-3). Where the voice of God "thunders" (Ps 29:2), Sophia's voice invites, "Come, eat of my bread" (Prov 9:5). While noting this I am not suggesting that Sophia is a timid shadow of God confined to the house. In Sirach 24 and Proverbs 8 her domain is the entire cosmos, and in the book of Wisdom

---

1. I refer to the two major sections within the Bible as the Old Testament (OT) and the New Testament (NT). Within the Old Testament there will be times when I refer to its Hebrew text and other times when I refer to the Greek translation of this known as the Septuagint (LXX). The designation "old" or "new" is simply a temporal statement referring to when these books were written. See further comments in the general editor's introduction, xxxix–xl.

she is credited with Israel's escape from Egypt (Wis 10:15-21) and their deliverance in the Sinai wilderness (Wis 11:1-14). Her protective care of Israel is a power to be reckoned with as "she drowned their enemies, and cast them up from the depth of the sea" (Wis 10:19). The poetic genre of Wisdom's speech allows for free ranging imagery and hyperbole. She is not tied to formulaic exactitude. In the words of Diego Irarrázaval: "Christian theology is not a mental and doctrinal labor. Rather, it is a loving relationship with God that leads to celebration, transformation, knowledge. It is, as Jon Sobrino puts it, an *intellectus amoris*."[2]

For feminist theologians the "maleness" of Jesus is a difficulty. It brings a male specificity to God imagery and language. But when the divine Sophia is brought into any thinking about Jesus, then the male specificity does not restrict divine imagery and language to "male only." Sophia breaks open the possibility for all women and men to find a place in divine friendship. That God became a particular human, Jesus, is called "the scandal of particularity." Adding to this is a further scandalous realization "that in various Second Testament and early church texts in which Jesus is celebrated as divine, Jesus is understood and celebrated as the *female divine*."[3] The study of early Christian texts leads Sally Douglas to conclude:

> Re-engaging with Jesus–Woman Wisdom honours the heart of Christian identity, as the incarnation is central and it is Christ who saves. Yet in re-recognizing Jesus–Woman Wisdom ancient claims about Christ are able to be liberated from cultural habits of seeing that diminish their audacity. Wisdom christology and Wisdom soteriology are widely, and wildly, accessible. Images and symbols of Jesus–Woman Wisdom have the potential to communicate with intensity and gripping power, as they dissolve within themselves humanly constructed dualism, between the divine and the earth, between male and female and between the church and the world.[4]

2. Diego Irarrázaval, "La otra globalización—anotación teológica," *Pasos* 77 (1998): 2. The phrase *intellectus amoris* means "love's understanding" through faith. See Sharon H. Ringe (*Wisdom's Friends: Community and Christology in the Fourth Gospel* [Louisville: Westminster John Knox, 1999], 1–5), who discusses the power and necessity of poetry to express religious experience in relation to the Gospel.

3. Sally Douglas, *Early Church Understandings of Jesus as the Female Divine: The Scandal of the Scandal of Particularity*, LNTS 557 (London: Bloomsbury T&T Clark, 2016), 2; italics in the original.

4. Douglas, *Early Church Understandings*, 202.

Wisdom Christology in the Fourth Gospel is well presented by Sharon Ringe, Martin Scott, and Ben Witherington III,[5] but it is also strongly critiqued by Judith Lieu, who writes, "John has no interest in 'wisdom.' . . .The Gospel itself shows no interest in them [the wisdom motifs]."[6] She acknowledges that the prologue draws on Wisdom traditions but then states correctly that Wisdom is not named in the narrative and that where there are links with the Wisdom tradition, "they are in no sense part of her gendered character and cannot be said to be an expression of the feminine (aspect of the divine or whatever)."[7] On this point I disagree with Judith Lieu.

Early in the narrative there is an encounter with Nicodemus, and in the dialogue and discourse that follows the Gospel uses a concept and terms that are unique to the wisdom literature. Briefly,[8] Jesus speaks of the reign of God (John 3:3, 5; βασιλεία τοῦ θεοῦ), an expression found only in the book of Wisdom (10:10). Similarly, the term "eternity life" (John 3:15, 16; ζωὴν αἰώνιον)[9] is unique to the book of Wisdom (5:15; εἰς τὸν αἰῶνα ζῶσιν), as is the theology of participation *now* in the life of God.[10] Pharisees, such as Nicodemus, considered this to be a feature of the "end time." It is in this context that Jesus speaks to Nicodemus of the need to be reborn (John 3:3, 5). The birth image is named specifically and is clearly a gendered image, much to Nicodemus's confusion (3:4). Following this dialogue, the discourse then introduces the concept of "eternity life" (John 3:15, 16), which is the quality of life that Sophia offers the righteous in the book of Wisdom (Wis 6:18; 8:17, 21). This concept clarifies what being "born again" means. It is to be born into a new quality of eternity life. Jesus

---

5. Ringe, *Wisdom's Friends*; Martin Scott, *Sophia and the Johannine Jesus*, JSNTSup 71 (Sheffield: JSOT Press, 1992); Ben Witherington III, *John's Wisdom: A Commentary on the Fourth Gospel* (Louisville: Westminster John Knox, 1995).

6. Judith Lieu, "Scripture and the Feminine in John," in *A Feminist Companion to the Hebrew Bible in the New Testament*, ed. Athalya Brenner, FCB (Sheffield: Sheffield Academic, 1996), 238.

7. Lieu, "Scripture and the Feminine in John," 238.

8. More will be said on these points within the commentary.

9. This Greek expression is usually translated "eternal life." I prefer to put the emphasis on the quality of life that is being described and not simply the length of life. I will argue that in this Gospel Jesus offers a new quality of life, that life God lives in eternity. The catchphrase "eternity life" expresses this richness and in the Fourth Gospel is the equivalent of the phrase "the reign of God," as used frequently in the Synoptic Gospels.

10. "The hour is coming and is now here" (John 4:23; 5:25).

speaks of himself as the only-*born* (μονογενῆ) of God (John 3:16)[11] and as Jesus/Sophia[12] offers eternity life to those who believe. From then on, the Gospel uses the term "eternity life" as a major motif of the narrative,[13] and this quality of life is grounded in the language of being born (John 3:3, 5). It is difficult *not* to see Sophia in this passage and, following this, whenever "eternity life" is mentioned.[14] At the cross, the image of being born is graphically shown in the birthing image when blood and water flow from the side of Sophia-Jesus.[15] As I will argue in the commentary, this is a moment when disciples are born to be children of God, as confirmed by Jesus to Mary Magdalene (John 20:17). As I elaborate on the Wisdom Christology throughout this commentary, I will be mindful to try to avoid the pitfalls Elisabeth Schüssler Fiorenza identifies. Similar to me, she thinks "the Fourth Gospel understands Jesus as making Sophia present in and through his/her work."[16] But she warns that Wisdom Christology can romanticize and divinize patriarchal notions of femininity, thereby unwittingly reinscribing gender dualism. In addition, she notes that wisdom literature came out of elite male circles. "Its function was to give instruction to the *pater familias*, legitimate male authority, and advance kyriarchal agenda."[17] In retrieving the submerged Sophia traditions, I will try to rearticulate them in such a way that questions the dominant male language for God and Christ in ways that open new possibilities for egalitarian practice.

In addition to drawing on wisdom traditions, a second interpretive strategy that I will use in this commentary is akin to the Jewish tradition of midrash. Many Gospel scenes are monochromatic, with only

---

11. Μονογενῆ has as its first meaning "to be born." It is a word found only in John (1:14, 18; and 3:16, 18). William F. Arndt, "γίνομαι," BDAG (2000): 197.

12. Sophia is also described as "the only born," although this word is usually translated as "unique" (Wis 7:22, μονογενές).

13. The expression ζωὴν αἰώνιον (eternity life) occurs in 3:15, 16, 36; 4:14, 36; 5:24, 39; 6:27, 40, 47, 54, 68; 10:28; 12:25, 50; 17:2; and αἰώνιος ζωὴ in 17:3.

14. Lieu does discuss the Nicodemus passage but does not relate it to the book of Wisdom and the concept of eternity life that follows the dialogue about being born again. Lieu, "Scripture and the Feminine in John," 237–38.

15. Barbara E. Reid, "Birthed from the Side of Jesus (John 19:34)," in *Finding a Woman's Place: Essays in Honor of Carolyn Osiek, R.S.C.J.*, ed. David L. Bach and Jason T. Lamoreaux (Eugene, OR: Pickwick, 2011). See excursus in this commentary at 19:34.

16. Elisabeth Schüssler Fiorenza, *Jesus: Miriam's Child, Sophia's Prophet; Critical Issues in Feminist Christology*, 2nd ed. (London: Bloomsbury T&T Clark, 2015), 167.

17. Barbara Reid and Shelly Matthews, *Luke 1–9*, WCS 43A (Collegeville, MN: Liturgical Press, 2021), 235.

men visible. The presence of women is taken for granted, forgotten, or unrecognized. Here, midrash is needed. As Jewish feminist theologian Judith Plaskow states: "Midrash expands and burrows, invents the forgotten and prods the memory, takes from history and asks for more. It gives us the inner life history cannot follow."[18] She also speaks of the "contradiction between the holes in the text and many women's felt experience."[19] Rather than continue the sins of my white European ancestors and see *terra nullius*, my reading insists on a text inhabited by women as well as men; I will draw Sophia to the foreground and bring women's discipleship from the shadows.

When reading any document, it is helpful to know basic information about it so that an interpretation is coherent with the document's original context, and its relevance to later times can then be extrapolated. Who was the author? When and where was it written? Why was it written? Who was the expected reader/audience? When asking these questions of the Fourth Gospel, there are immediate difficulties, as the earliest manuscripts available to scholars have no autograph to identify the author, nor is there certainty about the date and location of its writing. What follows is my position with a very brief discussion.[20]

Location and Dating

Early twentieth-century commentaries looked to a background in Greek thought because of the dualistic language of the Gospel; e.g., light, dark; above, below; heaven, earth. Since the discovery of the Dead Sea Scrolls in 1947 and their gradual dissemination to the wider scholarly community, scholars have been more convinced that the initial shaping of the Gospel was within a Judean context, as the type of dualism, the realized eschatology, the community-as-temple theology found in John is also found in the Scrolls. John's Gospel has its roots in the varieties of Jewish beliefs and groups found in first-century Judea and Galilee,

18. Judith Plaskow, *Standing Again at Sinai: Judaism from a Feminist Perspective* (New York: HarperCollins, 1990), 59.

19. Judith Plaskow, "Standing Again at Sinai: Jewish Memory from a Feminist Perspective," *Tikkun* 2 (1986): 28.

20. Further details can be found in Gail R. O'Day, "John," in *The Gospel of Luke; the Gospel of John*, ed. R. Alan Culpepper and Gail R. O'Day, NIB 9 (Nashville: Abingdon, 1995); Ruth B. Edwards, *Discovering John: Content, Interpretation, Reception*, DisBT (Grand Rapids: Eerdmans, 2015).

even if its final stages of development and editing occurred in the wider Greco-Roman world.

One early Christian writer, Irenaeus (c. 130–202 CE), named Ephesus as the place where the Gospel was written.[21] Notwithstanding this testimony, the Gospel could have been finally produced in any of the larger Greco-Roman cities where there were communities of Jews and Christians, such as Alexandria or Antioch. A clue within the Gospel that Ephesus may have been where the final form of the Gospel was written is the way John the Baptist is portrayed: John, like Jesus, is "sent from God" (1:6); the first disciples of Jesus come from within a group of John's followers. Later there is a glimpse of parallel baptizing ministries carried out by John's disciples and Jesus's disciples, leading to the affirmation by John that it is Jesus who is the bridegroom, while his role is to be the bridegroom's friend: "He must increase, but I must decrease" (3:30). Clearly, John's person and ministry are treated with honor, but just as clearly Jesus is the more important. One place outside the land of Judea/Galilee where John's ministry continued to have influence was Ephesus. In the Acts of the Apostles, when Paul and Barnabas arrive in Ephesus they find a group of Baptist followers who have received his baptism but not the baptism of the Spirit (Acts 19:1-7). The way John is treated in the Fourth Gospel, along with the fact that John's disciples were present in Ephesus, lends support to the written testimony of Irenaeus that the Gospel was finally recorded in Ephesus.

Most scholars consider that the final edition of the Gospel was written sometime in the late 90s. While this may be so, there are indicators in the text, to be discussed below, that it has gone through stages in its development. One reason why this Gospel is dated later than the Synoptics is because of its high Christology. Only John's Gospel affirms the divine status of the Word (1:1), and only John has a statement of faith that the risen Jesus is "my Lord and my God" (20:28). Such high Christology presumes a long process of theological thinking and development. Furthermore, within the Gospel there are three references to followers of Jesus being expelled from the synagogue (ἀποσυνάγωγος, 9:22; 12:42; 16:2). Even if this refers only to a local synagogue, such a decision may have come about following the rabbinic discussions at Jamnia/Yavneh

---

21. "Afterward, John, the disciple of the Lord, who also had leaned upon His breast, did himself publish a Gospel during his residence at Ephesus in Asia" (*Adv. Haer.* 3.1.1). Translation from New Advent website, https://www.newadvent.org/fathers /0103301.htm.

during the 80s.[22] These discussions sought to clarify issues facing the Jewish community after the destruction of the temple by the Romans in 70 CE. One decision made at this time was the introduction of a prayer into the Eighteen Benedictions that were part of the synagogue morning prayer service.[23] This new Benediction, the twelfth, was a curse against heretics:

> For those doomed to destruction may there be no hope
> And may the dominion of arrogance be quickly uprooted in our days
> And may the Nazarenes and the heretics be destroyed in a moment
> And may they be blotted out of the book of life
> And may they not be inscribed with the righteous.
> Blessed are you, O Lord,
> Who subdues the arrogant.[24]

In the aftermath of Jamnia, growing tensions between a local Christian group and the synagogue may well provide the context for the strong polemic in the Gospel against "the Jews" and the use of the term ἀποσυνάγωγος. But the waters here are muddy! There is little literary or archeological evidence from the late first century that can lead to certainty. Louis Martyn's hypothesis that the Gospel needs to be read on two levels makes good sense hermeneutically: it is narrating the story of Jesus in his time, while it is also literature with a stated aim to influence the listeners/readers some decades later.[25] But we also need to be cautious of ascribing to late first-century Judaism and Christianity clear boundaries that only become apparent centuries later. Judith Lieu points out that the important task of forming a self-identity can lead to the creation of an "other" as a

---

22. A recent discussion and evaluation of the ἀποσυνάγωγος statements can be found in Jörg Frey, *The Glory of the Crucified One: Christology and Theology in the Gospel of John*, trans. Wayne Coppins and Christoph Heilig, BMSEC (Waco, TX: Baylor University Press, 2018), 51–72.

23. According to the Talmud, "The benediction relating to the Minim was instituted in Jamnia" (t. Ber. 28b).

24. Joel Marcus, "*Birkat Ha-Minim* Revisited," *NTS* 55 (2009): 524. Marcus's article reviews the earlier proposal by J. Louis Martyn (that these three passages [9:22; 12:42; 16:2], which speak of being excluded from the synagogue, were the direct result of the Twelfth Benediction) and its critics before mounting a strong case that this prayer against heretics (*minim*) was a strategy developed by the rabbis to identify and exclude Jewish Christians and other forms of Judaism that were no longer considered orthodox.

25. J. Louis Martyn, *History and Theology in the Fourth Gospel* (New York: Harper and Row, 1968).

rhetorical image rather than a historical reality. Lieu writes, "It is in opposition that Christianity gains its true identity. So all identity becomes articulated, perhaps for the first time, in face of the 'other,' as well as in the face of attempts by the 'other' to deny its existence. Conversely, the uncompromising affirmation of identity constructs the boundary against 'the other.' "[26] So while the Gospel describes a distinction between believers and "Jews" where there is sufficient clarity to eject those confessing "Christ" from the synagogue, the actual historical situation is far from clear. An important Jewish voice that needs to be heard in evaluating Martyn's "expulsion" theory is that of Adele Reinhartz, who has challenged as simplistic and anachronistic any reading back into the Johannine text clear religious boundaries that emerged only in later centuries.[27] She considers "that the term *Ioudaios* had primarily rhetorical rather than denotative meaning. . . . From the Gospel's vantage point believers by definition are outside the group of *Ioudaioi*."[28] She sees the Gospel as looking forward to a time when there is a clear distinction between the Jesus believers and the *Ioudaioi*, and in looking to the future the narrative "pushes its audience to see such separation as essential to their own developing self-identification as children of God."[29] In other words, the Gospel is not describing a "casting out" that has happened but is part of the process of self-defining that will necessitate a stepping away.

The Gospel could not have been written much later than the final decade of the first century because a papyrus, $\mathfrak{P}^{52}$, with verses from this Gospel (18:31-33, 37-38) was found in Egypt, and this papyrus is dated between 125 and 150 CE.[30] Supporting this time-frame is an ancient text known as the *Epistle to Diognetus* where there are a number of passages

---

26. Judith M. Lieu, *Neither Jew nor Greek? Constructing Early Christianity*, SNTW (Edinburgh: T&T Clark, 2002), 215–16.

27. Adele Reinhartz, "Story and History: John, Judaism, and the Historical Imagination," in *John and Judaism: A Contested Relationship in Context*, ed. R. Alan Culpepper and Paul N. Anderson, RBS 87 (Atlanta: SBL Press, 2017); Adele Reinhartz, *Cast Out of the Covenant: Jews and Anti-Judaism in the Gospel of John* (Lanham, MD: Lexington Books, 2018).

28. Reinhartz, *Cast Out of the Covenant*, 161–62.

29. Reinhartz, *Cast Out of the Covenant*, 162.

30. The earlier dating, 125 CE, is proposed in Kurt Aland and Barbara Aland, *The Text of the New Testament: An Introduction to the Critical Editions and to the Theory and Practice of Modern Textual Criticism* (Grand Rapids: Eerdmans, 1987), 99. Caution about dating papyri based on paleographic evidence must allow for a range of plus or minus twenty-five years.

that are almost direct citations of John's Gospel: "Christians dwell in the world but are not of the world" (*Ad Diogn.* 6.3; compare John 17:11, 14, 16); "For God loved humanity . . . to them he sent his one and only Son" (*Ad Diogn.* 10. 2; compare John 3:16). This epistle was most likely written between 125 and 150.[31]

Authorship and the Beloved Disciple

Several questions overlap: Who was the actual author of the Fourth Gospel? What is the relationship of the author to the anonymous Beloved Disciple and the "other disciple" who appear in the text? Was the Beloved Disciple an actual historical person or a literary construct? In what follows, I offer my answers to these questions.

We do not have a clear indicator in any manuscript about the identity of the author.[32] The earliest manuscript with a superscription, "The Gospel according to John," is $\mathfrak{P}^{66}$, a Codex from Oxyrhynchus dated ca. 200.[33] In the second century, Irenaeus, the bishop of Lyons (ca. 180–200), attributed the Gospel to "John, the disciple of the Lord who also had leaned upon his breast" (*Adv. Haer.* 3.1.1). But this identification is open to question. In the second century the Fourth Gospel was popular among Gnostic sects, and Irenaeus may have attributed the Gospel to one of Jesus's close disciples in order to draw it within mainstream, rather than sectarian, Christianity. Even prior to Irenaeus another early witness, Papias (60–163), may be correct when he writes of two "Johns," one listed among the apostolic names, and another called "the presbyter John, the disciple of the Lord" (Eusebius, *Hist. eccl.* 3.39.4).[34]

---

31. Charles E. Hill, *The Johannine Corpus in the Early Church* (Oxford: Oxford University Press, 2004), 361–66.

32. The conventions within ancient writing meant that the "author" may not have been the person whose hand actually wrote the script. The author may have dictated to a scribal disciple who would have written his words, much like a modern-day secretary, or the author may have provided the ideas for another to shape and write the text, or the author may have been the writer (e.g., see Paul's comments on his own handwriting in 1 Cor 16:1; Gal 6:11; Col 4:18; 2 Thess 3:17). For this reason, some speak of the "authority" behind the text as distinct from the actual writer of the text.

33. Oxyrhynchus is an ancient Egyptian city located about 160 kilometers south of Cairo, where excavations since the mid-nineteenth century have yielded important papyrus documents.

34. This is the conclusion reached in a recent study of the ancient texts; Dean Furlong, *The Identity of John the Evangelist: Revision and Reinterpretation in Early Christian Sources* (Lanham, MD: Lexinton/Fortress Academic, 2020), 1.

The Gospel offers some clues about the author that led Brooke F. Westcott, writing toward the end of the nineteenth century, to state, "The writer of the Fourth Gospel was not only a Jew, but a Palestinian Jew of the first century."[35] He made this claim based on internal evidence such as the author's familiarity with Jewish customs, Jewish concepts (e.g., messianic ideas, religious schools, sin, hostility between Jews and Samaritans), Jewish laws, festivals; the Gospel's literary style and symbols; and the use of the Old Testament through both direct citations and allusions. He further argues that the author is a Palestinian Jew based on his detailed local knowledge of geography, e.g., Cana in Galilee (2:1), Bethany beyond the Jordan (1:28), the size of the Sea of Tiberias (6:19). He knows the topography of Jerusalem, such as the pool of Bethesda with its five porticos near the sheep-gate (5:2), the pool of Siloam (9:7), and the Kidron Valley (18:1). He is aware of Herod's long rebuilding program for the Jerusalem temple and the name of its cloisters (10:23).[36] Even the Gospel's use of creation occurring through the "Logos/word" reflects the Aramaic Scriptures read within the synagogues of Palestine and need not be explained in Hellenistic or Philonic terms. In these Scriptures, called the targums, God creates through the Word/*Memra*. "From the beginning with wisdom the *Memra* of the Lord created and perfected the heavens and the earth" (Tg. Neof. Gen 1:1). Further evidence from the discovery of the Dead Sea Scrolls in 1947 supports the Palestinian provenance of the traditions reflected in this Gospel.[37] This being so, it is highly doubtful that the author could have been John, the son of Zebedee. It is very unlikely that a Galilean fisherman would be so familiar with the topography of Jerusalem or have the level of education to write such an eloquent gospel.

There is another disciple present across the entire Gospel who may be the authority behind the text. When John the Baptizer, the only "John" mentioned in the Gospel, is introduced we hear of two disciples sent to follow Jesus—one is named Andrew, but the other remains anonymous (1:35-42). In other parts of the narrative where the setting is Jerusalem, an

35. Brooke Foss Westcott, *The Gospel According to St John: With Introduction and Notes* (London: John Murray, 1890), x.

36. A century of archaeology has provided further evidence of the historicity of places, customs, and Jewish thinking, which is reflected in this Gospel. See James H. Charlesworth, "The Historical Jesus in the Fourth Gospel: A Paradigm Shift?," *JSHJ* 8 (2010): 3–46.

37. Raymond E. Brown, *An Introduction to the Gospel of John: Edited, Updated, Introduced and Concluded by Francis J. Moloney*, ABRL (New York: Doubleday, 2003), 203–6.

anonymous disciple is also present (18:15, 16; 20:3, 4, 8). Then, in 20:2, this "other disciple" is identified with the Beloved Disciple: "So she [Mary Magdalene] ran and went to Simon Peter and the other disciple, the one whom Jesus loved." This Beloved Disciple is mentioned in 13:23 ("One of his disciples—the one whom Jesus loved—was reclining next to him"), is present at the cross (19:26), and then is explicitly said to be the author of the Gospel in chapter 21: "Peter turned and saw the disciple whom Jesus loved following them; he was the one who had reclined next to Jesus at the supper. . . . This is the disciple who is testifying to these things and has written them, and we know that his testimony is true" (21:20, 24). It is plausible that this disciple did not write/speak his/her name into the narrative and simply used the self-designation "the other disciple," but later, a final editor of the Gospel added the sobriquet "the disciple whom Jesus loved."

If the Beloved Disciple is the anonymous "other" disciple, then the Gospel gives us the following information. This disciple has been present from the beginning of Jesus's ministry (1:35), is one of his first disciples, and has heard John's testimony that Jesus is the Lamb of God (1:36). He demonstrates what discipleship means, namely, accepting the invitation of Jesus and then remaining with him (1:39). He is present reclining next to Jesus during the final meal (13:23) and thus hears Jesus's teaching and words of consolation. He is present in the garden scene of Jesus's arrest and then is able to follow him inside the grounds of the high priest's house (18:15). He stands at the foot of the cross (19:26) then runs with Peter to the tomb (20:2). This disciple can bear witness to what he has seen and heard across the full gamut of Jesus's ministry. He has a unique place among the disciples as the only one who has followed Jesus from the beginning, to the end. As such, this disciple stands as the authority, able to testify to the "truth" of this account.

Sandra Schneiders proposes that the authority behind the Gospel may be a woman.[38] Women were clearly leaders of some communities in early Christianity (e.g., Phoebe in Cenchreae, Rom 16:1-2), and in this Gospel women such as the Samaritan woman, Mary Magdalene, and Martha and Mary of Bethany are missionaries (John 4:39; 20:17-18), who engage in theological discussion (4:7-26; 11:21-27) and show theological insight into Jesus's identity (4:25; 11:27; 12:1-8). Schneiders's questions: What man would have assigned such prominent apostolically significant roles to

---

38. Sandra M. Schneiders, *Written That You May Believe: Encountering Jesus in the Fourth Gospel*, rev. and exp. ed. (New York: Crossroad, 2003), 233–54.

women, roles that in the Synoptic Gospels are assigned to the Twelve?[39] Schneiders then proceeds to analyze the function of the Beloved Disciple before arriving at a tentative conclusion about the identity of the author.[40]

Schneiders regards the "author" of the Gospel "to be both the authority from which the tradition stems (i.e., the Beloved Disciple) and the evangelist (a second-century Johannine Christian) mutually interacting in the production of the text."[41] At a later stage, there was also a redactor who edited the Gospel (see the next section of this introduction for an explanation of the various phases of production). The Beloved Disciple is "neither a pure literary symbol nor a single historical individual" but rather "a kind of textual paradigm who concretely embodies in the text the corporate authority of the Johannine School. The Beloved Disciple *in the text* is a kind of prism refracting the ideal of discipleship into a number of characters,"[42] including Nathanael, the Samaritan woman, the royal official, Martha, Mary, Lazarus, and Mary Magdalene. All of these characters are needed to give the reader a fuller picture of the ideal that the Beloved Disciple represents.[43] But if one of them embodies in the text an eyewitness source behind the Fourth Gospel, the one who most clearly does that is Mary Magdalene, who is a witness to the crucifixion (19:25-27), discovers the empty tomb, is the first to see the risen Christ and to be commissioned by him as an apostle (20:1-18).[44]

Mary Magdalene's story continues beyond the canonical Gospel into the apocryphal literature of the Gnostics, who were considered heretics by the greater church. And so, Schneiders explains:

> If we are looking for a motive for the evangelist's deliberate obscuring of the identity of the Beloved Disciple in the Fourth Gospel, what better reason could there be than that the authoritative source of the Gospel was, or was connected in some way with, Mary Magdalene, the problematic woman protagonist in literature regarded as heretical at precisely the time that this Gospel was beginning to circulate at the beginning of the second century.[45]

39. Schneiders, *Written That You May Believe*, 238.
40. Schneiders does not equate the "other disciple" with the Beloved Disciple. The "other disciple" is the evangelist's creation of an "empty set" into which the reader is intended to insert him- or herself, i.e., the implied reader (*Written That You May Believe*, 239).
41. Schneiders, *Written That You May Believe*, 246.
42. Ibid.; italics in the original.
43. Ibid., 248.
44. Ibid., 243.
45. Ibid., 245.

Schneiders's rigorous analysis, based on detailed exegesis and critical hermeneutical theory, offers important insights into the provenance of this Gospel and has gained acceptance by many feminists. Nonetheless, while agreeing with Schneiders on the important role of women in the Gospel, which may indicate women's authority behind its tradition, I consider the evidence insufficient to be able to make that conclusion.

Schneiders concludes with a tentative suggestion on the identity of the evangelist: we will never know who the historical author was, but the writer's *alter ego* or literary self-portrait in the text is the Samaritan woman, who receives Jesus's direct self-revelation, which constitutes her message and establishes her authority.[46] This is possible, but I am not convinced that the evangelist would take the radical literary step to be present in the text as a Samaritan, given the cultural/religious animosity between Samaritans and Jews. If the evangelist does use this literary technique of having a textual *alter ego*, then I suggest Thomas—who, like the Samaritan Woman, moves from utter doubt, to complete faith and makes the radical and perfect proclamation, "My Lord and my God" (20:28). This is the faith with which the Gospel opens (1:1) and closes. But this can only be conjecture.

I consider that there were two honored disciples in the community. A woman, Mary, always called the Magdalene (the great one),[47] remembered for her evangelizing the community with the Easter proclamation, "I have seen the Lord" (20:18). And a male disciple, present from the beginning of Jesus's ministry (the other disciple) to the end and remembered as the Beloved Disciple. He was the first to come to full Johannine faith by believing through signs, not sight. He did not see the Risen One but saw the sign of the face-veil (20:8) in the tomb and then the sign of the great draught of fish (21:7), and these were enough for him to know "it is the Lord" (21:7). The Risen Jesus commends such sign faith and calls those who come to faith in the future through such signs "Blessed" (20:29). The Samaritan woman and Mary the Magdalene are remembered for their evangelizing mission and duly honored by their prominence in the narrative. But there is another disciple, who remains anonymous, who is remembered as the model of faith. After his death, he remains anonymous but is given the sobriquet the Beloved Disciple: beloved by Jesus in the narrative and most likely beloved by the community for his role in their own foundation and formation.

---

46. Ibid., 251–53.

47. For further discussion about the likely meaning of Magdalene, see the contribution by Elizabeth Schrader, "One Woman or Three?," at 19:25.

The Johannine Community and Its Gospel

Linked to the question of authorship, date, and location is the likely development of a particular Christian community and the Gospel text produced from this community. Among the numerous hypotheses offered on this question, the work of Raymond Brown has gained the widest acceptance,[48] and based on his work I suggest the following stages in the development of the community.

Phase 1: Mid-50s to Late 80s

An originating group of Jews, probably in the region of Judea,[49] including disciples of John the Baptist, accepted Jesus, understanding him within traditional Jewish concepts as a Davidic messiah. To this group was added a second group of Jews and Samaritans who understood Jesus in terms of a "prophet like Moses" rather than as a Davidic figure. The addition of this group led to a deeper understanding of Jesus's relationship with God, which is called a high, preexistence Christology. These members of the community affirmed Jesus's divine status: "In the beginning was the Word, and the Word was with God, and the Word was God" (1:1). This led to conflict with other Jews, and eventually those believers openly confessing faith in Jesus were expelled from the synagogue (9:22; 12:42; 16:2) in this locale. During this time, the leader of the community, who came to be known as the Beloved Disciple, passed on the traditions of Jesus, shaping these oral traditions according to the pastoral needs of this community and possibly writing a first form of the Gospel.

Phase 2: During the 90s

By the 90s the group may have moved outside the Jewish homeland into the wider Greco-Roman world, and here they began to make Gentile converts. During this time the final form of the Gospel was produced.

---

48. Raymond E. Brown, *The Community of the Beloved Disciple: The Life, Loves, and Hates of an Individual Church in New Testament Times* (New York: Paulist Press, 1979). Brown, *Introduction to the Gospel of John*, 62–86.

49. I consider Judea a likely place for the group's origins, rather than Galilee, because of the many views shared with the Dead Sea Scrolls; see essays in Mary L. Coloe and Tom Thatcher, eds., *John, Qumran, and the Dead Sea Scrolls: Sixty Years of Discovery and Debate*, EJL 32 (Atlanta: SBL, 2011).

The christological debates with Judaism led some within the Johannine community to break away from the community (6:66; 8:31).[50]

Phase 3: Late 90s to 100

Toward the end of the first century some members of the breakaway group were placing such emphasis on the divinity of Jesus that they were losing sight of his humanity. The main group continued to emphasize the humanity of Jesus, and this group is responsible for the Johannine Epistles and the strong condemnation against the breakaway group (e.g., 1 John 2:18-19; 2 John 7). By this time the Beloved Disciple was probably dead (see John 21:20-23), and another within the community gave a final shape to the Gospel with the addition of chapter 21 and possibly other minor editorial additions.

Phase 4: The Second Century

The main group was assimilated into the broader apostolic church, while the breakaway group, who may have had greater numbers, moved toward other groups that so emphasized one aspect of Jesus, such as being a heavenly revealer,[51] that they lost sight of the total revelation.

It is important to realize that this is a hypothetical reconstruction of the Johannine community based on the writing found in the Gospel and Epistles attributed to "John."

Interpretive Approaches to the Gospel

The primary approach to studies of John through much of the twentieth century was using historical-critical methods in an attempt to understand the history, the community, and the sources behind the text.[52] The commentaries by Rudolph Bultmann, Raymond Brown, and C. K. Barrett typ-

---

50. It is only possible to hypothesize these debates from what the Gospel depicts since we do not have texts from the Jewish side. The Gospel depicts conflicts about the temple (chap. 2), about Jesus's identity and his claim to have the right to heal on the Sabbath (chaps. 5 and 9), about his claim to be the "bread of life" and that through eating his flesh one can gain eternity life (chap. 6).

51. Pheme Perkins, *Gnosticism and the New Testament* (Minneapolis: Fortress, 1993), chap. 7.

52. For earlier approaches, see the review in John Ashton, *Understanding the Fourth Gospel* (Oxford: Clarendon, 1996), 1–66.

ify this approach, which focuses on the world behind the text.[53] A major shift happened in 1983 with the publication of Alan Culpepper's *Anatomy of the Fourth Gospel*,[54] which brought narrative criticism into Johannine studies. Francis Moloney's, Andrew Lincoln's, and Marianne Thompson's commentaries offer such a reading of the world within the text.[55] Since then various other methods and hermeneutical approaches have offered new insights into the literary, rhetorical, theological, and ideological aspects of the Gospel, where the position of the reader, the world in front of the text, comes to the fore.[56] Feminist criticism is one of various ideological hermeneutics applied to the Gospel in recent decades.[57]

Feminist Studies and the Fourth Gospel

The general editor's introduction to this commentary provides an overview of feminist biblical interpretation; here I will mention briefly some of the Johannine studies. To commemorate the work of Elizabeth Cady Stanton in the 1890s,[58] *The Women's Bible Commentary* was published in

---

53. Rudolph Bultmann, *The Gospel of John: A Commentary*, trans. G. R. Beasley Murray et al. (Oxford: Blackwell, 1971); Raymond E. Brown, *The Gospel According to John*, 2 vols., AB 29, 29A (New York: Doubleday, 1966, 1970); Charles K. Barrett, *The Gospel According to St John*, 2nd ed. (London: SPCK, 1978).

54. R. Alan Culpepper, *Anatomy of the Fourth Gospel: A Study in Literary Design*, New Testament, FF (Philadelphia: Fortress, 1983).

55. Francis J. Moloney, *John*, SP 4 (Collegeville, MN: Liturgical Press, 1998); Andrew T. Lincoln, *The Gospel According to Saint John*, BNTC (London: Continuum, 2005); Marianne Meye Thompson, *John: A Commentary*, NTL (Louisville, KY: Westminster John Knox, 2015).

56. Two volumes edited by Fernando Segovia illustrate the wide range of possible readings when the focus shifts to how a real reader in front of the text may approach the Gospel. Fernando F. Segovia, ed., *What Is John?*, vol. 1: *Readers and Readings of the Fourth Gospel*, SBLSymS 3 (Atlanta: Scholars Press, 1996); Fernando F. Segovia, ed., *What Is John?*, vol 2: *Literary and Social Readings of the Fourth Gospel*, SBLSymS 7 (Atlanta: Scholars Press, 1998).

57. See, for example, Schneiders, *Written That You May Believe*; Adeline Fehribach, *The Women in the Life of the Bridegroom: A Feminist Historical-Literary Analysis of the Female Characters in the Fourth Gospel* (Collegeville, MN: Liturgical Press, 1998); Josephine Massyngbaerde Ford, *Redeemer—Friend and Mother: Salvation in Antiquity and in the Gospel of John* (Minneapolis: Fortress, 1997); Gail R. O'Day, "John," in *Women's Bible Commentary*, ed. Carol A. Newsom, Sharon H. Ringe, and Jacqueline E. Lapsley, 3rd ed. (Louisville: Westminster John Knox, 2012), 517–30.

58. Elizabeth Cady Stanton, *The Woman's Bible* (1895, 1898).

1992, and Gail O'Day contributed an essay on John.[59] Her essay focused primarily on the episodes in which women featured in the Gospel, with a brief discussion on some of the Johannine language such as "love," "abide," and "Father." Appearing around the same time was the study by Adele Reinhartz.[60] As a Jewish woman and feminist, Reinhartz explicitly raises the gender and Jewish biases of the text, such as the submersion of the female Sophia in the male son of God. Within the confines of a short study, she does engage with the entire Gospel, not simply the episodes with women, and concludes with a feminist-critical evaluation. At first reading, the Gospel can appear positive from a feminist perspective, but then she raises the negative portrayal of the Jews and dominant father-son language. The portrayal of "the Jews" leads her to self-identify as a resistant reader, one who is not compliant with the aims of the Gospel to come to faith in Jesus as the Messiah, Son of God (20:31). Nevertheless, she can applaud the "Johannine models that empower Christian women and validate their authority within the churches."[61]

In 1996, three essays on the Gospel of John appeared in *A Feminist Companion to the Hebrew Bible in the New Testament*, edited by Athalya Brenner.[62] Adele Reinhartz emphasizes how important it is for the reader or interpreter to recognize their own particular bias. She offers two contrasting views appraising the roles of Martha and Mary in both Luke and John: the view of Ben Withington III and that of Elisabeth Schüssler Fiorenza. She then adds her own reading as someone outside the Christian tradition. Judith Lieu's essay really challenges feminist interpreters. Not only does she deny the value of Wisdom/Sophia Christology for women, but she also points out that by focussing on the uniqueness of Jesus's supportive treatment of women, feminists may be colluding in anti-Judaism. Lyn Bechtel also raises the spectre of anti-Judaism in the Gospel in her discussion of the wedding at Cana, seeing a possible

---

59. O'Day, "John," 293–304. The second and third editions (1998, 2012) dropped "The" from the title.

60. Adele Reinhartz, "The Gospel of John," in *Searching the Scriptures*, vol. 2: *A Feminist Commentary*, ed. Elisabeth Schüssler Fiorenza (New York: Crossroad, 1994), 561–600.

61. Reinhartz, "The Gospel of John," 597.

62. Athalya Brenner, ed., *A Feminist Companion to the Hebrew Bible in the New Testament*, FCB (Sheffield: Sheffield Academic, 1996) includes: Adele Reinhartz, "From Narrative to History: The Resurrection of Mary and Martha," 197–224; Judith Lieu, "Scripture and the Feminine in John," 225–40; and Lyn M. Bechtel, "A Symbolic Level of Meaning: John 2.1-11," 241–55.

indication of Jesus's breaking his ties with Judaism. She points to the manner in which Jesus speaks to his mother as "Woman." See below at 2:1-11, where I take quite a different approach to this scene.

Two volumes on the Gospel of John appeared in 2003 in the Feminist Companion to the New Testament and Early Christian Literature series edited by Amy-Jill Levine with Marianne Blickenstaff. These two volumes offer seventeen studies addressing such issues as "Jesus and the Adulteress," "Cultural Stereotypes of Women," "Gender Matters," the use of "I am," and "Abiding."[63] The studies in these two volumes look beyond the episodes with women to how women and men are portrayed and to how gender and language function within the Gospel. Satoko Yamaguchi, for example, looks at the predicates of the "I Am" sayings to show that through metaphors such as life, bread, and light, "the imaginative world is not exclusively male."[64]

In addition to these collections of essays, there have also been monographs by individual writers. Two books bearing similar titles examine the roles of women and men in the Fourth Gospel. Colleen Conway offers a study of five women and five men:[65] the mother of Jesus, Nicodemus, the Samaritan woman, the man born blind, Martha and Mary of Bethany, Pilate, Simon Peter, the Beloved Disciple, and Mary Magdalene. To this list Margaret Beirne adds the royal official, Judas, and Thomas, while omitting Pilate.[66] Beirne presents her study as "gender pairs," such as Nicodemus and the Samaritan woman, Mary of Bethany and Judas. She proposes that these gender pairs are placed deliberately in the structure of the Gospel to display a genuine discipleship of equals. Although not going into a detailed historical reconstruction, Beirne suggests that such a portrayal was necessary at a time when the later epistles were proposing

---

63. Amy-Jill Levine, ed., with Marianne Blickenstaff, *A Feminist Companion to John*, vol. 1, FCNTECW 4 (London: Sheffield Academic, 2003) includes, among others, Holly J. Toensing, "Divine Intervention or Divine Intrusion? Jesus and the Adulteress in John's Gospel," 159–72; Jerome H. Neyrey, "What's Wrong with This Picture? John 4, Cultural Stereotypes of Women, and Public and Private Space," 98–125; vol. 2 (FCNTECW 5) includes Colleen M. Conway, "Gender Matters in John," 79–103; Satoko Yamaguchi, "'I Am' Sayings and Women in Context," 34–63; Dorothy A. Lee, "Abiding in the Fourth Gospel: A Case Study in Feminist Biblical Theology," 64–78.

64. Yamaguchi, "'I Am' Sayings and Women in Context," 60.

65. Colleen M. Conway, *Men and Women in the Fourth Gospel: Gender and Johannine Characterization*, SBLDS 167 (Atlanta: SBL, 1999).

66. Margaret M. Beirne, *Women and Men in the Fourth Gospel: A Genuine Discipleship of Equals*, JSNTSup 242 (London: Sheffield Academic, 2003).

a patriarchal household-code model. Conway gives more attention to the characterization and the relational aspects portrayed by the men and women that she considers highly significant in a discussion of gender.[67]

These are some of the feminist studies that this commentary will draw on.

While not engaging specifically with the Fourth Gospel, a significant collection edited by Elisabeth Schüssler Fiorenza also deserves our attention.[68] *Feminist Biblical Studies in the Twentieth Century: Scholarship and Movement; The Contemporary Period* provides a historical overview of feminist interpretation along with essays from around the globe and from different religious traditions, including Christianity, Judaism, and Islam, and uses different methodologies. An important contribution of this work is the insistence that any feminist study aims at societal transformation: "I understand feminism in a political sense as the radical notion that wo/men are fully entitled and responsible citizens in society, academy, and organized religions."[69] Schüssler Fiorenza provides a definition of feminist work:[70]

- must challenge/destabilize/subvert the subordination of wo/men, rather than strengthen or reinforce it;

- must reflect appreciation of and respect for wo/men's experience by acknowledging wo/men's capacities and agency;

- must be sensitive to context—both the immediate and possibly the larger context as well;

- must be critical of the manner in which wo/men have both aided and resisted oppression, subjugation, and violence;

- must have as its consequence far-reaching changes in religion and society, as well as political and revolutionary significance. Hence, it must be practical, this-worldly, transformative, renewing, and transitional.[71]

---

67. Conway, *Men and Women in the Fourth Gospel*, 48.

68. Elisabeth Schüssler Fiorenza, *Feminist Biblical Studies in the Twentieth Century: Scholarship and Movement; The Contemporary Period*, The Bible and Women: An Encyclopedia of Exegesis and Cultural History 9.1 (Atlanta: SBL, 2014).

69. Schüssler Fiorenza, "Between Movement and Academy: Feminist Biblical Studies in the Twentieth Century," in *Feminist Biblical Studies in the Twentieth Century*, 4.

70. She cites Monica Melanchthon as the source of this articulation at the 2010 SBL meeting.

71. Schüssler Fiorenza, "Between Movement and Academy," 4.

These words are a challenge to any author daring to offer a feminist interpretation of a Gospel for contemporary readers.

My own introduction to hermeneutical studies came through working with Sandra Schneiders whose *Revelatory Text* remains a foundational textbook for biblical students.[72] Schneiders draws particularly on the work of Paul Ricoeur, recognizing the metaphorical nature of biblical writing. Any attempt to speak of God needs to hold in tension both the "is" and "is not" of descriptive words. When the psalmist cries out, "God, my rock in whom I take refuge" (Ps 18:2), there is truth within the image, but literally God is not a rock! Once we move from a literalist reading this opens up a range of interpretive possibilities and brings with it ethical considerations. How can we read today a text written within a particular culture and patriarchal mind-set and allow the text to be revelatory of a God who created both male and female in God's own image (Gen 1:27)? How can we liberate a text that has been used to curtail the full discipleship of women?

Analysis of the text, asking questions about the culture of the time, the religious ideas, the meaning of a word, the circumstances of the community—all these steps are a necessary first step in the process of interpretation. In this commentary I attempt to understand the particular Jewish context in the first century, the world behind the text, and the dynamics of the evangelist's storytelling, the world within the text. A feminist hermeneutic then asks that the Scriptures be a revelation of God *now*, not simply a record of God's action in the past.

> In other words, the real referent of the New Testament text, what the text is primarily "about," is not the world of first century Christians which we are expected to reconstitute in the twentieth century but the experience of discipleship that is proposed to us and to each successive generation of readers as it was proposed by Jesus to the first generation.[73]

As Schneiders asserts, a valid interpretation should be emancipatory and transformative.

A feminist hermeneutic is both personal and political. It takes seriously that a text emerged from the experience of a person or community and that it is read by another person in their particular social and ethnic location. There can be no mechanistic approach to understanding a text that tries to bypass the personal. Writers are not robots, and readers are

---

72. Sandra M. Schneiders, *The Revelatory Text: Interpreting the New Testament as Sacred Scripture*, 2nd ed. (Collegeville, MN: Liturgical Press, 1999).

73. Sandra M. Schneiders, *Beyond Patching: Faith and Feminism in the Catholic Church* (New York: Paulist Press, 1990), 62.

not cyborgs. The historical-critical method can appear to be "scientific" in its search for evidence to know the intention of the writer, but such an approach overlooks the essence of the text as a work of literature, not an instruction manual for a device. There is a narrative art in storytelling—in the writer's selection and ordering of episodes; in the rhetoric, irony, imagery, and settings; in the characters and their interactions with other characters. The evangelist does not work in a vacuum but writes for real people and tells the story of Jesus in the light of Israel's ancient stories, songs, and prophecies. The writer is biased in his or her presentation, writing with the stated ideological purpose that readers will come to faith in Jesus "and have life in his name" (John 20:31).

Readers are also biased. I am a white, Australian, Roman Catholic woman, open to believe the theological propositions of this text. I read the Gospel as a valued canonical text that has shaped much of early Christian creeds. I read it as a Christian. And yet I read it with some suspicions, for my church has a long history of silencing women, and, in my tradition, most interpreters of the biblical texts are male celibate priests reading lectionaries compiled with androcentric language, and then they are the only ones authorized, by other men, to interpret these texts in a homily. The texts have been instruments of oppression for women, justifying male authority and female subservience. I have been privileged to receive a theological education. This was the first step in my feminist urge to liberate the text from its patriarchal founding context and misogynist historical context. When the text is free to be the Word of God, and not constrained to be the words of men, then it can be revelatory and liberative. That is my experience and my criterion for evaluating the validity of an interpretation. *Does it reveal the liberating God of the exodus and the Jesus willing to lay down his life that others may have the fullness of life?* This is where a feminist approach dares to be political as it asks questions of the text for real people today. Sharon Ringe states that a critical feminist interpretation involves a "commitment to the physical, psychological and social well-being of all women, through the unmasking, revisioning and transformation of the institutions, social systems and ideologies that define women's lives in 'kyriarchal' social realities—that is, those in which a small group of elite males is dominant over all women and many men."[74]

74. Sharon H. Ringe, "An Approach to a Critical, Feminist, Theological Reading of the Bible," in *A Feminist Companion to Reading the Bible: Approaches, Methods and Strategies*, ed. Athalya Brenner and Carole Fontaine (Sheffield: Sheffield Academic, 1997), 156.

This commentary falls under the broad umbrella of a feminist hermeneutical study using primarily narrative criticism. My interest is not so much in the history or the sources that may have contributed to the Gospel but rather how this text, taken as a unified whole, tells the story of Jesus and what, to my mind, are the major features of this particular story. In two previous monographs I have explored the narrative by tracing the symbol of the temple and the theme of the household across the Gospel.[75] These studies have opened my eyes to the deeply personal and intimate sense of the God who is portrayed.

The Use of "Father" to Speak of God

A particular difficulty for women reading this Gospel is the dominant "father" language to speak of God, more times in this Gospel than any other NT text.[76] It is important to be aware of just when and how this image is used. It is not scattered haphazardly across all chapters but comes to the fore in very particular episodes.

"Father" language is first employed in the prologue as a means of describing Jesus's relationship to God. In these first instances there is remarkable gender blurring, for Jesus is described as the "only son" of the father (1:14, 18). The Greek verb used in these two verses could be translated as the "only born son" since the first meaning ascribed to γίνομαι is "to come into being through process of birth or natural production, *be born, be produced.*"[77] Then, 1:18 continues by describing the only born son resting on the breast (Gk: κόλπον) of the one who gave him birth. It is not enough to speak of God solely as "father"; the imagery includes God as a birthing and nursing mother.

The next time "father" is used is to rename the Jerusalem temple, known as Israel's house of God, now named by Jesus as "my Father's house" (2:16). The temple imagery then shifts to the person of Jesus as God's dwelling place, but the "Father's house" language will reappear in Jesus's final discourse with his disciples where there is a further shift in its meaning to "the Father's household." This image incorporates all

---

75. Mary L. Coloe, *God Dwells with Us: Temple Symbolism in the Fourth Gospel* (Collegeville, MN: Liturgical Press, 2001); *Dwelling in the Household of God: Johannine Ecclesiology and Spirituality* (Collegeville, MN: Liturgical Press, 2007).

76. The term "father" occurs about one hundred times; "God," about sixty times. See the discussion of "the living father" in Marianne Meye Thompson, *The God of the Gospel of John* (Grand Rapids: Eerdmans, 2001), 57–100.

77. Arndt, "γίνομαι," 197; italics in the original.

believers into Jesus's relationship with God. It is a cultural, idiomatic way of naming the family and even the extended family. Today I could use another image and say we participate in God's DNA. Both images try to convey participation in the inner life of God, and neither can be read literally.

In John 5 a principle is stated to explain why the evangelist uses the "father-son" language so frequently.[78] In a situation of conflict, Jesus explains his authority to act by providing a parable based on ordinary family experience. The son within a family learns from his father and only then can he be authorized to act as his father (5:19). Similarly, a daughter would learn skills from her mother before she sets up in her home. The father-son language is therefore not an ontological statement about God, or about Jesus, but an image of Jesus's sense of union with God and subordination to the one who sent and authorized him. The principle of the authorizing father and the apprentice son continues in John 6.[79]

A new situation emerges in John 8 when Jesus is in a confrontation with his former disciples, those who once believed in him (8:31), but have now left him (see 6:66). The rhetoric is particularly harsh as both argue about who they belong to, in terms of their heredity. Jesus's opponents speak of Abraham as their father (8:39), while Jesus speaks of God as his father (8:38, 40). Jesus then points to the behavior of these opponents in seeking to kill him and refusal to believe in him. Their actions reveal who they belong to, who is their father (8:41). This was the principle from chapter 5, that sons do what their father teaches them to do (5:19). Jesus claims that their actions show they belong to the power of evil and are therefore children of the devil rather than Abraham's children (8:44). In response, they accuse Jesus of no longer belonging to the children of Israel and of being possessed by a demon (8:48). In this argumentative situation harsh language issues from both sides, and the identity of "your father" is a critical part of the argument.[80]

When Jesus names God as "Father" across chapter 10, he continues the principle from chapter 5 of only doing what he was commissioned to do, and in this cluster of images, the pathos of the "Father" is revealed as Jesus speaks of laying down his life for the sheep given to him by the Father (10:15, 29). The Father is not immune from what will happen to

---

78. 5:17, 18, 19, 23, 45.
79. 6:40, 45, 46, 57, 65.
80. 8:19, 27, 38, 41, 44, 49, 53.

Jesus. Doing the works given him by the Father will lead to his passion and death (18:11).[81]

The father image then dominates the discourse in chapters 14, 15, and 16. This discourse is introduced with Jesus speaking of the many dwellings in "my Father's household." In the commentary I will go into the details of this idiom and the important theological reasons for this terminology. It looks back to the term Jesus used to speak of the temple (2:16), but the Greek uses a different word, "household" (οἰκία, 14:1), rather than "house" (οἶκος, 2:16). In chapter 14, Jesus then speaks of God coming to dwell with and in his followers, drawing believers into his own intimate relationship with God. In and through Jesus, believers can become "children of God" as promised in the prologue (1:12-13). This is then confirmed in the final use of "Father" when Jesus commissions Mary Magdalene to "Go to my sisters and brothers and say to them, 'I am ascending to my Father and your Father, to my God and your God'" (20:17). The emphasis on "father" language across the discourse is a strategy to explain the meaning of the cross before it happens. It is as if Jesus is anticipating the new relationship he will establish between believers and God, that they, like himself, will be drawn into the life of God. This is the reason why "god" language is seldom used in the discourse and is replaced with "father" terminology.[82] The risen Jesus then speaks to the disciples in their commissioning, "As the Father has sent me, so I send you" (20:21).

Whenever Jesus turns to speak to God in prayer, he speaks from within his own sense of who God is for him and so uses the very personal and intimate term "Father" in the vocative form Πάτερ (11:41; 12:27, 28; 17:1, 5, 11, 21, 24, 25), and when his public ministry draws to its close there is a brief closing statement where Jesus affirms his subordination to only speak the words of the one who sent him, just as "the Father has told me" (12:49, 50).[83] In the first-century context the word "father" could take on many nuances and need not express intimacy. Mary Rose D'Angelo discusses Jesus's use of "Abba" and "Father" when speaking to God and to his contemporaries. This term was being used in Jewish

---

81. See also 10:18, 25, 32, 37.

82. The term "God" is used to speak of belief in God (14:1), worship of God (16:2), and that Jesus came from God (16:27, 30). "Father" occurs at 14:2, 6, 7, 8, 9, 12, 16, 21, 24, 28, 31; 15:10, 15, 16, 23, 24, 26; 16:3, 10, 17, 23, 25, 26, 28.

83. See Mary Rose D'Angelo, "Abba and 'Father': Imperial Theology and the Jesus Traditions," *JBL* (1992): 611–30.

literature of the time and so was not unique to Jesus; also, in the Roman context it could speak of power and dominion such as the authority of the "paterfamilias." Here, I have described "father" as an intimate term in John's presentation of Jesus, for Jesus associates the "Father" with love (5:19; 14:21, 23; 15:9; 16:27; 17:23, 24, 26), not simply with authority or dominion.

These are the primary times where Jesus speaks of God as "Father." It is a term rarely used by the narrator (5:18; 8:27; 13:1, 3) and never by other characters. As this survey shows it is used in quite specific scenes either for a rhetorical purpose, to attest to Jesus's authority by means of a cultural parable (chaps. 5 and 6), in a vituperative argument with former believers (chap. 8), or to express the evangelist's view of Jesus's identity and purpose, namely, to draw others into his personal living relationship with God (chaps. 14–16). It is not a statement about God's gender or identity but a statement of what must have been Jesus's particular sense of himself and his experience of God and then the community's experience. The difficulty has come when the text has been received literally, and within the tradition, particularly in the liturgy, God has been named only in male terms, predominantly "father," and never in female terms. While the Gospel uses "Father" and "God," it also presents the image of a birthing God (1:1, 18; 3:3, 5, 16) and a birthing Jesus (16:21; 19:34). This is a God who is vulnerable in giving the only born son. In the words of Dorothy Lee, "God's fatherhood, symbolically portrayed in the Father-Son relationship, is an outward movement of giving away power, surrendering selfhood as autonomous and self-sufficient. On the other hand, divine fatherhood draws others into the filial relationship between God and Jesus, so that the Father-Son language becomes the fundamental icon of God's relations with the world."[84] With this theological basis, it is not surprising to find that women in this Gospel are dramatized in an inclusive manner. Again quoting Lee, "Women are beloved in the gospel, established through the narrative as witnesses of faith, apostolic leaders, missionaries, and proclaimers."[85] Such an understanding of an intimate and personal God inviting all women and men into equal participation in a new quality of divine relationship characterized by friendship (15:14-15) and love (15:9) informs the approach taken in this Gospel.

The term "father" can be problematic, however, particularly when it is used so frequently in this Gospel. The reader can lose sight of it as a

---

84. Dorothy A. Lee, "The Symbol of Divine Fatherhood," *Semeia* 85 (1999): 181.
85. Lee, "Divine Fatherhood," 184.

metaphor and think that this is a declarative statement about the male "being" of God. This, of course, is heretical. God is not father, or mother, or parent, or bridegroom, or shepherd, or king, or lover—and yet, from within the limitations of our human need, an image may be helpful provided we acknowledge it is an image among many other possibilities, and not a definition. When the Gospel uses the personal image "father," it does so for a purpose.

Characters Called "the Jews"[86]

With the exception of a few characters such as Pilate (chaps. 18–19), the Greeks (12:20), the Samaritans (chap. 4), and the royal official (4:46), all the characters in the Gospel would self-identify as "children of Israel." To outsiders, such as the Romans, they would be called Jews (οἱ Ἰουδαῖοι). The expression οἱ Ἰουδαῖοι can also refer to those living in the region of Judea, thus, Judeans, but it would usually have a religious/ethnic sense of those daughters and sons of Abraham living according to the law of Moses. Historically, Jesus, his mother, his disciples, and his friends were all Ἰουδαῖοι. But the narrative of the Gospel creates another picture where Jesus and his followers are not part of this group. The great festivals of Israel are called "the feasts of the Jews" (6:4; 7:2; 11:55), and Jesus speaks about "your Law" (8:17; 10:34), and to the narrator, it is "their law" (15:25).

On this point we must distinguish between the actual time of Jesus's life and the decades later near the end of the first century, when the Gospel is written. These are two markedly different historical times, where the Jewish world has undergone the destruction of Jerusalem and its temple by the Romans (70 CE). This event destroyed the foundations of the Jewish religious practice: from this time there could be no sacrifices and no means of perpetual sanctification through the twice-daily holocausts; with no more sacrifice the priesthood was meaningless. In the post-70 decades, the lay teachers of Torah gradually took on the leadership of the Jewish people. During the time of Jesus, these were known as the Pharisees, and they were responsible for preserving what is now

---

86. On the characterization of "the Jews" in this Gospel, see the seminal work of R. Alan Culpepper, *Anatomy of the Fourth Gospel*. A more recent study is Ruben Zimmermann, " 'The Jews': Unreliable Figures or Unreliable Narration?," in *Character Studies in the Fourth Gospel: Narrative Approaches to Seventy Figures in John*, ed. Steven A. Hunt, D. Francois Tolmie, and Ruben Zimmermann, WUNT 314 (Tübingen: Mohr Siebeck, 2013), 71–109.

known as rabbinic Judaism, where Torah rather than temple shapes the religious life of Jews.

At the same time that the rabbis were trying to reconstitute Jewish life and practice focused on the law of Moses, another group of Jews was professing that Jesus had brought the definitive revelation of God. Over the next few centuries these two Jewish groups would draw apart and be known as the Synagogue and the Christian Church. In the late decades of the first century, this separation had not yet happened, and both groups were working to shape their distinctive identity. Both were looking at the other group as "other." The Fourth Evangelist writes as if the separation has occurred, and so the Pharisees and the crowds are labelled "the Jews," οἱ Ἰουδαῖοι. These are the characters presented as showing the greatest hostility to Jesus and even seeking his death (11:18). John Ashton poignantly writes, "Can one fail to recognize in these hot-tempered exchanges the type of family row in which the participants face one another across the room of a house which all have shared and all call home."[87] More will be said on this issue in the commentary, but it is important to know from the start that "the Jews" are characters in this story, created and shaped by the ideology of the evangelist.

"The Jews" in the Reception of the Gospel

> For a Jewish reader, the Gospel of John, in which Jews are portrayed as unbelieving descendants of the devil (8:44), blind, sinful, and incapable of understanding their own scriptures, is one of the most disturbing texts in the Christian canon.[88]

These words by Adele Reinhartz are painful to read. Writing as a Jewish woman, she gives expression to what happens when *she* reads

---

87. Ashton, *Understanding the Fourth Gospel*, 151. Much has been written on the identity formation of Jews and Christians. A sample of approaches can be seen in Ed P. Sanders, ed., *Jewish and Christian Self-Definition: The Shaping of Christianity in the Second and Third Centuries*, vol. 1 (London: SCM, 1980); James D. G Dunn, ed., *Jews and Christians: The Parting of the Ways A.D. 70 to 135* (Grand Rapids: Eerdmans, 1999); Daniel Boyarin, *Border Lines: The Partition of Judaeo-Christianity* (Philadelphia: University of Pennsylvania Press, 2004); Judith M. Lieu, *Neither Jew nor Greek?*; Raimo Hakola, *Identity Matters: John, the Jews and Jewishness*, NovTSup 18 (Leiden: Brill, 2005); R. Alan Culpepper and Paul N. Anderson, eds., *John and Judaism: A Contested Relationship in Context*, RBS 87 (Atlanta: SBL, 2017).

88. Adele Reinhartz, "A Nice Jewish Girl Reads the Gospel of John," *Semeia* 77 (1997): 177.

the text, with an awareness of how Christian texts have been used as a weapon to justify the pogroms, oppression, and murder of her people, still happening today. Some try to explain away the difficulty by translating the term as "Judeans"[89] or "Jewish authorities"[90] or "the successors to the Pharisees,"[91] but these lexical gymnastics are not satisfactory, for the most frequent term by which the opponents of Jesus are named is "the Jews." Even the few times when οἱ Ἰουδαῖοι describes those sympathetic to Jesus (7:35; 11:36), these rare mentions are far outweighed by the unremitting use of οἱ Ἰουδαῖοι as Jesus's persecutors, trying to stone (8:59) or kill him (7:1). The vilification of οἱ Ἰουδαῖοι comes to a head in chapter 8, when Jesus accuses them of being children of the devil (8:44).[92]

There has been a growing awareness of the role Christian texts have played in the long history of Jewish oppression, and some fine studies have been done on how to approach a text with this reception history, a text Christians yet call "Sacred Scripture."[93] My hope is that this commentary may offer further education about first-century Judaism and Christianity in their early decades, including an awareness of the painful process of identity formation when that involved separation.[94]

---

89. Malcolm Lowe, "Who Were the ΙΟΥΔΑΙΟΙ?," *NovT* 18 (1976): 101–30.

90. Urban C. von Wahlde, "The Johannine Jews: A Critical Survey," *NTS* 28 (1982): 33–60.

91. James D. G. Dunn, "The Embarrassment of History: Reflections on the Problem of 'Anti-Judaism' in the Fourth Gospel," in *Anti-Judaism and the Fourth Gospel*, ed. Reimund Bieringer, Didier Pollefeyt, and Frederique Vandecasteele-Vanneuville (Louisville: Westminster John Knox, 2001), 46.

92. In the commentary I will examine this passage in its narrative context where these particular "Jews" are introduced as former followers of Jesus (8:31), and in reply to Jesus's condemnation they charge him with being a Samaritan and being possessed by a demon (8:48).

93. Paula Fredriksen and Adele Reinhartz, eds., *Jesus, Judaism and Christian Anti-Judaism: Reading the New Testament after the Holocaust* (Louisville: Westminster John Knox, 2002); Culpepper and Anderson, *John and Judaism*; Bieringer, Pollefeyt, and Vandecasteele-Vanneuville, *Anti-Judaism and the Fourth Gospel*; Adele Reinhartz, *Befriending the Beloved Disciple: A Jewish Reading of the Gospel of John* (New York: Continuum, 2001); Reinhartz, *Cast Out of the Covenant*.

94. I must be succeeding in this educative task as my students sometimes think I am Jewish. One said to me, "Mary, I know you are a Jew but we Catholics believe . . ." She then went on to explain something "we Catholics" believe. I then had to explain that I wasn't a Jew, that I was a Catholic. In fact, I was a Catholic nun!

Women Characters in John

In the Fourth Gospel, five women characters have very significant roles.[95] The first is the mother of Jesus, who is not named and is known only as "woman" and "mother." She initiates Jesus's ministry with the first sign at Cana (2:1-13), acting with "prophetic knowledge and authority."[96] Then, at the cross (19:26), she is the one who carries the theological meaning of this event. Her role is critical for the fulfilment of Jesus's mission. "Apart from Jesus, no other character is as important to the ideological point of view of this Gospel's narrative than the Mother of Jesus."[97]

Two women have roles as evangelizers of their communities. First, there is the unnamed woman of Samaria and then Mary, "the Magdalene." The encounter with the Samaritan woman (4:1-42) follows the meeting with Nicodemus (3:1-10). But where his dialogue led to his exclamation, "it is not possible" (3:4), and "how is this possible?" (3:4), the Samaritan woman does not close off the conversation, and her questions lead her to discover the identity of the one to whom she is talking, "the Messiah" (4:25). She then returns with this revelation to her village. In John 19, Mary Magdalene is one of three women at the cross (19:25), and then she discovers the empty tomb (20:1). She is the first to see the Risen Jesus (20:16) and is sent back to the disciples with the Easter proclamation (20:17). She well deserves her title and feast as "the apostle to the apostles."[98]

The women in the household of Bethany have the major theological role in John 11. Their brother, Lazarus, says nothing. Mary and Martha are obviously friends of Jesus and so call him to come to their assistance (11:3), then greet him with their disappointments and hopes (11:21-22, 32) or, in Satoko Yamaguchi's words, "regret and grief . . . and trust in

---

95. I have not included in this description the episode of the woman caught in adultery (John 8:1-11) as this passage is not considered to be part of the original Gospel. The passage will be discussed in the commentary.

96. Adele Reinhartz, "Women in the Johannine Community: An Exercise in Historical Imagination," in *A Feminist Companion to John*, 2:19.

97. Mary L. Coloe, "The Mother of Jesus: A Woman Possessed," in *Character Studies in the Fourth Gospel*, 213.

98. In the early third century, Hippolytus of Rome calls the women who met the risen Christ "apostles to the apostles" in his commentary on the Song of Songs (25.6, 7). In June 2016, Pope Francis recognized this tradition and elevated the memorial of Mary Magdalene on July 22 to a feast day in the Catholic Church's liturgical calendar. Mass on that day now also includes a preface titled "Apostle of the Apostles."

Jesus."[99] They profess their faith in him,[100] and following the resuscitation of Lazarus Mary prophetically anoints Jesus's feet (12:1-8), an action that he will then repeat for his disciples (13:4-11).

With the exception of the Samaritan woman, four of these five Johannine characters are also in the Synoptic Gospels, which indicates the esteem in which they were held in the early tradition. But the Johannine Gospel gives a shape to these characters in quite a different manner to the mold in which they are cast in the Synoptics. All five women speak and act in ways that move the narrative forward and carry its theology. They are not incidental characters, and none of them are the recipients of a healing or exorcism. More on this in the commentary.

Gender in John

The author of the Gospel shapes our perception of characters by the way he constructs them.[101] We are seeing not the historical Martha or Jesus but a particular view of these persons so that the author's goal in writing the text succeeds. One aspect of the character is their gender. Male and female were seen as binary opposites, and, in ancient times, "biological sex and gender were inextricably bound together, the former constructing the identity and life expectations of the latter."[102] But when speaking about the portrayal of God and of Jesus there is a blurring of gender boundaries in this Gospel. When considering the Wisdom background of Johannine Christology, it requires reading the character "Jesus" with an eye on "Sophia." As Ingrid Rosa Kitzberger states, "He is definitely portrayed as a man, as the Son of his Father, but at the same time he is enriched with female traits that originate from Sophia/ Chokmah. . . . Gender boundaries are overcome in his person. And because Jesus is one with his Father . . . the Father's characterization is also affected. Consequently, the Johannine God-Father must also be

---

99. Satoko Yamaguchi, *Mary and Martha: Women in the World of Jesus* (Maryknoll, NY: Orbis Books, 2002), 117.

100. There are various views about the statement and actions of Martha and Mary and the quality of faith they profess. This will be discussed in the commentary.

101. For studies of individual characters, see Hunt, Tolmie, and Zimmerman, eds., *Character Studies in the Fourth Gospel*; Christopher W. Skinner, ed., *Characters and Characterization in the Gospel of John*, LNTS 461 (London: Bloomsbury, 2013).

102. Julia M. O'Brien, ed., *The Oxford Encyclopedia of the Bible and Gender Studies*, vol. 1 (Oxford: Oxford University Press, 2014), 264.

viewed in female terms."[103] In looking at the characterization of "God," one emphasis is that God is the creator of life, and with the ancient perception that life was generated through the male, this may explain the most frequent appellation of God as "father" to emphasize God as one who gives life and as a "living God" (6:57).[104] At times, when speaking of the life-giving qualities of God, the text uses the Greek expression for birthing (μονογενής, 1:18; μονογενῆ, 3:16), so that the apparent binary male-female perception is broken.

Some Major Theological Themes

The Gospel begins with the words of the creation account of Genesis 1 and closes with the hope that believers will have "life in his name" (20:31). Life, and the creation of a new quality of life, is the primary theme. Jesus states that he has come that "they may have life, and have it abundantly" (10:10), meaning the fulfilled hopes of eschatological life. In the narrative this theme emerges in the subthemes of birth, becoming children of God, and eternity life. Furthermore, the life being offered is a gift for *all* people and is not restricted by race, class, or gender: "And I, when I am lifted up from the earth, will draw all [πάντας] people to myself" (12:32). In late Second Temple literature such fullness of life is the gift of Sophia,[105] and so Jesus/Sophia acts in the world to bring the life that God desires for all people. God, as life giver and creator cannot be imaged solely in a male image, as Michelangelo depicted for the Sistine chapel! Jesus/Sophia incarnates "the wholeness of God's creative power expressed in both male and female terms."[106]

A second key theological theme is Jesus as the locus of God's presence. From the prologue introducing him as the tabernacling presence (1:14), the narrative then shows him disrupting the temple cult and taking over the function of the temple in his own body. Jesus is the dwelling place of God. This imagery continues throughout the narrative, coming to a

---

103. Ingrid Rosa Kitzberger, "Transcending Gender Boundaries in John," in *A Feminist Companion to John*, 1:193.

104. A study of how "God" is presented in the Fourth Gospel is Thompson, *The God of the Gospel of John*. "What it means to be a father is to be the origin or source of life of one's children" (71).

105. "Because of her I shall have immortality [ἕξω δι᾽ αὐτὴν ἀθανασίαν]" (Wis 8:13). "In kinship with Wisdom there is immortality [ἀθανασία ἐστὶν ἐν συγγενείᾳ σοφίας]" (Wis 8:17).

106. Scott, *Sophia and the Johannine Jesus*, 246.

climax at the cross when one temple is destroyed and a new temple is raised up (cf. 2:19). The temple was the center of Israel's religious practice, but women had limited access to it. They were permitted only in the outer courts and could not venture into the court where sacrifices took place, and no woman could ever pass beyond the outer curtain, into the holy place, let alone beyond the inner curtain, into the holy of holies. Women were clearly distanced from God. The Gospel redefines the meaning of the temple in terms of the person of Jesus and then in terms of the community of disciples in whom God dwells. The commentary will explore this further, particularly in the discussion of "my Father's house" in John 14:2. In overturning the tables in the temple (2:15), Jesus overturned the separating boundaries between women and the Divine. Women could make the household of God their own.

Literary Techniques

The primary literary feature of the Gospel is its continual drawing upon the Scriptures of Israel (intertextuality), Jewish festivals, symbols, and theology. At times this is stated explicitly, but often it is expected that the audience would be familiar with Jewish practice and thought, and so an oblique allusion such as "on the third day" (2:1) is considered enough.

There are times when the narrator steps into the scene to offer directions, such as giving the reader insight into the disciples: "His disciples remembered that it was written . . ." (2:17; similarly, 2:22). Sometimes we have privileged "inside" information about other characters, for example, "His parents said this because they were afraid of the Jews" (9:22), and Jesus, who "needed no one to testify about anyone; for he himself knew what was in everyone" (2:25).[107]

Another important Johannine technique is *inclusio*, the framing of the beginning and ending of sections through the repetition of words

---

107. These are a few examples of what Culpepper calls the omniscient point of view of the narrator. Culpepper, *Anatomy of the Fourth Gospel*, 20–26. Alan Culpepper was the first Johannine scholar to study the Gospel as literature, and he wrote of the ways an author communicates with a reader through "implicit commentary." See Culpepper, *Anatomy of the Fourth Gospel*, chap. 6. Since then there have been many studies of the narrative techniques in the Fourth Gospel; see, for example, Douglas Estes and Ruth Sheridan, *How John Works: Storytelling in the Fourth Gospel*, SBLRBS 86 (Atlanta: SBL, 2016); Tom Thatcher and Stephen D. Moore, eds., *Anatomies of Narrative Criticism: The Past, Present, and Futures of the Fourth Gospel as Literature*, SBLRBS 55 (Atlanta: SBL, 2008).

or symbols. For example, chapter 2 begins in Cana of Galilee (2:1) and chapter 4 concludes back in Cana of Galilee (4:46). The turning of water into wine is called "the first sign" (2:11), and the cure of the official's son is called "the second sign" (4:54). These repetitions create a literary frame around chapters 2, 3, and 4. Another example is the dialogue with Nicodemus that begins with him calling Jesus "a teacher who has come from God" (3:2) and ends with Jesus's ironic naming Nicodemus "a teacher of Israel" (3:10). The repetition of "teacher" indicates that 3:1-10 forms a section within a wider passage.

Another technique that engages the audience is the use of misunderstanding and irony.[108] Nicodemus misunderstands the meaning of Jesus's statement about being "born anew"; the Samaritan woman misunderstands what Jesus means by "living water." She then asks, "Are you greater than our ancestor Jacob?" (4:12). The audience, who know more than she does, would be saying, "Yes, yes, yes." They are ahead of her and can appreciate the irony of her question.

There are small parables in the Gospel that can be overlooked since they are not long narratives, as in the Synoptic Gospels. In John 5, for example, Jesus draws on the common experience of a parent showing a child how to do a particular work (5:19). He then uses this as an argument to speak of his own mission and being authorized by God. In John 8, Jesus employs this example to support his assertion, "if the Son makes you free, you will be free indeed" (8:36): only sons remain permanently within a household (8:35). Daughters leave to make a new home in the household of husbands. Slaves can be sold or freed. One other illustration: in his final discourse, Jesus speaks of his coming passion as being like a woman in labor who passes through anguish to joy (16:20-21). These brief statements offer an insight from ordinary life to make sense of a situation in the narrative. In the Synoptic Gospels the parables primarily point to an aspect of the reign of God; in John they are an integral part of the narrative context.

Outline of the Gospel

The Gospel has two major sections: chapters 1:19–12:50, the "Book of Signs," so designated as these chapters concern Jesus's miracles, which

---

108. For more detail, see Paul Duke, *Irony in the Fourth Gospel* (Atlanta: John Knox, 1985).

in this Gospel are called "signs" (e.g., 2:11; 4:54); and chapters 13:1–20:31, the "Book of Glory," focusing on Jesus's return to the Father, which in this Gospel is called his glorification (e.g., 13:31; 14:13; 17:1, 5, 24). A prologue (1:1-18) introduces these two major sections, and an epilogue (21:1-25) concludes them.[109]

Within the Book of Signs, subdivisions are suggested by the text. Chapter 1 begins with the ministry of John (1:19-34) and then presents a sequence of "days" designated by the repeated phrase, "the next day" (1:29, 35, 43). These days conclude with Jesus's promise to his disciples that they would see "greater things" (1:50-51). Chapter 2 begins in "Cana in Galilee" (2:1), and Jesus's mother initiates his public ministry. The changing of the water into wine is called "the first of his signs" (2:11). At the end of chapter 4 the narrative returns to "Cana in Galilee" (4:46), and the cure of the royal official's son is called "the second sign." These repetitions suggest that chapters 2, 3, and 4 are a literary unit, beginning and ending in Cana. Across this section there are various responses to Jesus, first within the Jewish world, characterized by "the Jews" in the temple (2:13-22), followed by the teacher, Nicodemus (3:1-21), and then John testifying that Jesus is the bridegroom (3:29). Jesus then travels outside the Jewish world into Samaria (4:1-42) and at a well meets one of the most significant Johannine characters, the Samaritan woman who comes for water. She engages with Jesus in a deep theological discussion and gains insight into his identity (4:25); she then leaves as a missionary to her people.

The next six chapters all deal with issues linked to specific Jewish feasts and are introduced with the phrase, "the feast of the Jews": the Sabbath (chap. 5), Passover (chap. 6), Tabernacles (7:1–10:21), and Dedication (10:22-42). In these chapters we see Jesus, the embodiment of Wisdom/ Sophia, reinterpreting the festivals and claiming them as her own. Only Sophia can offer eternity life (5:24), the ambrosia of paradise to nourish her children forever (6:27), life-giving water (7:37), and light that can never be extinguished (8:12). Only Jesus/Sophia can say, "the Father and I are one" (10:30).

---

109. This is the outline proposed by Raymond Brown in his 1966 commentary *The Gospel According to John*. Most other commentaries show a similar structure, e.g., Lincoln, *Gospel*, 4–5; George R. Beasley-Murray, *John*, WBC 36 (Waco, TX: Word Books, 1987), xci–xcii; Charles H. Dodd, *The Interpretation of the Fourth Gospel* (Cambridge: Cambridge University Press, 1970), 289–90.

Chapters 11 and 12 focus on the person of Lazarus, his death and resuscitation (11:1-44) and its consequences for Jesus (11:45-53; 12:10, 17-19). The death and raising of Lazarus make a transition from Jesus's public ministry to the final chapters dealing with a meal (13:2) where Jesus teaches his disciples the meaning of his departure (chaps. 13–16), prays for his disciples (chap. 17), then freely enters into the "hour" of his death (chaps. 18–19) and resurrection (chap. 20). In this final "hour" the promise of the prologue is fulfilled when believers are reborn as "children of God" (1:12-13). As noted above, many scholars today consider that the Gospel, at least in its earlier form, concluded with a brief statement of its purpose (20:30-31).

Chapter 21 appears to be an early editor's addition to the original text, an epilogue, which then has its own conclusion (21:24-25). This chapter establishes Peter as the pastoral leader of the group and explains that the death of the Beloved Disciple is not to be a cause of concern. The Gospel outline can be set out as follows.

1:1-18	Sophia finds her home
	THE BOOK OF SIGNS (Jesus's public ministry)
1:19-51	The First Days: Sophia Gathers Disciples
2:1–4:54	From a Jewish Mother to a Gentile Father at Cana
5:1–10:42	Sophia Celebrates the Jewish Festivals
11:1–12:50	Transition: The Household of Martha, Mary, and Lazarus
	THE BOOK OF GLORY (Jesus with his own)
13:1–17:26	Sophia's Friends Are Taught and Comforted
18:1–19:42	Sophia Births "the Children of God"
20:1-29	Raising Sophia's Household
20:30-31	Conclusion
21:1-24	Sophia's Bounteous Feast (Editorial Addition)
21:25	Editorial conclusion

John 1:1-18

Sophia Finds Her Home

At the beginning of God's work I [Wisdom] was created,
the first of God's acts of long ago;
Before the mountains had been shaped,
before the hills, I was born. (Prov 8:22, 25)[1]

There is in her a spirit that is intelligent, holy,
unique, manifold, subtle,
mobile, clear, unpolluted, . . .
overseeing all,
and penetrating through all spirits
that are intelligent, pure, and altogether subtle.
For wisdom is more mobile than any motion;
because of her pureness she pervades and penetrates all things. (Wis 7:22-24)

"In the beginning." With these words John plunges the reader back in time to that moment when energy and light exploded and the cosmos began. This author likewise begins the Jesus story as an explosion of light into darkness. The evangelist not only introduces the readers to John's cosmic compass but also alerts them to the way this narrative will develop. It will be a tapestry of memories of Jesus interwoven with the community's Spirit-guided experience, set against the writings,

1. Author's translation. In both the Hebrew (חוללתי) and the Greek (γεννᾷ) the term means to give birth, to labor. See William L. Holladay and Ludwig Köhler, "חיל," in *A Concise Hebrew and Aramaic Lexicon of the Old Testament* (Leiden: Brill, 2000), 102.

1

rituals, and wisdom of ancient Israel. In this kaleidoscopic manner, the evangelist sets out to tell the meaning of the Jesus event, to Israel, to all people, to the cosmos. In telling the Jesus story, the evangelist makes use of Israel's own narrative about a divine figure, present with God in the work of creation, who then comes to dwell in their midst. This was Wisdom (Gk.: σοφία; Heb.: חכמה).

Sophia/Wisdom

The wisdom traditions developed in the period after the exile in Babylon. The wisdom mentality was essentially a contemplative attitude, able to see God at the heart of the world. According to Sharon Ringe, "Wisdom is connected to the divine logic undergirding the creation—God's will or plan for the created order and for the structures and relationships that give the world meaning, shape, and coherence."[2] This wisdom, although immanent in creation, was differentiated from creation itself in the great poems of Job 28, Proverbs 8, Sirach 24, and Wisdom 7.[3] In the voice of Wisdom/Sophia a new bearer of divine revelation is introduced. The prophets spoke of the Word going forth from the mouth of God to accomplish God's purpose (Isa 55:10-11); of the Spirit being set within Israel (Ezek 22:26; 37:14). The sages in the postexilic community chose the term *Sophia*/Wisdom to describe God's self-communication in the world.

Wisdom's relationship to creation and to God is revealed clearly in Proverbs 8. Here, *Sophia* speaks publicly and directly, describing her origins at/as the beginning of God's creative activity and her role as that of a child or artisan.

> The LORD created me at the beginning of his work,
>   the first of his acts of long ago.
> Ages ago I was set up,
>   at the first, before the beginning of the earth . . .
>   then I was beside him, like a master worker [darling child];[4]
> and I was daily his delight,
>   rejoicing before him always,

---

2. Sharon H. Ringe, *Wisdom's Friends: Community and Christology in the Fourth Gospel* (Louisville: Westminster John Knox, 1999), 29.

3. The books of Wisdom and Sirach (Ecclesiasticus), were written late in Second Temple Judaism and were not written in Hebrew, but Greek. They were therefore not included in the Hebrew Bible but are in the Greek Septuagint. They are included in the Catholic canon and so are in Catholic Bibles. Within some Protestant traditions they are considered deuterocanonical and are not included in their Bibles.

4. The exact meaning of the Hebrew here is mysterious.

rejoicing in his inhabited world
>and delighting in the human race. (Prov 8:22-23, 30-31)

Sirach 24 follows Proverbs in describing Wisdom's origins in God, and
in this poem a new element is added, in that Wisdom is given a precise
location.

>Then the Creator of all things gave me a command,
>>and my Creator chose the place for my tent [LXX: τὴν σκηνήν μου].
>He said, "Make your dwelling in Jacob,
>>and in Israel receive your inheritance."
>Before the ages, in the beginning, he created me,
>>and for all the ages I shall not cease to be.
>In the holy tent [LXX: ἐν σκηνῇ ἁγίᾳ] I ministered before him,
>>and so I was established in Zion.
>Thus in the beloved city he gave me a resting place,
>>and in Jerusalem was my domain. (Sir 24:8-11)

Wisdom, who had dwelt in the heights of heaven (Sir 24:4), is now located within Israel's tabernacle (σκηνή). A later verse identifies Wisdom
with Torah,

>All this is the book of the covenant of the Most High God,
>>the law that Moses commanded us
>>as an inheritance for the congregations of Jacob. (Sir 24:23)

The book of Baruch makes a similar identification, "She is the book of the
commandments of God, the law that endures forever" (Bar 4:1). In the
postexilic period, it is in the living out of Torah that Israel is assured of
the divine presence.[5] Wisdom is the mode of expressing the immanence
of God, and in the final book of the Old Testament Wisdom is described in
ways that depict her intimate relationship with God and with humanity.[6]
Wisdom is the breath, the power, the pure emanation, the image of God
(Wis 7:25-26), and Wisdom passes into holy souls making them "friends
of God, and prophets" (Wis 7:27). Wisdom is God's gift (Wis 8:21) to the
righteous ones to draw them into an intimate communion of life. In the

---

5. The Aramaic targums speak of this divine presence of God in the world as the
Shekinah; see the excursus below.

6. In the book of Wisdom, *Sophia's* self-description of her works and qualities has
been likened to the literary genre known as "aretalogy," in particular the hymns
praising the Egyptian goddess Isis. For further discussion of this, see John S. Kloppenborg, "Isis and Sophia in the Book of Wisdom," *HTR* 75 (1982): 57–84; and Andrew
T. Glicksman, *Wisdom of Solomon 10: A Jewish Hellenistic Reinterpretation of Early Israelite
History through Sapiential Lenses*, DCLS 9 (Berlin: de Gruyter, 2011).

tradition of the sages, such a communion of life is found in the Torah, rather than in the rituals of the temple.[7] Through *Sophia*/Wisdom, a feminine voice is a new tone in the divine dialogue with humanity. For women, divine revelation is no longer spoken with an exclusively male timbre, and so women can now hear themselves echoed back to them.

The Gospel of John never uses the term "wisdom," and yet in its depiction of the Word, both preexistent and enfleshed, the attributes of Wisdom are also attributes of the Word.[8]

- Word and Wisdom have their origins in God (Prov 8:22; Sir 24:3; Wis 7:25-26; John 1:1-2)

- Wisdom preexisted and had a role in the task of creation (Prov 3:19; 8:22-29; Sir 1:4, 9-10; 16:24–17:7; Wis 8:4-6; John 1:2-3)

- Wisdom is infused in creation, giving it order and endurance (Wis 1:7; 7:24, 27; 8:1; 11:25; John 1:2, 10)

- Wisdom comes to the world with a mission (Prov 8:4, 31-36; Sir 24:7, 12, 19-22; John 1:14) to speak personally to the world (Sir 24:19-22; John 3:16-17), and to her followers she offers life and blessings (Sir 1:14-20; 6:18-31; 15:1-8; 24:19-33; John 3:10, 14)

- Wisdom draws people into friendship with God (Wis 7:27; John 15:13, 14, 15)

Making use of these OT images, the Fourth Gospel affirms that Wisdom, who was with God in the beginning, creating order in the world, has now found a resting place, has pitched her tent in human history. Where Israel sought Wisdom's resting place in Torah, for the Johannine community, *Jesus* is the incarnation of divine Wisdom, and this community bears witness to its experience. Within the earliest Church experience, still closely in touch with its Jewish roots and Scriptures, there was no difficulty proclaiming the divine presence of Sophia in the male Jesus; for those familiar with Israel's Scriptures she was not hidden. The works of Sally Douglas and Eva Günther demonstrate the way in which canonical Gospels and

7. Von Rad cautions against interpreting the various criticisms of the cult as outright rejection of cultic practices; he writes, "The wise men had, intellectually, outgrown the world of cultic action." See Gerhard von Rad, *Wisdom in Israel* (London: SCM, 1972), 186–89.

8. Sharon Ringe identifies numerous ways in which the motifs of *Logos* and *Sophia* continue across the Gospel narrative even though these terms do not appear as a christological title. Ringe, *Wisdom's Friends*, 53–61.

John 1:1-18

¹:¹In the beginning was the Word, and the Word was with God, and the Word was God. ²He was in the beginning with God. ³All things came into being through him, and without him not one thing came into being. What has come into being ⁴in him was life, and the life was the light of all people. ⁵The light shines in the darkness, and the darkness did not overcome it.

⁶There was a man sent from God, whose name was John. ⁷He came as a witness to testify to the light, so that all might believe through him. ⁸He himself was not the light, but he came to testify to the light. ⁹The true light, which enlightens everyone, was coming into the world.

¹⁰He was in the world, and the world came into being through him; yet the

letters found in Sophia the language and imagery needed to speak of Jesus and his mission.[9] A shift seems to occur in the middle of the second century, demonstrated particularly through Tertullian (ca. 155–240 CE).[10] By this time the good news of liberation and salvation has reached into the Greco-Roman world, and by doing this the Gospel has hit up against attitudes to women that go beyond patriarchy into the misogynism of Aristotelian anthropology and philosophy. Within this mind-set the woman is not made in the image of God (Gen 1:27) and her life is not celebrated as "bone of my bones and flesh of my flesh" (Gen 2:23); instead, women are malformed, imperfect men.[11] From this time on the maleness of Jesus casts a veil over Sophia that had been diaphanous in the New Testament texts.

Like the figure of Sophia, the Gospel presses Jesus's origins back to the beginning of time; the introductory prologue echoes the opening words of Genesis 1 and is guided by the seven-day structure of this creation account.

I structure the prologue with two parallel sections: one reporting or telling the story of Jesus (vv. 3-13), and one section then offering first person testimony to this story (vv. 14-17). These two sections are enclosed within an introduction (vv. 1-2) and conclusion (v. 18).

---

9. Sally Douglas, *Early Church Understandings of Jesus as the Female Divine: The Scandal of the Scandal of Particularity*, LNTS 557 (London: Bloomsbury T&T Clark, 2016) and Eva Günther, *Wisdom as a Model for Jesus' Ministry: A Study on the "Lament over Jerusalem" in Matt 23:37-39 Par. Luke 13:34-35*, WUNT 2/513, (Tübingen: Mohr Siebeck, 2020).

10. Douglas, *Jesus as the Female Divine*, 116–17.

11. Aristotle (384–322 BCE): "And a woman is as it were an infertile male; the female, in fact, is female on account of an inability of a sort. . . . The male provides the 'form' and the 'principle of movement,' the female provides the body, in other words, the material" (*On the Genesis of the Creatures* 1.20).

world did not know him. ¹¹He came to what was his own, and his own people did not accept him. ¹²But to all who received him, who believed in his name, he gave power to become children of God, ¹³who were born, not of blood or of the will of the flesh or of the will of man, but of God.

¹⁴And the Word became flesh and lived among us, and we have seen his glory, the glory as of a father's only son, full of grace and truth. ¹⁵(John testified to him and cried out, "This was he of whom I said, 'He who comes after me ranks ahead of me because he was before me.'") ¹⁶From his fullness we have all received, grace upon grace. ¹⁷The law indeed was given through Moses; grace and truth came through Jesus Christ. ¹⁸No one has ever seen God. It is God the only Son, who is close to the Father's heart, who has made him known.

Introduction: ¹In the beginning was the Word, and the Word was with God,

and the Word was God. ²He was in the beginning with God.

[Part A: The Story Told]

³ All things came into being through him,

and without him not one thing came into being. What has come into being ⁴in him was life,

and the life was the light of all people.

⁵The light shines in the darkness,

and the darkness did not overcome it.

⁶There was a man sent from God,

whose name was John. ⁷He came

as a witness to testify to the light,

so that all might believe through him.

⁸ He himself was not the light,

but he came to testify to the light.

[Part B: Personal Testimony]¹²

¹⁴And the Word became flesh

and lived [tabernacled: ἐσκήνωσεν] among us,

and we have seen his glory,

the glory as of a father's only son,

full of grace and truth.

¹⁵(John testified to him and cried out,

"This was he of whom I said,

'He who comes after me ranks ahead of me

because he was before me.' ")

---

12. Verses 1-13 are in reported speech; verses 14-17 use first-person pronouns, "I," "we," "us," giving these verses the character of eyewitness testimony.

⁹The true light, which enlightens
  everyone,

was coming into the world.

¹⁰He was in the world, and the world

came into being through him;

yet the world did not know him.

¹¹He came to what was his own,

and his own people did not accept
  him.

¹²But to all who received him,

who believed in his name,

he gave power to become children
  of God,

¹³who were born, not of blood

or of the will of the flesh or of the
  will of man,

but of God.

¹⁶From his fullness we have all
  received,

grace upon grace [χάριν ἀντὶ χάριτος].

¹⁷The law indeed was given through
  Moses;

grace and truth came through Jesus
  Christ.

Conclusion: ¹⁸No one has ever seen God.
It is God the only Son, who is close to the Father's
heart [κόλπον],¹³
who has made him known.

The Gospel opens with a hymn-like prologue (vv. 1-18) that has been likened to an overture of a grand opera.¹⁴ In these verses the audience hears of the major characters, namely, God and the Word (v. 1),¹⁵ who in the narrative will be named as Father and Son.¹⁶ Themes that will recur across the narrative are announced: life (v. 4), cosmos (v. 10), and

13. Κόλπος means "breast" rather than heart, which would be καρδία in Greek.

14. Brendan Byrne, *Life Abounding: A Reading of John's Gospel* (Collegeville, MN: Liturgical Press, 2014), 21.

15. A very rich study of the "character" of God in the Fourth Gospel is Marianne Meye Thompson, *The God of the Gospel of John* (Grand Rapids: Eerdmans, 2001).

16. While the names reflect the patriarchal culture of the time, the presentation of the "Father" in John subverts the image of patriarchy and depicts a nonauthoritarian father figure who displays vulnerability in loving and gifting the world with the beloved (3:16). See the insert by Dorothy Lee on the portrayal of the Father in John's Gospel, "The Iconic Father," p. 156; also Dorothy A. Lee, "Beyond Suspicion? The Fatherhood of God in the Fourth Gospel," *Pacifica* 8 (1995): 140–54.

tabernacle (v. 14).[17] The plot is poignantly described: "he came to what was his own [εἰς τὰ ἴδια], and his own people did not accept him" (v. 11). But there are some of "his own" who do receive him and these are given the promise that expresses the goal of this entire adventure,[18] that believers will be transformed into children (v. 12) who will participate in the intimate relationship of the only born Son, dynamically resting on the Father's breast (v. 18). Although *Sophia*/Wisdom is not named, her subtle presence suffuses the prologue.

Unfortunately, Christianity has moved away from its Jewish roots, and many Christians are not familiar with the wisdom literature or even do not have all of this literature within their Bibles. This means that Wisdom's presence is not obviously recognized, which can be problematic for feminists. That Wisdom is present but unnamed in the New Testament resonates with the experience of women in church communities today who are present and active, but their contribution and leadership is unrecognized and unnamed. Like *Sophia* of old, women today are crying out in the streets and raising their voices (Prov 1:20), demanding justice and equality for all human beings.

Distanced as we are by time, culture, and religious traditions, a Western, Christian, twenty-first-century audience may hear these verses but not be attuned to their deeper resonances. We are also listening to an evangelist who is both artist and theologian, employing the literary styles his original audience would have been accustomed to through the repeated hearing of their ancient Scriptures, the Old Testament.[19] There are times when the author will cite these Scriptures explicitly (e.g., 1:23), but more frequently the narrative will proceed through allusions and subtle echoes, relying on the audience's familiarity with these ancient texts and their appreciation of the author's artistic skill. While this is challenging for the modern reader, it is important to remember that the author's aim is to communicate in order to reveal and lead to belief in Jesus, and through believing, have life in his name (see 20:31).

---

17. Within the narrative, the cultic symbol of the tabernacle will be represented by the temple.

18. On this point I agree with Käsemann that v. 12 "could be the culmination . . . [of] what was achieved by the manifestation of the Revealer." See Ernst Käsemann, "The Structure and Purpose of the Prologue to John's Gospel," in *New Testament Questions of Today* (London: SCM, 1969), 152.

19. When referring to the Scriptures known and used in the first century, I will use the general expression the Old Testament (OT). At times I will refer specifically to the Greek text of these writings, the Septuagint (LXX), or the Hebrew text (MT) and sometimes the Aramaic text known as the targums.

Following the lead of Adele Reinhartz, we can read the Gospel as telling three different "tales." At one level the Gospel narrates the story of the historical person Jesus, situated in the regions of Galilee, Judea, and Samaria, in the early part of the first century CE. At another level, the story reveals something of the later experience of the Johannine community in their faith and struggle with early Judaism after the destruction of the temple in 70 CE. But beyond these two "tales" lies a larger "meta-tale" that has "the cosmos as its setting and eternity as its time frame."[20] The prologue takes the reader from the cosmological tale (v. 1) into the historical tale (v. 18) through the experience and witness of the ecclesiological tale (vv. 14-17).

Introduction (1:1-2)

The prologue begins by echoing the first words of Genesis, inviting listeners into a cosmic tale of God and the Word existing beyond space and time "in the beginning," whenever that may have been. The description of the Word "with [πρός] God" expresses a dynamic intimacy that will be recapitulated in the conclusion (v. 18), which describes the Son drawn "into" (εἰς) the Father's bosom (κόλπος),[21] a "vivid portrayal of maternal imagery of mother and child."[22]

The particular Greek construction of the third phrase, "the Word was God," makes it clear that the Word participates in the divinity without being totally identical with "the God" (ὁ θεός) of 1:1b. "The construction the evangelist chose to express this idea was the most concise way he could have stated that the Word was God and yet was distinct from the Father."[23]

Stanza 1 (1:3-5)

The structure presented above shows the prologue developing in two parallel arrays of three stanzas set within an introduction and a

---

20. Adele Reinhartz, *The Word in the World: The Cosmological Tale in the Fourth Gospel*, SBLMS 45 (Atlanta: Scholars Press, 1992), 4.

21. The Greek prepositions πρός and εἰς express movement toward; Bo Reicke, "πρός," *TNDT* 6 (1964): 721. The choice of the term "bosom" reflects the relational closeness between the "father" and "son" even as it blurs the gendered language, suggesting a maternal closeness of a child at the breast.

22. Adesola Joan Akala, *The Son-Father Relationship and Christological Symbolism in the Gospel of John*, LNTS 505 (London: Bloomsbury T&T Clark, 2014), 221.

23. See the lengthy discussion of this verse in Daniel B. Wallace, *Greek Grammar Beyond the Basics: An Exegetical Syntax of the New Testament* (Grand Rapids: Zondervan, 1996), 266–69.

conclusion.[24] The first stanza tells a story of the Word's relation to the cosmos as an agent of creation, recalling the breath and voice of God speaking over the waters to create light and to separate light from darkness (Gen 1:3-5). In stating that "the darkness did not overcome it," the prologue intimates a conflict between the light and the darkness, a conflict that will be played out in the ensuing narrative.[25]

Stanza 2 (1:6-9)

The second stanza introduces John as one "sent by God." John comes highly credentialed and yet John's role is not to be the light but to bear witness. The narrative will continue to make this distinction between John and Jesus.

Stanza 3 (1:10-13)

The third stanza briefly narrates the experience when the creative Word, already present in the cosmos, is revealed to "his own." Here a distinction is made between some of his own who reject him and some who receive him in faith. These believers in "his name" (v. 12) will become "children of God" and will be "born" of God (ἐγεννήθησαν, v. 13). In both the Pauline and Johannine literature, being a child of God is a metaphorical way of stating a close and personal relationship with God, made possible through Jesus. The metaphor draws on the OT sense of Israel as God's own people, expressed in Hosea as God's children (Hos 11:1-4). For Paul, "The status of son implies full freedom and adulthood as compared with legal servitude and restriction. It means freedom from all cosmic powers, Gal. 3:25 ff.; 4:1 ff., 9; Rom. 8:31 ff."[26] It is also important for readers today to understand that in the ancient world adults could become closely affiliated with another adult through a process of adoption, a process not restricted to children. Wisdom speaks of initiating a close relationship between the righteous and God, but rather than

---

24. For a summary of other ways of structuring the prologue, see Mary L. Coloe, "The Structure of the Johannine Prologue and Genesis 1," *ABR* 45 (1997): 40–43.

25. Light and darkness will be two key symbols expressing the cosmological drama. For an examination of the dramaturgical and revelatory function of the "light" metaphor, see Jörg Frey, *The Glory of the Crucified One: Christology and Theology in the Gospel of John*, trans. Wayne Coppins and Christoph Heilig, BMSEC (Waco, TX: Baylor University Press, 2018), 126–37.

26. Albrecht Oepke, "Divine Sonship," *TDNT* 5 (1967): 652.

the metaphor of "adoption," she uses the model of friendship (Wis 7:27). This model is also used by Jesus in his final discourse when he calls his disciples "friends" (15:15). While the language of becoming "children of God" may suggest childishness for a reader today, culturally the metaphor included chosen adult relationships, and in the narrative this model shifts to one of adult friendship.

Becoming children of God is the ultimate goal of the narrative. Not only does the Word reveal God, but also through him believers will be drawn into the very life of God and be transformed into brothers and sisters of Jesus and daughters and sons of God (20:17).[27] This transformation will be depicted at the cross. A very frequent way of designating all Israel was to say, "the children of Israel." The evangelist situates the origin of believers not in a human patriarch (Jacob/Israel) but in God, and this God is depicted as giving "birth" (γεννάω) to her children.[28]

The image of God as a birthing mother would be familiar to a Jewish audience whose Scriptures describe God as "the Rock that bore you" and Israel is chastised for forgetting "the God who gave you birth" (Deut 32:18). Similarly, God "will cry out like a woman in labor, I will gasp and pant" (Isa 42:14). The image of God as a birthing and nurturing mother is a promise of hope for the returning exiles: "Shall I open the womb and not deliver? says the LORD. . . . As a mother comforts her child, so I will comfort you" (Isa 66:9a, 13). God challenges Job to recognize that creation itself is born from her womb: "From whose womb did the ice come forth, and who has given birth to the hoarfrost of heaven?" (Job 38:29). Thus, the Law, the Prophets, and the Writings bear witness that God images and language must be inclusive of women's experience. The birthing language introduced in the prologue cuts across the primary narrative language of God as "Father" and prepares the reader to encounter further "birthing" imagery.

---

27. Mary Magdalene is given the Easter proclamation: "Go to my sisters and brothers [ἀδελφούς] and say to them, 'I am ascending to my Father and your Father, to my God and your God.'" Although the word ἀδελφοί is grammatically masculine, according to H. G. Liddell, it is in fact a generic plural meaning both brothers and sisters. Henry G. Liddell, "ἀδελφός," in *A Lexicon: Abridged from Liddell and Scott's Greek-English Lexicon* (Oak Harbor, WA: Logos Research Systems, 1996), 12.

28. Although γεννάω may be used for both "the 'begetting' of the father and the 'bearing' of the mother," it is only rarely used to speak of God. Psalms 2 and 109 speak of the king being begotten/born of God, and Sophia/Wisdom in Proverbs 8. See Karl Heinrich Rengstorf and Friedrich Büchsel, "γεννάω," *TDNT* 1 (1964): 665–75.

Stanza 4 (1:14)

In verse 14 a major shift occurs. The story told across verses 2-13 is repeated, but now it has the character of first-person testimony. The incarnate Word dwelt among "us"; we hear directly the voice of believers witnessing to what "*we* have seen" (v. 14); John's witness in his own words, "This was he of whom *I* said, 'He who comes after *me* ranks ahead of *me* because he was before *me*'" (v. 15); and what they know through experience, "from his fullness *we* have all received" (vv. 16-17). The change from narration to testimony at verse 14 led to my structure shown above.

> [14]The Word became flesh and tabernacled among us, and we have seen his glory,
> the glory as of a father's only son [μονογενοῦς], the fullness of a gift that is true.[29]

In the first stanza, verses 3-5 speak of life and light shining in the darkness. When story becomes testimony, verse 14 proclaims, "*we saw* his glory." The Word, present as the life-force within creation, has become visible; light has brought perception. When we hear the statement, "The Word became flesh [σάρξ]," we may understand this as simply a statement of the Word becoming human. A common creed affirms, "by the Holy Spirit was incarnate of the Virgin Mary, and became *man*."[30] This is not accurate according to the biblical sense of "flesh." The Hebrew word בשׂר, "flesh," in the OT means more than a physical attribute of biological life experienced by humans and animals. In both Hellenistic Greek and early Judaism "flesh" "can also be used to emphasize the corruptibility of man [*sic*] and the lowliness of the creature over against the Creator."[31] Thus "flesh" is a quality of all created things—*ta panta*. Under the influence of Platonic and Epicurean philosophy, "flesh" became associated with materiality and sin in later Jewish and Christian writings, but this is not its primary sense in the OT or in the Fourth Gospel. In the OT "flesh" is the perception of the human person "in relation to God. As

---

29. Author's translation. "The LXX uses μονογενής for יָחִיד, e.g., Ju. 11:34, where it means the only child; cf. also Tob 3:15; 6:11." Friedrich Büchsel, "Μονογενής," *TDNT* 4 (1967): 738. In Tob 6:11 it is used to speak of Sarah, the only daughter of Raguel. In v. 14 the adjective has a masculine ending giving "only son."

30. This statement is from the Profession of Faith based on the Nicean-Contantinopolitan Creed, as expressed in the latest English translation of the Roman Catholic Eucharist (2010).

31. Eduard Schweizer and Friedrich Baumgärtel, "Σάρξ, Σαρκικός, Σάρκινος," *TDNT* 7 (1971): 111.

a creature of God he [sic] is flesh, always exposed to death."[32] Flesh emphasizes the corruptibility of human life, its temporality as distinct from the incorruptibility of the eternal God. Within the Fourth Gospel σάρξ is the human, earthly sphere without knowledge of God. This does not mean it is sinful, simply ignorant. It is the choice for unbelief, not σάρξ, that gives the world its sinful state. In 1:13 σάρξ refers to ordinary human birth as distinct from birth of God. In becoming flesh the Word enters fully into a world bound by space and time, and like all creation the enfleshed Word will experience death. Flesh means anything that has been created and is therefore bound by time and the ordinary material processes of death and decay.

> All flesh is grass, and all its beauty is like the flower of the field. The grass withers, the flower fades, when the breath of the LORD blows upon it; surely the people is grass. The grass withers, the flower fades; but the word of our God will stand for ever. (Isa 40:6-9; RSV)

Σάρξ, "flesh," in verse 14 therefore balances πάντα, "all things," in verse 3 to describe the entry of the Word into the "stuff" of creation. It is all inclusive, male and female, human and nonhuman, living and nonliving. As Dorothy Lee states, "It is not the maleness of Jesus that has symbolic significance in this world view but rather his embodiment in material/ human form."[33]

And herein lies a great paradox, not only that flesh reveals divine glory, but also that the incarnation destroys dualistic views of spirit/matter, male/female. Under the later influence of Greek philosophy Christianity moved away from an incarnational theology. "It has set in place a hierarchy with God and spirit presiding and various manifestation of the flesh in descending order. Women, and nature itself, are at the bottom since man has claimed for himself rationality and spirituality which are nearer to divinity than are matter and flesh."[34] The Neoplatonic philosopher Plotinus (205–270 CE) was the first philosopher to emphasize the connection of matter with evil. He wrote, "When something is absolutely deficient—and this is matter—this is essential evil without any share of

32. Eduard Schweizer and Friedrich Baumgärtel, "Σάρξ, Σαρκικός, Σάρκινος," *TDNT* 7 (1971): 123.

33. Dorothy A. Lee, *Flesh and Glory: Symbolism, Gender and Theology in the Gospel of John* (New York: Crossroad, 2002), 29.

34. Lisa Isherwood and Elizabeth Stuart, *Introducing Body Theology*, IFT 2 (Sheffield: Sheffield Academic, 1998), 16. See also Marie J. Giblin, "Dualism," in *Dictionary of Feminist Theologies*, ed. Letty M. Russell and J. Shannon Clarkson (Louisville: Westminster John Knox Press, 1996).

good."[35] Since women were associated with materiality, under the influence of Neoplatonism, women became identified with evil.[36] Against such centuries-old dualism, feminists and eco-theologians today are reclaiming incarnational theology. "'Flesh' is a far broader reality than 'humanity' and, as we are learning from the geneticists and biologists, we are not a solo species; we are related to all other 'flesh' with whom we share the same remote origin in the dust of exploding stars."[37]

In the first stanza the Word was described as "life" and "light." In verse 14, a community bears witness to what the light has revealed—"*we* have seen his glory." This glory is described as πλήρης χάριτος καὶ ἀληθείας, "the fullness of a gift that is true." This verse is frequently translated using the Pauline word "grace," but χάρις usually means "gift."[38] Furthermore, in Greek when the two nouns "gift" and "truth" are connected by "and" the second noun can be understood not as an addition to but as a quality of the first noun. The phrase χάριτος καὶ ἀληθείας is thus better translated as the fullness of a "true gift," or the fullness of a "gift that is true."[39]

In describing the flesh-taking of the Word, John uses the verb ἐσκήνωσεν from the word σκηνή, which means "tent" or "tabernacle," so the expression could read, "The Word became flesh and *tabernacled* among us." The word σκηνή was used in the OT to speak of the tent/tabernacle that symbolized God's presence with Israel when they left Sinai (Exod 40). This same word was then used to describe Sophia finding her place "in the holy tent" (LXX: σκηνή, Sir 24:10). By using this cultic term, John evokes the long memory of the Divine Presence dwelling within Israel and associated with the ark of the covenant, the temple, and the tabernacle.[40]

---

35. Plotinus, *Enneads* in *Plotinus* (Cambridge: Harvard University Press, 1966), 3:256.

36. See Prudence Allen, *The Concept of Woman: The Aristotelian Revolution, 750 B.C.–A.D. 1250* (Grand Rapids: Eerdmans, 1985). The Plotinus citation is on p. 203.

37. Margaret Daly-Denton, *John: An Earth Bible Commentary; Supposing Him to be the Gardener*, Earth Bible Commentary (London: Bloomsbury T&T Clark, 2017), 35. See also Lee, *Flesh and Glory*, 61.

38. In English we use the words "charism" to speak of a gift and "charismatic" to describe a gifted individual.

39. This grammatical form will also be significant in translating v. 16. For further explanation, see Francis J. Moloney, *John*, SP 4 (Collegeville, MN: Liturgical Press, 1998), 45; Ruth B. Edwards, "ΧΑΡΙΝ ΑΝΤΙ ΧΑΡΙΤΟΣ (John 1:16): Grace and the Law in the Johannine Prologue," *JSNT* 32 (1988): 3-15.

40. For a more detailed discussion of this cultic presence, see Mary L. Coloe, *God Dwells with Us: Temple Symbolism in the Fourth Gospel* (Collegeville, MN: Liturgical Press, 2001), chap. 3.

Following the exile, God's presence was seen beyond the cult, within the very order of the universe with its rhythms of times and seasons. This presence of God was named divine Wisdom, Σοφία (*Sophia*). The sages found *Sophia* not only in the order of the cosmos but also in the orderly life of the community living according to God's law—the Torah—and so they spoke of *Sophia* making her home within Israel, coming to dwell in the tent/tabernacle and later enscripted in Israel's Torah (Sir 24).

Stanza 5 (1:15)

Following the personal testimony of the community, who have seen the Word tabernacling "among *us*," the next stanza returns to the witness of John, where he speaks in his own voice, "He who comes after *me* ranks ahead of *me* because he was before *me*." In the context of the Fourth Gospel's theology of the preexistent Word, the verse as it now stands is a reference to Jesus, who ranks higher than John and whose existence has already been situated "in the beginning."[41]

Stanza 6 (1:16-17)

[16]From his fullness *we* have all received, a gift instead of a gift [χάριν ἀντὶ χάριτος].
[17]For the law was given through Moses; the true gift [ἡ χάρις καὶ ἡ ἀλήθεια] came through Jesus Christ.[42]

Testimony continues in the final stanza, which speaks of a gift that "*we* have received." Where stanza 3 made a distinction between those of his own who did not receive the Word and those who did, stanza 6 makes a distinction between two "gifts"—χάριν ἀντὶ χάριτος. Once again most translations follow the Pauline sense of χάρις as "grace" rather than the usual translation as "gift." The following verse elaborates further on these two gifts. The first gift was the law, "given through Moses"; now in Jesus another gift is being offered, described as the fullness of a true

---

41. John Meier considers that since a similar phrase is attested in the Synoptic Gospels, "we have good reason to accept that this is substantially the Baptist's own teaching." Most likely the historical John was referring to an expectation of Elijah returning before the eschatological Day of the Lord (Mal 4:6). See John P. Meier, *A Marginal Jew: Rethinking the Historical Jesus*, vol. 2: *Mentor, Message, and Miracles*, ABRL (New York: Doubleday, 1994), 27–40.
42. Author's translation.

gift (v. 17). The tragedy is that some of "his own" who received the first gift of the Mosaic law are unable to see in Jesus the second gift, which this community believes to be in continuity with and fulfilling the hope expressed in Israel's law.

The parallel stanza, verses 11-13, clarifies what this further gift is. Those who believe in his name "are given the power to become the children of God" (v. 12). Within the Gospel narrative, some of "his own" will claim to be followers of Moses (9:28) and children of Abraham (8:33). The Johannine community claims that a greater lineage is now possible, that through Jesus they have become children of God.

These two verses can be read falsely as supersessionism, particularly when the preposition ἀντὶ is read as a *contrast* between two gifts. Ἀντί is a preposition that can mean replacement or "equivalent in estimation" or "similarity."[43] The Gospel narrative does not show Jesus replacing the gift of the law or denying its validity. In fact, when there is a conflict about Jesus's act of healing on the Sabbath (chap. 5), Jesus draws on the law to support his actions (7:19-24). Therefore, it is best to read χάριν ἀντὶ χάριτος as a gift just as once Moses received a gift, where the emphasis is on the bounty of God's free giving, once to Moses and now to "us" (1:14). In the estimation of the Johannine community, this gift, becoming children of God (1:12), is the full expression of the first gift. Daniel Boyarin proposes the following understanding of these verses (1:16, 17): "Although the Word is the creator of all, as we learned in v. 3, all were not capable alone of receiving him. Indeed, his own people did not receive him when he came in the form of the Torah . . . but God performed the extraordinary act of incarnating his Logos in flesh and blood. . . . Jesus comes to fulfill the mission of Moses, not to displace it. The Torah simply needed a better exegete, the *Logos Ensarkos*, a fitting teacher for flesh and blood."[44]

Conclusion (1:18)

> [18]No one has ever seen God. It is the only Son, who is close to the Father's heart [κόλπον] who has made him known.

---

43. Friedrich Büchsel, "Ἀντί," *TDNT* 1 (1964): 372–73.

44. Daniel Boyarin, "The Gospel of the Memra: Jewish Binitarianism and the Prologue to John," *HTR* 94 (2001): 280.

The introduction began with the mythic language of *Logos* and *Theos* "in the beginning." When the *Logos* enters human history in verse 14, the language shifts to metaphor, and the prologue now expresses the dynamic unity of verse 1 in the familial image of an only child nestled in the bosom (κόλπος)[45] of a parent. Against claims that some of Israel's great holy ones went up to heaven and saw God, the Gospel asserts that this has never happened (see also 3:13). The only one who can reveal God is the one who has always been in God's presence and now has come into history. There are difficulties with the text in that some manuscripts read "the only God" (μονογενὴς θεὸς) and others read "the only son" (μονογενὴς υἱὸς). For consistency with the image of "father" I prefer the only "son" even though it has the weaker attestations; also as noted in the introduction, the first meaning ascribed to γίνομαι is "to come into being through process of birth or natural production, *be born, be produced.*"[46] While masculine language is used, the imagery is of an only born child resting at the mother's breast.

In the introduction I noted the "blurring of gender boundaries" that occurs in the Gospel, and 1:18 is another clear example of this. The prologue begins with mythic cosmic language of God and the Word, but now that the Word has entered corporeal existence as "flesh" the language changes to that of person—and in this case the image of father and son is used. This will be the primary overt image throughout the narrative, but it is interrupted by other times of gender blurring, as will be shown, when Jesus speaks and acts as Sophia and when birthing is attributed to himself (19:34) and God (cf. 1:13). The feminine gender is regularly lost in translation. In 1:18 Jesus is spoken of as the μονογενής, from two adjectives μόνος and γένος related to the verb γίνομαι, a term that can mean both "begotten" as from a man or "birthed" as from a woman. But as Gail O'Day notes, "Most translations favor the 'begotten' side, of that translation choice."[47] This results in the feminine imagery of God as a birthing and nursing mother (e.g., Isa 49:15; 66:13) being lost, as well as the feminine face of Sophia-Jesus.

---

45. As noted above, κόλπος means bosom, not heart, as NRSV renders it. The Greek word for heart is καρδία.

46. BDAG, 197. Italics in the original.

47. Gail R. O'Day, "John," in *Women's Bible Commentary*, ed. Carol A. Newsom, Sharon H. Ringe, and Jacqueline E. Lapsley, 3rd ed. (Louisville: Westminster John Knox, 2012), 520.

Old Testament Resonances

Creation

The prologue immediately sets up an echo of Genesis in its opening phrase—"In the beginning." As well as this there are strong similarities between the structure of the first creation account and the prologue. Like the prologue, the creation account can be set out in two parallel arrays of three stanzas covering the first six days. The first three days are works involving separations: light/darkness; waters above/waters below; water/land. In the prologue, the first three stanzas establish clear distinctions: light/darkness; witness/Light; belief/rejection.

In Genesis there is a relationship between the work of the first three days and the work of the next three days. The light and darkness of day one are populated by the greater and lesser lights in day four. The firmament above, created on day two, is populated by birds on day five, while the waters below are populated by fish. Then on day six, the land formed on day three is populated by animal life, including humanity made in God's image. These three days lead into the divine rest on the seventh day—the Sabbath.

The structure can be shown schematically as:[48]

Introduction: In the beginning (1:1-2)

Separation	Population
A (1:3-5) light/darkness	**A'** (1:14-19) sun, stars
B (1:6-8) heaven/earth	**B'** (1:20-23) birds, fish
C (1:9-13) land/waters	**C'** (1:24-31) animals, humans

Climax: The Sabbath (2:1-3)

Conclusion: The generations of heaven and earth (2:4a)

Similarly, in the prologue there is a parallelism between the first three stanzas and the final three. The first stanza introduces the Light. The fourth stanza testifies that the Light, now incarnate, has been seen (v. 14). Stanza two describes the witness of John, while in stanza five we hear John's own testimony. Stanza three describes the two responses to the Word; in stanza six we learn of two gifts, the Mosaic law and a true gift

---

48. This structure is noted by many scholars; see Joseph Blenkinsopp, *Creation, Un-creation, Re-creation: A Discursive Commentary on Genesis 1–11* (London: T&T Clark, 2011), 20.

through Jesus, which the parallelism reveals to be the power to become children of God (v. 12).

The structure of the prologue can be shown schematically as:

Introduction (1:1-2)   *Logos/Theos* in eternity

Part 1 (story told)		Part 2 (testimony)
A (1:3-5) light	have seen	**A'** (1:14) glory
B (1:6-8) John	have heard	**B'** (1:15) John
C (1:9-13) two responses	have experienced	**C'** (1:16-17) two gifts

Conclusion (1:18) *Son/Father* in history

The Johannine prologue thus mirrors the structure of Genesis 1 as the following diagram demonstrates:

GENESIS

Introduction (1:1-2)

Separation	*Population*
A (1:3-5) light/darkness	**A'** (1:14-19) sun, stars
B (1:6-8) heaven/earth	**B'** (1:20-23) birds, fish
C (1:9-13) land/waters	**C'** (1:24-31) animals, humans

Climax: The seventh day (2:1-3)
"On the seventh day God finished the work" (Gen 2:2)

Conclusion (2:4a)

JOHANNINE PROLOGUE

Introduction (1:1-2)

Story Told	*Testimony Given*
A (1:3-5) light	**A'** (1:14) we saw
B (1:6-8) John	**B'** (1:15) I said
C (1:9-13) children of God	**C'** (1:16-17) gift

Conclusion (1:18)

A comparison of these structures offers further insight into John's theology that will become clearer as the narrative develops. One significant difference between these two structures is that the prologue has no equivalent to the seventh day divine rest. According to Johannine theology, God did not complete the work of creation "in the beginning," for Jesus declares, "My Father is still working, and so am I" (5:17; see also 4:34; 9:4; 17:4). It is not until Jesus's work is completed and from the cross he announces, with words echoing Genesis, "It is finished," that there can be a great Sabbath.[49]

Logos/Sophia

Two questions follow John's Wisdom Christology. Why was Wisdom/ *Sophia* such a dominant motif in Israel's postexilic theology? Why did John use *Logos*/Word rather than *Sophia*/Wisdom to introduce Jesus?

The destruction of Jerusalem in 587 BCE resulted in many children of Israel leaving the land of Canaan and going into exile, either in Babylon (forced) or by fleeing to Egypt. This diaspora brought them into contact with many other forms of worship, including the worship of feminine goddesses such as Astarte in Babylon and Isis in Egypt. Later, under Hellenistic influence, the cult of Isis spread across the Mediterranean world. "Personified Wisdom was the answer of orthodox Judaism to this threat."[50] It was Wisdom, *Sophia*, not Isis, who brought forth creation, who sustains the world, and who saved Israel across generations. This is very clear in the book of Wisdom, where from chapter 10 Israel's history is retold and *Sophia*/Wisdom is named as the savior who delivered Israel from Egypt, guiding them by day and night, leading them through deep waters, and drowning their enemies (e.g., Wis 10:15-19). Similarly, the images in the poem of Sirach 24:1-34 hark back to the wilderness wanderings, only now the pillar of cloud is the throne of Wisdom (Sir 24:4) and the tent that had been the tabernacle of God's dwelling is now the place of Wisdom's dwelling (Sir 24:10). But within the book of Wisdom, a change occurs in chapter 18, where the savior "Wisdom" shifts to the masculine-gendered "Word/*Logos*." This may have been needed because the savior figure is imaged in masculine terms as a "stern warrior."

---

49. "When Jesus had received the wine, he said, 'It is finished.' Then he bowed his head and gave over the spirit. Since it was the day of Preparation, the Jews did not want the bodies left on the cross during the Sabbath, especially because that Sabbath was a great day [μεγάλη ἡ ἡμέρα]" (19:30-31).

50. Elizabeth A. Johnson, "Jesus, the Wisdom of God: A Biblical Basis for Non-Androcentric Christology," *ETL* 61 (1985): 269.

For while gentle silence enveloped all things,
and night in its swift course was now half gone,
your all-powerful word [*logos*] leaped from heaven, from the royal throne,
into the midst of the land that was doomed,
a stern warrior
carrying the sharp sword of your authentic command,
and stood and filled all things with death,
and touched heaven while standing on the earth. (Wis 18:14-16)

In much the same way, the maleness of Jesus may have necessitated using the masculine-gendered *Logos*/Word rather than the feminine *Sophia*/Wisdom in the prologue. Also, the image of *Logos* would resonate with both a diaspora Jewish audience through their Scriptures (LXX) and the Stoic *logos* philosophy of Philo:[51] "Let us, then, pay no heed to the discrepancy in the gender of the words, and say that the daughter of God, even Wisdom, is not only masculine but father, sowing and begetting in souls aptness to learn, discipline, knowledge, sound sense, good and laudable actions" (*Flight* 52).[52] Wisdom mythology, particularly her rejection, shapes the Johannine narrative so much so that Elisabeth Schüssler Fiorenza writes: "The logos title of the prologue, therefore, seems not to lessen but to increase the possibility that the Fourth Gospel understands Jesus as making Sophia present in and through her/his work."[53] The term *Logos* would also be familiar to a Gentile audience where the *Logos* is part of the "cosmological speculations of Hellenism."[54]

---

51. William Loader, "Wisdom and Logos Tradition in Judaism and John's Christology," in *Reading the Gospel of John's Christology as Jewish Messianism: Royal, Prophetic, and Divine Messiahs*, ed. Benjamin E. Reynolds and Gabriele Boccaccini, AGJU 106 (Leiden: Brill, 2018), 313.

52. Cited in Loader, "Wisdom and Logos Tradition," 306, n. 8. This philosophy is based on Aristotelian thought where only the male is responsible for procreation. "And a woman is as it were an infertile male; the female, in fact, is female on account of an inability of a sort. . . . The male provides the 'form' and the 'principle of movement,' the female provides the body, in other words, the material" (*Generation of Animals* 1.20). Tragically, this incorrect biology remained a significant influence on Western religion and society until the discovery of the female ovum by Karl Ernst von Baer in 1827 using a microscope. A more critical approach to Philo's blending of Sophia and Logos is taken by Elisabeth Schüssler Fiorenza, *Jesus: Miriam's Child, Sophia's Prophet; Critical Issues in Feminist Christology*, 2nd ed. (London: Bloomsbury T&T Clark, 2015), 150–51.

53. Schüssler Fiorenza, *Jesus: Miriam's Child, Sophia's Prophet*, 167.

54. Rudolph Bultmann, *The Gospel of John: A Commentary*, trans. G. R. Beasley Murray et al. (Oxford: Blackwell, 1971), 24.

Even though Jesus is introduced as the incarnate *Logos*, this title is not used within the narrative, and, paradoxically, the narrative depicts Jesus as the embodiment of *Sophia*, acting as she did offering nourishment, life, light, and salvation. But her presence is obscured by the predominance of the "Son-Father" language. This language "reinscribes the metaphorical grammatical masculinity of the expressions 'logos' and 'son' as congruent with the biological masculine sex of the historic person of Jesus."[55] Schüssler Fiorenza names this as the "genderization" of both Christology and theology.[56] The danger of such predominantly masculine metaphorical language is that it can lead to *ontological* thinking that only a male can be *in persona Christi* and that God is also male. The grammatical forms of human language thus define the "being" of the risen Christ and God.

For those wishing to read John in an inclusive and liberative way two hermeneutical shifts are needed: first, to bring into the reading the strong consciousness of Wisdom's embodied presence in Jesus; second, to read the "Father-Son" language aware of how it is used in a particular narrative context as described in the introduction and freed from the usual patriarchal dynamic. The essay by Dorothy Lee (p. 156), "The Iconic 'Father' of Jesus," shows how the Johannine presentation of "Father" in fact subverts the patriarchal image.

Prologue and Gospel

In my reading of the prologue and the following narrative, there are such strong theological links that I can only conclude that the prologue comes from the same theological mind as the rest of the Gospel.[57] The theme of creation continues across the Gospel expressed in terms such as "life" (ζωή) and "eternity life" (ζωὴν αἰώνιον),[58] in images of birth and

---

55. Schüssler Fiorenza, *Jesus: Miriam's Child, Sophia's Prophet*, 168.

56. Ibid., 168–69.

57. The earliest major twentieth-century commentary on the Gospel was by Rudolph Bultmann (*The Gospel of John: A Commentary*, 17–18; the original German commentary was published in 1941), who proposed that the prologue was originally a cultic hymn within the community of John the Baptist. Raymond E. Brown (*The Gospel according to John*, 2 vols., AB 29–29A [New York: Doubleday, 1966, 1970], 1:20) also sees traces of an original hymn but proposes that this hymn arose from within the Johannine community.

58. The expression ζωὴν αἰώνιον occurs frequently across the narrative (3:15, 16, 36; 4:14, 36; 5:24, 39; 6:27, 40, 47, 54, 68; 10:28; 12:25, 50; 17:2, 3) and is usually translated as "eternal life"; I prefer to translate this expression as "eternity" life to focus on a new quality of life that Jesus is offering, i.e., the life God lives in eternity, which is now accessible in the present.

rebirth (3:3-8; 16:21; 19:34), and in the creation imagery in chapters 18–20. The assertion that believers will become God's children (1:12) is depicted in the passion (19:25-27). The cultic symbolism expressing the incarnation of the Word (v. 14) is reiterated in Jesus's identification with the temple (2:19-21). *Logos/Sophia* speaks through the words and action of Jesus; Wisdom offers salvation (3:17) and eternity life; she will teach and nourish her children (6:35, 48-51).

The Aramaic Targums

By the time of Jesus, Hebrew was no longer spoken in the regions of Galilee and Judea. For this reason, in the synagogue, after the Scriptures were read in Hebrew, they were then reread in Aramaic. These Aramaic readings were known as the targums (meaning "translation"), but they were not an exact translation, rather a transliteration, where the original Hebrew was often given a further elaboration.[59] Because the targums continued to develop into later centuries, it is difficult to determine the dating of texts; however, since the discovery of the Dead Sea Scrolls, scholars have some comparative Jewish literature, including targum fragments, that can help to assess whether ideas in the targums were current in late Second Temple Judaism.

Like the earlier Deuteronomic and Priestly traditions, the targums grapple with the paradox of speaking about an omnipresent and infinite God being located in this world with its limitations of time and space.[60] Where the Deuteronomist spoke of God's *name* dwelling in the temple (e.g., Deut 12:5; 14:23; 16:6; 1 Kgs 3:2) and the Priestly tradition spoke of God's *glory* filling the tabernacle and temple (Exod 40:34; Ezek 8:4; 43:5), the targums use a nonscriptural term and speak of God's *Shekinah*, which, like Wisdom/*Sophia*, is grammatically feminine. "And the cloud covered the tent of meeting, and the Glory of *the Shekinah of* the Lord filled the Tabernacle" (Tg. Neof. Exod 40:34).[61]

As a cognate of the verb שכן (dwell), *Shekinah* is used

59. The practice of explaining the reading seems to go back to the time of Ezra explaining the readings for the people who had returned from exile in Babylon: "So they read from the book, from the law of God, with interpretation. They gave the sense, so that the people understood the reading" (Neh 8:8).

60. C. G. Montefiore and H. Loewe, *A Rabbinic Anthology* (New York: Schocken, 1974), 15.

61. Martin McNamara and Michael Maher, *Targum Neofiti 1: Exodus; Targum Pseudo-Jonathan: Exodus*, The Aramaic Bible 2 (Edinburgh: T & T Clark, 1994). A detailed introduction to the Palestinian targums can be found in Martin McNamara, *Targum Neofiti 1: Genesis*, The Aramaic Bible 1A (Edinburgh: T & T Clark, 1992), 1–46. The dating of Neofiti is problematic since it shows evidence of a number of reworkings.

primarily to describe God's numinous immanence and is commonly used in association with the term "glory" (יקרא—*Yichra*).[62] Both terms, *Shekinah* and *Yichra*, preserve the holy transcendence of God while acknowledging God's presence within Israel's midst, and both are associated with fiery light. "And the appearance of the glory *of the Shekinah* of the Lord (was) like a devouring fire, *a devouring fire* on the top of the mountain, in the eyes of the children of Israel" (Tg. Neof. Exod 24:17).

By using terms such as *Shekinah* and *Yichra*, the targums avoid any naive anthropomorphic ideas about God and thus interpret the Hebrew text for the listeners. By such instructive interpretation, the Targumist stands as heir to a tradition that had its beginnings with Ezra the scribe, who not only read the text but interpreted it for the people to ensure accurate understanding (Neh 8:1-3, 8).[63] *Shekinah* and *Yichra* are used at times as a reverent alternative to speaking of God.[64]

A further term, *Memra* (word), is found in the targums and is used in a similar way to *Shekinah* and *Yichra*. *Memra* is not simply a translation of דבר־יהוה (the Word of the Lord), when this conveys the sense of the prophetic word; rather, *Memra* is used to express God's self-manifestation within this world,[65] and, like *Sophia* and *Shekinah*, it is grammatically feminine. In Targum Neofiti, God creates through the *Memra*: "From the beginning with wisdom the *Memra* of the Lord created and perfected the heavens and the earth" (Tg. Neof. Gen 1:1). It is the *Memra* of the Lord that gives the

---

62. The term "glory," כבוד, in the Hebrew text is associated with "weightiness" that gives a person importance or honor. When used of God, the term, while associated with the visible storm cloud, refers to the invisible essence of God. The cloud appears necessary to veil the radiance of God's presence. The LXX text translates כבוד with the term δόχα. As used in the LXX, δόχα takes on a distinct meaning quite different from its use in secular Greek literature. In the secular sense it usually means "opinion," while in the LXX is comes closer to the sense of כבוד, meaning the divine revelation of God's essential nature in the created world. In the targums כבוד is always rendered יקרא, *yichra*. See G. von Rad and G. Kittel, "δόξα," *TDNT* 2 (1964): esp. 238–46.

63. Martin McNamara, *Targum and Testament: Aramaic Paraphrases of the Hebrew Bible; A Light on the New Testament* (Grand Rapids: Eerdmans, 1972), 35.

64. A. Unterman, "Shekinah," *Encyclopedia Judaica* 14 (1971): 1349–50. Etan Levine argues that the primary concern of the targums is not to eliminate anthropomorphisms, but to avoid the direct use of God's name. See Etan Levine, *The Aramaic Version of the Bible: Contents and Context* (Berlin: de Gruyter, 1988), 57.

65. George F. Moore, *Judaism in the First Centuries of the Christian Era: The Age of the Tannaim*, 3 vols. (Cambridge, MA: Harvard University Press, 1927–1930), 1:417–19.

command, "Let there be light" (Gen 1:3).

All three words—*Shekinah*, *Yichra*, and *Memra*—are ways of speaking of that which is of God and which goes forth from God into the world, so that where the *Shekinah* or *Yichra* or *Memra* is present, there is God. By means of these expressions, the Targumist avoids expressions such as "God dwelt" or "departed" or "ascended." Such expressions seem to be too anthropomorphic and beneath the dignity of God. Where the Hebrew reads, "The Lord appeared to Abram" (Gen 17:1) and "God went up from Abraham" (17:22), Neofiti renders this "The *Memra* of the Lord was revealed to Abram" and "the glory of the *Shekinah* of the Lord went up from Abraham."[66] The targums expand our vocabulary of the divine world, adding Aramaic feminine terms *Shekinah* and *Memra* to counterbalance the masculine *Logos*.

The targums show a close parallel with a number of Johannine terms and concepts. If clear dating can be proven, then these Scriptures from the Palestinian synagogues provide a more likely Johannine source for the *Logos* concept than Stoic philosophy or Philo of Alexandria. Following a very detailed study of this issue, Craig Evans concludes:

> The point of all this is that the Christology of the Fourth Evangelist is fundamentally indebted to the language, concepts and institutions of the Old Testament and first-century Judaism. . . . It has come as no surprise then to find the Fourth Gospel permeated by the language, exegesis and presuppositions of the synagogue.[67]

In verse 14 of the prologue three terms used in the targums to speak of God's presence in this world are combined—*Memra*, *Shekinah*, and *Yichra*. "The Word [*Memra*] was made flesh and dwelt among us [he made his *Shekinah* dwell among us] and we have beheld his glory

---

66. John Ronning argues that in fact the targums provide the best solution for why the evangelist called Jesus "the Word"; John Ronning, *The Jewish Targums and John's Logos Theology* (Grand Rapids: Baker Academic 2010). At the time when post-70 Judaism is seeing the Torah as the embodiment of *Sophia*, the Johannine community asserts that Jesus is *Sophia* incarnate. On this point, see the excellent article by Warren Carter, "The Prologue and John's Gospel: Function, Symbol and the Definitive Word," *JSNT* 39 (1990): 35–58. Like other scholars, I consider the evangelist's use of *Logos* rather than *Sophia* was determined by the gender of Jesus and possibly influenced by Philo's philosophical thinking, "where Wisdom tradition is enriched by Stoic logos tradition." See Loader, "Wisdom and Logos Tradition," 313.

67. Evans, *Word and Glory*, 184.

[*Yichra*]."[68] In commenting on the distinction between the terms *Memra and Shekinah*, Frédéric Manns links *Memra* with the creative and revelatory word, while *Shekinah* describes God's dwelling among humanity.[69] Whether it is God's word in creation, or the manifestation of God's glory, or God's abiding presence, all three terms express a relationship between God and humanity that is accessible to human senses. The word can be heard, the glory can be seen, albeit veiled, and God's dwelling among us can be experienced. These terms from the targums used in Jewish synagogue worship may have provided the Johannine author with the theological tools to express the divinity they saw, heard, and experienced in Jesus.

The Mystical Journey from Light to Darkness

The terms "light" and "dark" will be used across the narrative with a symbolic sense primarily in terms of Jesus's presence associated with light (8:12; 9:5) and Jesus's absence associated with darkness (6:17). The metaphor of light is extended to include belief (12:36, 46), while that of darkness is extended to include willful unbelief (13:30), the domain of evil (3:19), and Satan (13:27). In a culture without modern technology, the nighttime was a state of intense darkness and to be feared, with only moonlight to offer relief. Whether from the ready use of light/dark as symbols in the religious world or arising from a natural fear of the darkness of night when vision fails, the words developed a pejorative sense when used anthropologically to describe people.[70] As mentioned in the introduction, when white Europeans landed on Australian soil they dismissed the existence of the dark-skinned indigenous

68. R. Le Déaut, *The Message of the New Testament and the Aramaic Bible (Targum)*, SubBi 5 (Rome: Biblical Institute Press, 1982), 43. Le Déaut is here using the work of Alejandro Díez Macho, "Targum y Nuevo Testamento," in *Mélanges Eugène Tisserant* (Vatican: Biblioteca apostólica vaticana, 1964), 153–85.

69. Frédéric Manns, *L'Évangile de Jean à la lumière du Judaïsme*, SBFA 33 (Jerusalem: Franciscan Printing Press, 1991), 41.

70. David Goldenberg, "Racism, Color Symbolism, and Color Prejudice," in *The Origins of Racism in the West*, ed. Miriam Eliav-Feldon, Benjamin Isaac, and Joseph Ziegler (Cambridge: Cambridge University Press, 2009).

people who were already settled on the land with skills in agriculture, aquiculture, forest management, and water locating and protecting, and with arts such as dance, music, and painting. This culture was dismissed and also the land management of thousands of years was lost.

When darkness has gathered to itself a history of negative associations that are then ascribed to people of color, religious literature can reclaim the godliness of "dark" and "black." A place to start could be the Song of Songs that was considered by the rabbis to be the holy of holies.[71] In this song the woman celebrates her color—

> I am black and beautiful,
>   O daughters of Jerusalem,
> like the tents of Kedar,
>   like the curtains of Solomon.
> Do not gaze at me because I am
>   dark,
>   because the sun has gazed
>   on me.
> My mother's sons were angry
>   with me;

> they made me keeper of the
>   vineyards,
> but my own vineyard I have not
>   kept! (Song 1:5-6)

Just as in the OT the term "glory" was used to express the magnificent dark thundercloud of God's presence at Sinai (Exod 19:16), so within the Christian tradition, darkness has long been associated with mysticism and the impenetrable "cloud of unknowing."[72] Garry Poe writes, "Gregory was able to demonstrate how the Christian life is a progressive journey from light to darkness."[73] The Flemish mystic Hadewijch of Brabant wrote of "the deep, insurmountable darkness of love."[74] Evelyn Underhill writes of her conviction to "start definitely learning God is in the darkness for me as well as light."[75]

If we could embrace the whole religious tradition surrounding words such as "black" or "dark," we may overcome the racial prejudices and stereotypes causing so much personal and social damage in our time.

---

71. The Mishnah records that at the Council of Yavneh (ca. 80), Rabbi Aquiba stated: "All the scriptures are holy, but the Canticle is the Holy of Holies" (m. Yad. 3.5).

72. The tradition continues, as shown in modern poetry; see Peter O'Leary, *Thick and Dazzling Darkness: Religious Poetry in a Secular Age* (New York: Columbia University Press, 2017).

73. Gary R. Poe, "Light to Darkness: From Gnosis to Agape in the Apophatic Imagery of Gregory of Nyssa," *Baptist History and Heritage* 53 (2018): 58.

74. Douglas E. Christie, "The Insurmountable Darkness of Love: Contemplative Practice in a Time of Loss," *Cross Currents* 69 (2019): 107.

75. Robyn Wrigley-Carr, "Darkness and Light in Evelyn Underhill," *Journal of Spiritual Formation and Soul Care* 12 (2019): 141.

This painting evokes the "earthiness" and vulnerability of 1:14, of Sophia pitching her tent in our midst. The tabernacle/tent was a temporary habitation as God moved with the people of Israel during their wilderness time. There is no grandeur of temple or rituals—just people gathered in wonder.

Painting by Sr. Dorothy Grills, CSJ, †, He Pitched His Tent among Us, 2011. Used with permission from Eva Solomon.

Symbolism in the Fourth Gospel[76]

The fact that John, despite a few minor challenges in the first two centuries, has always been accepted as a Gospel on a par with the Synoptics[77] testifies to early ecclesial consensus that it is essentially, even if not primarily, historical. Its designation in the late second century as the "spiritual gospel" witnessed to the recognition from the very beginning that it is also a highly symbolic work.[78] The tendency, however, of modern critics to see "historical" and "symbolic" as contrary (if not contradictory) terms led many nineteenth- and early twentieth-century exegetes to regard the Fourth Gospel as historically worthless and led some contemporary

76. This essay is a synthesis of my previous work on symbolism in the Fourth Gospel. For further detail, see Sandra M. Schneiders, *Written That You May Believe: Encountering Jesus in the Fourth Gospel*, rev. and exp. ed. (New York: Crossroad, 2003), 63–77.

77. See Rudolph Schnackenburg, *The Gospel According to St John*, trans. K. Smyth et al., 3 vols., HTCNT (London: Burns & Oates, 1968–1982), 1:192–93.

78. According to Eusebius (*Eccl. Hist.* 6.14.7), Clement of Alexandria, who died c. 200 CE, was the first to call the Fourth Gospel the "spiritual gospel."

scholars to an extreme reserve about its symbolism.

The new manuscript and archaeological evidence, which continues to appear, is steadily reinforcing the judgment of contemporary scholarship on the historical reliability of John.[79] And the growing interest in the study of all of Scripture, including John, as literature is steadily focusing more positive attention on such essential elements of literature as structure and symbolism.[80] These facts of contemporary biblical scholarship almost force the student of the Fourth Gospel to reexamine the relationship between history and symbolism in John, and such a reexamination has convinced me that this relationship is not simply a literary characteristic of this Gospel but an integral part of Johannine theology.

I would like to suggest that this aspect of Johannine theology, namely, the relation between history and symbolism, constitutes, in itself, a *sacramental* principle. John's understanding of history itself as symbolic revelation is that principle. Several consequences flow from this. First, because history itself is John's symbolic material, the more historical something is, the more symbolic potential it possesses. Second, symbolism in John is not an element *in* the Gospel but a dimension *of* the Gospel as a whole, namely, its characteristic revelatory mode. Third, because the Fourth Gospel is thoroughly symbolic, the individual parts have to be understood in function of the whole rather than the whole in function of the parts. Fourth, Johannine symbolism is not extrinsicist allegorism.[81] Fifth, since the genuine symbol is polyvalent by nature and therefore open to a surplus of meaning, it is open to multiple valid interpretations, but this does not mean that all interpretations are valid or even equally insightful. While there

---

79. See Raymond E. Brown, *An Introduction to the Gospel of John: Edited, Updated, Introduced and Concluded by Francis J. Moloney*, ABRL (New York: Doubleday, 2003), 90–114.

80. The work of Alan Culpepper laid the foundation for a growing repertoire of studies approaching John's Gospel as literature. See R. Alan Culpepper, *Anatomy of the Fourth Gospel: A Study in Literary Design*, New Testament: FF (Philadelphia: Fortress, 1983).

81. Actually, the term "allegory" as it was used by the patristic writers included all figurative or more-than-literal uses of language and not merely the kind of one-to-one correspondence of the *roman à clef* that the term suggests today. For a fuller treatment of the ancient theory of the "senses of scripture," see Sandra M. Schneiders, "Scripture and Spirituality," in *Christian Spirituality: Origins to the Twelfth Century*, ed. Bernard McGinn and John Meyendorff, *World Spirituality: An Encyclopedic History of the Religious Quest* (New York: Crossroad, 1985), 1–20.

are no rules for the "decoding" of symbols, since they are not signs, there are criteria for the valid interpretation of symbolic works.[82]

All of these consequences explicate the basic hypothesis that the Fourth Gospel is essentially symbolic and that taking this fact into account in its interpretation is not an optional exercise but a condition of validity.

The Meaning of Symbol

Before discussing symbolism in itself, and symbolism in the Fourth Gospel, it would be well to call attention to the semantic confusion sometimes occasioned by John's use of the term *sēmeion*, which is usually translated "sign." John's choice of *sēmeion* rather than *symbolon* perhaps reflects the Septuagint's use of *sēmeion* to translate '*ōt* (sign), the Old Testament designation of the great revelatory and salvific acts of God in the history of Israel (e.g., Exod 10:1-2; Num 26:10; Deut 34:11). But whatever the reason for John's choice of *sēmeion*, there is growing consensus among scholars that "sign" and "symbol" are very different realities and that using the two terms interchangeably leads to substantial confusion. The Johannine *sēmeia* are, in contemporary terms, not signs, but symbols.[83]

Although there is much theoretical diversity among those working in the several disciplines concerned with symbolism, there is today broad consensus at least on the nature and function of the symbol, and the following definition would, I think, be generally acceptable.[84] Symbol can be defined as (1) a sensible reality (2) that renders present to and (3) involves a person subjectively in (4) a transforming experience (5) of the mystery of the Transcendent. Of the five elements of this definition only the first is common to both sign and symbol. A brief consideration of each of the five elements of the definition will clarify this point.

82. An excellent start in developing criteria for the handling of Johannine symbolism was made by Juan Leal, "El simbolismo histórico del IV Evangelio," *EstBíb* 19 (1960): 329–48.

83. Willem Nicol takes the opposite position on terminology but comes to the same conclusions on content, that is, on the significant difference between sign and symbol. See Willem Nicol, *The Semeia in the Fourth Gospel: Tradition and Redaction*, NovTSup 32 (Leiden: Brill, 1972), 123.

84. When I developed this definition of symbol I was making use of the monograph of Gilbert Durand, *L'imagination symbolique*, Initiation philosophique (Paris: PUF, 1968). This book unfortunately is not available in English. Although I have since refined my definition, my debt to this text remains.

1) Both sign and symbol are sensible realities. Not only things (such as bread, wine, and water) but also words, gestures, and combinations of things, words, and gestures can constitute the sensible dimension of the symbol. The importance of the sensible element in the symbol is that it renders the Transcendent, which is by nature purely spiritual, intersubjectively available. In the Fourth Gospel, Jesus of Nazareth is the great symbol of God. John's audacious and fundamental affirmation that the "Word became flesh" (1:14) is the basis for regarding the incarnation as genuinely symbolic. In the "Word made flesh" the Wisdom of God, which is invisible by nature, becomes "what we have seen with our eyes, what we have looked at and touched with our hands . . . what we have seen and heard" (1 John 1:1-3), and in Jesus the God whom "no one has ever seen" (John 1:18) is revealed.

2) Unlike the sign, which merely points to or stands for an absent reality that is totally other than itself, the symbol renders present the Transcendent because and insofar as it participates in what it re-presents. The symbol is an epiphany of a present reality,[85] not an indication of an absent one. Nevertheless, although the symbol renders the Transcendent really present, it renders it present in a limited and sensible mode, thus simultaneously revealing and concealing what it re-presents. This is the basis of the essential ambiguity of the Johannine *sēmeia* in the face of which the blind see and those who see become blind (9:39). The symbol, although sensibly perceptible, is by nature revelatory only to spiritual intuition. Everyone present could see Jesus, but not everyone could see in him the glory of the only Son.

3) The symbol, unlike the sign, is not an objective communication. Rather, it reveals by involving the person in a *subject-to-subject relationship* with the Transcendent. This characteristic of the symbol has two implications. First, unlike the sign, which designates the known by means of an unambiguous one-to-one correspondence, the symbol leads a person into the unknown by rendering present the mystery of the Transcendent, which is essentially many-faceted. Because the symbol

---

85. This is the point made by Paul Ricoeur when he distinguishes between meta-phor, which is a purely linguistic reality, and symbol, which stands on the threshold between reality and language, participating in the former and giving rise to the lat-ter. See Paul Ricoeur, *Interpretation Theory: Discourse and the Surplus of Meaning* (Fort Worth: Texas Christian University Press, 1976), 45–69.

involves a one-to-many relationship, it resists translation or explanation.[86] The question, "What does this symbol stand for?" shows that the questioner takes the symbol for a sign. Second, the symbol does not give objective information; it initiates into an experience that is open-ended. The man born blind, in John 9, in the *sēmeion* of his healing, encountered the glory of the living God in Jesus and progressed in that experience even before he could name his healer (9:17, 30-31, 33, 36).

4) The involvement of a person with the Transcendent rendered present in the symbol is necessarily a transformative experience. By nature, the symbol demands involvement as a condition for entering into the revelation of which it is the locus.[87] The blind man knew that only those who wished to become Jesus's disciples could understand the *sēmeion* of his healing (9:27). The initial commitment that enables one to encounter the Transcendent in the symbolic, however, is only the beginning of the relationship that must develop in a continuously deepening commitment or die. It is this relationship of ever deepening commitment that gradually transforms the person. All of the encounter narratives in the Fourth Gospel illustrate this characteristic of the symbol as dynamically involving.

5) Finally, the symbol mediates the Transcendent or some aspect of the Transcendent. From all that has been said, it is clear that only the personal can be symbolized, either a person him- or herself or some aspect of personal existence such as life, truth, or love. Therefore, all symbolism is potentially religious in that the symbolic opens out on personhood and ultimately on the divine. Only in the incarnation, however, according to the Fourth Gospel, did God adequately self-symbolize in the human sphere. It was the Word of God, Holy Wisdom, that became flesh. And that symbol, Jesus of Nazareth, constitutes the sensible locus of relationship with God.

It is only in terms of symbol, correctly understood, that we can grasp John's presentation of the incarnation as salvation. According to John, the incarnation was the inauguration of a symbolic or sacramental economy of salvific revelation in which the history of Jesus, and eventually the history of his disciples, constitutes the symbolic material.

---

86. See Paul Ricoeur, *The Symbolism of Evil*, trans. Emerson Buchanan (Boston: Beacon, 1967), 347–57.

87. Thomas Fawcett, *The Symbolic Language of Religion: An Introductory Study* (London: SCM, 1970), 42–46.

The sacramental/symbolic principle in the Fourth Gospel is, in other words, the basis of the extraordinary realism of its theology and spirituality rather than, as some positivist exegetes have feared, the source of confusion and obscurity. What it precludes is not clarity but detachment. This Gospel cannot be understood by simply reading it as a detached observer. The only path to understanding is participation, and such participation is supremely dangerous. One who sees the light of the world in Jesus is caught up in the existential crisis of choosing or refusing to believe. And this is a choice for or against eternal life.

Sandra Schneiders, IHM

John 1:19-51

The First Days:
Sophia Gathers Disciples

Come to her [Wisdom] with all your soul,
and keep her ways with all your might.
Search out and seek, and she will become known to you;
and when you get hold of her, do not let her go. (Sir 6:26-27)

As in the Synoptics, and probably recalling a historical memory, the Gospel narrative begins with John in Bethany across the Jordan,[1] although in this Gospel he is seen, not baptizing, but bearing witness. The episode unfolds across four days, indicated by the repeated

---

1. "The most plausible identification for Bethany beyond the Jordan is the region of Batanaea, which is termed *Bashan* in the Old Testament. (i) As a northern Transjordan area, Batanaea would fit both the geography and chronology portrayed in the Gospel of John; (ii) the Septuagint (Num 32:32-33; Deut 3:8; 4:47) characterizes Bashan by the phrase *beyond the Jordan* (πέραν τοῦ Ἰορδάνου); (iii) this region would have been outside the rule of Herod, who would later execute John the Baptist, and this theory would explain the apparent reference to it as a region in John 10:40. If this identification is accurate, it is unclear why the text reads *Bethany* and not *Batanaea*." See William B. Fullilove, "Bethany beyond the Jordan," in *The Lexham Bible Dictionary*, ed. John D. Barry et al. (Bellingham, WA: Lexham Press, 2016).

phrase "the next day" (v. 29, 35, 43), leading into the announcement, "On the third day there was a wedding in Cana of Galilee" (2:1). The specifying of "days" links the Cana miracle (2:1-12) both back to chapter 1 and to the following chapters until the second Cana miracle in chapter 4. The technique of overlapping sections will continue into chapters 2 and 3.[2] As in the prologue, the evangelist draws on first-century Jewish theology, social customs, and religious traditions, along with OT allusions. All of these Jewish features add a particular depth to this episode of the disciples gathering around Jesus.

John's Witness (1:19-28)

Within first-century Judaism, there was a strong hope that the end times, spoken of by the prophets, were imminent. This is the context for understanding the preaching and ministry of John. Judaism had various rituals for purification. Immersion in water was a common and even regular practice for purification—not necessarily for sin, but for seeking worthiness to come before God.[3] In the Synoptic Gospels there are accounts of John's immersion ministry (Mark 1:1-11; Matt 3:1-17; Luke 3:1-22), but not in the Fourth Gospel. Here, John's task is to bear witness (1:6). An aspect of the thinking about this eschatological age was the expectation that various figures from Israel's history would return in fulfilment of the Scriptures.

> Lo, I will send you the prophet Elijah before the great and terrible day of the LORD comes. (Mal 4:5)

> I will raise up for them a prophet like you [Moses] from among their own people; I will put my words in the mouth of the prophet, who shall speak to them everything that I command. (Deut 18:18)

Texts like these led to a general hope that God would raise up an "anointed one" (Heb.: משיח; Gk.: χριστός) who would overcome the powers of evil and usher in the new age of God's reign. There was no single

---

2. It is also important to remember that chapters and verses were not marked in the original manuscript. These were introduced in 1551 by Robert Stephanus. In its original form, there would have been no break between 1:51 and 2:1.

3. Archaeology has revealed many ritual immersion pools (*mikvot*) in first-century Jerusalem. See Hannah K. Harrington, "Clean and Unclean," *NIBD* 1 (2006): 681–89. It would be more appropriate to describe John's ministry as "immersing" rather than baptizing since this latter term now has a particular Christian meaning.

¹⁹This is the testimony given by John when the Jews sent priests and Levites from Jerusalem to ask him, "Who are you?" ²⁰He confessed and did not deny it, but confessed, "I am not the Messiah." ²¹And they asked him, "What then? Are you Elijah?" He said, "I am not." "Are you the prophet?" He answered, "No." ²²Then they said to him, "Who are you? Let us have an answer for those who sent us. What do you say about yourself?" ²³He said,

"I am the voice of one crying out in the wilderness,

'Make straight the way of the Lord,'"

as the prophet Isaiah said.

²⁴Now they had been sent from the Pharisees. ²⁵They asked him, "Why then are you baptizing if you are neither the Messiah, nor Elijah, nor the prophet?" ²⁶John answered them, "I baptize with water. Among you stands one whom you do not know, ²⁷the one who is coming after me; I am not worthy to untie the thong of his sandal." ²⁸This took place in Bethany across the Jordan where John was baptizing.

or unified doctrine of the end times but what was consistent was the conviction that "human failure has so corrupted life on this earth that only a radical transformation initiated by God alone could make things right."[4] It is this hope in the imminent arrival of the end times that leads some from Jerusalem to ask John if he is the Messiah or Elijah or the prophet-like-Moses. John denies these titles and describes himself, citing Isaiah, as "the voice of one crying out in the wilderness" (Isa 40:3). He then testifies, as in the prologue, that there is one, in their midst already, who is greater than he.

Day 2 (1:29-34)

Jesus arrives on the scene "the next day," leading to John's declaration that Jesus is the "Lamb of God who takes away the sin of the world" (v. 29). Apart from immersion there were other rituals that involved the sacrifice of an animal, usually bulls or goats (Lev 4:1-31), to atone for personal and communal sin.[5] Also, every morning and evening a lamb

---

4. Donald E. Gowan, *Eschatology in the Old Testament* (Philadelphia: Fortress, 1986), 122. A helpful discussion of Jewish "end-time" thinking can be found in J. Julius Scott Jr., *Jewish Backgrounds of the New Testament* (Grand Rapids: Baker Books, 1995), esp. chap. 14, "The Final Age."

5. Susan E. Hylen, "Lamb," *NIDB* 3 (2008): 563.

²⁹The next day he saw Jesus coming toward him and declared, "Here is the Lamb of God who takes away the sin of the world! ³⁰This is he of whom I said, 'After me comes a man who ranks ahead of me because he was before me.' ³¹I myself did not know him; but I came baptizing with water for this reason, that he might be revealed to Israel."

³²And John testified, "I saw the Spirit descending from heaven like a dove, and it remained on him. ³³I myself did not know him, but the one who sent me to baptize with water said to me, 'He on whom you see the Spirit descend and remain is the one who baptizes with the Holy Spirit.' ³⁴And I myself have seen and have testified that this is the Son of God."

was sacrificed as a continual (*Tamid*) offering for Israel's purification.[6] The image of the lamb that takes away sin may allude to the suffering servant of Isaiah 53 who "is compared to a lamb (53:7), which vicariously bears (53:5, 8, 10-12) our sins (53:4) and finally dies (53:12)."[7]

Another possibility is the Passover lamb. Although this lamb was not expiatory but rather had an apotropaic function (i.e., to turn away evil),[8]

6. This lamb holocaust is prescribed in Num 28:2-6. For more details on the *Tamid* service, see Mary L. Coloe, " 'Behold the Lamb of God': John 1:29 and the Tamid Service," in *Rediscovering John: Essays on the Fourth Gospel in Honour of Frédéric Manns*, ed. L. Daniel Chrupcala, Studium Biblicum Franciscanum 80 (Milan: Edizioni Terra Santa, 2013), 337–50. In this essay I suggest that the *Tamid* lamb may lie behind the expression "the Lamb of God" in John 1:29. Further reflection and research on the "sin of the world" has led me to give greater weight to the Passover lamb as the referent.

7. Daniel Stökl Ben Ezra, *The Impact of Yom Kippur on Early Christianity: The Day of Atonement from Second Temple Judaism to the Fifth Century*, WUNT 163 (Tübingen: Mohr Siebeck, 2003), 177.

8. A late Jewish text (probably 160 BCE) rewrites the account of the first Passover and clearly indicates that the Passover lamb was for protection from evil. "For on this night . . . we were eating the Passover in Egypt, when all the powers of Mastema had been let loose to slay the first-born in the land of Egypt. . . . And this is the sign which the Lord gave them: Into every house on the lintels of which they saw the blood of a lamb of the first year, into (that) house they should not enter to slay, but should pass by (it), that all those should be saved that were in the house because the sign of the blood was on its lintels" (Jub. 49:2-4). By late Second Temple Judaism, the tenth plague is attributed to Mastema, a spirit of evil, similar to the figure of Belial mentioned frequently in the Dead Sea Scrolls. "Both are malevolent beings, are engaged in pestering humans, chiefly Israelites, and both perform their malicious activity with the help of their subordinate evil spirits." See Devorah Dimant, "Between Qumran Sectarian and Non-Sectarian Texts: The Case of Belial and Mastema," in *The Dead Sea Scrolls and Contemporary Culture: Proceedings of the International Conference Held at the Israel Museum, Jerusalem (July 6–8, 2008)*, ed. Shani Tzoref, Lawrence H. Schiffman, and Adolfo Daniel Roitman (Leiden: Brill, 2011), 255.

the Fourth Gospel clearly identifies Jesus as the Passover lamb in the passion narrative: Pilate hands Jesus over for execution on the same day and at the same time as the Passover lambs are being killed in the temple (19:14); the hyssop branch used to raise vinegar to Jesus (19:29) is the same branch used to smear the blood of the lamb on the lintels of the Hebrew houses in Egypt (Exod 12:22); and the Scripture citation (19:36) links Jesus with the instructions for the Passover lamb (Exod 12:46). As well as looking at the possible "lambs" the evangelist may have in view, it is also important to look at the function of this lamb, namely, to take away the sin of the *cosmos*. Here, we are once again dealing with John's cosmic tale, and the sin is not personal or even national but cosmic.[9]

It is premature to expand further here on the Johannine understanding of the crucifixion, but the Passover symbolism challenges other models of salvation that portray Jesus's death as being representative for sinners and thus making atonement for sin.[10] Even though atonement became the dominant model of salvation through the teaching of Anselm (1033–1109), atonement theology is foreign to John's Gospel. Such a theology places emphasis on Jesus as the suffering victim, and women in particular have been encouraged to develop a false spirituality identifying silently with the wrongly crucified one. Expecting women and children to endure abuse in the name of Christ crucified is itself an abuse of the Gospel.[11]

Elisabeth Schüssler Fiorenza was one of the first feminists to offer a critique of the atonement model and describe various responses in moving away from what I call a "salvation through suffering" approach. She rightly points out that there are various NT interpretations of Jesus's death. In itself, the cross was a violent, painful form of Roman execution of Jesus. The question is, what did it come to mean for the early Christians? She writes, "Feminist theologians might learn from the early

9. On this cosmic tale, see the study by Adele Reinhartz, *The Word in the World: The Cosmological Tale in the Fourth Gospel*, SBLMS 45 (Atlanta: Scholars Press, 1992).

10. For a discussion of the various NT models of salvation, see Scot McKnight, *Jesus and His Death: Historiography, the Historical Jesus, and Atonement Theory* (Waco, TX: Baylor University Press, 2005).

11. For a more thorough critique of the atonement theology of the cross, see Elisabeth Schüssler Fiorenza, *Jesus: Miriam's Child, Sophia's Prophet; Critical Issues in Feminist Christology*, 2nd ed. (London: Bloomsbury T&T Clark, 2015), 106–18; Barbara E. Reid, *Taking up the Cross: New Testament Interpretations through Latina and Feminist Eyes* (Minneapolis: Augsburg Fortress, 2007), 17–56; Linda D. Peacore, *The Role of Women's Experience in Feminist Theologies of Atonement*, PrTMS 131 (Eugene, OR: Pickwick Publications, 2010), chap. 5.; Elizabeth A. Johnson, *Creation and the Cross: The Mercy of God for a Planet in Peril* (Maryknoll, NY: Orbis Books, 2018).

Christians, who used a great diversity of formulas to make sense of the cruel death of Jesus."[12] She then goes on to describe many interpretations of the cross in the NT literature, with a particular focus on Paul and Mark. These interpretations begin with "God raised him from the dead" (Rom 10:9) and move to the concept of exaltation and vindication (Phil 2:9). Ideas of a friend giving life for a friend (Rom 5:7-8), present in the Jewish and Hellenistic worlds, lead to the notion of the innocent martyr (Rom 3:25), to the cultic atonement language (Rom 3:24) and a life given to bring about reconciliation (2 Cor 5:19), to restore the covenant relationship, to free those enslaved by sin (Mark 10:45), and as the ultimate gift of a loving God (Rom 8:32). These were various ways of making sense of the death of the righteous one by drawing on OT writings and are all aspects of the NT with no one model dominating.[13] Schüssler Fiorenza finishes by offering "a feminist discourse of liberation" through the image of the empty tomb.[14] In this context she gives no attention to the Gospel of John, except for mentioning God's love for the world (John 3:16). She holds out hope that a new model of salvation may be found through the rediscovery of Sophia. "A feminist exegetical attempt to reconstruct the traces of Sophia as emancipatory Christology invites us to develop a critical praxis of reflective sophialogy. Such a critical feminist practice has to sort out and evaluate those traces of emancipatory Christology in general and biblical Wisdom theology in particular that open up possibilities of liberation and well-being but have not yet been fully realized in history."[15] It is my hope that this commentary may help to construct a liberative model of salvation that can be life-giving for all women and men. In the next paragraph I give a brief overview of how this may develop across the Johannine narrative and in this commentary.

First-century Jewish apocalyptic theology perceived that this world was held captive to the dominion of an evil power sometimes named Belial (Jub. 1:20, 15:34)[16] or Mastema (e.g., Jub. 10:7; 11:5; 49:2) or Beelzebub (e.g., Mark 3:22; Matt 10:25), and, in the Fourth Gospel, "the devil" (6:70; 8:44; 13:2), "Satan" (13:27), and "the ruler of this world" (12:31; 14:30; 16:11). According to this theological vision, "taking away" sin will

---

12. Schüssler Fiorenza, *Jesus: Miriam's Child, Sophia's Prophet*, 117.
13. Ibid., 121–29.
14. Ibid., 135–38.
15. Ibid., 178.
16. See the article by Dimant, "Between Qumran Sectarian and Non-Sectarian Texts," for the many references to Belial and Mastema in the Dead Sea Scrolls.

not be an act of atonement or expiation but an act of liberation from a power opposing the power of God.[17] Jesus comes to bring freedom to those held captive by this cosmic power of sin by transferring those who believe in him from living under the power of the ruler of this world, to living within the freedom of the household of God. This liberation from a cosmic power of sin lies behind the dialogue in John 8. In a conflict with some who had believed in him, Jesus speaks of the true freedom that believers in him will know (8:31). When these followers object and reply that they are children of Abraham and have always been free and never slaves (8:33), Jesus replies, "everyone who commits sin is a slave to sin.[18] The slave does not have a permanent place in the household [οὐ μένει ἐν τῇ οἰκίᾳ εἰς τὸν αἰῶνα]; the son has a place there forever. So if the son makes you free, you will be free indeed" (8:34-36).[19] When Jesus's mission is seen in this cosmic dimension as a struggle with the "ruler of this world," in order to achieve for his followers the freedom of belonging in God's household (1:11) and liberation from the power of cosmic sin, then the Passover lamb symbolism is appropriate and in keeping with the evangelist's theology. Just as the Passover lamb achieved liberation from captivity in Egypt, so Jesus in his life and death brings liberation for those who believe in him, making them "children of God" (1:12).[20]

17. Of course, the overcoming of the evil one by the power of God was thought to belong to the "end time," as Lovell comments: "Because the workings of God's kingship in the present world are inhibited by the evil of the present age the expectation is for a future age or world to come where the quality of the world is changed by the ultimate rule of God enacted in the world." See Beth M. Lovell, *Mapping Metaphorical Discourse: John's Eternal King*, LBS 5 (Leiden: Brill, 2012), 200.

18. Slavery was accepted practice within the Jewish and Greco-Roman culture. There is no evidence that Jesus or his first followers challenged the institution of slavery.

19. This statement will be discussed later in the commentary. At this point note that Jesus offers his opponents a brief parable comparing the place in the household of a slave and a son and the son's authority. The slave's place can change for numerous reasons. The son always remains within his family's house, even when he marries and brings his bride to join the household. A daughter, on marriage, will leave her family's house to live with her husband's family. Jesus likens his role to that of the household son who has a permanent place and is able to offer freedom to those in slavery. On this statement as a parable, see Barnabas Lindars, *The Gospel of John*, NCB (London: Oliphants, 1972), 325–26.

20. This synthesis of the Gospel's sense of cosmic sin has drawn on the work of a number of scholars: Sandra M. Schneiders, "The Lamb of God and the Forgiveness of Sin(s) in the Fourth Gospel," *CBQ* 73 (2011): 1–29; Craig R. Koester, "The Death of Jesus and the Human Condition: Exploring the Theology of John's Gospel," in *Life in Abundance: Studies of John's Gospel in Tribute to Raymond E. Brown*, ed. John R.

Liberation for All

The lamb image, I believe, points to the liberative symbol of the Passover lamb, and this is supported in the narrative by Jesus's discussion of slavery and freedom in John 8. In its first-century setting the text speaks of "sons," as the place of women in that patriarchal world was not considered. Sandra Schneiders raises the critical question, "How can a text which is oppressive of women open a world of liberating possibilities for its readers?"[21]

Using the studies of Hans-Georg Gadamer and Paul Ricoeur she answers the question by seeing that the text can be liberative as it is a dynamic medium where meaning is not fixed in a determined manner *in* the text, but meaning is open to future possible interpretations. "It is no longer determined by the author's intention."[22] The real referent of the text "is not the experience of those first Christians but the experience that is made possible for the reader by the text."[23] The world of those reading the text today "is the world structured by the paschal mystery of Jesus, in which life issues from death, and by the eschatological hope of liberation for all in the boundless shalom of the reign of God."[24] Over the course of centuries Christian reflection on the meaning of the Jesus event has brought a change of consciousness. The values taken for granted in the past have been and continue to be critiqued against the Jesus proclamation of a new law of love, where all are included.

Day 3 (1:35-42)

John's declaration that Jesus is the "Lamb of God" (v. 35) prompts two of John's disciples to follow Jesus, who invites them to "come and see" (v. 39). They accept this invitation and dwell (ἔμειναν) with him.[25]

Donahue (Collegeville, MN: Liturgical Press, 2005), 141–57; also Brendan Byrne, *Life Abounding: A Reading of John's Gospel* (Collegeville, MN: Liturgical Press, 2014), 42–44. It is only in the light of a total reading of the narrative that some of this symbolism will become clearer as themes will develop.

21. Sandra M. Schneiders, "Feminist Ideology Criticism and Biblical Hermeneutics," *BTB* 19 (1989): 3.

22. Schneiders, "Feminist Ideology Criticism," 7.

23. Ibid., 7–8.

24. Ibid., 8.

25. The verb μένω (to dwell) will become a very important term in the second part of the Gospel, where it expresses the intimate mutual relationship between Jesus, God, and believers. This will be developed in the commentary on chap. 14.

[35]The next day John again was standing with two of his disciples, [36]and as he watched Jesus walk by, he exclaimed, "Look, here is the Lamb of God!" [37]The two disciples heard him say this, and they followed Jesus. [38]When Jesus turned and saw them following, he said to them, "What are you looking for?" They said to him, "Rabbi" (which translated means Teacher), "where are you staying?" [39]He said to them, "Come and see." They came and saw where he was staying, and they remained with him that day. It was about four o'clock in the afternoon. [40]One of the two who heard John speak and followed him was Andrew, Simon Peter's brother. [41]He first found his brother Simon and said to him, "We have found the Messiah" (which is translated Anointed). [42]He brought Simon to Jesus, who looked at him and said, "You are Simon son of John. You are to be called Cephas" (which is translated Peter).

Believing in and dwelling with Jesus describes discipleship in this Gospel. Where the Synoptics have Jesus sending disciples out on mission during his own ministry in Galilee (Mark 6:6-13 and par.), in the Fourth Gospel such missioning occurs only following the resurrection (John 20:21). Searching, seeking, and abiding in Jesus, who lies in the embrace of God (1:18), draws disciples into relationship with God.[26] One of the two disciples who follow Jesus is named Andrew; the other remains anonymous. This "other" disciple may be the one who is later known as "the Beloved Disciple" (13:23; 19:26).[27]

Day 4 (1:43-51)

Andrew, the "other" disciple, and Simon/Peter are joined on this fourth day by Philip and Nathanael. By the end of this section the reader/audience has heard many titles applied to Jesus. John testifies that he is the Son of God (1:34) and the Lamb of God (1:29, 36); Andrew tells Peter, "We have found the Messiah" (1:41); Philip speaks of him as the one "about whom Moses in the law and also the prophets wrote" (1:45); and finally Nathanael names Jesus as "Rabbi," "Son of God," and "King

---

26. For a feminist discussion of the significance of the concept of "abiding," see Dorothy A. Lee, "Abiding in the Fourth Gospel: A Case-Study in Feminist Biblical Theology," *Pacifica* 10 (1997): 123–36.

27. Susan E. Hylen, *Imperfect Believers: Ambiguous Characters in the Gospel of John* (Louisville: Westminster John Knox, 2009), 93.

⁴³The next day Jesus decided to go to Galilee. He found Philip and said to him, "Follow me." ⁴⁴Now Philip was from Bethsaida, the city of Andrew and Peter. ⁴⁵Philip found Nathanael and said to him, "We have found him about whom Moses in the law and also the prophets wrote, Jesus son of Joseph from Nazareth." ⁴⁶Nathanael said to him, "Can anything good come out of Nazareth?" Philip said to him, "Come and see." ⁴⁷When Jesus saw Nathanael coming toward him, he said of him, "Here is truly an Israelite in whom there is no deceit!" ⁴⁸Nathanael asked him, "Where did you get to know me?" Jesus answered, "I saw you under the fig tree before Philip called you." ⁴⁹Nathanael replied, "Rabbi, you are the Son of God! You are the King of Israel!" ⁵⁰Jesus answered, "Do you believe because I told you that I saw you under the fig tree? You will see greater things than these." ⁵¹And he said to him, "Very truly, I tell you, you will see heaven opened and the angels of God ascending and descending upon the Son of Man."

of Israel" (1:49). This array of male titles begs the question of Jesus's identity. Are these disciples correct? Or is their patriarchal mind-set blinding them from seeing something more—namely, Sophia, who takes the initiative and reveals herself in the following response to Nathanael?

Jesus's words to Nathanael provide an insight into the evangelist's point of view. Jesus begins by identifying Nathanael as "a true Israelite" (v. 47; author's translation). This ancient title reflects the self-designation of Jews at this time as "children of Israel," recalling their eponymous ancestor Jacob, whose name was changed to Israel (Gen 32:28; 35:10). When Nathanael asks how Jesus knew him, Jesus replies, "I saw you under the fig tree before Philip called you" (v. 48). This phrase alludes to aspects of Jewish theology and Scripture. An article by Craig Koester relates Jesus's words to a number of OT passages where the phrase "under his vine and under his fig tree" occurs (1 Kgs 4:25; Mic 4:4; Zech 3:10; 1 Macc 14:12).[28] In particular, Koester looks to the passage in Zechariah that speaks of a coming messianic figure called "the Branch."

> Now listen, Joshua, high priest, you and your colleagues who sit before you! For they are an omen of things to come: I am going to bring my servant the Branch. For on the stone that I have set before Joshua, on

---

28. Craig Koester, "Messianic Exegesis and the Call of Nathanael (John 1.45-51)," *JSNT* 39 (1990): 34.

a single stone with seven facets, I will engrave its inscription, says the
LORD of hosts, and I will remove the guilt of this land in a single day.
On that day, says the LORD of hosts, you shall invite each other to come
under your vine and fig tree.[29] (Zech 3:8-10)

The symbolic name "Branch" alludes to the messianic prophecy of Isaiah:
"A shoot shall come out from the stump of Jesse, and a branch [נצר; *netzer*]
shall grow out of his roots" (Isa 11:1). The word "branch" in Hebrew has
the same root as the word "Nazareth/Nazarene."[30] In the Fourth Gospel
Jesus is never named Jesus *of* Nazareth,[31] but in the passion he is named
Jesus *the* Nazarene on three occasions, including the unique title Pilate
has affixed to the cross: Ἰησοῦς ὁ Ναζωραῖος ὁ βασιλεὺς τῶν Ἰουδαίων;
"Jesus the Nazarene, King of the Jews" (19:19; also 18:5, 7).[32] Knowing
the linguistic links between Nazareth, *netzer*/branch, it is as if Pilate had
written, "Jesus the *Branch*, the King of the Jews."

Another passage in Zechariah further explains why the evangelist
makes use of this unique title, Jesus the Nazarene/Branch: "Thus says the
LORD of hosts, Here is a man whose name is *Branch*: for he shall branch
out in his place, and he shall build the temple of the LORD" (Zech 6:12).
The strange title, "the Branch," names the eschatological figure who is
to build the new temple. In the Fourth Gospel, Jesus claims that he is the
one who will raise up the temple in three days (2:19).[33] The exchange with
Nathanael thus alludes to what will unfold in the following narrative.
That the evangelist alludes to this Zechariah passage is strengthened

29. Koester provides textual arguments to show that this phrase could be read to
apply to Philip calling Nathanael when Nathanael was already under the fig tree.
See Koester, "Messianic Exegesis," 25.

30. See my more detailed arguments on this in Mary L. Coloe, *God Dwells with
Us: Temple Symbolism in the Fourth Gospel* (Collegeville, MN: Liturgical Press, 2001),
171–74, 185–90. Hebrew has two words meaning branch: נצר, *netzer*, and צמח, *tzamah*;
references in the Dead Sea Scrolls show that the two words for branch used in Isaiah
and Zechariah were being used interchangeably in a Messianic sense.

31. It is important to note that Philip speaks of "Jesus, son of *Joseph from Nazareth*"—not "Jesus of Nazareth" as some earlier translations wrongly state (Authorized
Version, King James). Also, this is the only place in John where the word Nazareth
is used, which further suggests the author has the "branch" of Zechariah in mind.

32. The Synoptic Gospels have "The king of the Jews" (Mark 15:26; Matt 27:37;
Luke 23:38).

33. More will be said on this in discussing the Johannine passion. This brief synopsis
is necessary here in order to make sense of Jesus's response to Nathanael about seeing him under a fig tree, and also Nathanael's comment, "Can anything good come
out of Nazareth?" (1:46).

by the reference to removing "the guilt of this land" (Zech 3:9). In the Hebrew it reads, ומשתי את־צון הארץ־ההיא ביום, "and I will take away the sin of the land on that day." This is very close to John's description of Jesus as the lamb who will "take away the sin of the world" (1:29).

Jesus's final words to Nathanael promise that he will see greater things, and these "greater things" are then described as a vision of angels ascending and descending on "the human-one" (v. 51).[34] With these words, Nathanael, who has been called a true Israelite, is promised that he will see what his ancestor Jacob/Israel saw.

> And he [Jacob] dreamed that there was a ladder set up on the earth, the top of it reaching to heaven; and the angels of God were ascending and descending on it. . . . So Jacob rose early in the morning, and he took the stone that he had put under his head and set it up for a pillar and poured oil on the top of it. He called that place Bethel. (Gen 28:12, 18-19)

In the later book of Wisdom, Sophia herself reveals heavenly things to Jacob.

> When a righteous man fled from his brother's wrath,
> she [Wisdom] guided him on straight paths;
> she showed him the kingdom of God [βασιλείαν θεοῦ],
> and gave him knowledge of holy things. (Wis 10:10)

Nathanael, a son of Israel/Jacob, will in fact see far more than his ancestor. The allusion to Jacob's dream situates the opening of the heavens at a place Jacob named as Beth-el, i.e., "the house of God." In the prologue the evangelist spoke of the incarnation with reference to Israel's tabernacle (1:14); here, the allusion to Jacob's dream at Bethel continues the prologue's theological vision of Jesus as the one who embodies Israel's cultic traditions of the tabernacle and "house of God," which was the most frequent OT way of referring to the Jerusalem temple.[35] In Jesus/Sophia, the "house of God" is now accessible to Nathanael. Against the background of Wisdom 10:10, Jesus's words to Nathanael maintain the active presence of Jesus/Sophia within the narrative, as the revealer of

---

34. See the excursus at the end of this chapter (p. 50) on the phrase "The Son of Man—ὁ υἱὸς τοῦ ἀνθρώπου," which is an idiomatic expression referring to an apocalyptic figure (Dan 7:13) who has access to the heavens.

35. Koester comments: "The evangelist expected readers to catch the allusions to the Jacob story in order to make sense of the narrative." See Koester, "Messianic Exegesis," 24.

"holy things." The revelation of Sophia also corrects the male-only titles that Nathanael ascribed to Jesus (1:49).

Jesus has acted as Wisdom incarnate in inviting disciples to her lodgings and promising that she will reveal to Jacob/Israel's children the very dwelling of God. Although no women have been called directly in these opening scenes, it would be inaccurate to assume that there are no women disciples within the Gospel or that this scene records all the disciples. Later in the narrative, named women have a significant role as close friends of Jesus, e.g., Martha and Mary of Bethany (11:1–12:8) and Mary Magdalene (19:25; 20:1-18), and other male disciples are named: Thomas (11:16; 14:5; 20:24), Judas Iscariot (12:4; 13:26; 18:3), and another Judas (14:22). Apart from the unidentified women disciples, we know that Simon/Peter was married (Mark 1:30), and it is likely that some of these disciples also had wives who joined the discipleship group following Jesus. The men named in this scene have cameo roles, representative of the many other women and men who follow and dwell with Jesus. Possibly they are named because they are Galileans and Jesus is in this northern region. We are told that Peter, Andrew, and Philip were from Bethsaida (1:44), and later we hear that Nathanael was from Cana (21:2).

The Johannine gathering of disciples is quite different from what is recorded in the Synoptics. Discipleship begins with John directing two of his disciples toward Jesus (1:36), and then they are invited to "Come and see" (1:39). There is no mention of a future ministry, nor that they are fishermen. Simon is not the first called. In fact, Jesus does not "call" Simon to discipleship; he simply changes his name to Cephas/Peter (1:42). The usual pattern in this Gospel is that one comes to faith not by a direct encounter with Jesus but through the witnessing word of another.[36] So John bears witness to his disciples who go to Jesus; then Andrew bears witness to Simon; then Philip bears witness to Nathanael. Later, two exceptional witnesses are the Samaritan woman, whose testimony draws her village to faith (4:39), and Mary Magdalene, whose witness rekindles faith in the disciples (20:18). This pattern establishes the truth of the opening verse, "In the beginning was the *Word*" (1:1). Faith begins not through sight but through the witness of the word. Furthermore, this pattern also establishes the priority of human experience as the foundation of faith, a claim supported by many feminist theologians, as Linda D. Peacore states:

36. Philip is the exception to this pattern since he is called directly by Jesus (1:43).

An understanding of religious experience is often relevant to and influential upon the theology being constructed. According to Rosemary Radford Ruether, reaction to patriarchal distortions of the Christian tradition forces feminist theology to utilize the "primary intuitions of religious experience itself" as a theological resource.[37]

Sandra Schneiders writes of the community's lived experience of the risen Jesus that led to their articulation of a theology to make sense of this experience, and then this theology led to the narrative of the Fourth Gospel.[38] The pattern of bearing witness to one's own experience established in John 1:19-51 is the model of evangelization and is a model at the fore of all feminist theology.

Cultural Background to John's Role

The opening days of the narrative provide the reader with a particular, symbolic perspective on John and Jesus that will be developed further in the following chapters. Unlike the Synoptic traditions, we do not see John baptizing; instead, the focus in the Fourth Gospel is on his role as a witness. Then, in chapter 3, John speaks of himself as the "friend of the bridegroom" (3:29), indicating his lesser role, with Jesus the more important figure, the bridegroom. Within that culture, the "friend of the bridegroom" had an important role from betrothal to the marriage ceremony.[39] Because of the possibility of loss of face, when a marriage was being considered neither the groom nor his father dealt directly with the family of the prospective bride. Instead, both families worked through proxies or deputies. When the father of the groom and his deputy, the friend of the bridegroom, came to negotiate a possible marriage with the bride's family, this family also brought in a deputy. It was the two deputies who negotiated the amount of the dowry, the amount to be given at the betrothal, the date of the wedding, and other details, thus sparing either family shame if the negotiations broke down.

---

37. Peacore, *The Role of Women's Experience*, 16. Peacore then states that "Carter Heyward outlines human experience as the fundamental source for theology, also calling it her starting point, and Daphne Hampson states explicitly that experience is the 'basis' for theology" (22). Here, Peacore is quoting Rosemary Radford Ruether, "The Future of Feminist Theology in the Academy," *JAAR* 53 (1985): 703–13, citing p. 710.

38. Sandra M. Schneiders, *Written That You May Believe: Encountering Jesus in the Fourth Gospel*, rev. and exp. ed. (New York: Crossroad, 2003), 48.

39. For more details on these arrangements and references to research see Mary L. Coloe, *Dwelling in the Household of God: Johannine Ecclesiology and Spirituality* (Collegeville, MN: Liturgical Press, 2007), 29–36.

If the deputies came to agreement, then the fathers were brought in to seal the betrothal. At this stage the contract would be prepared by the deputies, signed by the two fathers, and then "committed into the trusty hands of the best man."[40] Also at this time, a small token was given by the bridegroom's friend as a promise of the future dowry that would be given at the time of the wedding.

In these negotiations the bridegroom's friend had a critical role. He witnessed to and testified about the virtues and worthiness of the groom. He was the "voice" of the bridegroom, who was not present. So important was this role that there were ancient laws forbidding the "friend" from ever marrying the prospective bride should the negotiations fail. The woman could never be his spouse.[41] At the time of the wedding, the deputy was often the one to lead the young woman from her father's house to the groom's father's house where she would make her home.[42]

These cultural practices shed light on John's role. He is the voice, sent by God (the "father") to witness to Jesus, to testify to his greatness, and he directs two of his disciples to Jesus as the "friend" leads the bride to her betrothed. The narrative comment on the time, "it was about four o'clock in the afternoon" (1:39; literally, the tenth hour), indicates the traditional time of a wedding celebration in the late afternoon toward sunset.[43] The time detail, which seems to have no other purpose in the narrative, is one indicator to the reader that the evangelist may be working with symbolism; that is, the meaning of this detail is to be found beyond the narrative.[44]

40. J. Jeremias, "νύμφη, νυμφίος," *TDNT* 4 (1967): 1101 n. 20.

41. A. van Selms, "The Best Man and Bride: From Sumer to St. John," *JNES* 9 (1950): 65–70.

42. M. Emile Boismard, "L'ami de l'Époux (Jo. III, 29)," in *A la recontre de Dieu: Mémorial Albert Gelin*, ed. A. Barucq et al., Bibliothèque de la Faculté Catholique de Théologie de Lyon 8 (Le Puy: Xavier Mappus, 1961), 292. Boismard refers also to a number of rabbinic texts where God is considered to have had the role of the friend of the bridegroom when, following the creation of Eve, God brought her to Adam.

43. Edmond Stapfer, *Palestine in the Time of Christ*, trans. A. H. Holmden (New York: Armstrong and Son, 1885), 163. This late afternoon time is also indicated in the parable of the ten women waiting for the bridegroom to arrive, but he arrives late (Matt 25:1-13).

44. In an article on Johannine symbolism, Juan Leal offers four criteria that can indicate when the narrative has a symbolic as well as a literal meaning: (1) the presence of inconsequential details that seem to play no part in the narrative, (2) a discourse set within the narrative of an event such that they are mutually illuminating, (3) the evangelist's accentuating the importance of a person who has no significant role in the context, (4) the use of later liturgical and Christian expression. See Juan Leal, "El simbolismo histórico del IV Evangelio," *EstBib* 19 (1960): 344–46.

Missing from this description of the cultural background is the role of women in this practice. The negotiations seem to involve only men, talking about a possible groom and possible bride. No other types of committed relationships would be considered in that culture. In these negotiations the prominence given to the issue of the dowry gives the appearance of being a fiscal transaction. How much is this object worth? The women's absence in these negotiations, like the unnamed women disciples in John 1, calls for a hermeneutic of remembrance.

Conclusion

These opening verses, like the prologue, introduce the reader not only to the themes of the Gospel and the identity of Jesus but also to the evangelist's particular writing style. While passages can be read and understood to some extent on a first reading, the hints and allusions will not be fully grasped until the whole Gospel has been read. In his work on interpreting texts, Paul Ricoeur speaks of a "second naïveté" to describe the process of returning to a literary work a second time, bringing to this second reading the insights gained from the first reading.[45] The second reading, therefore, has a certain level of perception that makes possible the disclosure of deeper levels of meaning. Thus, the reader is involved in an ongoing hermeneutical circle of reading, understanding, raising questions, new readings, new perceptions, and new questions. Such is the ongoing nature of interpretation. Biblical scholarship today has been enriched by a wide range of new critical readings by women and men from various cultures, social classes, and gender identifications.

"The Son of Man"—
ὁ υἱος τοῦ ἀνθρώπου

Traditionally, the phrase ὁ υἱος τοῦ ἀνθρώπου (which first appears in 1:51) has been translated as "the Son of Man." Géza Vermes proposed that the expression has its origin in an Aramaic idiom, בר אנש (*bar-'anash*), a term of self-reference meaning "I" or "me."[46] While at the level of the Aramaic-speaking historical

---

45. Paul Ricoeur, *Interpretation Theory: Discourse and the Surplus of Meaning* (Fort Worth: Texas Christian University Press, 1976), 4.

46. A recent synopsis of his argument can be found in Géza A. Vermes, "The Son of Man Debate Revisited (1960–2012)," in *Parables of Enoch: A Paradigm Shift*, ed. Darrell L. Bock and James H. Charlesworth, JCTCRS 11 (London: Bloomsbury T&T Clark, 2013), 293.

Jesus this may explain the origins and frequency of this phrase,[47] it does not explain the way each evangelist has incorporated this phrase into his Gospel. Within the Fourth Gospel the phrase occurs thirteen times in contexts that bring a theological meaning to this expression, rather than a simple circumlocution.[48] Four occurrences are associated with lifting up/exaltation (3:14; 8:28; 12:34 [2x]); two speak of glorification (12:23; 13:31);[49] two assert that ὁ υἱος τοῦ ἀνθρώπου is the one able to give life/eternity life (6:23, 53); two refer to his heavenly origins (3:13; 6:22); in John 1:51 ὁ υἱος τοῦ ἀνθρώπου is to be a source of revelation, and in 5:27 he is a locus of judgment. In 9:35, in the context of Israel's profession of faith in God within the morning ritual of tabernacles, the man born blind is challenged to profess belief in ὁ υἱος τοῦ ἀνθρώπου.

The roles and attributes of ὁ υἱος τοῦ ἀνθρώπου in the Fourth Gospel lead many to see an allusion to Daniel 7:13, where one ὡς υἱὸς ἀνθρώπου comes from heaven at the time of eschatological judgment and is given "dominion and glory and kingship" (Dan 7:14).

Two things are to be noted in this Daniel reference. First is the use of the comparative conjunction ὡς (like), indicating that the seer is trying to describe the heavenly figure of his vision and says this figure is "human-*like*." Second, this is an apocalyptic figure who appears when the cosmic powers of evil have been defeated, and he is the one given glory and sovereignty. Where Daniel situates this eschatological revelation in the future, the Gospel of John draws this revelation into the "now" in the historical person of Jesus, and the Gospel never uses the comparative conjunction ὡς (like). Jesus is not "human-like"; he is the enfleshed *Logos*—the mortal human-one. Jesus, in his humanity, can be lifted up on the cross, and this is the climax of his revelation of God, his defeat of the "ruler of this world" (12:31; 14:30; 16:11), and his glorification when he completes the "work" of God ("it is finished," 19:30). In a

---

47. On the historical probability that the idiom was used by Jesus, see the discussion in Dale C. Allison Jr., *Constructing Jesus: Memory, Imagination, and History* (Grand Rapids: Baker Academic, 2010), 293.

48. For this position, see the arguments by Francis J. Moloney, "The *Parables of Enoch* and the Johannine Son of Man," in Bock and Charlesworth, *Parables of Enoch*, 269–93.

49. A scholar who has studied this Johannine expression for over thirty years is Francis Moloney. For him, the title speaks of "the presentation of the revelation of God in the human event of Jesus Christ, especially in his being 'lifted up' on a cross (cf. 3:14; 8:28; 12:32; 19:5)." See Francis J. Moloney, "The Johannine Son of Man Revisited," in *Theology and Christology in the Fourth Gospel*, ed. Gilbert Van Belle, Jan G. van der Watt, and P. Maritz, BETL 184 (Leuven: Peeters, 2005), esp. 181, 202.

paradoxical manner, the title ὁ υἱος τοῦ ἀνθρώπου, "the human-one," expresses both his full humanity and his unique origins in and with God (1:1).

In its English translation, the doubling of masculine language in "son" and "man" leads many feminists to prefer the gender-neutral expression "the human one." In this commentary I will use "the human-one" to show by using quotation marks and the hyphen that this is an idiomatic phrase, alluding to the apocalyptic figure of Daniel 7:13.

John 2:1-12

A Jewish Mother Takes
the Initiative at Cana

[Sophia calls,]
"Come, eat of my bread
and drink of the wine I have mixed.
Lay aside immaturity, and live,
and walk in the way of insight." (Prov 9:5-6)

The opening phrase, "On the third day," links the Cana episode with the previous chapter and its sequence of days.[1] Remember, the original text had no breaks or numbering of chapters and verses, since these were introduced by Robert Stephanus in 1551. Although linked to the preceding days of chapter 1, Cana is a distinct episode delineated by the repetition of "Cana of Galilee" (vv. 1, 11), while also introducing a new section of the Gospel that begins with this first sign in Cana (2:11) and concludes with a second sign, also in Cana (4:54). This section is often called "From Cana to Cana."[2]

---

1. A link is also made through Nathanael, who was the final disciple named in chap. 1, and later in the Gospel we read that he is from Cana in Galilee (21:2).

2. In what follows I will continue to examine the text through the symbolism associated with John, the witness and friend of the bridegroom, and what this reveals

53

2:1On the third day there was a wedding in Cana of Galilee, and the mother of Jesus was there. 2Jesus and his disciples had also been invited to the wedding. 3When the wine gave out, the mother of Jesus said to him, "They have no wine." 4And Jesus said to her, "Woman, what concern is that to you and to me? My hour has not yet come." 5His mother said to the servants, "Do whatever he tells you." 6Now standing there were six stone water jars for the Jewish rites of purification, each holding twenty or thirty gallons. 7Jesus said to them, "Fill the jars with water." And they filled them up to the brim. 8He said to them, "Now draw some out, and take it to the chief steward." So they took it. 9When the steward tasted the water that had become wine, and did not know where it came from (though the servants who had drawn the water knew), the steward called the bridegroom 10and said to him, "Everyone serves the good wine first, and then the inferior wine after the guests have become drunk. But you have kept the good wine until now." 11Jesus did this, the first of his signs, in Cana of Galilee, and revealed his glory; and his disciples believed in him.

12After this he went down to Capernaum with his mother, his brothers, and his disciples; and they remained there a few days.

The "wedding at Cana" continues the narrative symbolism associated with John as the witness and friend of the bridegroom, discussed in the previous chapter, for this episode clearly identifies Jesus as the bridegroom. When the wine runs out, and at his mother's prompting, Jesus provides an abundance of good quality wine, and the chief steward mistakenly praises the bridegroom at the wedding for providing such good wine at this later stage of the festivities (2:10). The reader knows who really provided the wine and thus identifies Jesus as the real bridegroom at this feast. The "miracle" functions as a symbolic act, pointing to a far deeper meaning than abundant wine; it visibly expresses Jesus's identity as the Messianic Bridegroom,[3] and the evangelist calls this action "the first sign" (ἀρχὴν τῶν σημείων, v. 11).

---

about Jesus. An alternative and more frequent approach examines the faith response to Jesus of the various characters across this section. An example of this approach can be found in Francis J. Moloney, "From Cana to Cana (Jn. 2:1–4:54) and the Fourth Evangelist's Concept of Correct (and Incorrect) Faith," *Salesianum* 40 (1978): 817–43. These alternative perspectives complement each other in bringing out the multiple interpretations of the text for different readers.

3. Several biblical passages associate the coming of the Messiah with abundant wine (Gen 49:10-12; Amos 9:11, 13-14; 2 Bar 29:3, 5). For further discussion see Jocelyn

Present at this first sign is a woman who is never named in the narrative but known only as "the mother of Jesus" by the narrator and addressed by Jesus as "Woman." Although appearing only twice, here and at the cross, I have argued that this woman is theologically the most important character in the Gospel, other than Jesus; through her the theological goal of the narrative is achieved.[4] At Cana, her significance is emphasized by being the first identified character in this episode, and by the strange, somewhat jarring, dialogue between mother and son. Also, she is the one to initiate the action by pointing to the lack of wine. She is the one who seems to have "prophetic knowledge and authority."[5] Jesus responds—"what concern is that to you and to me"—followed by the enigmatic statement, "My hour has not yet come."

For modern, Western readers who hear a rebuke in Jesus's words,[6] the surprise is that his mother responds by presuming that he will act, for she instructs the servants to "do whatever he tells you" (v. 5). Clearly, there is more to this dialogue than what meets our Western ears! At this point, the work of the sociolinguist Deborah Tannen on gender-related communication can enable our understanding of this strange dialogue.[7] Tannen looks beyond the spoken words to the quality and type of relationship between the speakers. The mother's apparently neutral comment, "they have no wine," can be understood as a linguistic strategy of indirectness, where without making an explicit request, she presumes because of her relationship with her son that he will hear the implicit request: "Could you do something about this?" Notwithstanding the apparently harsh

---

McWhirter, *The Bridegroom Messiah and the People of God: Marriage in the Fourth Gospel*, SNTSMS 138 (Cambridge: Cambridge University Press, 2006), 47–50; Adeline Fehribach, *The Women in the Life of the Bridegroom: A Feminist Historical-Literary Analysis of the Female Characters in the Fourth Gospel* (Collegeville, MN: Liturgical Press, 1998), 29–30.

4. Mary L. Coloe, "The Mother of Jesus: A Woman Possessed," in *Character Studies in the Fourth Gospel: Narrative Approaches to Seventy Figures in John*, ed. Steven A. Hunt, D. Francois Tolmie, and Ruben Zimmermann, WUNT 314 (Tübingen: Mohr Siebeck, 2013), 202–13.

5. Adele Reinhartz, "Women in the Johannine Community: An Exercise in Historical Imagination," in *A Feminist Companion to John*, vol. 2, ed. Amy-Jill Levine with Marianne Blickenstaff, FCNTECW 5 (London: Sheffield Accademic, 2003), 19.

6. It is an indictment of our times that in domestic and even work situations men of any age can speak dogmatically, patronizingly, and correctively to women and presume this as their right. While this is more obvious in some cultures, such abuse of women continues to be a global issue for all societies.

7. Deborah Tannen, *Gender and Discourse* (New York: Oxford University Press, 1996), 584.

words, Jesus's response contains an implicit acquiescence, "yes," leading to her instructions to the servants. His acquiescence to provide the wine also implies his acceptance of the role of being the messianic bridegroom[8] and his assuming the role of YHWH, the bridegroom of Israel.[9]

Jesus's sharp response is puzzling; it reads literally, "Woman, what to me and to you?" (2:4). In all its uses in the LXX[10] this statement has a corrective, if not harsh, tone in a situation "in which two parties have nothing in common, or no relationship to each other."[11] The reply to his mother is strange, but then the puzzle deepens when Jesus acts in accordance with her wishes. Calling her "woman" may sound odd to our ears, but it is not discourteous; it is used to speak to the Samaritan woman (4:21), to the woman brought to Jesus for judgment (8:10), again to his mother (19:26), and to Mary in the garden (20:15). Adele Reinhartz concludes that calling his mother " 'woman' does not belittle his relationship to her but rather recognizes its intimacy."[12] Furthermore, the contradiction between Jesus's words and his later actions suggests that his response is not a rebuff of his mother's request. Tannen states that many cultures see "arguing as a pleasurable sign of intimacy," and in this mother-son context she notes that among men and women of Jewish backgrounds "a friendly argument is a means of being sociable" and that when a Jewish couple appear to be arguing "they are staging a kind of public sparring match, where both fighters are on the same team."[13] Adding to Tannen's approach to look below the spoken words to

8. Fehribach, *Women in the Life of the Bridegroom*, 30.

9. Sandra M. Schneiders, *The Revelatory Text: Interpreting the New Testament as Sacred Scripture*, 2nd ed. (Collegeville, MN: Liturgical Press, 1999), 187.

10. Judg 11:12; 2 Sam 16:10; 19:22; 1 Kgs 17:18; 2 Kgs 3:13; 2 Chr 35:21. Similarly in the New Testament it has the negative sense "leave me alone" (Matt 8:29; Mark 1:24; 5:7; Luke 4:34; 8:28). None of these cases is a dialogue between a mother and her son.

11. Arthur H. Maynard, "TI EMOI KAI ΣOI," *NTS* 31 (1985): 584. For a discussion of its use in the LXX and the possible Semitism lying behind the expression, see Jean-Paul Michaud, "Le signe de Cana dans son contexte johannique," *LTP* 18 (1962): 247–53. Supporting Tannen's approach, Ritva Williams cautions that context is important to interpret the meaning of this exchange and not presume that words and phrases remain constant over time or remain constant regardless of context; see Ritva H. Williams, "The Mother of Jesus at Cana: A Social-Science Interpretation of John 2:1-12," *CBQ* 59 (1997): 687.

12. Adele Reinhartz, "The Gospel of John," in *Searching the Scriptures*, vol. 2: *A Feminist Commentary*, ed. Elisabeth Schüssler Fiorenza (New York: Crossroad, 1994), 569.

13. Tannen, *Gender and Discourse*, 44. Tannen works in linguistics and discourse analysis and so her methodology is based on twentieth-century research data. Whether

deeper levels of communication, Jane Kopas comments, "As we ponder the kind of communication that was going on, we realize that there was an exchange of invitation and response, initiated and answered from each side. The words themselves are not the most important vehicle of meaning; the relationship is."[14]

The very strangeness of the exchange draws the reader's attention to the relationship between Jesus and his mother and to the indication that this relationship will be particularly significant in the future, when "the hour" arrives. The theme of Jesus's "hour" will develop across the narrative and take on a meaning related to the passion, as the "hour" of Jesus's death, exaltation, and glorification (7:30; 8:20; 12:23, 27; 13:1; 17:1). The presence of the woman/mother at Cana and at the cross link these two scenes and require that the "hour" named here be understood in terms of the passion. In the first sign at Cana the passion is initiated. Considering Jesus's subsequent actions in changing the water into wine, his words to his mother must be understood primarily as a narrative strategy directing the reader's attention to the future "hour."[15] It is then that the relationship between Jesus and his mother will be critical. The importance of her relationship as mother of Jesus in this Gospel will only be revealed in "the hour." The problem at Cana is resolved, but Jesus's apparent reprimand creates a puzzle that will not be resolved until the passion.

Adeline Fehribach argues that at Cana the woman is portrayed as a character type, "the mother of an important son." She looks back to the "Mothers of Israel" whose behind-the-scenes actions "actually determined the future of Israel."[16] According to Fehribach, this character type diminishes the individual personality of the woman in naming her, following patriarchal customs, solely in terms of her relationship to her son.[17] Against this view, I consider it wiser to wait for her appearance in the "hour" before making this judgment, where naming her "mother" and "woman" is vital to the theological purpose of the Gospel.

---

this applies to ancient cultures is open to question, but this is true of any evaluation of a dialogue weighed against modern and cultural presumptions.

14. Jane Kopas, "Jesus and Women: John's Gospel," *ThTo* 41 (1985): 202.

15. So also Lieu: "We are led to look for a deeper meaning that has yet to be revealed. There is unfinished business." Judith Lieu, "The Mother of the Son in the Fourth Gospel," *JBL* 117 (1998): 66.

16. See Fehribach, *Women in the Life of the Bridegroom*, 26.

17. Ibid., 32–40.

Old Testament Resonances

The opening words, "on the third day," the situation of a wedding, and the phrase "revealed his glory" (2:11) indicate an allusion to the great covenant ceremony of Sinai, which happened "on the third day," culminating in the revelation of God's glory. The mother's words, "do whatever he tells you," recall also the words of the assembly at Sinai, "All the words that the LORD has spoken we will do" (Exod 24:3). The liturgical celebration of the Sinai covenant also explains the repetition of the phrase "the next day" across chapter 1 (1:29, 35, 43) followed by "on the third day" (2:1).

At Sinai, Moses is instructed that the people are to be consecrated and prepared "for the third day, because on the third day the LORD will come down upon Mount Sinai in the sight of all the people" (Exod 19:10-11). Moses then informs the people, "Prepare for the third day" (Exod 19:15). The narrative continues, "On the morning of the third day there was thunder and lightning, as well as a thick cloud on the mountain" (Exod 19:16). Following the covenant ceremony in chapter 24, Moses ascends the mountain and God's glory settles on the mountain (Exod 24:16, 17).[18] The experience at Sinai is the first covenant made with *all the people* of Israel, as previous covenants were made with individuals such as Noah (Gen 9:8) and Abraham (Gen 15:18). At Sinai, the whole people are to witness and participate in the covenant. This covenant begins a long relationship between God and Israel, a relationship that is frequently described using nuptial imagery as a relationship between a husband and wife (Isa 54:5; Jer 31:32; Ezek 16), betrothed and beloved (Hos 2), bride and bridegroom (Isa 61:10). The wedding at Cana, understood against the background of Sinai, identifies Jesus as the presence of the covenanting God of Israel, and this revelation is possible because of the initiative of his mother.

Jewish Liturgical Background

By New Testament times the Sinai event was linked to the annual pilgrim festival of Weeks (*Shavu'oth*), which is also known as First Fruits

---

18. Within the LXX, the term δόξα comes to mean the divine revelation of God's essential nature in the created world. See R. G. Bratcher, "What Does 'Glory' Mean in Relation to Jesus? Translating *doxa* and *doxazo* in John," *BT* 42 (1991): 401–8; and Gerhard von Rad and Gerhard Kittel, "δόξα," *TDNT* 2 (1964): 238–46.

and in the later Greek books as Pentecost.[19] In its origins, this festival was simply a harvest festival, a day of thanksgiving for God's care and bounty in the harvest. In response to God's gifts of the grain, the people brought offerings of their first fruits. For most of the Old Testament period, there is no indication that this is linked to an event in Israel's history, but by the time of the book of Jubilees (ca. 150 BCE) First Fruits is associated with a series of covenant rituals (Noah in Jub. 6:1, 18; Abraham and the Sinai covenant in Jub. 15:1; 6:11). According to Jubilees, all the covenants were made in the third month, which is the month the Israelites arrived at Sinai (Exod 19:1). Following the destruction of the temple in 70 CE, the rabbis shifted the focus from the celebration of the covenants to the celebration of the gift of the law on Sinai. The earliest reference to this association with Torah is attributed to Rabbi El'azar ben Pedath (ca. 270 CE): "Pentecost is the day on which Torah was given" (b. Pesaḥ 68b).

In the celebration of Weeks, the three days of Exodus 19 were prefaced by four days of earlier or remote preparation. The fourth day of this remote preparation is also the first of three days of immediate preparation according to the Exodus account. These preparations culminate therefore on "the third day," or the sixth from the beginning of the sequence. This time scheme of Exodus "shapes the order of the events reported in John 1:19–2:12."[20]

The structure can be shown schematically:

Day 1 (vv. 19-28): John the Baptizer's testimony to the Jerusalem delegation.

Day 2 (vv. 29-34): John's testimony to Jesus's baptism.

Day 3 (vv. 35-42): Two of John's disciples follow Jesus. Andrew brings Peter to Jesus.

Day 4/1 (vv. 43-51): Day 1 of the Exodus three days of preparation. Philip and Nathanael.

Day 5/2

---

19. Feast of the Harvest (Exod 23:16), Feast of Weeks (Deut 16:10), day of the First Fruits (Num 28:26; Exod 23:16; 34:22; Lev 23:17), Pentecost (Tob 2:1; 2 Macc 12:32). See James C. vanderKam, "Weeks, Festival of," *ABD* 6 (1992): 895.

20. Francis J. Moloney, *John*, SP 4 (Collegeville, MN: Liturgical Press, 1998), 50.

Day 6/3 (vv. 2:1-12): "On the third day," the revelation of Jesus's glory in Cana.

This naming of days in a sequence is similar to the targum version of the Sinai revelation (Ps-Jon Exodus 19:1-4), which gives the following:

On the first day of the month, they came to the wilderness of Sinai (19:1).

On the second day, Moses went up to the top of the mountain (19:3).

On the third day the Lord said to Moses, "Behold, I will reveal myself to you in the thickness of the cloud of glory" (19:9).

On the fourth day the Lord said to Moses, "Go to the people and prepare them today and tomorrow. . . . Let them be ready for the third day; for on the third day the Lord will reveal himself" (19:10-11).

On the third day, on the sixth of the month . . . the Lord was revealed on Mount Sinai (19:16, 20).

When considering the likelihood that John 1:19–2:12 is shaped by the festival of First Fruits, I have given attention to the similarities between words found in the Cana pericope and the Sinai covenant found in Exodus 19–24. From the evidence of the book of Jubilees, the Sinai covenant was memorialized in the Pentecost festival by the first century. The targums offer support for this thesis and add the possibility that in the synagogue liturgy the Exodus account had enumerated a sequence of six days.[21] In beginning the Gospel narrative with allusions to the covenant of Sinai and its celebration in the festival of First Fruits, the evangelist suggests that the gathering of disciples around Jesus and his mother constitute the "first fruits" of Jesus's ministry.[22]

The sign of Cana concludes with the statement that "the disciples believed in him" (2:11), which is followed by their joining Jesus, his mother, and siblings to journey and dwell/abide (μένω) in Capernaum. The next scene will show them in Jerusalem with Jesus in his "Father's house" (2:16).

---

21. For further detailed discussion see Mary L. Coloe, "The Johannine Pentecost: John 1:19-2:12," *ABR* 55 (2007): 41–56.

22. Later, in John 4, Jesus will speak explicitly of his ministry using harvest imagery (4:35-38).

So far, from 1:19–2:13, John has been depicted as the witness and friend, while Jesus has been revealed as the bridegroom. The question must be asked—where or who is the bride? In most commentaries this question is not asked, or if it is, the answer is sought in John 4 with the Samaritan woman;[23] while McWhirter posits that the bride is representative of believers, and that they are characterized in the gospel by the Samaritan Woman, Mary of Bethany and Mary Magdalene.[24] Within the narrative, the characters who function in this role are the disciples.[25] They are the ones directed by the witness of John to Jesus. They attend a wedding with him, come to believe in him, then dwell (ἔμειναν) with him and his family in Capernaum (2:12). They then enter into "the Father's house," which is where the bride and groom consummate their marriage. Even though only male disciples have been named so far, the bride image needs to be read inclusively and analogically. In using the image "bride" to depict disciples, when so far only males have been named, the evangelist transcends the socially constructed sense of who a bride is and focuses instead on how the character(s) functions in the narrative. Just as a male Jesus can be depicted as Sophia, so also disciples can be the bride of the divine bridegroom. Narrative allows such ambiguity of images.[26]

Within the OT, nuptial imagery was used to express the loving and idealized relationship between God and all Israel, both men and women,[27] "and quality wine in abundance was sometimes employed as a symbol of messianic blessing (Isa 25:6; Jer 49:11-12; Joel 4:18; Song 1:2; 2:3; 2 Bar. 29:5)."[28] In symbolizing the covenant in terms of nuptial imagery, the prophets of Israel were working with patriarchal presumptions that gave

23. Andrew T. Lincoln, *The Gospel according to Saint John*, BNTC (London: Continuum, 2005), 134; Fehribach, *Women in the Life of the Bridegroom*, 47–51.

24. Jocelyn McWhirter, *The Bridegroom Messiah and the People of God: Marriage in the Fourth Gospel*, SNTSMS 138 (Cambridge: Cambridge University Press, 2006), 130.

25. Adele Reinhartz also argues that the disciples are the referent of the bridal image; see Adele Reinhartz, "The 'Bride' in John 3:29: A Feminist Perspective," in *The Lost Coin: Parables of Women, Work and Wisdom*, ed. Mary Ann Beavis, BibSem 86 (London: Sheffield Academic, 2002), 238–41.

26. See the discussion by Ingrid Rosa Kitzberger, "Transcending Gender Boundaries in John," in *A Feminist Companion to John*, vol. 1, ed. Amy-Jill Levine with Marianne Blickenstaff, FCNTECW 4 (London: Sheffield Academic, 2003), 173–207.

27. Exod 34:10-16; Deut 5:10; Isa 54:4-8; Jer 2:2; 11:15; Ezek 16:8-13; Hos 1:2-9; 2:2-10.

28. Adeline Fehribach, "The 'Birthing' Bridegroom: The Portrayal of Jesus in the Fourth Gospel," in *A Feminist Companion to John*, vol. 2, ed. Amy-Jill Levine with Marianne Blickenstaff, FCNTECW 5 (London: Sheffield Academic, 2003), 105.

all the privileges and authority to men in society and readily portrayed God in the same manner. When Israel was chastised for being unfaithful to the covenant, Israel was always cast as the faithless or adulterous wife (Jer 2:2; 3:1-10) and never as the deceitful husband. In real life, statistics show that more men than women are unfaithful marriage partners.[29]

Across the narrative, the intimate and mutual relationship between Jesus and disciples is expressed by the verb "to abide" or "to dwell" (μένω).[30] In the final chapters of the Gospel this verb carries the highly charged sense of the mutual loving relationships between Jesus, the Paraclete, and the Father, as well as the intimacy between Jesus and disciples who are called to abide in him, as a branch in a vine (chap. 15). Already in chapter 1, John witnesses to the Spirit coming upon and abiding in Jesus (1:32, 33). When John directs the disciples to Jesus they abide with him (1:39). Later Jesus will speak of his love and friendship toward his disciples (15:15). Just as Jesus is the manifestation of Israel's divine bridegroom, the disciples, who are the first to experience his love both individually and collectively (i.e., Mary, Martha, Lazarus, the Beloved Disciple), can appropriately be referred to as "the bride."

The Mother of Jesus Was There

In the preparations for the covenant making at Sinai, Moses explicitly tells the men of Israel, "do not go near a woman" (Exod 19:15). But these are Moses's words and *not* the words of God. God gives Moses a number of instructions about what he is to say, but the prohibition against women is not part of these divine instructions—this is Moses, thinking perhaps that he is "improving" the divine words! In fact, when God speaks, the whole people (19:9-12, 21), all the children of Israel (19:3, 6), are included, and not just the men. "We all stood at Sinai."[31] Women were at Sinai, and men were not singled out by God. But when divine

---

29. "In general, men are more likely than women to cheat: 20% of men and 13% of women reported that they've had sex with someone other than their spouse while married, according to data from the recent General Social Survey (GSS)." *Institute of Family Studies*, January 10, 2018; https://ifstudies.org/blog/who-cheats-more-the-demographics-of-cheating-in-america.

30. See the excursus below, "Abiding in the Fourth Gospel," by Dorothy Lee.

31. Rabbi Julie K. Gordon, "Yitro: We All Stood at Sinai," in *The Women's Torah Commentary: New Insights from Women Rabbis on the 54 Weekly Torah Portions*, ed. Rabbi Elyse Goldstein (Woodstock, VT: Jewish Lights, 2000), 143–47.

words are passed on Moses adds, "Prepare for the third day; do not go near a woman" (19:15).

At Cana, in the sign that the covenant is being renewed in Jesus,[32] the Gospel makes explicit that women must be included by giving the mother of Jesus pride of place (John 2:1). Jesus's mother is present at this first sign, when his ministry begins, and present also at the cross (19:25-27), when his ministry achieves its goal and Jesus can say, "it is finished" (19:30). Not only is she present, but here at Cana she initiates the action, and at the cross she is essential for Jesus's final words to have meaning. Barbara Reid describes these two scenes as "bookmarks, framing the whole gospel" and the mother/woman as "midwife" in that she recognized that the right time had come for the "birthing" of Jesus's public ministry.[33]

"Abiding in the Fourth Gospel"[34]

Abiding is an expression of the divine life revealed in the Johannine Jesus, who lives in profound union with God, the source of all being. God's nature is thus revealed in the Fourth Gospel as relational and immanent.[35] The implicitly Trinitarian share of revelation is not self-sufficient and isolating, but the source and heart of intimacy. Into this abiding, human beings are drawn not as objects but subjects. The mutuality of the language of abiding is important here. The divine is not presented in this gospel as paternalistic and condescending; rather, the love of God for the world is vulnerable and self-giving (1:11-12; 3:16), calling disciples not into slavish or even childish obedience and servitude but intimate friendship (15:15). Through indwelling, human beings come to relate to God as subject to subject; indeed they find authentic subjectivity

---

32. The covenant theme is well argued in Rheka M. Chennattu, *Johannine Discipleship as a Covenant Relationship* (Peabody, MA: Hendrickson, 2006).

33. Barbara E. Reid, *Wisdom's Feast: An Invitation to Feminist Interpretation of the Scriptures* (Grand Rapids: Eerdmans, 2016), 133.

34. Excerpt from Dorothy A. Lee, "Abiding in the Fourth Gospel: A Case-Study in Feminist Biblical Theology," *Pacifica* 10 (1997): 123–36.

35. Catherine Mowry LaCugna, *God for Us: The Trinity and Christian Life* (San Francisco: HarperCollins, 1991).

in the encounter which, for John, lies at the heart of redemption. The divine "I am" stands in personal relation to human becoming, so that human beings find in themselves a subjective "I am,"[36] a sense of selfhood that is itself the gift of an incarnate God. Abiding defines the divine-human relationship as one of immanence: subject to subject, face-to-face, I-Thou, redeeming the world from the terror of objectification, the fear of alterity, the dread of intimacy.

Dorothy A. Lee

36. John S. Dunne, *The Homing Spirit: A Pilgrimage of the Mind, of the Heart, of the Soul* (New York: Crossroad, 1987), 83–91.

John 2:13-22

Sophia Claims Her Dwelling

8"Then the Creator of all things gave me [Wisdom] a command,
*   and my Creator chose the place for my tent [σκηνήν].*
He said, 'Make your dwelling in Jacob,
*   and in Israel receive your inheritance.'*
9Before the ages, in the beginning, he created me,
*   and for all ages I shall not cease to be.*
10In the holy tent [σκηνῇ ἁγίᾳ] I ministered before him,
*   and so I was established in Zion.*
11Thus in the beloved city he gave me a resting place,
*   and in Jerusalem was my dominion."*
23All this is the book of the covenant of the Most High God,
*   the law which Moses commanded us*
as an inheritance for the congregations of Jacob. (Sir 24:8-11, 23)

According to the book of Sirach, Jerusalem was the place assigned by God for Wisdom's dwelling. The "holy tabernacle" looks back prior to the construction of the temple, to the time following the exodus, when God's presence was symbolized by a simple "tent of meeting" (Exod 33:7-11; Num 11:16, 24; 12:4-5, 10; Deut 31:14). Formal cultic practices developed after the temple was built, which suggested that God now had a permanent dwelling place. It took the prophets and the sages to remind Israel that their relationship with God was not permanent but conditional on covenant obligations, on living just and righteous lives.[1] The wisdom books of Sirach and Baruch remind Israel that the temple cults do not guarantee God's presence; rather, Wisdom is inscribed in the covenant, the "law that endures forever" (Bar 4:1), where the Gospel announces that she is enfleshed in Jesus (John 1:14). Following the initiative of his mother and the first sign, Jesus begins his public ministry in the temple that Wisdom claims to be the place of her ministry (Sir 24:10).

From Marketplace to Sophia's Dwelling

The temple scene in John 2 is shared by all four Gospels, but the Fourth Gospel has a number of significant differences: Passover (v. 13) and the larger animals (v. 15) are mentioned, a different Scripture passage is cited (v. 17), the disciples have a role (vv. 17, 22), and the scene is followed by a dialogue with the Jewish authorities about destroying and raising the temple (v. 19). The most significant change is the location of this scene within the narrative, as the Synoptic Gospels all record this scene at the close of Jesus's ministry (Mark 11:15-19; Matt 21:12-13; Luke 19:45-48), and his words about destroying the temple are then part of the accusations made during his trial (Mark 14:57; Matt 20:61). Clearly, in spite of the differences, there is a historical memory underlying this event, even if an accurate reconstruction of what happened and Jesus's motives are elusive.

Many Bibles present this episode under a heading—"The Cleansing of the Temple." This title is grossly inadequate and reflects an unfamiliarity with first-century Jewish practices. Far more than a "cleansing," Jesus's actions challenge Israel's central sacrificial practice. Whatever this prophetic demonstration meant for the historical Jesus, the Johannine account is a highly condensed theological presentation that Jesus/ Sophia, not the temple system, is now the means of encountering God.

Jewish Liturgical Background

The passage begins by noting that it was the time of Passover (v. 13). This was one of three major pilgrimage festivals when Jews from all the surrounding regions and countries would try to be present for the cele-

---

1. For more information on this "spiritualization" of the temple cult, see Mary L. Coloe, *God Dwells with Us: Temple Symbolism in the Fourth Gospel* (Collegeville, MN: Liturgical Press, 2001), 42–58.

John 2:13-22

¹³The Passover of the Jews was near, and Jesus went up to Jerusalem. ¹⁴In the temple he found people selling cattle, sheep, and doves, and the money changers seated at their tables. ¹⁵Making a whip of cords, he drove all of them out of the temple, both the sheep and the cattle. He also poured out the coins of the money changers and overturned their tables. ¹⁶He told those who were selling the doves, "Take these things out of here! Stop making my Father's house a marketplace!" ¹⁷His disciples remembered that it was written, "Zeal for your house will consume me."

¹⁸The Jews then said to him, "What sign can you show us for doing this?" ¹⁹Jesus answered them, "Destroy this temple, and in three days I will raise it up." ²⁰The Jews then said, "This temple has been under construction for forty-six years, and will you raise it up in three days?" ²¹But he was speaking of the temple of his body. ²²After he was raised from the dead, his disciples remembered that he had said this; and they believed the scripture and the word that Jesus had spoken.

brations in Jerusalem. There were two aspects of this festival: the slaying of the paschal lamb (Exod 12:1-13) followed by the seven-day celebration of unleavened bread (Exod 12:14-20). Because there was only the one temple in Jerusalem, this was the only place where the Passover lambs could be sacrificed.² Those unable to come to Jerusalem would celebrate only with the unleavened bread. In fact, Passover was so important that allowance was made for a second Passover to be celebrated the following

2. The only other Jewish temples were in Egypt. The earliest appears to have been built in Elephantine at the onset of the Babylonian exile when many Jews fled to Egypt (cf. Jer 43:5-7). This temple was later destroyed by rival Egyptian priests in 410 BC, then rebuilt on condition that it had no animal sacrifices and was eventually abandoned sometime after 400 BCE; see Stephen G. Rosenberg, "The Jewish Temple at Elephantine," *NEA* 67 (2004): 6–9. At the time of the Hellenization of the Jews inflicted by Antiochus IV, a temple was built at Leontopolis in the district of Heliopolis (ca. 170 BCE). This temple, erected by Onias IV, the son of the Jerusalem high priest, was destroyed in 73 CE under the orders of Vespasian; see Stephen G. Rosenberg, "Two Jewish Temples in Antiquity in Egypt," *BAIAS* 19–20 (2001–2002): 182. Even though lambs were sacrificed at these temples, at least while they existed, the Jews in Egypt continued to support the Jerusalem temple, and from the evidence of Philo of Alexandria they likely attended its services when possible and contributed to the temple tax; see C. T. R. Hayward, *The Jewish Temple: A Non-Biblical Sourcebook* (London: Routledge, 1996), esp. 109–41.

month for those unable to celebrate at the proper time, either because of ritual impurity or because of travel (Num 9:9-14).[3]

With the large influx of pilgrims to Jerusalem, this was also the time when the annual temple tax, the half-shekel, was collected. This tax could be paid only in Tyrian coinage because of its standard of pure silver.[4] Pilgrims would therefore need to exchange their money for this coinage before paying their taxes. According to the Mishnah, the rabbis permitted tables to be set up in the outer courts of the temple prior to Passover for the money changers and those collecting the temple tax (m. Šeqal. 1:3).

This tax, obligatory for all Jewish males, was essential for the upkeep of Israel's sacrificial system. It paid for the morning and evening daily holocaust of a lamb for Israel's purification.[5] In addition, it paid for the upkeep of the temple officials and all the paraphernalia such as the oil, wood, candles, and vestments. This half-shekel tax was the continuation of Israel's offering in the wilderness (Exod 30:14-16). Through the payment of this offering, all Israelites participated in the twice-daily holocaust, "which accomplished atonement for sin on behalf of the holy people as a whole."[6]

3. Michael A. Daise, *Feasts in John: Jewish Festivals and Jesus' "Hour" in the Fourth Gospel*, WUNT 2:229 (Tübingen: Mohr Siebeck, 2007), 118–19. This second Passover can often be overlooked, but, as Daise notes, it "enjoyed great currency in Second Temple and Tannaitic discussion" (118). As this Passover is discussed in Philo and in the Qumran literature, he considers it was known to the Fourth Evangelist. This second Passover will be very significant in discussing John 6.

4. The rabbis prescribed that the half-shekel temple tax was to be paid in Tyrian coins (m. Bek. 8.7). These coins, although bearing a "graven image," seem to have been tolerated because of the purity of the silver. The shekel was approximately fourteen grams of pure silver, and during the Roman occupation the Jews were not permitted to mint their own silver coins, which became one of the causes for the Jewish revolt in 66 CE. Roth comments, "It is true that the Tyrian shekel bore the head of Heracles (Melkart) and the Ptolemaic eagle, but it did not have the head of the Roman emperor or any reference to him and it is conceivable that in the eyes of the Zealots a conventional pagan symbol was preferable to one which implicitly recognized a gentile ruler." See Cecil Roth, "The Historical Implications of the Jewish Coinage of the First Revolt," *IEJ* 12 (1962): 35.

5. The holocaust was the sacrifice where the entire animal was burnt, signifying its total offering to God. In some sacrifices only part of the animal was burnt and part shared with the person making the offering.

6. Jacob Neusner, "Money-Changers in the Temple: The Mishnah's Explanation," *NTS* 35 (1989): 289.

An Alternative Model of Worship

While a modern reader may be offended by the thought of animals within a place of worship, in fact one of the major aspects of any ancient temple was the slaying and offering of animals. Worshipers would continually be bringing their offerings of sheep, goats, pigeons, cattle, according to their wealth and the purpose of the sacrifice. As an aid to the many pilgrims coming to Passover from distant places, animals for sale in the outer courts would be a great assistance and not be offensive to first-century Jews.[7] When commenting on the money changers, Jacob Neusner comments, "Their presence made possible the cultic participation of every Israelite, and it was not only not a blemish on the cult but part of its perfection."[8]

Jesus's actions therefore are not a response to the profaning of the temple because of the presence of the money changers and the animals.[9] All these things are essential elements for Israel's worship. His actions are best understood as a prophetic sign that the temple worship system is no longer needed. The Jerusalem temple, as the great symbol of God's presence in Israel's midst, is now embodied in Jesus. It is important to remember that by the time the Fourth Gospel was taking its final shape, the temple had been destroyed by the Romans. The evangelist considers that even prior to its destruction the temple was no longer necessary, because Jesus was the incarnate Word and the presence of divine Sophia.

Jesus's words are important for understanding the particular theology of this Gospel. The most frequent name for the temple in the OT was the Lord's house, בית יהוה (*bayt YHWH*). By renaming the temple "my Father's house" Jesus claims a uniquely personal relationship with God, which to this point only the readers of the prologue know.[10] This name

---

7. Donald A. Carson, *The Gospel according to John* (Grand Rapids: Eerdmans, 1991), 178.

8. Neusner, "Money-Changers in the Temple," 289.

9. Nor are they a protest against exploitation of the poor by the temple authorities. See further James McLaren, "Corruption among the High Priesthood: A Matter of Perspective," in *A Wandering Galilean: Essays in Honour of Séan Freyne*, ed. Zuleika Rodgers with Margaret Daly-Denton and Anne Fitzpatrick McKinley, JSJS 132 (Leiden: Brill, 2009), 141–57.

10. At this point it is important to realize the double meaning of the expression the "father's house," which in the OT is the idiomatic way of referring to the household and so always carries a personal sense. Many Bibles today translate the idiom as "family." The "father's house" reflects the patriarchal social structures of the times and refers to all those within his authority—his wife, children, slaves, grandchildren,

also continues the nuptial symbolism initiated by John; Jesus's disciples have been brought to him by John's witness; they have participated in a wedding, then joined Jesus's mother and siblings, and now have entered into his "father's house," which is the traditional place for the consummation of a marriage. The contrast between τὸν οἶκον τοῦ πατρός μου (house of my father) and the οἶκον ἐμπορίου (house of trade) echoes the language of Zechariah when speaking about the eschatological temple, "And there shall no longer be traders in the house of the LORD of hosts on that day" (Zech 14:21).[11] In Jesus, the *eschaton* has arrived.

The narrative comments that the disciples remembered (vv. 17, 22) are reminders to the reader that the Gospels are a postresurrection reflection on and interpretation of Jesus.[12] The comment suggests that during Jesus's ministry the disciples did not fully comprehend their experience, but this recollection and understanding was possible later, through the gift of the Paraclete (14:26). The Scripture verse that they recall, in the context of the temple and its sacrificial animals, indicates that Jesus's actions, which set him in conflict with the authorities, will ultimately lead to his being consumed in death. In Psalm 69:10, the psalmist is not speaking of a zeal that totally dominates him, but one that brings him close to death. This is also the meaning in John 2:17.[13]

By What Authority?

In response to these actions, "the Jews" do not ask what they mean; rather, they ask for a sign of Jesus's authority. This implies that they have understood his actions, to some extent, as a prophetic action, since

---

and extended family. This "household" meaning of the expression will recur later in the Gospel, as the meaning of the temple is transferred from a building to the person of Jesus and ultimately to the community of believers.

11. Andrew T. Lincoln, *The Gospel according to Saint John*, BNTC (London: Continuum, 2005), 138.

12. This post-Easter perspective has been the particular focus of Franz Mussner, *Die johanneische Sehweise und die Frage nach dem historischen Jesus*, QD 28 (Freiburg: Herder, 1965), and Christina Hoegen-Rohls, *Der nachösterliche Johannes: Die Abschiedsreden als hermeneutischer Schlüssel zum vierten Evangelium*, WUNT 2.84 (Tübingen: Mohr Siebeck, 1996). A brief summary of their work can be found in Mary L. Coloe, *Dwelling in the Household of God: Johannine Ecclesiology and Spirituality* (Collegeville, MN: Liturgical Press, 2007), 14–15.

13. Maarten Menken, *Old Testament Quotations in the Fourth Gospel: Studies in Textual Form*, CBET 15 (Kampen: Kok Pharos, 1996), 41.

prophets were authenticated by the "signs and wonders" that they were able to perform, e.g., Moses (Exod 7:3). The sign Jesus offers that points to his authority from God is the destroying and raising of a temple (v. 19). The Gospels of Mark (14:58) and Matthew (26:61) record a statement that Jesus spoke about the destruction and rebuilding of the temple. This saying is not unique to Jesus; within Jewish apocalyptic thinking was the scenario of the temple's destruction in the last days (e.g., Dan 9:26; Tob 14:4) and then it being rebuilt (Dan 9:24; Tob 13:16-18; 14:5; Jub. 1:28; 4Q174 1:1-3). It is conceivable that the historical Jesus echoed these sentiments as part of his belief in the imminent advent of the end times, symbolized by his participating in John's baptism. When the temple was destroyed by the Romans in 70 CE, the Johannine community could recall Jesus's words and give them now the status of a prophecy and also reinterpret the meaning of the event. This is not supersessionism when seen within the context of first-century Jewish eschatology; rather, it is the ancient prophecies now being accomplished.[14]

Understandably, Jesus's listeners think he is speaking of the temple building and scoff, replying that Herod's recent renovations had taken forty-six years (v. 20). The narrator interprets from a Johannine theological perspective and informs the reader that "he was speaking of the temple of his body" (v. 21). The reader has already been introduced to the concept of Jesus as the dwelling place of God in the prologue, which referred back to Israel's tabernacle to describe the flesh-taking of the Word (1:14). Just as the tabernacle was the visible symbol of God's presence among Israel, so too, the human flesh of Jesus makes God's presence visible for those with eyes to see. As the Gospel narrative continues, the reader will need to bring to the reading task this understanding of Jesus's identity as a living temple of God's presence.

The scene closes with the disciples once again remembering these words in the post-Easter time. The implication is that the disciples participating in the scene were as bewildered as "the Jews." Only the readers, guided by the reading so far and the narrative comments, have inside information about Jesus's identity.

---

14. For more on the temple and its restoration, see Ed P. Sanders, *Jesus and Judaism* (Philadelphia: Fortress, 1985), 77–90. On the historicity of this statement, see Dale C. Allison Jr., *Constructing Jesus: Memory, Imagination, and History* (Grand Rapids: Baker Academic, 2010), 236, esp. n. 63.

From Division to Sophia's Welcome Table

The temple, the great symbol of God's presence in Israel, was also a visible expression of a society that was both hierarchical and patriarchal.[15] The many walls, gates, and doors of the physical building established clear boundaries and what might be termed "grades of holiness." Gentiles were permitted in the outer courtyard but were not permitted beyond a marble screen (the *soreg*) on pain of death. Israelite men and women could pass through the many gates into the sanctuary, which was further divided into the court of women and the court of Israel. Only men could walk up the fifteen steps and pass through the elaborate Nicanor gate into the court of Israel. This court was also divided by a low balustrade and steps leading up to the court of the priests. Further steps and a veil screened the court of Israel from the inner room of the holy place where a priest would enter to burn incense. A further veil separated the holy place from the holy of holies, which was entered only by the high priest on the Day of Atonement.[16] Apart from the many physical boundaries built into the architecture of the temple, there were other religious boundaries that barred some men and women from the temple because of some level of defilement.[17]

The very architecture of the temple is divisive. The steps, gates, and walls configure in space a hierarchical social mind-set. This continued when Christian churches were allowed to be built in the fourth century. Archaeologists have discovered, however, the remains of an alternative octagonal space in Capernaum that was built over what was believed to be "the House of Peter." This is one of the earliest worship spaces for the Jesus believers discovered so far (ca. mid-first century).[18] The octagonal-

---

15. Schüssler Fiorenza provides a diagrammatic representation of a patriarchal/kyriarchal state and then how that was transposed onto a Constantinian patriarchal model of church, in Elisabeth Schüssler Fiorenza, *Wisdom Ways: Introducing Feminist Biblical Interpretation* (Maryknoll, NY: Orbis Books, 2005), 132–33. She then offers an alternative circular model of a discipleship of equals (134).

16. For details of the temple and its rituals, see Alfred Edersheim, *The Temple: Its Ministry and Services*, updated ed. (Peabody, MA: Hendrickson, 1994).

17. For further details on Israel's purity laws and defilement, see Hannah K. Harrington, "Clean and Unclean," *NIDB* 1 (2006): 681–86.

18. The graffiti, "O Lord Jesus Christ—have mercy . . ." and the pottery and the design have pointed to this being a very early house church for the followers of Jesus in Capernaum. The eight-sided shape testifies to early theology of a new creation on the eighth day, i.e., the day after the Sabbath, which for Christians is the day of the resurrection. More will be said on this when looking at John 20. For further details on this early church, see Jerome Murphy-O'Connor, *The Holy Land: An Oxford Archaeologi-*

shaped church was built in the fifth century. It is close to being a "church in the round" and suggests a nonhierarchical gathering of disciples, where there is equality of gender and class. This house church witnesses to Letty Russell's idea of what the Christian Church should be:

> *Church in the Round* describes a community of faith and struggle work-ing to anticipate God's New Creation by becoming partners with those who are at the margins of church and society. The metaphor [Church in the Round] speaks of people gathered around the table and in the world, in order to connect faith and life in action/reflection (the round table), work for justice in solidarity with those at the margins of society (the kitchen table), and to welcome everyone as partners in God's world house (the welcome table).[19]

Sophia's Dwelling

During the historical life of Jesus, he enacted some form of prophetic demonstration about the temple, probably in the light of Jewish apocalyptic hopes. Following his death and resurrection, this action was reflected on and given deeper meaning by the Christian communities, as shown by the different manner of reporting the event in the four Gospels. For the Johannine community, Jesus's temple actions and dialogue with "the Jews" signified an end to the temple system and pointed to a new way of encountering God in his own person. When the temple was destroyed by the Romans in 70 CE, it marked the end of sacrifices and the Jewish priesthood. Following this event, the rabbis shifted the focus from the temple to living out the Torah (Law) as the means of encountering God. The transition from sacrifice to Torah is illustrated in this later rabbinic tale.

Once, as Rabban Yohanan ben Zakkai was coming forth from Jerusalem, Rabbi Joshua followed him and beheld the Temple in ruins.

"Woe unto us," Rabbi Joshua cried, "that this, the place where the iniquities of Israel were atoned for, is laid waste!"

"My son," Rabban Yohanan said to him, "be not grieved. We have an-other atonement as effective as this. And what is it? It is acts of loving kindness, as it

---

cal Guide from Earliest Times to 1700, 5th ed. (Oxford: Oxford University Press, 2008), 252–55; Virgilio C. Corbo, "Capharnaüm," *RB* 78 (1971): 588–91.

19. Letty M. Russell, *Church in the Round: Feminist Interpretation of the Church* (Lou-isville: Westminster John Knox, 1993), 12.

is said, *For I desire mercy and not sacrifice"* (Hos 6:6). (Avot de Rabbi Natan, chap. 6)[20]

Where the Jewish community looked to the Law, the early Jesus believers looked to Jesus as the way to encounter God. The destruction of the temple was therefore a major impetus for the development of Christology. As the Johannine narrative progresses, this living temple will be shown to be nonhierarchical and open to all who make the choice to believe. As Sophia incarnate, who makes people "friends of God, and prophets" (Wis 7:27), Jesus's relationship to believers will be that of mutual friendship (John 15:15) and self-sacrificing love (John 15:13).[21]

Of course, this is only one understanding of the Jesus event and one expression of living out the Gospel's vision and values. Even in the New Testament other theologies are present and other models of community living and leadership structures are proposed.[22] Some of these issues are reflected in John 21 and in the Johannine epistles, witnessing that there was tension from the beginning between the ideal and the social reality. In time, particularly after Constantine, the hierarchical model of leadership prevailed. This Gospel dares to challenge such a model and proposes an alternative where love and friendship prevail.

The Father's House

The basic unit in Israelite society was the בית אב, "father's house,"[23] which would include two or three generations of consanguineal or blood relationships and affinal relations based on marriage or adoption, unrelated servants, and even sojourners. Editions of the Bible frequently translate בית אב as "family." The Bible is a text produced by educated scribes and so can be called a

---

20. Quoted in Jacob Neusner, "Judaism in a Time of Crisis: Four Responses to the Destruction of the Second Temple," *Judaism* 21 (1972): 324.

21. This theme of friendship will dominate the final discourse (chaps. 13–17).

22. E.g., the household codes of Eph 5:22–6:9; Col 3:18–4:1. The description of roles in 1 Tim 2:1, 8-15; 3:1-13; Titus 2:1-19.

23. More accurately it could be termed the "father's household" as it always referred to people, rather than a building. A good example of this is Josh 2, where after requesting that her "father's house" be saved Rahab then names the members of the household "save alive my father and mother, my brothers and sisters, and all who belong to them, and deliver our lives from death" (Josh 2:12-13).

patriarchal text, shown in its bias to use male-gendered language and providing information predominantly about the male figures;[24] so the terminology of the "father's house" suggests a hierarchical structure within the household, where all power is held by the eldest male. This configuration is termed "patriarchy." With little in the way of archaeological remains or other nonbiblical texts, the assumption is made that the Israelite household functioned as a patriarchal unit. Thus, some readers of the Gospel will find the term "Father's house" affronting and even abusive.

With more knowledge about the ancient agricultural economy, characterizing the ancient Israelite household as "patriarchal" needs to be nuanced. Processing the grain for food and the skills in textile production meant that women accrued power since they contributed to the economic well-being of the household.[25]

The tasks that involved working in groups established women's networks wherein lay an elusive and invisible source of women's power.[26]

Carol Meyers writes: "Because the household in Iron Age settlements was the primary unit of society, and because women had significant power in household social spaces, it may be better to consider the gendered spheres of these settlements as complementary rather than hierarchical."[27] She then uses the term "heterarchy" rather than "patriarchy" to more accurately describe "the variability, context, and fluctuation of social relations in peasant societies."[28]

Because of this study she cautions against assumptions based on modern evaluations of household work. "Newer studies of traditional societies show that women's household economic roles, in both subsistence tasks and craft production, functioned in ways that contest our often

---

24. "The OT is the product of a patriarchal world, and more specifically, of a literate, urban elite of male religious specialists." See Phyllis A. Bird, "Women: Old Testament," *ABD* 6 (1992): 951.

25. "The gender attribution of these processes can be established with reasonable certainty"; see Carol Meyers, "Material Remains and Social Relations: Women's Culture in Agrarian Households of the Iron Age," in *Symbiosis, Symbolism, and the Power of the Past: Canaan, Ancient Israel, and Their Neighbors from the Late Bronze Age through Roman Palaestina*, ed. William G. Dever and Seymour Gitin (Winona Lake, IN: Eisenbrauns, 2003), 431. She bases this statement on ethnographic, ethnohistorical, and iconographic evidence.

26. "The presence of female work groups, whether for food-processing or crafts production, signals the existence of women's networks"; see Meyers, "Material Remains and Social Relations," 435.

27. Ibid.," 437.

28. Ibid.

unexamined but persistent notions of female dependency and patriarchal dominance. The work patterns and authority structures in premodern societies meant that daily life was rarely hierarchical along gendered lines."[29]

While Meyers's critique offers a more positive evaluation of women's position, this does not mean there was an egalitarian society. There were differences along gendered lines between the private sphere of the household, where women could be managers, teachers of younger children, revenue makers, and providers, and the public sphere of the wider society, where the male head represented the household in legal matters such as land ownership, arranging

marriages, and negotiating with civil and religious authorities.[30] The designation "father's house" reflects the male authority in the public sphere, but within the household, the term must be nuanced by recognizing the power of women and women's networks.

The custom and bias of using the term "father's house" continues in the Fourth Gospel, but the characterization of women in the text counters an assumption that the term means women are subservient in this household. On the contrary, women in this Gospel, like the mother of Jesus at Cana, will demonstrate strong missionary roles (the Samaritan woman, Mary Magdalene) and will bear prophetic witness (Mary of Bethany).

"The Jews" (οἱ Ἰουδαῖοι) in the Gospel of John

The term οἱ Ἰουδαῖοι (hoi Ioudaioi) occurs roughly seventy times in the Gospel of John, referring to a character group largely depicted as Jesus's persistent adversaries.[31] Most English editions of the New Testament translate οἱ Ἰουδαῖοι as "the Jews." At face value, we

could categorize the use of the term οἱ Ἰουδαῖοι in the Gospel along an evaluative continuum, with many references considered "negative" (e.g., 2:18, 20; 5:10, 15, 16, 18; 6:41), some "neutral" (e.g., 2:6, 13; 5:1), and a smaller number "positive" (e.g., 1:38, 49; 3:2; 4:9, 22).[32] While such a categorization can be useful, it would be erroneous to assume that John's

---

29. Meyers, "Material Remains and Social Relations," 434.

30. Bird, "Women: Old Testament," 953.

31. The approximation ("roughly seventy") is due to manuscript variations.

32. For a more extensive list of examples, see Ruth Sheridan, *Retelling Scripture: 'The Jews' and the Scriptural Citations in John 1:19–12:15*, BibInt 110 (Leiden: Brill, 2012), 3–4.

presentation of "the Jews" can be wholly evaluated in terms of statistical assessment.[33] Discussion of the Johannine portrait of οἱ Ἰουδαῖοι, and whether the Gospel could be termed "anti-Jewish" or not, needs to consider the broad rhetorical effect of the Gospel's connotative characterization of "the Jews" and the way this characterization is built into the Gospel's dualistic and mythical worldview.[34] For example, "the Jews" are frequently depicted as wishing to kill Jesus (5:18; 7:1, 20; 8:37, 40; 11:53; 18:28-32; 19:7, 12) and as inciting fear in believers (7:13; 20:19); they are "from below" (8:23), and the "devil" is said to be their "father" (8:44). Their behavior and origins fit within the underside of the Gospel's binary rhetoric.[35]

Evaluating if and to what extent the Gospel's presentation of "the Jews" is anti-Jewish would involve a number of hermeneutical and definitional considerations beyond the scope of this short study.[36] In what follows I will restrict my focus to discussing the term οἱ Ἰουδαῖοι but also touch on some hermeneutical points toward the end of the essay.

In the secondary literature, the subject of the "sense and referent" of the term οἱ Ἰουδαῖοι has been much debated.[37] Studies on the referent of οἱ Ἰουδαῖοι are predominantly conducted within the remit of historical-critical exegesis. Most often, the same studies ask whether the term οἱ Ἰουδαῖοι should be thought of as

---

Cf. Stephen Wilson, *Related Strangers: Jews and Christians, 70–170 CE* (Minneapolis: Fortress, 1995), 74.

33. I explain my preference for using quotation marks to signify "the Jews" in Ruth Sheridan, "Issues in the Translation of οἱ Ἰουδαῖοι in the Fourth Gospel," *JBL* 132 (2013): 671–95.

34. Cf. Judith M. Lieu, "Anti-Judaism, the Jews, and the Worlds of the Fourth Gospel," in *The Gospel of John and Christian Theology*, ed. Richard Bauckham and Carl Mosser (Grand Rapids: Eerdmans, 2008), 178.

35. Cf. Adele Reinhartz, " 'Jews' and Jews in the Fourth Gospel," in *Anti-Judaism and the Fourth Gospel*, ed. Reimund Bieringer, Didier Pollefeyt, and Frederique Vandecasteele-Vanneuville (Louisville: Westminster John Knox, 2001), 217.

36. A good overview of such issues can be found in Terence L. Donaldson, *Jews and Anti-Judaism in the New Testament: Decision Points and Divergent Interpretations* (Waco, TX: Baylor University Press, 2010). The definitive discussion, to my mind, is still Judith Lieu, "Anti-Judaism in the Fourth Gospel: Explanation and Hermeneutics," in *Anti-Judaism and the Fourth Gospel*, ed. Reimund Bieringer, Didier Pollefeyt, and Frederique Vandecasteele-Vanneuville (Louisville: Westminster John Knox Press, 2001), 110–17.

37. The first to make this distinction between the connotative "sense" and historical "referent" of the term was John Ashton, "The Identity and Function of the *Ioudaioi* in the Fourth Gospel," *NovT* 27 (1985): 40–75. Since then, scholarship has largely followed this trend; see further literature cited below.

"anti-Jewish" from an authorial perspective. The first scholar to posit an alternative referent for the term (i.e., other than "the Jews") was Malcom Lowe in 1976.[38] Lowe correctly argued that the term οἱ Ἰουδαῖοι can be translated as either "Jew" or "Judean," the former option functioning as a religious descriptor and the latter referring to an inhabitant of the land of Judea. Given that many of the references to οἱ Ἰουδαῖοι in the Gospel are negative, Lowe championed the adoption of "Judean" in all future English translations. Despite Lowe's noble intentions, some problems with his thesis are evident. One counterargument is that the term οἱ Ἰουδαῖοι underwent semantic expansion in the Hasmonean period, when the term οἱ Ἰουδαῖοι came to embrace religious and political aspects of Jewish self-understanding (cf. John 9:28) as well as ethno-geographical aspects, making a sharp separation between these aspects difficult to maintain.[39]

Another approach to the referent of οἱ Ἰουδαῖοι has been to opt for a loose equivalent translation and to render the term "the authorities" or "the Jewish authorities." This is based on the argument of Urban C. von Wahlde, who claimed that, according to the Gospel text, "the Jews" function in a comparable way to the Pharisees in the Synoptic Gospels.[40] The problem with von Wahlde's suggestion is that it does not reflect, in a consistent manner, the evidence in the Gospel. For example, the Ἰουδαῖοι are sometimes equated with, or found among, the common "crowd" (ὄχλος) in Galilee (e.g., 6:22; 41), and other times "the Jews" fear the authorities rather than functioning in an authoritative manner themselves (cf. 7:11-13). Translating οἱ Ἰουδαῖοι as "the (Jewish) authorities" may not necessarily defuse the anti-Jewish potential contained in the standard translation "the Jews." This is because, whatever we call this group—"the Jews" or "the Jewish authorities"—their connotative characterization still encourages the reader to view them negatively from within the story, and their being "Jewish" is still self-evident.

Other studies on the referent of οἱ Ἰουδαῖοι tend to work on

---

38. Malcolm Lowe, "Who Were the ΙΟΥΔΑΙΟΙ?," *NovT* 18 (1976): 101–30.

39. See Shaye J. D. Cohen, *Boundaries, Varieties, Uncertainties* (Berkeley: University of California Press, 1999), 70, 137. Josephus's writings indicate that Ἰουδαῖοι can denote the entire country of ancient Palestine, not just the postexilic temple precinct of Judea (*A.J.* 17.253-254; 18.2; 20.43); see also Tacitus, *Annals* 22.54. Cited in Lars Kierspel, *'The Jews' and the World in the Fourth Gospel: Parallelism, Function and Context*, WUNT 2/20 (Tübingen: Mohr Siebeck, 2006), 22, n. 44.

40. Urban C. von Wahlde, "The Johannine Jews: A Critical Survey," *NTS* 28 (1982): 33–60.

assumptions about the symbolic function of language, even as they make historicist claims. That is, "the Jews" in John's Gospel are thought to function as a cipher for some (presumably other) group. This reasoning is often indebted to J. Louis Martyn's "two-level" reading of John's Gospel, which proposes that the Gospel tells the story of Jesus and is thus set in or around the 30s CE but that it simultaneously tells the story of the Johannine community in the 90s CE.[41] According to Martyn, Jesus and the disciples stand for the believing Johannine Christians in the community, and "the Jews" stand for the Jewish (proto-rabbinic or Pharisaic) authorities who were responsible for ejecting the believers from the synagogue (cf. 9:22; 12:42; 16:2). Even though the basic premise of the Gospel as a "two-level drama" has become paradigmatic in the scholarship, it has also been critiqued.[42] But Martyn's reasoning about the symbolic function of "the Jews" has been shared by various other scholars, who have posited that "the Jews" stand for, among others, the rabbis at Yavneh,[43] a more religiously observant segment of the Jewish populace,[44] the crypto-Christians who were afraid to confess belief in Jesus,[45] or the *yehudim* resident in the temple state following the exile.[46] In the view of some commentators and scholars, the symbolic function of the term οἱ Ἰουδαῖοι is taken to the extreme—Rudolf Bultmann, for example, offers an existentialist

41. J. Louis Martyn, *History and Theology in the Fourth Gospel*, 2nd ed. (Nashville: Abingdon, 1979).

42. See Tobias Hägerland, "John's Gospel: A Two-Level Drama?," *JSNT* 25 (2003): 309–22; cf. Burton L. Visotsky, "Methodological Considerations on the Study of John's Interaction with First-Century Judaism," in *Life in Abundance: Studies of John's Gospel in Tribute to Raymond E. Brown*, ed. J. R. Donahue (Collegeville, MN: Liturgical Press, 2005), 91–107; Edward W. Klink III, *The Sheep of the Fold: The Audience and Origin of the Gospel of John*, SNTSMS 141 (Cambridge: Cambridge University Press, 2007), 107–51. See also Adele Reinhartz, *Cast Out of the Covenant: Jews and Anti-Judaism in the Gospel of John* (Lanham, MD: Lexington Books 2018), 111–30.

43. James D. G. Dunn, "The Embarrassment of History: Reflections on the Problem of 'Anti-Judaism' in the Fourth Gospel," in Bieringer, Pollefeyt, and Vandecasteele-Vanneuville, *Anti-Judaism and the Fourth Gospel*, 42.

44. K. B. Bornhäuser, *Das Johannesevangelium: Eine Missionsschrift für Israel* (Gütersloh: Bertelsmann, 1928).

45. Henk Jan de Jong, "'The Jews' in the Gospel of John," in Bieringer, Pollefeyt, and Vandecasteele-Vanneuville, *Anti-Judaism and the Fourth Gospel*, 121–40.

46. Daniel Boyarin, "The Ioudaioi in John and the Prehistory of Judaism," in *Pauline Conversations in Context: Essays in Honor of Calvin J. Roetzel*, ed. Janice Capel Anderson, Philip Sellew, and Claudia Setzer (Sheffield: Sheffield Academic, 2002), 216–39.

interpretation, arguing that "the Jews" in John represent "the unbelieving world in general" from the "standpoint of Christian faith."[47]

There is therefore no consensus about the historical referent of οἱ Ἰουδαῖοι in the scholarship. But an assumption is shared, namely, that in John "the Jews" represent only a small part of a larger and more variegated Jewish community in the first century CE. Whatever profile the Johannine "Jews" are made to fit—whether they are defined by their geography, their leadership roles, or their degree of religious observance— the idea is that they constitute, or represent, "some" Jews, not "all" Jews.[48] The implication of this reasoning is that John's use of οἱ Ἰουδαῖοι does not denote "Jews *qua* Jews" and cannot therefore be considered "anti-Jewish." This is indeed sometimes the stated rationale for placing the translated term "the Jews" in quotation marks when commenting on the text.[49] On this understanding, the Johannine Jews ought not to be considered coterminous with real Jews of Jesus's day, or of any age, but must be thought of as rhetorical ploys, whose negative traits are perhaps

magnified or exaggerated but who nevertheless represent (albeit, real) antagonists in the evangelist's day.

These methods of ameliorating John's harsh rhetoric against "the Jews" are evidently well-meaning, and they come some way toward making sense of the fact that οἱ Ἰουδαῖοι sometimes has a positive sense in the Gospel (e.g., 4:22). Also, these solutions attempt to contain the vitriol of John's text by situating it within a putative historical situation, thus qualifying the referent to encompass only "some" Jews. The most basic problem, however, is that John does not refer to "some" Jews; he mostly uses the unqualified term with the definite article, οἱ Ἰουδαῖοι (but see "a Jew" in 3:25; 4:9; 18:35; the qualifications in 8:31; 11:31, 33; and the split between "the Jews" in 11:37). More important, there is the problem of the connotative sense of John's term, which aligns "the Jews" overwhelmingly with adversarial, negative, and even demonic traits (cf. 8:44), while carrying the potential of semantic crossover (there are today millions of people who identify themselves, or are identified by others, as "the Jews"). That point strikes at

---

47. R. Bultmann, *The Gospel of John: A Commentary*, trans. G. R. Beasley Murray et al. (Oxford: Blackwell, 1971), 86.

48. Cf. Stephen Motyer, "Bridging the Gap: How Might the Fourth Gospel Help Us Cope with the Legacy of Christianity's Exclusive Claim over against Judaism?," in Bauckham and Mosser, *The Gospel of John and Christian Theology*, 143–67.

49. Cf. Francis J. Moloney, *John*, SP 4 (Collegeville, MN: Liturgical Press, 1998), 9.

deeper hermeneutical issues. Contemporary reader-response criticism asks about the effect of the text on the reader rather than what the original author might have intended. Adele Reinhartz, one modern Jewish interpreter of the Gospel, has alerted scholars that placing quotation marks around the translated term "the Jews" might have the effect of "whitewashing" the text and of illegitimately defusing the anti-Jewish tenor of the text instead of appropriately exposing it in order to address it.[50] The various historical referents posed for "the Jews" do not alter the way the text is heard and the damage that can be done in the hearing (e.g., Reinhartz wrote of feeling addressed by the term and thus also feeling like each reference was a "slap in the face").[51]

The more pressing problem may be that in trying to understand John's Jews as "ciphers" for another group in the evangelist's time, or as mere symbols of the force of unbelief, we ignore the negative uses to which the Gospel was later put vis-à-vis real Jews, in the sense that an assumed irenic intention on the part of the evangelist was simply "misunderstood" by later Christian history and practice, when the Gospel's teaching was harshly applied to actual Jews. This is not to argue that understanding what we can about John's first-century setting is futile, only to caution that the limitations affecting our evidence prevent us from gaining certainty in our results. The Johannine community is a heuristic construct used to interpret the Gospel text but can only be deduced from the text itself. Furthermore, John's story is skewed toward the victors, the "believers," who have light and life (cf. 3:16-20). The risk in reading the tale, on either of its "two-levels," too simply is that we might end up arguing that John's "Jews" were responsible for ejecting the Johannine believers from synagogues and that this "explains" (or even justifies) John's harsh rhetoric against them. It is wise to keep all of these issues in mind when encountering "the Jews" in John's narrative and perhaps also to bravely face the discomfort of John's negative rhetoric rather than covering it up, thus allowing it to pull readers toward a "hermeneutic of repentance."[52]

Ruth Sheridan

50. Reinhartz, " 'Jews' and Jews," 225–27.

51. Adele Reinhartz, *Befriending the Beloved Disciple: A Jewish Reading of the Gospel of John* (New York: Continuum, 2001), 13.

52. Mary L. Coloe, "Response: The Beyond Beckons," in *What We Have Heard from the Beginning: The Past, Present and Future of Johannine Studies*, ed. Tom Thatcher (Waco, TX: Baylor University Press, 2007), 213.

John 2:23–3:36

Nicodemus:
The Labor of New Birth[1]

*In kinship with [Sophia] there is immortality [ἀθανασία],
and in friendship with her, pure delight. (Wis 8:17-18)*

Sophia-Jesus is obviously present in this dialogue with Nicodemus, which speaks of birth (3:3, 5) and then clarifies that this birth is not into ordinary mortal life but into the eternity life (3:16) of God—a gift that only Sophia can provide. The chapter needs to be read with the book of Wisdom as its primary intertext.

Transition from the Temple Scene (2:23–3:2)

The transition between the temple scene and the episode with Nicodemus (2:23-25) clearly links the two. It is still Passover; the setting is Jerusalem, and the narrator refers to many believing in Jesus "because they saw the signs" (v. 23; cf. 2:18). But faith based on seeing signs is inadequate. A deeper commitment that believes without seeing (6:26) is required. While looking back to the temple scene, these verses also serve to

---

1. I am rewording a phrase used by R. Alan Culpepper, "Nicodemus: The Travail of New Birth," in *Character Studies in the Fourth Gospel: Narrative Approaches to Seventy Figures in John*, ed. Steven A. Hunt, D. Francois Tolmie, and Ruben Zimmermann, WUNT 314 (Tübingen: Mohr Siebeck, 2013), 249.

²³When he was in Jerusalem during the Passover festival, many believed in his name because they saw the signs that he was doing. ²⁴But Jesus on his part would not entrust himself to them, because he knew all people ²⁵and needed no one to testify about anyone; for he himself knew what was in everyone.

³:¹Now there was a Pharisee named Nicodemus, a leader of the Jews. ²He came to him by night and said to him, "Rabbi, we know that you are a teacher who has come from God; for no one can do these signs that you do apart from the presence of God."

introduce the next episode through the repetition of the words ἄνθρωπος (human/man), τὰ σημεῖα (signs) and γινώσκω; οἶδα (know).[2] There is rich irony in the passage where many come to trust (ἐπίστευσαν) in Jesus, but he cannot entrust (ἐπίστευεν) himself to them; also the contrast between Jesus's knowledge (γινώσκειν) of these people and Nicodemus's claim to knowledge (οἴδαμεν) of Jesus.

TRANSLATION MATTERS

*The word ἄνθρωπος (translated by NRSV as "anyone" and "everyone" in v. 25) is an inclusive generic term accurately translated as a human (when referring to an individual), or humanity (when referring to humankind in general). But in order to bring out the ironic connections between these transitional verses and the Nicodemus episode, which are obvious in the Greek, I will translate these verses using "man": "Now when he was in Jerusalem at the Passover feast, many trusted in his name when they saw the signs which he did; but Jesus did not entrust himself to them, because he knew all *men* [πάντας] and needed no one to bear witness of *man* [ἀνθρώπου]; for he himself knew what was in *man* [ἀνθρώπῳ]. Now there was a *man* [ἄνθρωπος] of the Pharisees . . ."

The Waters and Breath of Life (3:1-10)

As the two male teachers dialogue, a mother's experience must be borne in mind. Dorothy Lee writes: "At the first level, for birth to be successful, the infant must pass through the waters of childbirth and

---

2. Other connections are: when Nicodemus is introduced, the text simply says, "He came to *him* by night," and the reader is meant to understand that the "him" is Jesus from 2:24; in fact most translations write Jesus instead of "him" in 3:1. The connective δέ (translated "now") relates what follows to what has gone before.

3:1Now there was a Pharisee named Nicodemus, a leader of the Jews. 2He came to Jesus by night and said to him, "Rabbi, we know that you are a teacher who has come from God; for no one can do these signs that you do apart from the presence of God." 3Jesus answered him, "Very truly, I tell you, no one can see the kingdom of God without being born from above." 4Nicodemus said to him, "How can anyone be born after having grown old? Can one enter a second time into the mother's womb and be born?" 5Jesus answered, "Very truly, I tell you, no one can enter the kingdom of God without being born of water and Spirit. 6What is born of the flesh is flesh, and what is born of the Spirit is spirit. 7Do not be astonished that I said to you, 'You must be born from above.' 8The wind blows where it chooses, and you hear the sound of it, but you do not know where it comes from or where it goes. So it is with everyone who is born of the Spirit." 9Nicodemus said to him, "How can these things be?" 10Jesus answered him, "Are you a teacher of Israel, and yet you do not understand these things?"

breathe into its nostrils the breath of life (cf. Gen 2:7). . . . The 'labor' to enter life . . . is difficult and painful, and the outcome uncertain, as Nicodemus' own story indicates."[3]

The dialogue between Nicodemus and Jesus, and the following discourse, are a rich and complex theological exposition of Jewish theology conducted by two Jewish teachers on matters of life and death. Nicodemus greets Jesus as "Rabbi," literally "my great one," and "teacher who has come from God" (v. 2). The dialogue concludes with Jesus's question to Nicodemus, "a teacher of Israel" (v. 10).

First-Century Jewish Background

Nicodemus is introduced as a Pharisee, which means he is a lay teacher of Israel's law in both its written (Scripture) and oral (tradition) forms.[4]

---

3. Dorothy A. Lee, *Flesh and Glory: Symbolism, Gender and Theology in the Gospel of John* (New York: Crossroad, 2002), 69. The expression "breath of life" is also found in Genesis 6:17 and 7:22. On the relationship between breath and life, as well as the Hebrew and Greek translations, see Matthew Edwards, *Pneuma and Realized Eschatology in the Book of Wisdom*, FRLANT 242 (Göttingen: Vandenhoeck & Ruprecht, 2012), 92–96.

4. The Pharisees are one of several groups to emerge within the Second Temple period, following the Maccabean revolt against Greek oppression in 160 BCE. While much about them is still obscure, a general portrait has emerged from the sources. They had a reputation as students and teachers of the Mosaic law, but they extended

One aspect of the developing oral tradition in late Second Temple Judaism was the question of life after death. Up until quite late, Israel had no theology of life beyond the grave. At death, one's personal life was over; one was cut off from the loving God and departed to the shadowy world of Sheol, from which there was no return.

In the postexilic time, and in response to the oppressive rule of the Greeks, which led some Jews to choose death rather than apostasy, the issue of God's justice arose. Surely the righteous, who died for their faith, would not remain in death forever. Surely God's justice demanded some postmortem restitution for these martyrs. The hope developed that at the end of time God would raise the righteous, restoring them to life in order to participate in the end-time reign of God, which is called in the Synoptic Gospels the βασιλεία τοῦ θεοῦ (usually translated the "kingdom/reign of God"). This final reign of God would come about when the world was liberated from the oppressive rule of evil. At such time the dead would be restored to life, they would face God's judgment, and the righteous would continue to live in God's presence.

This thinking about "the reign of God" and life after death was such a late development that there is nothing written on these beliefs within the Hebrew Scriptures. But we do find such concepts within the Greek Old Testament, the Septuagint. In the account of the martyrdom of the Maccabees, the second brother being tortured declares, "You accursed wretch, you dismiss us from this present life, but the King of the universe [κόσμου βασιλεὺς] will raise us up to an everlasting renewal of life [εἰς αἰώνιον ἀναβίωσιν ζωῆς], because we have died for his laws" (2 Macc 7:9). The third son "put out his tongue and courageously stretched forth his hands, and said nobly, 'I got these from Heaven, and because of his laws I disdain them, and from him I hope to get them back again'" (2 Macc 7:10-11).

Belonging to a group open to both the written and oral traditions, Nicodemus would have accepted this theology of a future resurrection

---

the law to include later traditions of the elders. For further discussion on the origins and beliefs of this group, see Bruce Chilton and Jacob Neusner, eds., *In Quest of the Historical Pharisees* (Waco, TX: Baylor University Press, 2007); Lawrence H. Schiffman, "Pharisees," in *Jewish Annotated New Testament*, ed. Amy-Jill Levine and Marc Zvi Brettler, 2nd ed. (Oxford: Oxford University Press, 2017), 619–22; and the proceedings from a conference held in 2019 in Rome titled "Jesus and the Pharisees: An Interdisciplinary Reappraisal," forthcoming from Eerdmans and available online at https://www.jesusandthepharisees.org.

and participation in the βασιλεία τοῦ θεοῦ. This is the issue at the heart of the discussion between these two Jewish teachers—the possibility (or not) of participating in the reign of God.

The following translation, which is my own, better shows the rhetoric and structure of the dialogue:

> ¹Now there was a man [ἄνθρωπος] of the Pharisees, named Nicodemus, a ruler of the Jews.
> ²He came to Jesus by night and said to him
> "Rabbi, we know that *you are a teacher* come from God;
> for it is *not possible* [οὐδεὶς δύναται] for anyone to do these signs that you do, unless God is with him."

Parable of Birth/Rebirth (vv. 3-5)[5]

> ³Jesus answered him saying,
> "Amen, Amen, I say to you, unless one is *born anew* [γεννηθῇ ἄνωθεν]
> it is *not possible* [οὐ δύναται] to see the reign of God [βασιλείαν τοῦ θεοῦ]."
> ⁴Nicodemus said to him,
> "How is it *possible* [δύναται] for a person to be born [γεννηθῆναι] when he is old?
> It is *not possible* [μὴ δύναται] to enter into the mother's womb a second [δεύτερον] time and be born."
> ⁵Jesus answered,
> "Amen, Amen, I say to you, unless one is born of water and the Spirit,
> it is *not possible* [οὐ δύναται] to enter into the reign of God [βασιλείαν τοῦ θεοῦ].

Principle

> ⁶What is born of the flesh is flesh,
> and what is *born of the Spirit* [πνεύματος] is spirit.

---

5. I consider that the imagery of birth and then the image of the wind (vv. 7-8) fit the definition of a parable. In a study of parable research and genre Ruben Zimmermann offers: "[T]the following criteria are employed for the 'parable' genre: A parable is a short, narratival (1), fictional (2) text that is related in the narrated world to known reality (3), but, by way of implicit or explicit transfer signals, makes it understood that the meaning of the narration must be differentiated from the literal words of the text (4). In its appeal structure (5) it challenges the reader to carry out a metaphoric transfer of meaning that is steered by co-textual and contextual information (6)." Ruben Zimmermann, "Are There Parables in John? It Is Time to Revisit the Question," *JSHJ* 9 (2011): 266. Rushton also names John 3:3-5 a parable: Kathleen P. Rushton, "The (Pro)creative Parables of Labour and Childbirth (John 3:1-10 and 16:21-22)," in *The Lost Coin: Parables of Women, Work, and Wisdom*, ed. Mary Ann Beavis, BibSem 86 (Sheffield: Sheffield Academic, 2002), 206–29.

Parable of the Wind (vv. 7-8)[6]

[7]Do not marvel that I said to you, 'You must be born from above [ἄνωθεν].'[7]

[8]The wind/spirit [πνεῦμα] blows where it wills, and you hear the sound of it,

but you do not know whence it comes or whither it goes;

so it is with everyone who is *born of the Spirit* [πνεύματος]."

Conclusion

[9]Replying, Nicodemus said to him, "How is this *possible* [δύναται]?"

[10]Replying, Jesus said to him "Are you *a teacher of Israel*, and yet you do not understand these things?"

"Secret Women's Business"[8]

Nicodemus approaches Jesus at night and recognizes him as a "teacher who has come from God" (v. 2) but does not grasp the deeper truth of his words.[9] Nicodemus considers that Jesus has "come" in much the same manner as the "sign-prophets" of Israel, such as Moses or Elijah, whose signs and wonders (Exod 7:3) testified to their being called to speak God's word. Jesus not only speaks the words of God but *is* the

---

6. A similar image based on the ephemeral nature of the "wind," "breath" is found in Wisdom 5:

All those things have vanished like a shadow,

as, when a bird flies through the air, no evidence of its passage is found;

the light wind [πνεῦμα] lashed by the beat of its pinions and pierced by the force of its rushing flight,

is traversed by the movement of its wings and afterward no sign of its coming is found there. (Wis 5:9, 11)

7. In this context, speaking of the Spirit (πνεύματος), I translate the term ἄνωθεν as "from above" rather than "again"; similarly in this parable πνεῦμα is best translated as "wind" rather than "spirit." The evangelist is exploiting the double meaning of these Greek terms.

8. Among Australian Aborigines, certain knowledge, rituals, and even sites are considered to be accessible only to women. Women pass on these traditions orally to trusted elders, called "aunties." Anything to do with procreation, pregnancy, or birth would be known as "secret women's business." Certainly, this would not be a fit topic for discussion by men—even respected teachers.

9. There are various suggestions why the evangelist has placed this encounter "at night." The most likely reason is that this is a discussion about Jewish belief between two teachers; the night meeting is in accord with Jewish practice of coming together to study the law at nighttime. See the many references to this practice in Craig S. Keener, *The Gospel of John: A Commentary*, 2 vols. (Peabody, MA: Hendrickson, 2003), 1:536 n. 24.

Word made flesh (1:14), present with God from all time (1:1), and now "come from God" as the unique revealer (1:18).

Echoing Nicodemus's own words, "not possible," Jesus responds by speaking of an aspect of Pharisaic teaching, namely, belief in a future reign of God that the righteous will share. Jesus teaches that it is possible to see the reign of God only by being born anew (ἄνωθεν). This word can mean to be born again/anew, and it could also mean to be born from above.[10] Nicodemus's response indicates that he has understood the first meaning but in a literal sense. He replies by speaking of being born a second (δεύτερον) time and offers the grotesque image of a person reentering a mother's womb to achieve such "second" birth, which he imagines is "not possible," as he states (v. 4).[11]

Jesus then clarifies what he means by being born anew, and who is the agent of this birth. "Unless one is born of water *and the Spirit*, it is not possible to enter into the reign of God" (v. 5; author's translation). This statement is followed by a principle that he would expect Nicodemus to agree with: "What is born of the flesh is flesh, and what is born of the Spirit is spirit" (v. 6). Jesus is speaking of a different type of birth, a different agent for this birth, and a different quality of life.[12]

A child enters into this world and is born into human life through the breaking of the mother's waters. This is the first birth, "born of water."[13]

---

10. While it does have these two senses, I agree with Ben Witherington, who states, "We are not dealing with a double entendre or a pun here (Nicodemus thinking Jesus means born again while Jesus means born from above), but rather the characteristic Johannine problem of two levels of understanding. Both Jesus and Nicodemus are referring to being born anew or again; the problem lies not in the meaning of the word, but in what it refers to." See Ben Witherington III, *John's Wisdom: A Commentary on the Fourth Gospel* (Louisville: Westminster John Knox, 1995), 95.

11. Behind Nicodemus's words about being born a second time may lie the platonic idea of the transmigration of the soul, where the soul had existence before entering the mother's body and survived beyond death. But the Pharisees did not believe in reincarnation of the soul; they believed in resurrection of the body. Nicodemus refutes the idea of being reincarnated through a second birth. See further Martha Himmelfarb, "Afterlife and Resurrection," in *The Jewish Annotated New Testament*, ed. Amy-Jill Levine et al. (Oxford: Oxford University Press, 2017), 691–95.

12. I agree with Witherington that when writing about "water and spirit" the evangelist is writing about "two parallel but different realities—physical birth and spiritual birth." See Ben Witherington III, "The Waters of Birth: John 3.5 and 1 John 5.6-8," *NTS* 35 (1989): 155.

13. Witherington examines both ancient Near Eastern literature and the OT and concludes that "in the ancient Near Eastern literature the word 'water' can be and is used as a *terminus technicus*, or at least a well-known circumlocution to matters involving procreation, . . . a circumlocution for semen, for amniotic fluid, or for the

Through this natural birth, the child enters into ordinary human life, sharing the conditions of all flesh, and will eventually die.[14] Ordinary human life has an end point in death. Jesus then speaks of another type of birth, that is, to be born of the Spirit. This birth brings one into a different quality of life, the life of the Spirit of God, and this life does not end in death. This life is the quality of God's own life in eternity, and the one who is born into this life can therefore participate in the reign of God.[15]

At this point further clarification is needed about the Johannine meaning of "the reign of God" (βασιλεία τοῦ θεοῦ) and what is meant by "life" within this reign.[16]

A Second Approach to Life after Death[17]

As noted above, one late concept in Second Temple Judaism was that of the future reign of God and the resurrection of the righteous at the end of time. This was one way of thinking about life after death, which

---

process of birth itself." Witherington, "The Waters of Birth," 156. This article gives details from ancient Jewish and non-Jewish sources.

14. See the discussion on the biblical meaning of "flesh" in the analysis of John 1:14. Flesh designates that which is bound by time and will eventually decay.

15. This new quality of life will be called by the evangelist ζωὴν αἰώνιον—which is usually translated "eternal life," but I prefer to translate as "eternity life" to emphasize that it is a new quality of life, not simply human life, but the life of the Spirit of God. More will be said on this when discussing John 3:15, which is the first occurrence of this expression in the Fourth Gospel. Second Temple Judaism had already begun to see a connection between God's eternal reign and life beyond death; this was clear in the citation above of 2 Macc 7:9. In her study of the theme of kingship in John, Beth M. Lovell (*Mapping Metaphorical Discourse: John's Eternal King*, LBS 5 [Leiden: Brill, 2012]) uses discourse analysis to draw together a number of related themes, such as the eternal reign of God and the gift of eternity life to God's children. John 3 is where some of these metaphors begin to coalesce.

16. See the excursus "ἡ βασιλεία τοῦ θεοῦ: The Kindom of God" at the end of this chapter.

17. A more detailed discussion of Jewish eschatological views and further references can be found in Mary L. Coloe, " 'The End Is Where We Start From': Afterlife in the Fourth Gospel," in *Living Hope—Eternal Death?! Conceptions of the Afterlife in Hellenism, Judaism and Christianity*, ed. Manfred Lang and Michael Labhan (Leipzig: Evangelische Verlagsanstalt, 2007), 177–99; also Sandra M. Schneiders, "The Resurrection (of the Body) in the Fourth Gospel: A Key to Johannine Spirituality," in *Life in Abundance: Studies of John's Gospel in Tribute to Raymond E. Brown*, ed. John R. Donahue (Collegeville, MN: Liturgical Press, 2005), 168–98.

Sandra Schneiders calls "resurrection eschatology."[18] But there was a second stream of thought emerging, perhaps even contemporary with the life of Jesus that is found in the book of Wisdom.[19] This book is possibly the latest in the Greek Old Testament, and it may have been written as late as 70 CE.[20] Here, probably influenced by Hellenistic views, we find a new thinking about human life in relationship with God, a new anthropology, and a new conception of eschatology.[21]

The Greeks considered that the gods were immortal because they were able to feed on heavenly ambrosia, which prevented their "atoms" from dissipating and corrupting.[22] Humans did not have access to this nectar of the gods, and so human life knew death, disintegration, and decay. When considering God's response to the death of the righteous, the book of Wisdom postulates that God gave the righteous, those who choose the way of Sophia, the gift of immortality, which is usually a quality of divine life, "For righteousness is immortal [δικαιοσύνη γὰρ ἀθάνατός ἐστιν]" (Wis 1:15). The righteous one already participates in the life of God and can be called a "child of the Lord" (παῖδα κυρίου, Wis 2:13), who "boasts that God is his father" (Wis 2:16). Drawing on the creation account of Genesis 1, the writer makes the bold claim, "for God created us for incorruption, and made us in the image of God's own eternity" (Wis 2:23). According to the book of Wisdom, the righteous only seem to die (Wis 3:2); in fact, they already have the gift of God's own "immortal [ἄφθαρτόν] spirit" (Wis 12:1), enabling them to live on "in the hand of God" (3:1) and "live forever" (εἰς τὸν αἰῶνα ζῶσιν, Wis 5:15).

What is noticeable in the book of Wisdom's concept of what it means to be human is that the divine gift of immortality is a gift given *prior* to death. The righteous, who have chosen the way of Sophia, live *now* with this gift of eternity life. Their mortal bodies will experience death, but

---

18. Schneiders, "The Resurrection (of the Body)," 174.

19. Bibles within the Catholic tradition consider the Book of Wisdom as deutero-canonical and include this book in their Bibles; in other Christian traditions these books are regarded as Apocrypha, and so many editions of the Bible do not include them. The theology of the book of Wisdom is essential for understanding John 3.

20. See John J. Collins, *Jewish Wisdom in the Hellenistic Age* (Edinburgh: T&T Clark, 1997), 179. More conservatively, David Winston places this book in Alexandria during the time of Caligula (37–41 CE); see David Winston, *The Wisdom of Solomon*, AB 43 (New York: Doubleday, 1979), 23.

21. These complex concepts involving both Hellenistic philosophy and Jewish theology are well treated by Edwards, *Pneuma and Realized Eschatology*, esp. chap. 7.

22. Collins, *Jewish Wisdom in the Hellenistic Age*, see 186, n. 16.

the eternity life they *now* possess will continue. Thus the righteous are able to see and enter into the reign of God.

One passage in the Book of Wisdom seems particularly appropriate to this meeting between two teachers:

> ¹⁷The beginning of wisdom is the most sincere desire for instruction [παιδείας],
> and concern for instruction is love of her,
> ¹⁸and love of her is the keeping of her laws [νόμων],
> and giving heed to her laws is assurance of immortality [ἀφθαρσίας],
> ¹⁹and immortality brings one near to God;
> ²⁰so the desire for wisdom [σοφίας] leads to a kingdom [βασιλείαν]. (Wis 6:17-20)

Nicodemus, a Pharisee, has a desire for instruction (παιδείας) and for the Torah (νόμων). He had thought that this was the way to "immortality [ἀφθαρσίας]" and nearness to God, and was the means of entry into the "kingdom [βασιλείαν]."[23] But Jesus challenges this perception. While we seem to be listening to the words of Jesus, we can also "overhear" the claims being made by members of the later Johannine community, who have come to believe that it is through Jesus, not the Torah, that one encounters Wisdom/Sophia. Jesus incarnates Sophia, and by committing oneself to Jesus one is brought near to God, thereby gaining immortality and entry into the reign of God. The book of Wisdom does not explicitly presume an end-time resurrection, although there seem to be hints of some future judgment of the wicked (Wis 4:20–5:13). But, as Sandra Schneiders comments, "while nothing is said of bodily resurrection in sapiential eschatology, it is fundamentally susceptible to it."[24]

The Nicodemus encounter is drawing on, and even developing further, sapiential ideas found across the book of Wisdom. It must also be noted that in the discussion with Nicodemus, Jesus speaks twice of "the reign of God" (τὴν βασιλείαν τοῦ θεοῦ) (3:3, 5). These are the only times in the Fourth Gospel where this expression is found. While Christian readers are very familiar with this expression from the Synoptic Gospels, it is a phrase that is not found in the Hebrew Old Testament and found only

---

23. The anarthrous βασιλείαν, "a kingdom," makes it unclear if this kingdom is the political kingdom gained by Solomon or the "reign of God." Whichever is intended, it is a present reality.

24. Schneiders, "The Resurrection (of the Body)," 175. More will be said on this when discussing John 6.

once in the Septuagint, in the book of Wisdom: "When a righteous man [Jacob] fled from his brother's wrath, she guided him on straight paths; she showed him the kingdom of God [βασιλείαν θεοῦ]" (Wis 10:10). The constellation of images across these verses (John 3:1-4), along with the use of this phrase found only in the book of Wisdom, makes a strong case for reading this Nicodemus passage in the light of the sapiential eschatology that Schneiders calls "exaltation eschatology."[25]

Born of Water (3:5-7)

In my reading of John 3, I understand the expression "born of water" as a reference to natural birth when a mother's waters break preceding the birth; this is the "first" birth experienced by all human beings, while to be "born again" refers to birth of the Spirit. More needs to be said about this interpretation as scholars are divided in their understanding. Raymond Brown, for example, interprets the expression γεννηθῇ ἄνωθεν to describe the begetting of a child through the male principle.[26] To be born of water would therefore refer to conception through male seminal fluid. Brown and C. K. Barrett then continue by interpreting "water and the Spirit" (v. 5) in terms of Christian baptism. On the contrary, although members of a Christian community may have heard echoes of its own water rituals, a sacramental interpretation must be secondary.[27]

---

25. Schneiders, "The Resurrection (of the Body)," 174.

26. Raymond E. Brown, *The Gospel according to John*, 2 vols., AB 29–29a (New York: Doubleday, 1966, 1970), 1:130. To be born "from above," born "of the Spirit," is then understood as a rather crude metaphor for being begotten by God. "A man takes on flesh and enters the kingdom of the world because his father begets him; a man can enter the kingdom of God only when he is begotten by a heavenly Father" (Brown, *The Gospel according to John*, 1:138). Similarly, Barrett speaks of "spiritual semen"; see Charles K. Barrett, *The Gospel according to St John*, 2nd ed. (London: SPCK, 1978), 209.

27. "Although the practice of baptism may stand somewhere behind the text, nothing stated by the narrator or by Jesus makes an association with baptism concrete"; see Larry Paul Jones, *The Symbol of Water in the Gospel of John*, JSNTSup 145 (Sheffield: Sheffield Academic, 1997), 76. Dorothy Lee (*Flesh and Glory*, 71) also comments, "It is likely that water, as a symbol, evokes both birth and baptism in this passage, the text making no attempt to delimit the symbolic meaning. While Christian baptism is not the primary focus of the dialogue, John's symbolism is evocative in a number of directions and suggests a wider field of meaning." Ben Witherington (*John's Wisdom*, 97) is even more forceful: "The Johannine community was interested in focusing on Christological, not ecclesiological or sacramental matters." For a discussion of criteria

The Nicodemus passage uses the word "born" several times: born anew/from above (3:3, 7), born having grown old (3:4), enter the mother's womb and be born (3:4), born of water and the Spirit (3:5), born of the flesh (3:6), born of the Spirit (3:6, 8). In all of these cases the Greek verb used is γεννάω. In Greek there are two verbs used to denote both begetting by a male or birthing by a female, γίνομαι and γεννάω. While both can be used of either male begetting or female birthing, γίνομαι "tends to be used more frequently for male begetting" and γεννάω to describe a woman giving birth.[28] In this passage, the meaning of the verb is clarified by Nicodemus's statement (3:4) when the verb is used to speak of reentering the mother's womb to be born (γεννηθῆναι) a second time. Disagreeing with Brown's view that this passage is an image of God as a father begetting (conceiving) children, I believe that the passage presents an image of God as mother giving birth to her children. This image of a birthing mother also suggests the labor and suffering such womb-birth entails. Here we may have a suggestion of the cross, just as at Cana it was suggested by the use of "the hour" (2:4) and in the temple by the Psalm citation, which spoke of an all-consuming zeal (2:17).[29] This Gospel has previously blurred gender boundaries in the prologue: "But to all who received him, who believed in his name, he gave power to become children of God [τέκνα θεοῦ γενέσθαι], who were born, not of blood or of the will of the flesh or of the will of man, but [born] of God [ἐκ θεοῦ ἐγεννήθησαν]" (1:12-13).[30] Both verbs γίνομαι and γεννάω are used here. The prologue then concludes with the image of the Son nestled close to the Father's *breast* (κόλπον).[31]

---

for reading passages sacramentally, see Francis J. Moloney, "When Is John Talking about Sacraments?," *ABR* 30 (1982): 10–33.

28. Barbara E. Reid, "Birthed from the Side of Jesus (John 19:34)," in *Finding a Woman's Place: Essays in Honor of Carolyn Osiek, R.S.C.J.*, ed. David L. Balch and Jason T. Lamoreaux (Eugene, OR: Pickwick, 2011), 192.

29. A first-time reader may miss these hints of the passion, but the Johannine community, knowing this Gospel's Christology, style, and narrative, can read this passage and marvel at its artistry and depth. When discussing John 1:19-51 I referred to the work of Paul Ricoeur who speaks of a "second naïveté" in returning to a literary work a second time, bringing to this second reading the insights gained from the first reading. The second reading brings a deeper level of perception that makes possible the disclosure of deeper levels of meaning; see Ricoeur, *Interpretation Theory: Discourse and the Surplus of Meaning* (Fort Worth: Texas Christian University Press, 1976), 4.

30. When discussing these verses in the prologue (1:10-13) I presented a number of passages from the OT where God is portrayed as a mother, so the image of a birthing mother would not be foreign to the evangelist's community.

31. Reid, "Birthed from the Side of Jesus," 192–93.

The Parable of the Wind (3:8)

To further clarify his teaching, Jesus offers a parable drawing on the verbal similarity between the Spirit (πνεύματος) and the wind (πνεῦμα). The parable emphasizes hearing rather than seeing; "the sound of it you hear, but you do not know [οὐκ οἶδας] whence it comes or whither it goes" (3:8; author's translation). The verb "to know" that is used here is the same verb used to describe Nicodemus "knowing" that Jesus is a teacher come from God (3:2), and this knowledge is based on seeing signs. It is knowledge in the sense of perception.[32] Jesus is challenging Nicodemus to move beyond faith based on *seeing* to faith based on *hearing*, i.e., to hearing and entrusting himself to Jesus's words, even though these words may be mysterious, like the wind.

Spirit and Wisdom: Pneuma and Sophia

In the Hebrew Scriptures both Spirit (רוח) and wisdom (חכמה) are grammatically feminine words and have similar functions, particularly in the task of creation and giving life. In Genesis the spirit (רוח) hovers over the waters and ushers in God's work of creation (Gen 1:2). As well as the task of creation, the spirit is also an agent in God's salvific work, in raising up leaders (e.g., Joshua, Num 27:18; David, 1 Sam 16:13; Saul, 1 Sam 10:10) and prophets (1 Kgs 18:12; Mic 3:8; Ezek 2:2; Zech 7:12). Then when Israel is in exile Ezekiel has a vision of the spirit rushing into the dry bones and restoring them to life (Ezek 37:1-10); this vision of resurrection holds the promise of what God can do for Israel.

These functions of creation and salvation aligned with God's Spirit are transposed to Sophia in the wisdom literature. Sophia is the agent of creation and life in the great songs of Proverbs (8:22-31) and Sirach (24:1-17). The book of Wisdom describes Sophia's role in creation as a "craftswoman" (τεχνῖτις) and the source of all Solomon's knowledge, "for wisdom, the fashioner of all things, taught me" (ἡ γὰρ πάντων τεχνῖτις

---

32. Throughout this passage the verb used to describe Jesus's "knowing" is γινώσκω (2:24, 25; 3:10), which has the sense of coming to understand something, of acquiring knowledge. Another verb for "knowing" (οἶδα) is related to sight (εἰδέα) and has the sense of certain conviction or intuitive knowing. Nicodemus knows with certainty that Jesus is a man of God because he has seen the signs (3:2). At the close of the dialogue Jesus asks, "Are you a teacher of Israel and have not come to (understand) this?" (3:10). On the use of these two verbs, see Ignace De La Potterie, "Οἶδα et γινώσκω: Les deux modes de la connaissance dans le quatrième évangile," *Bib* 40 (1959): 709–25.

ἐδίδαξέν με σοφία; Wis 7:22).[33] Sophia "reaches mightily from one end of the earth to the other, and she orders all things well" (Wis 8:1), thus she was present when God made the world and knows God's works (9:1). For this reason Solomon prays for Wisdom, which can only come as God's gift. Here, the parallelisms bring Wisdom and Spirit together.

> Who has learned your counsel,
> unless you have given wisdom
> and sent your holy spirit from on high? (Wis 9:17)

Wisdom is known on earth, not only in the cosmic order, but also in Israel's history of salvation. Solomon's prayer concludes with

> And thus the paths of those on earth were set right,
> and people were taught what pleases you,
> and were saved by wisdom [καὶ τῇ σοφίᾳ ἐσώθησαν]. (9:18)

The prayer then leads into a description of Sophia's saving acts, as Solomon narrates Israel's story, beginning with Adam (10:1). Sophia then steered Noah's boat (10:4), saved Lot (10:5), guided Jacob (10:10), delivered Joseph (10:13), and rescued Israel from Egypt, "a nation of oppressors" (10:15). In the wilderness journey it was Sophia who provided water (11:4, 7), quails (16:2), and the food of angels as bread ready to eat (16:20).[34]

In this book, Wisdom and Spirit are both described as agents of immortality:

"In kinship with wisdom there is immortality [ἀθανασία]" (Wis 8:17), and later, "for your immortal [ἄφθαρτόν] spirit is in all things" (12:1). In his study of the spirit and eschatology in the book of Wisdom, Matthew Edwards concludes that wisdom and spirit are so closely coupled that he uses the term *pneuma*-Sophia[35] and describes three times where the phrase, "the Spirit of wisdom" (חכמה רוח) occurs (Exod 28:3; Deut 34:9; Isa 11:2). Although Sophia is not named in John 3, her close association with creation, life, and the Spirit, in addition to the strong resonances with the book of Wisdom, provides traces of her subtle presence in this narrative.

---

33. Sophia the craftswoman is also described in Wis 8:6; 14:2.

34. The feminine pronoun "she" (Αὕτη) is used at the beginning of chapter 10, referring back to Sophia at the end of Solomon's prayer (9:18). Sophia is then named explicitly in 10:4, 8, 10, 21. She is not explicitly named beyond chapter 10.

35. Edwards, *Pneuma and Realized Eschatology*, 131, 82.

A Pregnant Pause (3:9-10)

The dialogue ends with Nicodemus unable to move beyond the literalness of Jesus's words and he asks, "How is this possible?" (author's translation). Jesus ironically replies, "Are you a teacher of Israel and yet you do not understand these things?"[36] Although Nicodemus leaves, apparently baffled by Jesus's words, his journey is not yet complete and his story will continue in chapters 7 and 19. In a sense Nicodemus has begun the passage to birth into the *basileia*, but at this point his bewilderment puts him on hold. He can get no further but must wait with puzzlement and uncertainty. As a mother knows, birthing takes time and cannot be rushed. The labor for Nicodemus will continue in chapter 7, where his question about proper process is met with hostility. Only in chapter 19 do we see signs that Nicodemus has been born anew; with tender yet dramatic irony he is the one to anoint and wrap the body of Jesus in death (19:39-40). While Raymond Collins describes Nicodemus as a representative figure of "official Judaism,"[37] I consider he is too sharply drawn as a character to be merely a spokesperson for a group. He engages with Jesus in this dialogue, keeps asking questions, and remains baffled within the limits of his Pharisaic traditions. As Alan Culpepper states, "The character is never merely a cipher for a statement about a theme, and as a character Nicodemus transcends the themes with which he is linked."[38]

Passage toward Light (3:11-21)

Nicodemus seems to depart following verse 11, and Jesus's audience is no longer σύ, "you" singular, but ὑμῖν, "you" plural (v. 12); Jesus also speaks as if he is representing a group: "we speak," "we know," "we have seen," "our testimony" (v. 11). Although the characters seem to be different, the discourse follows the literary shape of the preceding dialogue and continues its themes.

---

36. I consider Jesus's response to be ironic rather than "accusatory," which is how Reinhartz reads this conclusion. Adele Reinhartz, "The Gospel of John," in *Searching the Scriptures*, vol. 2: *A Feminist Commentary*, ed. Elisabeth Schüssler Fiorenza (New York: Crossroad, 1994), 570.

37. Raymond F. Collins, *These Things Have Been Written: Studies on the Fourth Gospel*, Louvain Theological and Pastoral Monographs 2 (Louvain: Peeters, 1990), 14–16, 56–67.

38. Culpepper, "Nicodemus: The Travail of New Birth," 249.

John 3:11-21

¹¹"Very truly, I tell you, we speak of what we know and testify to what we have seen; yet you do not receive our testimony. ¹²If I have told you about earthly things and you do not believe, how can you believe if I tell you about heavenly things? ¹³No one has ascended into heaven except the one who descended from heaven, the Son of Man. ¹⁴And just as Moses lifted up the serpent in the wilderness, so must the Son of Man be lifted up, ¹⁵that whoever believes in him may have eternal life.

¹⁶"For God so loved the world that he gave his only Son, so that everyone who believes in him may not perish but may have eternal life.

¹⁷"Indeed, God did not send the Son into the world to condemn the world, but in order that the world might be saved through him. ¹⁸Those who believe in him are not condemned; but those who do not believe are condemned already, because they have not believed in the name of the only Son of God. ¹⁹And this is the judgment, that the light has come into the world, and people loved darkness rather than light because their deeds were evil. ²⁰For all who do evil hate the light and do not come to the light, so that their deeds may not be exposed. ²¹But those who do what is true come to the light, so that it may be clearly seen that their deeds have been done in God."

The introduction to the discourse (v. 11) repeats the themes of knowing, seeing (ἑωράκαμεν), and witnessing (μαρτυροῦμεν) found in the introduction to the dialogue with Nicodemus (2:23–3:2). This leads into the contrast between earthly things and heavenly things (v. 12), which parallels the contrast established in the dialogue between two births— ordinary birth of water and a new birth of the Spirit that enables access to the reign of God (3:3-5). In the dialogue and discourse principles are announced (vv. 6, 13), followed by an image: in the dialogue it has the form of the parable of the wind (v. 8); in the discourse it has the form of the typology of the bronze serpent (vv. 14-15). Both images conclude with the phrase "so it is" (οὕτως; vv. 8, 14). The conclusion (vv. 16-21) brings to an end the issue raised in the dialogue with Nicodemus, the issue of the Pharisaic belief in life after death when there will be a final judgment before the righteous enter the reign of God. Just as in the dialogue Jesus made birth in the Spirit a present reality, in these concluding verses he brings into the present both judgment (κρίσις) and eternity life (ζωὴν αἰώνιον, v. 15); these are conditional upon the choice to believe or not believe in him.

The structure enables further clarification of the issues raised in the dialogue. The phrase "everyone who is born of the Spirit" (v. 8) is clarified by the parallel statement "everyone who believes in him" (v. 18; author's translation), where "him" refers to the "human-one" (ὁ υἱὸς τοῦ ἀνθρώπου).[39] Belief is the means of being born anew. In the dialogue, being born of the Spirit/born anew gives one access to the reign of God (vv. 3, 5). In the discourse, one may have "eternity life" through belief in "the human-one" (v. 15). The phrase "the reign of God" will no longer appear in the Fourth Gospel, but this reality will be expressed by the Johannine equivalent "eternity life."[40] This phrase draws on the book of Wisdom's theology that God gives the righteous a share in God's own immortal Spirit (Wis 12:1), enabling the righteous to live forever (εἰς τὸν αἰῶνα ζῶσιν, Wis 5:15). In Johannine terms, those who believe participate already in the life of God. They need not wait in death for an end-time resurrection. Eternity life is brought into the present in and through Jesus. Eternity life is now!

The principle stated in verse 13 speaks of "the human-one" as the only one who can reveal heavenly things. This statement counters claims made within first-century Judaism that Moses ascended to heaven and then returned with divine revelation.[41] Jesus, the incarnate Word, is the only one who has come from God and is the unique revealer. The figure of "the human-one" is then compared to the figure of the bronze serpent that Moses made and raised on a pole to protect the Israelites in the wilderness. Just as the bronze serpent was lifted up and brought salvation to Israel, so also "the human-one" must be lifted up as a means of salvation. Once again the book of Wisdom provides a likely background for this typology. Here we find an account of the episode found in Numbers that has a number of associations with Johannine thought.

---

39. See the excursus (p. 50) on the origin and meaning of ὁ υἱὸς τοῦ ἀνθρώπου.

40. The expression ζωὴν αἰώνιον (which I translate "eternity life") occurs in 3:15, 16, 36; 4:14, 36; 5:24, 39; 6:27, 40, 47, 54, 68; 10:28; 12:25, 50; 17:2; and αἰώνιος ζωὴ in 17:3. The translation "eternity life" places emphasis on the quality of life offered, the life of God in eternity.

41. For a detailed discussion of these verses, see Francis J. Moloney, *The Johannine Son of Man*, 2nd rev. ed., Biblioteca di Scienze Religiose 14 (Rome: LAS, 1978), 42–67.

Numbers 21:6-9	Wisdom 16:5-6	John 3:14-15
⁶Then the LORD sent poisonous serpents among the people, and they bit the people, so that many Israelites died. ⁷The people came to Moses and said, "We have sinned by speaking against the LORD and against you; pray to the LORD to take away the serpents from us." So Moses prayed for the people. ⁸And the LORD said to Moses, "Make a poisonous serpent, and set it on a standard [ἐπὶ σημείου; LXX]; and everyone who is bitten shall look at it and live." ⁹So Moses made a serpent of bronze, and put it upon a standard [ἐπὶ σημείου]; and whenever a serpent bit someone, that person would look at the serpent of bronze and live.	⁵For when the terrible rage of wild animals came upon your people and they were being destroyed by the bites of writhing serpents, your wrath did not continue to the end; ⁶they were troubled for a little while as a warning, and received *a symbol of salvation* [σύμβολον ἔχοντες σωτηρίας] to remind them of your law's command. ⁷For the one who turned toward it was saved, not by the thing that was beheld, but by you [Sophia], the Savior of all [τὸν πάντων σωτῆρα].	¹⁴As Moses lifted up the serpent in the wilderness, so it is that "the human-one" must be lifted up, ¹⁵that everyone who believes in him may have *eternity life*. (Author's translation)

In Numbers, Moses is told to make a serpent and set it upon a standard, נס, usually translated "pole." In the Septuagint, it is rendered σημείον, which in the Fourth Gospel has already been used to speak of the "signs" of Jesus. The book of Wisdom then develops this sense of σημείον and speaks of the raised serpent as a *symbol of salvation*; in the Gospel, the uplifted "human-one" is to be a sign and source of eternity life (v. 14), which the following verses show to be equivalent to salvation.

For God so loved the world	For God sent the Son into the world
that s/he gave the only-born Son,	
that whoever believes in him should not perish	not to judge the world
but have *eternity life*. (v. 16)	but that through him the world might be *saved*. (v. 17)

Since the fundamental symbol in the pericope relies on birth from the mother's womb, it seems appropriate to continue the image of birth and to speak of Jesus as "the only-born" (μονογενῆ) Son of God in verses 16 and 18.[42]

The Gospel draws the parallel between the lifted-up serpent and the lifted-up "human-one" as a symbol of salvation, or, in Johannine terms, eternity life.[43] The serpent is the type of a savior; Jesus is the antitype. The serpent narrative, told through the lens of Wisdom, provides the most likely background for the theme of salvation introduced in the Nicodemus passage and rarely used in the Fourth Gospel. The book of Wisdom makes clear that it is not the serpent itself that is the source of salvation but Sophia, who is called "the savior of all" (Wis 16:7).

The Johannine use of the phrase "the human one," both here and throughout the Gospel, establishes that the title refers to the crucified and exalted Jesus.[44] The Greek verb ὑψόω means both to lift up literally, as on a cross, but also figuratively with the sense of "to exalt." In John both meanings must be held together in the one act of Jesus's "return to

---

42. On the symbol of divine motherhood, see Lee, *Flesh and Glory*, 135–65. Its purpose here is to signify the uniqueness of Jesus vis-à-vis the believers, who are also to be "born" of God and be called "children of God" (1:12-13).

43. Moloney (*The Johannine Son of Man*, 64) writes: "The point of comparison between the raised serpent and the elevated Christ is that all who believe may have eternal life in him." While the typology of the Serpent-Jesus is strange, it is found in the Letter of Barnabas 12:5-7: "Finally Moses . . . made them a symbol of Jesus. So Moses made a bronze serpent and set it up conspicuously." Through this typology the evangelist reverses the symbol of the cross from a sign of degradation to a sign of triumph.

44. On the use of this title refer to the excursus (p. 50): "The Son of Man"; ὁ υἱὸς τοῦ ἀνθρώπου.

the Father" via the cross. It is not exaltation *following* crucifixion but exaltation *in and through* the cross, the great symbol of salvation (Wis 16:6).

This last sentence is problematic and must be understood in its context and as a later interpretation of a horrific event. Suffering and the cross can be misused in ways that contribute to the ongoing oppression of people. Simplistic platitudes such as "offer it up" or "think of Jesus" distort the Gospel and are used to keep vulnerable people, such as children, the elderly, and women who are abused, in silence. The Gospel is a message of life in its fullness (10:10), and anything that detracts from such fullness of life is not to be spiritualized. When this is done deliberately to maintain the subjugation of another, it must be named as evil.

Within the early community of believers, the cross became the great enigma. How could a crucified savior be proclaimed? Or where is God in the crucifixion of Jesus? Within Paul's preaching and the Gospels we find many and quite different approaches to this question, and most responses draw on Jewish theological thinking about the world, the powers of evil apparently loose within the world, and yet a hope for the in-breaking of God's spirit.[45] From this maelstrom of conflicting ideas, images, and memories, the Fourth Evangelist offers his insight.

The meaning of the cross will become clearer as the narrative progresses, but put simply here, the evangelist does not present Jesus as a victim of external forces. Jesus has come as the one sent from God to engage in battle with evil powers. Jesus makes choices, and we will see that, against the advice of his disciples, he chooses to return to Bethany in Judea. It is his choices that set in process the choices of other people and ultimately the decision by the Roman procurator Pilate. Before Pilate Jesus asserts that the procurator has no power over him (19:11) and then carries his own cross to Golgotha (19:17). Even on the cross his mission actively continues until he breathes down the Spirit on a fledgling community and knows that his mission is now complete. From John's perspective Jesus triumphs over the powers of evil. Suffering is *not* the agent of salvation but results from the choices made by Jesus, which he describes as *love*: "No one has greater love than this, to lay down one's life for one's friends" (John 15:13).

Conclusion

Jesus's opening remarks to Nicodemus spoke of being born anew as the requirement for accessing the reign of God. Set against the back-

---

45. See the earlier discussion of this at John 1:29-34, pp. 39–42.

ground of the book of Wisdom, Jesus speaks of a Spirit-generated birth through which a believer enters into not simply ordinary, mortal life but a quality of heavenly or eternity life. As a Pharisee, Nicodemus could have been expected to have some perception of a renewal of life, but he understood this in terms of a future resurrection. The Johannine Jesus speaks as divine Sophia, whose children (Prov 2:1; Sir 2:1; 4:10-11; Wis 2:13) participate in the life of God *now*, sharing God's own eternity life, which is this Gospel's understanding of what salvation means. God's gift of salvation for the world is the loving gift of the "only-born son" (3:16). Belief in him brings about a new birth making eternity life possible now. In words reminiscent of the prologue, the discourse concludes with images of light and darkness to convey that judgment is *already* operative in the choices people make now in response to Jesus. The dialogue with Jesus began in the night and these final words about light and darkness reflect back across this entire encounter. Nicodemus has come at night; thus he is associated with darkness, and his perception of Jesus as a sign prophet is inadequate. The dialogue dramatizes the choice that must be made, a choice for the light, through belief in Jesus, or a choice to remain in the dark. At this point in the Gospel Nicodemus must remain an ambiguous character. In coming to Jesus he has begun to move from the darkness to the light, but this initial encounter is inconclusive. As Jouette Bassler writes, "This text does not provide the final word on this figure."[46] His journey will continue (7:50; 19:39).

John's Testimony (3:22-30)

Following the Nicodemus passage, the figure of John returns, reminding the reader that the sequence from 1:19 has been initiated by John and has followed the normal sequence in establishing a household. The bridegroom's friend initiates the process by being the voice and witness to the bridegroom in the prenuptial negotiations. He is the one through whom the bride is introduced to the groom, who often leads the bride to the wedding feast, who conducts the groom into the wedding chamber in the father's house, and who bears witness to the consummation of the marriage, which would lead hopefully to the birth of a child. In a sense, John has overseen the progression of the narrative so far, from the initial gathering of disciples, their participation in a wedding, then

---

46. Jouette M. Bassler, "Mixed Signals: Nicodemus in the Fourth Gospel," *JBL* 108 (1989): 635–46.

John 3:22-30

²²After this Jesus and his disciples went into the Judean countryside, and he spent some time there with them and baptized. ²³John also was baptizing at Aenon near Salim because water was abundant there; and people kept coming and were being baptized ²⁴—John, of course, had not yet been thrown into prison.

²⁵Now a discussion about purification arose between John's disciples and a Jew. ²⁶They came to John and said to him, "Rabbi, the one who was with you across the Jordan, to whom you testified, here he is baptizing, and all are going to him." ²⁷John answered, "No one can receive anything except what has been given from heaven. ²⁸You yourselves are my witnesses that I said, 'I am not the Messiah, but I have been sent ahead of him.' ²⁹He who has the bride is the bridegroom. The friend of the bridegroom, who stands and hears him, rejoices greatly at the bridegroom's voice. For this reason my joy has been fulfilled. ³⁰He must increase, but I must decrease."

being included with the brothers and sisters of Jesus in going with his mother to Capernaum, then entering with Jesus into his Father's house (2:16). The Nicodemus episode concludes this sequence in its teaching that these disciples, who are believing in Jesus, are experiencing a process of new birth enabling them to see the reign of God and hear the voice of the Spirit (3:8) dwelling in Jesus (1:33). New life is beginning in the household. John's role is now complete. He now explicitly names himself as the bridegroom's friend and withdraws from the narrative, saying, "He must increase, but I must decrease" (3:30).

John's statement can cause disquiet for some reading this as a reflection of social mores when women were expected to be subservient to their father, husband, and, later, adult sons. But this is to take John's words out of context. He is speaking theologically, noting his important role to be one sent from God to bear witness. His task is now complete. His witness has borne fruit in the gathering of disciples around Jesus. It is a statement of his fulfilment allowing him now to withdraw from this ministry, as Jesus has now begun his own task. Facing the envious words of his disciples, comparing themselves to the disciples of Jesus, John challenges them with the truth of his identity and therefore their own. This is no competition. John is secure in his own identity, role, and integrity. He has no need to compete with Jesus, nor does he need to put another in a subservient role to increase his stature. We know from history that John continued to bear prophetic witness against Herod, leading ultimately to his death.

Conclusion to This Section (3:31-36)

The sequence from John's opening words to his final testimony (1:19–3:30) is set within the world of Judaism. As we have seen, some Jews, Jesus's mother and disciples, respond positively to him by accepting his words of invitation and enter into his household of disciples. These believers have eternity life. But there are others, like Nicodemus, who cannot yet receive Jesus's words but require signs that they can perceive and comprehend. The only sign that Jesus will offer is the lifting up of the human-one as a symbol of the world's salvation. And there are some, like "the Jews" in the temple, who completely reject his words and person. The conclusion to this section recalls Jesus's identity and mission as the one who has come from above and as Son can reveal God.

There is no explicit mention of Sophia, or citation from the book of Wisdom, but this chapter draws on Wisdom's theology to speak of the *kindom* of God, of eternity life, and of salvation. The chapter has also brought into the foreground the image of God as a birthing mother, an image that will recur later in the Gospel (16:21-22; 19:34). Jesus is the embodiment of Sophia, and belief in Jesus will lead to friendship (John 15:14-15) and kinship (John 20:17) and so

> In kinship with *Sophia* there is immortality [ἀθανασία],
> and in friendship with her, pure delight. (Wis 8:17-18)

ἡ βασιλεία τοῦ θεοῦ: The Kindom of God

In the Fourth Gospel we find this expression only at 3:3, 5, whereas it is a key part of Jesus's preaching in the Synoptic Gospels. It is frequently translated as "the kingdom of God." The phrase is a shorthand means of expressing the full eschatological and liberative plan of God. It is God's desire for the world, and when this comes to fruition all the forces that mitigate against or crush the fullness of life will be overcome.[47] Rather than this image of the βασιλεία, the Fourth Gospel describes the fullness of life with the expression "eternity life" (ζωὴ αἰώνιος).[48] This fullness of life is what Jesus came to bring (John 10:10), and in his teaching and praxis he demonstrated that it is life for the poor,

---

47. This apocalyptic perspective of late Second Temple Jewish theology was discussed previously when examining John 1:29-34, (pp. 39–42).

48. 3:15, 16, 36; 4:14, 36; 5:24, 39; 6:27, 40, 47, 54, 68; 10:28; 12:25, 50; 173.

John 3:31-36

[31]The one who comes from above is above all; the one who is of the earth belongs to the earth and speaks about earthly things. The one who comes from heaven is above all. [32]He testifies to what he has seen and heard, yet no one accepts his testimony. [33]Whoever has accepted his testimony has certified this, that God is true. [34]He whom God has sent speaks the words of God, for he gives the Spirit without measure. [35]The Father loves the Son and has placed all things in his hands. [36]Whoever believes in the Son has eternal life; whoever disobeys the Son will not see life, but must endure God's wrath.

the ill, the tax collectors, the lepers, the prostitutes, and all those considered outcasts. The clearest image of this praxis is companionship with Jesus around the meal table (Luke 15:1-2).

A study of this expression in its earliest, pre-Gospel form in the Q source reveals that images of ἡ βασιλεία emerge from within women's everyday experience—sweeping, spinning, singing, grinding grain, cooking, tending children.

> Specifically, Q creates a new metaphor of "the *basileia* of God as a homey place" through its metonymic mappings of domestic reality. . . .
> A striking fact is that this domestic setting of the *basileia* of God is more concretely depicted by the metonymy of women's daily labors and activities: cleaning the house (15:8-9; 11:24-26), making food (13:20-21; 14:34), birthing children (7:26), feeding children (11:11-12), spinning cloth for clothes (12:26-27), being concerned about providing bread (11:2), grinding grain (17:35). Most references to the *basileia* of God in Q are related to women's daily labors, with the exceptions of the Beelzebub debate (11:14-22), the parable of "the Builders" (6:47-49), and Q 11:52; 16:16.[49]

The study by In-Hee Park of the *ur-source* Q takes the βασιλεία from the military realm of men and royal courts into the domestic world.

> These domestic, and generally peaceful, images supplant the masculinist image of the Kingdom of God (His Kingdom), with its connotation of the cruelty of war. Scenes of violent battle give way to the rhythms and warmth of home life through the vivid meton-

---

49. In-Hee Park, "Women and Q: Metonymy of the *Basileia* of God," *JFSR* 35 (2019): 47.

ymy of the daily life of ordinary women (Q 6:20-21, 35, 36; 10:2-9, 10:21; 11:3, 9-13; 12:22-31; 13:20-21; 15:8-9). Domestic space—traditionally deemed marginal or secondary to a male public sphere and representative of women's submission to male rule—becomes the scene of God's reign.[50]

Park's study may explain why the phrase is used here in John, in the context of a discussion about birth, which is clearly women's business. Kathleen Rushton also notes that the juxtaposition of birth and βασιλεία is noteworthy. "It is significant that this female image is found in association with the only explicit mention of the metaphor 'the reign of God' (ἡ βασιλείαν τοῦ θεοῦ) in the Fourth Gospel (3.3, 5)."[51] Because the English term "kingdom" has come to be equated with male military and political power, the expression "kingdom of God" no longer conveys the apocalyptic, feminine, and liberative force of the βασιλεία and is now a dead metaphor. While some use "the reign of God" as an alternative, I prefer the expression "kindom" of God, for its evocation of kinship, intimacy, and being in relationship. Kindom also refers to the means of gaining immortality through Sophia (Wis 8:17).

---

50. Park, "Women and Q," 48.
51. Rushton, "The (Pro)creative Parables," 226.

John 4:1-45

A Woman's Witness
in Samaria[1]

It [Wisdom/Law] runs over, like the Euphrates, with understanding,
  and like the Jordan at harvest time.
It pours forth instruction like the Nile,
  like the Gihon at the time of vintage.
The first [person] did not know wisdom fully,
  nor will the last one fathom her.
For her thoughts are more abundant than the sea,
  and her counsel deeper than the great abyss. (Sir 24:26-29)[2]

1. For detailed analysis and further arguments on issues raised in this commentary, see chap. 5 of Mary L. Coloe, *God Dwells with Us: Temple Symbolism in the Fourth Gospel* (Collegeville, MN: Liturgical Press, 2001), 285. Along with a number of other scholars I do not consider that this encounter records a historical event, but it has been developed as an aspect of the Gospel's theology and to support the likely participation in the post-Easter community of Samaritans along with Jews and Gentiles. This is the position argued in Sandra M. Schneiders, *Written That You May Believe: Encountering Jesus in the Fourth Gospel*, rev. and exp. ed. (New York: Crossroad, 2003), 134–35. Jean Zumstein accurately states: "Critics are unanimous in discerning in John 4 a masterpiece of the Johannine school's reworking an ancient tale whose origin remains uncertain." Jean Zumstein, *L'Évangile selon Saint Jean (1–12)*, CNT 4a 2nd ser. (Genève: Labor et Fides, 2014), 143–45. Zumstein then shows that the scene may have developed from an OT "type-scene" of a man and a woman meeting at a well leading on to a marriage. Brown also raises questions about the plausibility of the encounter but allows for the possibility of a "substratum of traditional material, the evangelist has taken . . . and formed it into a superb theological scenario." Raymond E. Brown, *The Gospel according to John*, 2 vols., AB 29–29A (New York: Doubleday, 1966, 1970), 1:176.

2. The book of Sirach, also known as Ecclesiasticus or Ben Sira, is a later biblical book (ca. 200 BCE) written in Greek, and so not included in the Hebrew canon but

In the previous chapters the setting has been in the Jewish regions of Galilee and Judea. In chapter 4, Jesus moves beyond Jewish territory into Samaria. The statement "he had to go through Samaria" (4:4) reflects a theological necessity linked to Jesus's mission that the world might be saved (3:17). Geographically there were alternate routes that would usually have been taken by a Jewish person to avoid going through Samaria.

In order to understand this rich theological discussion with the Samaritan woman there are a number of important OT texts to be aware of and two primary symbols of Jesus's identity revealed in the narrative so far to be conscious of—that Jesus is the bridegroom and the temple. In this chapter, an understanding of these two symbols is necessary if a modern reader is to follow the narrative.

Wells and Betrothals (4:1-6)

The introductory verses provide essential information for interpreting the following dialogue. Jacob is named twice (vv. 5, 6) and reference is made to his well. Jesus rests on the well, and the time is given literally as "about the sixth hour," i.e., the middle of the day.[3] These associations reverberate with the episode in Genesis 29:1-9 where Jacob comes to a well in the middle of the day and meets Rachel, his future wife.

The meeting of a man and a woman at a well is called a "type" scene. The well is the typical meeting place that will lead to betrothal and marriage: e.g., where Abraham's servant meets Rebecca, the future wife of Isaac (Gen 24:10-33); Jacob meets Rachel (Gen 29:1-14); and Moses meets

---

found in the Septuagint (LXX). It is included in the Catholic canon a deuterocanonical book; Protestant Christian denominations consider it Apocrypha and so it is excluded from some Bibles.

3. There were two different ways of telling time in the first century. The official Roman time, according to the priests, went from midnight to midnight, as is customary today. In the agricultural peasant culture of the ancient Near East the day began at dawn, and so the sixth hour would be the middle of the day. Because this scene has resonances with the meeting of Jacob and Rachel, I think there is no doubt that this encounter took place at "high day" (Gen 29:7, LXX: ἡμέρα πολλή). See the work of J. Edgar Bruns, "Use of Time in the Fourth Gospel," *NTS* 13 (1967): 285–90; Norman Walker, "The Reckoning of Hours in the Fourth Gospel," *NovT* 41 (1960): 69–73; Eric Rowe and Jerome H. Neyrey, "Christ and Time Part Three: 'Telling Time' in the Fourth Gospel," *BTB* 402 (2010): 79–92.

⁴˸¹Now when Jesus learned that the Pharisees had heard, "Jesus is making and baptizing more disciples than John" ²—although it was not Jesus himself but his disciples who baptized— ³he left Judea and started back to Galilee. ⁴But he had to go through Samaria. ⁵So he came to a Samaritan city called Sychar, near the plot of ground that Jacob had given to his son Joseph. ⁶Jacob's well was there, and Jesus, tired out by his journey, was sitting by the well. It was about noon.

Zipporah (Exod 2:15-22).[4] So when a woman comes to this well the reader, familiar with the OT patterns, will be expecting this encounter to lead to a marriage, especially since Jesus has already been identified as the bridegroom at Cana (John 2:1-11) and in the testimony of John the Baptizer (3:29).

The Greek text states that Jesus sat "on" (ἐπὶ) the well, often translated as "beside the well," thus placing Jesus on the ground beside or near the well. This may make more sense for modern readers with images of modern wells, but this does not do justice to the Middle Eastern culture, Johannine symbolism, or grammatical considerations. The preposition best suited to express the idea of "beside" or "near" is παρά; the preposition ἐπί with the dative usually means "on" or "upon." So Jesus is literally resting on the well, presumably on the rock slab that lies across the well opening. Wells were usually simple boreholes with a rock covering them. Someone wanting water would lift the stone from the mouth of the well, then use a rope to lower a bucket or jug that they brought with them to reach down to the water (see the description of Rebecca drawing water in Gen 24:10-21). When the evangelist states that Jesus sat *on* the well, this would place Jesus on the stone covering the mouth of the well. At this point the symbolism of Jesus as the temple is at the forefront.

There were Jewish traditions that the temple rested on the fissure above the great abyss that was the source of the creative waters in Genesis

4. Robert Alter finds five repeated characteristics in this type-scene: (1) the bridegroom travels to a foreign land where (2) he encounters a woman or group of women at a well; (3) one of the characters draws water; (4) the woman returns home to tell about the encounter with the stranger; (5) there is an invitation to a meal and a betrothal followed by a wedding. See Robert Alter, *The Art of Biblical Narrative* (New York: Basic Books, 1981), 51–52.

2:8.[5] After the flood, the rock of Noah's altar sealed up the waters of the abyss. Noah's altar became the foundation stone of a new creation. Jewish traditions link the altar of Noah with the foundation stone in the holy of holies supporting the ark of the covenant.[6] According to this mythology, the temple lies on the wellspring of the earth, the center and source of creation. "The waters under the earth were all gathered beneath the temple, they believed, and it was necessary to ensure that sufficient [water] was released to ensure fertility, but not so much as to overwhelm the world with a flood."[7] The temple was the meeting point between heaven and earth and was called the Earth's "navel."[8] This mythology lies behind the passage in Ezekiel 47:1, 3, 5, 8-9, 12 describing the water flowing from the temple.

In chapter 2, within the temple courtyard, Jesus was revealed as the new temple. That image is now relocated from Sion to Sychar. Just as the temple rested on the foundation stone above the waters of the great abyss, now Jesus, the new temple, sits *on* the rock over the waters of Jacob's well. The betrothal and temple imagery would be familiar to first-century readers who had been prepared, by the narrative so far and by this introduction, for a woman to arrive at this well.[9]

The Samaritan Woman Arrives (4:7-15)[10]

Jesus's request for a drink is met with initial hostility as the woman's response reflects centuries of animosity between Jews/Judeans and

---

5. Frédéric Manns, *Le Symbole Eau-Esprit dans le Judaïsme Ancien*, SBFA 19 (Jerusalem: Franciscan Printing Press, 1983), 285.

6. Frédéric Manns, *L'Evangile de Jean à la lumière du Judaïsme*, SBFA 33 (Jerusalem: Franciscan Printing Press, 1991), 135.

7. Margaret Barker, *The Gate of Heaven: The History and Symbolism of the Temple in Jerusalem* (London: SPCK, 1991), 18.

8. Ezek 38:12 calls the region around Jerusalem the earth's navel (τὸν ὀμφαλὸν τῆς γῆς). For more on the mythology of Jerusalem, see Georg Fohrer, "Σιών," *TDNT* 7 (1971): 317–18.

9. Unlike Nicodemus, this woman is not named. See the excursus at the end of this chapter for a discussion of "Anonymity and Characterization."

10. The narrative establishes a contrast between a learned Jewish man coming at night (Nicodemus) and an unnamed woman of Samaria coming in the middle of the day. For more on these contrasts, see Colleen M. Conway, "Gender Matters in John," in *A Feminist Companion to John*, vol. 2, ed. Amy-Jill Levine with Marianne Blickenstaff, FCNTECW 5 (Sheffield: Sheffield Academic, 2003), 81–86; Margaret M. Beirne, *Women and Men in the Fourth Gospel: A Genuine Discipleship of Equals*, JSNTSup 242 (London: Sheffield Academic, 2003), 67–104.

John 4:7-15

[7]A Samaritan woman came to draw water, and Jesus said to her, "Give me a drink." [8](His disciples had gone to the city to buy food.) [9]The Samaritan woman said to him, "How is it that you, a Jew, ask a drink of me, a woman of Samaria?" (Jews do not share things in common with Samaritans.) [10]Jesus answered her, "If you knew the gift of God, and who it is that is saying to you, 'Give me a drink,' you would have asked him, and he would have given you living water." [11]The woman said to him, "Sir, you have no bucket, and the well is deep. Where do you get that living water? [12]Are you greater than our ancestor Jacob, who gave us the well, and with his sons and his flocks drank from it?" [13]Jesus said to her, "Everyone who drinks of this water will be thirsty again, [14]but those who drink of the water that I will give them will never be thirsty. The water that I will give will become in them a spring of water gushing up to eternal life." [15]The woman said to him, "Sir, give me this water, so that I may never be thirsty or have to keep coming here to draw water."

Samaritans. This conflict goes back to the time when the one kingdom of David and Solomon was divided into two separate kingdoms: Israel in the north with its capital Samaria, and Judea in the south with its capital Jerusalem. In 721 BCE the Assyrian Empire captured the Northern Kingdom and dispersed thousands of its people. They then brought into this area thousands of foreigners from other captured nations. This brought about a mixing of peoples that was considered by Jews to make Samaritans ritually impure. The encounter between a man from the Southern Kingdom of Judea[11] and a woman from the Northern Kingdom of Samaria bristles with centuries of antagonism.[12] "What! You a Judean ['Ιουδαῖος] ask a drink from me, a woman of Samaria!"[13] The long history of national conflict is clear.

Jesus then shifts the encounter from physical water to speak of "living water," which he can provide. The background to this gift of "living water" lies in the passage from Ezekiel 47:8 describing the water flowing from the temple bringing life, even to the Dead Sea. Jesus has been identified as the temple, the source of all the waters of creation, and so

---

11. See comments at 4:43 on Jesus's identification with Judea.

12. By the time of Jesus these two kingdoms had long ceased, but the centuries of animosity were still keenly felt.

13. Because the geographical differences are highly significant in this encounter, I will translate 'Ιουδαῖος as Judean, rather than "Jew," which has more religious connotations.

he is able to offer living or perhaps "life-giving" water to this woman. The discussion with Nicodemus and the following discourse establishes Jesus as God's gift of salvation for the world (3:16), where salvation means eternity life (3:16-17). The living water Jesus offers symbolizes this salvific gift of eternity life (ζωὴν αἰώνιον).[14]

The woman understands his reference to water literally and rightly objects. Jesus has no bucket and no means of drawing water from the well, and so she challenges him with the question, "Are you greater than our father Jacob?" Underlying her question is the meeting of Jacob and Rachel, not the narrative as it is found in the Hebrew or Greek Scriptures, but as this meeting was recounted in the Aramaic Scriptures in the Palestinian synagogues. These Aramaic versions, called the targums, were developed after the exile when the language spoken in the land of Israel gradually changed from Hebrew to Aramaic. This version was not an exact translation, but it offered further explanation of, and elaboration on, the original Hebrew text. The Aramaic account of the meeting between Jacob and Rachel is noticeably different from the scriptural accounts in either Hebrew or Greek.

From the original Hebrew:

> Now when Jacob saw Rachel, the daughter of his mother's brother Laban, and the sheep of his mother's brother Laban, Jacob went up and rolled the stone from the well's mouth, and watered the flock of his mother's brother Laban. (Gen 29:10)

From the Aramaic versions:

> *Targum Pseudo-Jonathan*:
> And when Jacob saw Rachel, the daughter of Laban, his mother's brother, and the flock of Laban, his mother's brother, Jacob drew near and, *with one of his arms*, rolled the stone from the mouth of the well; *and the well began to flow, and the waters came up before him*, and he watered the flock of Laban, his mother's brother; *and it continued to flow for twenty years*. (Gen 29:10)[15]

---

14. In most Bibles ζωὴν αἰώνιον is translated as "eternal life," but I wish to emphasize the new quality of life that Jesus offers—the quality of God's life in eternity.

15. Kevin Cathcart, Michael Maher, and Martin McNamara, eds., *Targum Pseudo-Jonathan: Genesis*, The Aramaic Bible 1B (Collegeville, MN: Liturgical Press, 1992), 101. In this series of the targums, the additions or changes made by the Targumist are written in italic to show the contrast with the original text.

Targum Neofiti:
Five miracles were worked for our father Jacob the time that he went forth from Beersheba to go to Haran. . . .
And the third miracle: when our father Jacob raised his feet to go to Haran the earth shrank before him and he was found dwelling in Haran.
And the fourth miracle: the stone which all the pastors had come together to roll away from over the mouth of the well and could not, when our father Jacob came he raised it with one hand and gave to drink to the flock of Laban, his mother's brother.
And the fifth: when our father Jacob raised the stone from above the mouth of the well, the well overflowed and came up to its mouth, and was overflowing for twenty years—all the days that he dwelt in Haran. (Gen 28:10)[16]

In the targums there are a number of miracles ascribed to "our father Jacob" that are highly relevant to the Samaritan woman episode:[17] the waters gush up from the well and so Jacob has no need of a bucket; the waters keep flowing for twenty years; and Jacob is miraculously transposed from Bethel to Haran. The synagogue traditions clearly associate the cultic site of Bethel with a miraculous gift of water at the well of meeting between Jacob and Rachel. The woman's question to Jesus, in the light of the targum traditions about Jacob, could be rephrased, "Are you greater than our father Jacob who was able to make the waters gush up without needing a bucket?"

Jesus's reply indicates that, yes, he is greater than "our father Jacob." The waters from Jacob's well gushed up for twenty years; the waters that Jesus offers well up for "eternity life." There are various opinions about what is meant by the symbol of "living water." Some link the water with the outpouring of the Spirit,[18] while others consider it a reference to revelation or Wisdom.[19] Symbols can be polyvalent, and it need not be a

---

16. Kevin J. Cathcart, Michael Maher, and Martin McNamara, eds., *Targum Neofiti 1: Genesis*, The Aramaic Bible 1A (Collegeville, MN: Liturgical Press, 1992), 139–40.

17. It is not possible to ascribe a date to the targums as the traditions found there continued to develop well into the Common Era; however, much of the discussion in John 4 presupposes many of the Jacob traditions found in the targums. Neyrey concludes from this that "these traditions certainly existed prior to John." See Jerome H. Neyrey, "Jacob Traditions and the Interpretation of John 4:10-26," *CBQ* 41 (1979): 420.

18. So Rudolph Schnackenburg, *The Gospel according to St John*, trans. K. Smyth et al., 3 vols., HTCNT (London: Burns & Oates, 1968–1982), 1:431–32; Brendan Byrne, *Life Abounding: A Reading of John's Gospel* (Collegeville, MN: Liturgical Press, 2014), 83.

19. Rudolph Bultmann, *The Gospel of John: A Commentary*, trans. G. R. Beasley Murray et al. (Oxford: Blackwell, 1971), 182–87; Brown, *The Gospel according to John*, 1:179.

matter of either-or when determining what the water could symbolize. It can hold a number of associations. In my view the strongest association is to life, that quality of divine life that is called in this Gospel "eternity life."[20] Just as the temple waters in Ezekiel brought life to the Dead Sea, so the waters that Jesus, the living temple of God, offers are life-giving waters for eternity life. The woman responds positively to Jesus's offer, even though she is still thinking literally.

In this encounter at a well between a man and a woman, the man's offering of living water carries sexual overtones. When discussing John 3:5, I referred to the work of Ben Witherington III and his comment that "in ancient Near East literature the word 'water' can be and is used as a *terminus technicus* or at least a well-known circumlocution, for matters involving procreation, . . . for semen, for amniotic fluid, or for the process of birth itself from the breaking of the waters to the actual delivery."[21] The Song of Songs makes use of the image of water to speak of the lover's desire for his bride: "A garden locked is my sister, my bride, a garden locked, a fountain sealed . . . a garden fountain, a well of living water, and flowing streams from Lebanon" (Song 4:12, 15). The offer of living water presumes the woman thirsts, and when the following scene moves to a discussion about husbands it becomes clear that the woman's "thirst" has not been satisfied by her six previous husbands. Her "thirst" can only be met by finding a seventh husband who will quench "in a radical way the thirst for life."[22]

The Woman Recognizes the Messiah (4:16-26)

The woman's positive response brings a shift of dialogue topics from water to marriage. Knowing the background of well meetings between women and men leading to marriage, especially the meeting of Jacob and Rachel, the topic ought not to come as a surprise. When the woman replies to Jesus, "I have no husband," he commends the truth of her an-

20. In agreement with Charles H. Dodd, *The Interpretation of the Fourth Gospel* (Cambridge: Cambridge University Press, 1970), 311–13.

21. Ben Witherington III, "The Waters of Birth: John 3.5 and 1 John 5.6-8," *NTS* 35 (1989): 156.

22. Bultmann, *The Gospel of John: A Commentary*, 186. See also the discussion in Dorothy A. Lee, *Flesh and Glory: Symbolism, Gender and Theology in the Gospel of John* (New York: Crossroad, 2002), 69–70, 72–74; and Barbara E. Reid, "Birthed from the Side of Jesus (John 19:34)," in *Finding a Woman's Place: Essays in Honor of Carolyn Osiek, R.S.C.J.*, ed. David L. Balch and Jason T. Lamoreaux (Eugene, OR: Pickwick, 2011), 192.

[16]Jesus said to her, "Go, call your husband, and come back." [17]The woman answered him, "I have no husband." Jesus said to her, "You are right in saying, 'I have no husband'; [18]for you have had five husbands, and the one you have now is not your husband. What you have said is true!" [19]The woman said to him, "Sir, I see that you are a prophet. [20]Our ancestors worshiped on this mountain, but you say that the place where people must worship is in Jerusalem." [21]Jesus said to her, "Woman, believe me, the hour is coming when you will worship the Father neither on this mountain nor in Jerusalem. [22]You worship what you do not know; we worship what we know, for salvation is from the Jews. [23]But the hour is coming, and is now here, when the true worshipers will worship the Father in spirit and truth, for the Father seeks such as these to worship him. [24]God is spirit, and those who worship him must worship in spirit and truth." [25]The woman said to him, "I know that Messiah is coming" (who is called Christ). "When he comes, he will proclaim all things to us." [26]Jesus said to her, "I am he, the one who is speaking to you."

swer and offers further revelations that she has had five husbands, plus one current man who is not her husband, to give a total of six. Following the discussions with Nicodemus about being born "anew" and with the woman about "living waters," the reader ought to be alert to look beyond the literal words in this exchange. The issue is not the moral life of this woman, and Jesus passes no further comment on this. The discussion is moving forward at a symbolic level, and this woman is able to follow the deeper nuances and recognizes Jesus as a prophet.

Marital imagery was a familiar theme in the prophetic literature. The infidelity of Samaria and their worship of foreign gods (*ba'alim*) was depicted as adultery (Hos 2:2-5).[23] In John 4 there is a play on the double meaning of the word for a husband, which in Aramaic is *ba'al*, the same word that can mean "master," "owner," or "lord."[24] "Jesus's declaration that Samaria 'has no husband' is a classic prophetic denunciation of

23. In words that parody a marital commitment, God speaks to Israel, "she is not my wife, and I am not her husband" (Hos 2:2). See comments on pp. 61–62 on the problematic aspects of the symbolism of Israel always being cast as the adulterous wife and never as the deceitful husband.

24. A similar play on the double meaning of *ba'al* is found in Hosea: "And in that day, says the Lord, you will call me, 'My husband [אישׁ],' and no longer will you call me, 'My Baal [בעל]'" (Hos 2:16).

false worship."[25] The woman's five previous husbands plus her current one give a total of six, which symbolically indicates the inadequacy of Samaritan worship.[26] At Cana, in a Jewish context, the six jars of water symbolized the lack of perfection of Jewish rituals; now, in a Samaritan context, the six "husbands" indicate the less-than-perfect worship of the Samaritans. The true "husband" of Samaria stands before this woman in the person of Jesus, the bridegroom.

Reading the narrative with its symbolism explains the shift from a discussion about husbands to the woman's growing understanding of Jesus's identity as a prophet who can both reveal extraordinary knowledge and challenge her. Identifying Jesus as a prophet leads to the woman's question about worship, which is not a ploy on her part to change the subject, as commentators sometimes suggest. Evidence from Josephus shows that there were Samaritan traditions in the first century that Moses had hidden the sacred vessels of the temple on Mount Gerizim.[27] Also, biblical and Qumran traditions looked to an eschatological figure who would be a prophet like Moses,[28] leading to a belief that this prophetic figure would reveal these sacred vessels and establish true worship on Mount Gerizim.[29]

Such traditions about a prophet coming to reveal hidden things on Gerizim may well lie behind the woman's perception that Jesus might be

---

25. Sandra M. Schneiders, *The Revelatory Text: Interpreting the New Testament as Sacred Scripture*, 2nd ed. (Collegeville, MN: Liturgical Press, 1999), 191.

26. Seven is the number that symbolizes wholeness, completion, and perfection, both within Israel and also in other ancient cultures. Within the Bible it is the most common sacred number. From this symbolic meaning of seven, the number six takes on the sense of incompleteness, less than perfect, inadequate. See M. Eugene Boring, "Seven, Seventh, Seventy," *NIDB* 5 (2009): 197–99.

27. "But the nation of the Samaritans did not escape without tumults. The man who excited them to it was one who thought lying a thing of little consequence, and who contrived everything so that the multitude might be pleased; so he bade them get together upon Mount Gerizim, which is by them looked upon as the most holy of all mountains, and assured them that, when they were come thither, he would show them those sacred vessels which were laid under that place, because Moses put them there" (*Ant.* 18.4.1). Flavius Josephus and William Whiston, *The Works of Josephus: Complete and Unabridged* (Peabody, MA: Hendrickson, 1987), 482.

28. Deut 18:18; 4Q Testimonia; 4Q Biblical Paraphrase 158; and 1QS 9.11.

29. Meeks discusses the passage from Josephus along with other Samaritan traditions about Moses's eschatological role. Wayne A. Meeks, *The Prophet-King: Moses Traditions and the Johannine Christology*, NovTSup 14 (Leiden: Brill, 1967), 248. This work on Samaritan traditions has been developed further by Marilyn F. Collins, "The Hidden Vessels in Samaritan Traditions," *JSJ* 3 (1973): 97–116.

such a prophet; after all, he has just revealed things to her that would be beyond normal human perception. If he is this prophet like Moses then he will surely know where true worship should take place.

In this discussion about the correct place of worship the figure of Jacob is still present. He was the great ancestor who established the first "house of God" following his dream of the open heavens.

> Then Jacob awoke from his sleep and said, "Surely the LORD is in this place—and I did not know it." And he was afraid, and said, "How awesome is this place! This is none other than the house of God [*Beth-el*], and this is the gate of heaven." (Gen 28:16-17)

Both Samaritans and Jews look back to Jacob traditions to claim the holiness of their sacred sites—Mount Gerizim or Mount Sion. Abraham's first altar was built at Shechem at the bottom of Mount Gerizim (Gen 12:6-7), and later Jacob also built an altar there (Gen 33:18-20). As such, in Samaritan traditions Mount Gerizim has priority over Mount Sion, which became a site of worship much later under David. Also, Mount Gerizim is called the navel of the earth (τοῦ ὀμφαλοῦ τῆς γῆς) in Judges 9:37 (LXX); later, the prophet Ezekiel will make the same claim for Jerusalem (Ezek 38:12). As noted in the targum above, when Jacob awoke from his dream at Beth-El, "the earth shrank before him" and he found himself miraculously by the well where he met Rachel. These traditions of the House of God (Bethel), of ancestral worship, and of the meeting of heaven and earth all authenticate Mount Gerizim as an ancient site of worship.

But Jacob is also associated with the Jerusalem temple. One of the most frequent names for the temple is *Beth YHWH*—which is etymologically similar to *Beth-El*. We find a passage in the Temple Scroll from Qumran referring to a future temple that was dependent on the covenant made with Jacob at Bethel.

> ⁷I shall accept them. They shall be for me a people and I will be for them forever; and I shall dwell ⁸with them forever and always. I shall sanctify my [te]mple with my glory, for I shall make my glory reside ⁹over it until the day of creation, when I shall create my temple, ¹⁰establishing it for myself for all days, according to the covenant which I made with Jacob at Bethel.³⁰

---

30. 11Q19 col. 29. Translation from Florentino Garcia Martinez and Eibert J. C. Tigchelaar, *The Dead Sea Scrolls Study Edition (Translations)*, 2 vols. (Leiden: Brill, 1997–1998), 1251. See further discussion on the relationship between Bethel and the Jerusalem temple in Joshua Schwartz, "Jubilees, Bethel and the Temple of Jacob," *HUCA* 56 (1985): 63–85.

So traditions of Jacob at *Beth-El* were called on by both Samaritans from the north and Judeans from the south to legitimize their places of worship.

Jesus's response to the woman's question about worship is to move beyond physical sites and ancestral legitimation to point to a new reality of God's presence in and toward the world. Since God's movement toward humanity is in Spirit, the same Spirit who can bring about new birth (3:3), humanity's response to God must be "in Spirit" (ἐν πνεύματι). At this point Jesus names God as "Father," moving God beyond the limited views of Samaritans or Judeans, but the God now revealed before her in Jesus. Central to this passage is the affirmation: "You [plural: ὑμεῖς] worship what you [plural] do not know; we worship what we know, for salvation is from the Jews [Ἰουδαίων]. But the hour is coming, and is now here, when the true worshipers will worship the Father in spirit and truth" (vv. 22-23). Two significant shifts happen in these verses. First, a shift from a conversation between Jesus and one woman to an affirmation made by a group, "we," to another group, "you" (plural). Second, two time frames come together—a future hour, which is *coming* and yet is now *present*. As was the case in the Nicodemus dialogue (3:11), Jesus is here giving voice to the later Johannine community. In knowing the Father whom Jesus revealed, the Christian community can claim, "we worship what we know."

The statement "salvation is from the Jews/Judeans [τῶν Ἰουδαίων]" in this context could be continued "and not from the Samaritans," in keeping with the polemic that has been present from the beginning of this dialogue. The passage began identifying Jesus as a Judean (Ἰουδαῖος, v. 7), and when this passage concludes Jesus returns to Galilee because he "has no honor in his own country [πατρίδι]" (4:43), which indicates that his *patris* is considered to be Judea. The phrase depicts the journey of the Judean Jesus, the Father's gift for the salvation of the world (3:16-17), to Samaria. In him, "salvation has come from the Judeans/Jews [τῶν Ἰουδαίων]."

Jesus's answer to the woman's question about the place to worship causes her to see that he is more than a prophet and to consider that he might be the expected Messiah (Μεσσίας), called the Christ (χριστός) (v. 25). She raises this possibility because of Jesus's revelations. For the first time in the Gospel, Jesus responds: ἐγώ εἰμι, ὁ λαλῶν σοι, "I am, the one who is speaking to you."[31] The expression ἐγώ εἰμι, "I AM," is the consistent translation in the LXX of the great revelation of God's name to Moses, "I

---

31. Jesus's words are remarkably close to the LXX version of Isa 52:6: ἐγώ εἰμι αὐτὸς ὁ λαλῶν, "it is I who speak; here am I."

AM who I AM; ἐγώ εἰμι ὁ ὤν" (Exod 3:14). Therefore, there must be some correspondence between the woman's perception of Jesus's identity as a Messiah and his own self-perception, in Johannine terms.[32] Later in the Gospel, other figures will speak of Jesus as the Messiah (7:26-27, 41; 10:24), but Jesus will not accept the title as it reflects narrow, nationalistic, Davidic expectations. But this woman speaks of the Christ as a revealer, one who "will proclaim all things to us."[33] Jesus can accept her perception of the Messiah as a revealer, and so she, and not one of the male disciples, is "the first recipient of a direct revelation of who Jesus is."[34]

Disciples Return (4:27-38)

With the revelation of Jesus as the "I AM," the dialogue with the woman ends and the disciples return. The woman leaves her water jar behind, a sign that her deeper thirst has now been quenched. She offers her villagers the same invitation Jesus offered to his disciples, "Come, see . . ." (4:29; cf. 1:39, 46). Just as Jesus's first disciples then invited others, now this woman disciple invites the people of her village to see the revealer and then poses the question, "Perhaps he is the Messiah/Christ." While some see her question as an expression of doubt on her part, I believe it is a rhetorical device allowing the villagers to hear her words as an invitation and to make their own journey of faith.[35]

---

32. Within the narrative Jesus accepts the woman's understanding of the messiah as one who can reveal God. In the postresurrection time, the community came to perceive that Jesus was the revealer of God in his own person, and so the Gospel affirms his divine status (1:1; 20:28). The evangelist expresses this spirit-guided faith in Jesus through the use of the expression "I AM."

33. It is possible that Samaritan traditions of a Messiah focused more on a revealer than a Davidic king, as suggested by Josephus in the passage above. Four centuries later a Samaritan document called the *Memar Marqah* speaks of a revelatory figure called the *Taheb*. See Brown, *The Gospel according to John*, 1:72; also Craig R. Koester, *The Dwelling of God: The Tabernacle in the Old Testament, Intertestamental Jewish Literature, and the New Testament*, CBQMS 22 (Washington, DC: Catholic Biblical Association of America, 1989), 55–59.

34. Martin Scott, *Sophia and the Johannine Jesus*, JSNTSup 71 (Sheffield: JSOT Press, 1992), 191.

35. Teresa Okure suggests that the woman's comments are "a veiled confession couched in the form of a question in order to appeal to the personal judgment of the Samaritans, get them to reflect, and so arouse their interest in Jesus." See Teresa Okure, *The Johannine Approach to Mission: A Contextual Study of John 4:1-42*, WUNT 2, Reihe 32 (Tübingen: Mohr Siebeck, 1988), 174. See also the discussion of the woman's role as a missionary/witness in Scott, *Sophia and the Johannine Jesus*, 192–97.

27 Just then his disciples came. They were astonished that he was speaking with a woman, but no one said, "What do you want?" or, "Why are you speaking with her?" 28 Then the woman left her water jar and went back to the city. She said to the people, 29 "Come and see a man who told me everything I have ever done! He cannot be the Messiah, can he?" 30 They left the city and were on their way to him.

31 Meanwhile the disciples were urging him, "Rabbi, eat something." 32 But he said to them, "I have food to eat that you do not know about." 33 So the disciples said to one another, "Surely no one has brought him something to eat?" 34 Jesus said to them, "My food is to do the will of him who sent me and to complete his work. 35 Do you not say, 'Four months more, then comes the harvest'? But I tell you, look around you, and see how the fields are ripe for harvesting. 36 The reaper is already receiving wages and is gathering fruit for eternal life, so that sower and reaper may rejoice together. 37 For here the saying holds true, 'One sows and another reaps.' 38 I sent you to reap that for which you did not labor. Others have labored, and you have entered into their labor."

The dialogue with the woman was about water, understood symbolically as a gift of eternity life (4:14); when the disciples return they engage Jesus with a dialogue about food, which also has a deeper meaning than physical nourishment. The imagery of sowing, reaping, and harvesting speaks of Jesus's ministerial work while also recalling prophetic images of the eschatological harvest when divisions between Samaria and Judea will be healed and the scattered tribes will be gathered together.

> Lift up your eyes and look around;
> > they all gather together; they come to you. (Isa 60:4)

> For you also, O Judah, a harvest is appointed.
> When I would restore the fortunes of my people,
> > when I would heal Israel. (Hos 6:11–7:1)[36]

Through his dialogue with the woman of Samaria, Jesus's ministry has begun to bear fruit, and while she has had her thirst quenched, he has also been nourished by this exchange.

36. See also Isa 11:11; 27:12; Jer 23:3; 29:14; Ezek 20:34; 34:13; 37:21.

Because of Her Testimony (4:39-42)[37]

The final verses (39-45) confirm the meaning of the harvest image in the preceding section (35-38). The Samaritans at first believe because of the witness of the woman (v. 39), but finally their belief is based on their own experience of hearing Jesus, "we have heard for ourselves" (v. 42). From their personal encounter with the Word they proclaim their faith in Jesus as "Savior of the world" (v. 42, cf. 3:17).[38]

OT Insight into This Meeting

A passage from Ezekiel can help elucidate the deeper significance of the meeting between Jesus, a man from Judea, and the woman of Samaria. In Ezekiel 37, the prophet is told:

> Son of man, take a stick and write on it, "For Judah, and the children of Israel associated with him"; then take another stick and write upon it, "For Joseph (the stick of Ephraim) and all the house of Israel associated with him"; and join them together into one stick, that they may become one in your hand. (Ezek 37:16-17; RSV)

Following this action, the prophetic sign is explained:

> Behold, I will take the people of Israel from the nations among which they have gone, and will gather them from all sides, and bring them to their own land; and I will make them one nation in the land, upon the mountains of Israel; and one king shall be king over them all; and they shall be no longer two nations, and no longer divided into two kingdoms. (Ezek 37:21-22; RSV)

The passage from Ezekiel, addressed to the exiles in Babylon, looks to a future when the divided kingdoms will be joined and Israel will be reconstituted as one. One stick is named "for Judah," and one "for Joseph (the stick of Ephraim)."[39] At the time, when Judah and Israel are

---

37. See the excursus below, p. 126, on "A Woman's Witness" for evidence of this woman's esteem in the church traditions.

38. See comments at 1:44-51 on the Johannine pattern of gathering disciples. The usual pattern is that one comes to faith not by a direct encounter with Jesus but through the witnessing word of another.

39. After the exodus, when the Israelites move into the land of Canaan, Moses is reputed to have divided the land among the twelve ancient tribes. In this division the tribe of Levi was not allocated a portion; instead, the tribe of Joseph was allocated a double settlement named for his two sons, Ephraim and Manasseh (Josh 14:3-4).

John 4:39-42

39Many Samaritans from that city believed in him because of the woman's testimony, "He told me everything I have ever done." 40So when the Samaritans came to him, they asked him to stay with them; and he stayed there two days. 41And many more believed because of his word. 42They said to the woman, "It is no longer because of what you said that we believe, for we have heard for ourselves, and we know that this is truly the Savior of the world."

reunited, then the promise is made that the covenant will be renewed: "they shall be my people, and I will be their God" (Ezek 37:23).

The episode by the well of Jacob symbolically presents the fulfillment of Ezekiel's prophetic action. Jesus, a "bridegroom" (3:29) from Judea, has come to a well, a typical meeting place for a betrothal. With strong echoes of the meeting between Jacob and Rachel, Jesus meets a woman of Samaria, and in this meeting he reveals himself as one "greater than our father Jacob." Without needing a bucket, Jesus is able to offer the woman waters welling up to eternity life. When the woman responds positively to his offer, the conversation moves to discussion of her husbands. At this point it becomes clear that that woman has been in six relationships prior to meeting Jesus; this number suggests both the inadequacy of these prior relationships and the arrival of the "seventh" bridegroom—Jesus. The symbolism of marriage, which runs through this entire encounter, recalls the OT covenant relationship between God and Israel, which was frequently likened to a marriage. In this "betrothal-type" meeting between a Judean man and a Samaritan woman, Judah and Samaria are once again united into one covenant people of God.

The dialogue then shifts to speak of the right place of worship and the necessity to worship "in Spirit." The mention of the Spirit leads the woman to consider if Jesus could be the Messiah associated with the end-time outpouring of the Spirit and the one who, according to Samaritan traditions, would reveal the hidden sanctuary. Once again, the passage from Ezekiel 37 provides the theological background to the flow of this dialogue. In Ezekiel, when the two kingdoms are united then God will dwell with them.

The Samaritans consider themselves to be the direct descendants of these two tribes, Ephraim and Manasseh. See Robert T. Anderson, "Samaritans," *ABD* 7 (1996): 941.

I will make a covenant of peace with them; it shall be an everlasting covenant with them; and I will bless them and multiply them, and will set my sanctuary in the midst of them forevermore. My dwelling place [κατασκήνωσίς] shall be with them; and I will be their God, and they shall be my people. (Ezek 37:26-27)

In the final scene with the Samaritan villagers Jesus is present to them as the covenanting God of Israel, the bridegroom, the I AM, and the temple dwelling place of God. When the Samaritans come to Jesus, they ask him "to dwell [μεῖναι] with them; and he dwelt [ἔμεινεν] there two days" (4:40).[40]

Welcome by Galileans (4:43-45)

The journey into Galilee completes the movement begun in verse 3 and establishes a stark contrast between two groups, namely, the Ἰουδαῖοι (2:18), who did not accept Jesus, and the Γαλιλαῖοι, who do. The named disciples of Jesus were all Galileans: Phillip, Andrew, and Peter from Bethsaida (1:44), and Nathanael from Cana (21:2).[41] The proverb about the prophet rejected by his own was common within the tradition and usually referred to the Galileans (Mark 6:4; Matt 13:57; Luke 4:24), but from the Johannine perspective the Ἰουδαῖοι are Jesus's own people (1:11; οἱ ἴδιοι). Judea is the πατρίς of Jesus.[42] Jesus has spent considerable time in Judea (2:13–3:36), and although Joseph is from Nazareth (1:45), there is nothing in the Gospel so far to suggest that Jesus is a Galilean. In fact, the Samaritan woman has just called him a Judean (4:9), and he was in his "Father's house" (2:16) in Jerusalem. In the rejection by the Ἰουδαῖοι, the words of the prologue are exemplified, "He came to his own and his own did not receive him" (1:11; author's translation).

---

40. In the Last Discourse, especially 15:1-11, the verb "to dwell" (μένω) takes on a rich theological meaning describing the mutual indwelling of the Father, Son, Spirit, and believer.

41. The evangelist considers that Bethsaida lies in Galilee (12:21).

42. The term *patris* means "the region or population center from which a person comes, that is to say, the place of one's birth or childhood or the place from which one's family has come." Johannes P. Louw and Eugene Albert Nida, "πατρίς," in *Greek-English Lexicon of the New Testament: Based on Semantic Domains*, vol. 1, 2nd ed. (New York: United Bible Societies, 1996), 15. For an alternative position, that Jesus's *patris* is Galilee, see Gilbert van Belle, "The Faith of the Galileans: The Parenthesis in Jn 4,44," *ETL* 74 (1998): 27–44.

⁴³When the two days were over, he went from that place to Galilee ⁴⁴(for Jesus himself had testified that a prophet has no honor in the prophet's own country). ⁴⁵When he came to Galilee, the Galileans welcomed him, since they had seen all that he had done in Jerusalem at the festival; for they too had gone to the festival.

The encounter with the Samaritan woman is a symbolic enactment of the words of Ezekiel—Samaria and Judea are joined as one covenant people, and God's living temple, Jesus/Sophia, dwells in their midst. Here in Samaria Jesus is recognized not simply in terms of Jewish or Samaritan messianic hopes but in terms of his divine purpose for *all* people: "God did not send the Son into the world to condemn the world, but in order that the *world* might be saved through him" (3:17; emphasis added). Such a fulfilment of Ezekiel's words could not have happened if the character Jesus met was not a Samaritan and not a woman. Here, gender and race are critical to Johannine theology that Jesus is to be the "Savior of the world" (4:42), and the encounter with this woman of Samaria is the first enactment and recognition of Jesus's world-saving mission (4:42). Through the character of the Samaritan woman, the harvest that Jesus spoke about to his disciples has begun; "look around you, and see how the fields are ripe for harvesting" (v. 35). With no citations from the wisdom literature, nonetheless, Jesus has embodied Sophia, and her life-giving waters have been fruitful.

> It [Wisdom] runs over, like the Euphrates, with understanding,
> and like the Jordan at harvest time. (Sir 24:26)

A Woman's Witness

In bearing witness to Jesus the woman functions as an apostle to her village. In the narrative so far, Jesus has called disciples but has not yet sent them out on mission. Missioning does not happen in John until the appearance of the risen Christ (20:21). This woman is the only one in the narrative who is seen bearing witness to others. Although Jesus's command was, "Go call your husband," her subsequent proclamation in the village led Origen (185–ca. 251) to state: "But he used that woman as an apostle to those in the town. She was so inflamed by his words that, abandoning her water-jar and returning to the town, the woman said to the men: 'Come, see a man who has told me everything I have done'" (*Comm. on John* 13.169).[43] Similarly, Theophylact of Bulgaria (ca. 1050–1108), archbishop of Ochrid, in his commentary on John 4:28 claims that she became an apostle and received a laying on of hands because of her faith-filled heart (*Joan.* 4.28ff., PG 123:1241D).[44] A Byzantine chant in which she is named Photina, "enlightened one," declaims:

Thou wast illumined by the Holy Spirit
And refreshed by the streams of Christ the Saviour.
Having drunk the Water of Salvation,
Thou didst give copiously to the thirsty.
O Holy Great Martyr Photina,
Equal-to-the-Apostles,
Entreat Christ our God that our souls may be saved.[45]

Anonymity and Characterization

By chapter 4, much is known about Jesus; indeed, his name is known from the prologue even before the formal narrative begins, but the woman he meets remains nameless. Why? In a study of anonymity in the OT, Adele Reinhartz notes that the general assumption by literary critics is that anonymity means the character is unimportant.[46] By contrast, key figures have names (e.g., Moses, David, Bathsheba, Samson) while Manoah's wife and the wise woman of Tekoah (2 Sam 14:2) are nameless. Feminists often see in this a deliberate way of suppressing the woman's identity and that it

43. Translation from Joseph W. Trigg, *Origen*, ed. Carol Harrison, ECF (New York: Routledge, 1998).

44. "Theophylacti," ed. Jacques-Paul Migne, vol. 123, *Patrologiæ cursus completus* (1864–), http://books.google.com/books?id=mL7UAAAAMAAJ.

45. From Antiochian Orthodox Christian Archdiocese of North America: http://ww1.antiochian.org/node/22317. For additional information and legends about the Samaritan woman/Photina, see http://www.orthodoxchristian.info/pages/photini.htm and Barbara E. Reid, *Wisdom's Feast: An Invitation to Feminist Interpretation of the Scriptures* (Grand Rapids: Eerdmans, 2016), 102.

46. Adele Reinhartz, *"Why Ask My Name?" Anonymity and Identity in Biblical Narrative* (New York: Oxford University Press, 1998), 5.

"symbolizes her lack of power and personhood within her narrative context."[47] Reinhartz summarizes her findings on the use of a name in the biblical texts:

> The proper name therefore defines biblical character. In doing so, it ascribes unity and a full identity to the character and gives the reader a convenient way of referring to the figure and distinguishing it from others. The name may also carry symbolic meaning, which provides insight into the nature, appearance, or significance of the character in the larger story of the Israelite people.[48]

From looking at characteristics of those who are named and those left nameless she then comments that the anonymous characters "surprise exegetes with the amount and detail of their portrayal."[49] Furthermore, even the anonymous person can be referred to either by what they do or say or some other identity marker. With no name, they are frequently given a quasi-title—the wise woman of Tekoa, the witch of Endor (1 Sam 28:7), Pharaoh's daughter (Exod 2:5), the mother of Jesus (2:1; 19:25), the Samaritan woman (John 4), the man born blind (John 9).

Another approach to anonymity is offered by David Beck, who contends that this is a deliberate ploy by the evangelist that allows readers to identify with the unnamed faithful ones.[50] But as Judith Redman argues, this "notion of allowing readers to identify more closely with appropriate belief paradigms comes from the psychology of today and would not have been part of the mindset of the first-century author."[51] Rather than look to psychological motives, she proposes that the anonymity of characters is more likely because the names were not known to members of the intended

---

47. Reinhartz, *Why Ask My Name?*, 6.

48. Ibid., 8.

49. Ibid., 9.

50. David R. Beck, *The Discipleship Paradigm: Readers and Anonymous Characters in the Fourth Gospel*, BibInt 27 (Leiden: Brill, 1997), chap. 8.

51. Judith C. S. Redman, "Eyewitness Testimony and the Characters in the Fourth Gospel," in *Characters and Characterization in the Gospel of John*, ed. Christopher W. Skinner and Mark Goodacre, LNTS 461 (London: Bloomsbury, 2013), 64. On this critique of Beck's argument I agree with Redman and add that each character needs to be assessed in the narrative context. There may well be a reason for presenting a character without a name, e.g., the mother of Jesus. More will be said on this in examining chap. 19.

audience and so the names were not important.[52]

The woman in John 4 is usually simply known by her ethnic and gender identity—the Samaritan woman. Later, because of her insight, she has been known in the Orthodox tradition as Photina, from *phōs* ("light"). Apart from the unanswerable historical questions, I believe that in calling this character *woman* and *Samaritan*, the evangelist has made a theological decision that further reveals the mission of Jesus. By leaving her nameless, *woman* and *Samaritan* are emphasized and thus her importance to the narrative as an agent in Jesus's mission is given prominence. This episode in Samaria would not achieve its purpose if the character were a man or a Jew.

52. Redman, "Eyewitness Testimony and the Characters in the Fourth Gospel," 64. Of course, with the mother of Jesus and the Beloved Disciple their names were known within the Johannine community. With the mother of Jesus I have argued that the purpose of using "Woman" and "Mother" was made for a significant theological reason, which will become clearer when discussing John 19. See Mary L. Coloe, "The Mother of Jesus: A Woman Possessed," in *Character Studies in the Fourth Gospel: Narrative Approaches to Seventy Figures in John*, ed. Steven A. Hunt, D. Francois Tolmie, and Ruben Zimmermann, WUNT 314 (Tübingen: Mohr Siebeck, 2013), 202–13. In the introduction, when discussing the author of this Gospel, I propose that this author wrote of himself simply as the "other disciple" (1:35-42; 18:15, 16; 20:3, 4, 8), but shortly after his death the final editor of the text gave him the title "the Beloved Disciple" (13:23; 19:26; 20:2; 21:20).

John 4:46-54

The Household of Faith

God did not make death,
  and does not delight in the death of the living.
God created all things so that they might exist.
  (Wis 1:13-14; author's translation)

John 4 concludes with another episode of a person coming to faith in Jesus's word. Like the Samaritan woman, the official (βασιλικός, 4:46) is not a Jew.[1] This episode follows the typical structure of a miracle story,[2] with the additional Johannine feature of an initial

---

1. Although there is some uncertainty about the status of this man, the term βασιλικός is probably a reference "to a royal official." See Karl L. Schmidt, "Βασιλικός," *TDNT* 1 (1964): 591. Capernaum, although small, was an important Roman town with a Roman tax station and a Roman milestone inscribed "Imperator Caesar Divi . . ." Luke describes a centurion living there who was a friend of the Jewish community (Luke 7:4), while Matthew speaks of an official (ἄρχων, 9:18). As a border town on the road to Damascus, it is likely that there was a Roman official there. See Melton B. Winstead, "Capernaum," in *The Lexham Bible Dictionary*, ed. John D. Barry et al. (Bellingham, WA: Lexham Press, 2016). Since the scene appears to be the Johannine version of the healing of the centurion's servant (cf. Matt 8:5-13; Luke 7:1-10), Moloney suggests that this official was a Gentile; see Francis J. Moloney, *Belief in the Word: Reading John 1–4* (Minneapolis: Fortress, 1993), 183.

2. Miracle stories have the following typical structure: (a) a problem described; (b) request made; (c) the miracle performed accompanied by a gesture, touch, word, or

refusal or rebuke to the request (see 2:4; 11:6). The apparent rebuke to this Gentile father in Cana establishes a balance with the apparent rebuke to the Jewish mother in Cana (1:1-12), and this episode brings this first section of the Gospel to its conclusion. The bridegroom established at Cana brings life to a child in Cana.[3]

The royal official from Capernaum is facing an illness unto death, for although his son is not dead the language suggests this extremity.[4] Following the pattern of a miracle story the request is made that Jesus come so that healing can happen, but Jesus rebukes the official for expecting "signs and wonders" (4:48). The official responds by making the request again, now reported in the first person: "Sir, come down before my little boy dies" (4:49). Usually miracle workers interact directly with the person to be healed through touch (e.g., Mark 1:41; 5:41), spittle (Mark 7:33), or breath (Mark 7:34). In reply, Jesus gives his authoritative word, "Go; your son lives" (4:50).[5] Jesus's word is enough to ensure life for this child; his physical presence is not necessary. The official trusts this word and returns home.

On his way home he is met with the message that his boy is alive (4:51) and that his recovery began at the same time as Jesus's words, namely, the seventh hour (ὥραν ἑβδόμην). In response, the whole household becomes a household of faith even without seeing Jesus. The naming of a specific time, particularly the *seventh* hour, suggests a deeper symbolic significance. Within the theological world of Judaism seven had come to represent completion or wholeness. "The number seven thus bears the

---

name; (d) the successful accomplishment is described; (e) the response of wonder by the onlookers. The recognition and naming of this fivefold pattern is based on the work of Bultmann and the description here follows the wording of Moloney (*Belief in the Word*, 90). For a comparison of the structure of the miracle accounts in this section of the Gospel, see Marianne Meye Thompson, *John: A Commentary*, NTL (Louisville: Westminster John Knox, 2015), 114. Michael Labahn discusses this structure and its significance and also brings in the Bethany household. See Michael Labahn, "Between Tradition and Literary Art: The Miracle Tradition in the Fourth Gospel," *Bib* 80 (1999): 178–203.

3. The child who is ill lies in Capernaum, but the life-giving encounter between the official and Jesus takes place in Cana.

4. The boy is "at the point of death" (v. 47); Jesus says, "Your son will live," rather than "your son is healed."

5. Thompson (*John*, 114) sees in Jesus's words an echo of Elijah's words to the Sidonian woman when he restored life to her child (1 Kgs 17:17-24). A further similarity is that both the Sidonian woman and the royal official are Gentiles.

⁴⁶Then he came again to Cana in Galilee where he had changed the water into wine. Now there was a royal official whose son lay ill in Capernaum. ⁴⁷When he heard that Jesus had come from Judea to Galilee, he went and begged him to come down and heal his son, for he was at the point of death. ⁴⁸Then Jesus said to him, "Unless you see signs and wonders you will not believe." ⁴⁹The official said to him, "Sir, come down before my little boy dies." ⁵⁰Jesus said to him, "Go; your son will live." The man believed the word that Jesus spoke to him and started on his way. ⁵¹As he was going down, his slaves met him and told him that his child was alive. ⁵²So he asked them the hour when he began to recover, and they said to him, "Yesterday at one in the afternoon the fever left him." ⁵³The father realized that this was the hour when Jesus had said to him, "Your son will live." So he himself believed, along with his whole household. ⁵⁴Now this was the second sign that Jesus did after coming from Judea to Galilee.

character of totality, i.e., of the totality desired and ordained by God."[6] The narrative sequence describing various forms of faith in Jesus began in Cana (2:1) and now has been brought to completion in Cana. In this seventh hour the official expresses absolute faith in Jesus's word, and simultaneously life comes to his household. This short episode, bringing together faith and life in the seventh hour, could be seen as "the whole gospel in a nutshell: 'that you may come to believe (or continue to believe) that Jesus is the Messiah, the Son of God and that believing you may have life in his name' (20:31)."[7]

While we do not see the actual household at Capernaum, the narrative indicates that the royal official is changed through his encounter with Jesus. He is introduced at first in terms of his role as an official (βασιλικός, 4:46). No doubt in his position this man is used to having his wishes carried out. Jesus's rebuke must come as a shock to one in his position of authority. Jesus will not do the usual wondrous things associated with a miracle worker. There will be no incantations, no special potions, and no

6. Karl Heinrich Rengstorf, "Ἑπτά, Ἑπτάκις, Ἑπτακισχίλιοι, Ἕβδομος, Ἑβδομήκοντα, Ἑβδομηκοντάκις," *TDNT* 2 (1964): 628.

7. Bernadeta Jojko, "Eternity and Time in the Gospel of John," *Verbum Vitae* 35 (2019): 272.

strange gestures. With the rebuke the official speaks again, and now with a polite form of address, "Sir" (v. 49). He is shifting from his position as one with authority over another to one recognizing the authority of the other. Jesus responds then with his word, "Go; your son lives" (v. 50). At this point the courtier is simply called a human being (ἄνθρωπος, v. 50); he has been stripped of the trappings of royal status and now shares the experience of all humanity before the authoritative *logos*. When he returns to his household context, the emphasis is now on his relationship with his child, and he is called father (πατήρ, v. 53). Within the household, his identity is now found in terms of his relationship to his child and no longer in terms of his official status. A child in this household of faith has found life, and a father has found his humanity.

The Missing Mother

The focus of this scene is the meeting between the official and Jesus some distance away from the house, where his child lies close to death, and the official's expression of faith in Jesus's words. We read/hear the anguish of the father, but the narrative says nothing of the mother. While this makes sense culturally, and humanly, since her place is by the side of her sick child (cf. Mark 5:40), it means we miss the woman's experience of this illness unto death and also her experience of the word of Jesus that brings joy and life to the whole household. The wife and mother has "disappeared" from this narrative. We can only imagine her prayers and lamentations and then her tears of joy and faith in Jesus through her son's recovery.

While speaking of the missing mother, it is worth noting that in the Fourth Gospel we also miss the many healings of women recorded in the Synoptics. The only healings in this Gospel are the royal official's son (4:46-54), the man at the pool of Bethesda (John 5), the man born blind (John 9), and Lazarus (John 11). We hear nothing of Peter's mother-in-law (Mark 1:31), Jairus's daughter (Mark 5:42), the Syrophoenician woman's daughter (Mark 7:29), the woman with persistent bleeding (Mark 5:29), or the woman with an infirmity (Luke 13:13). In their place we read of women missionaries and evangelists, such as the Samaritan woman (John 4), Mary the Magdalene (John 20), and of women prophets, such as Mary of Bethany who anoints Jesus (John 12). It is quite the reversal of the portrayal of women in the Synoptics. In John they are agents of faith and change: Mary and Martha of Bethany bring about the raising of their brother (11:3), the mother of Jesus initiates the abundance of wine (2:3), and Mary the Magdalene is the first apostle of the Risen One (John 20:17). As agents in the narrative, they are never portrayed as victims—either of illness, of sin,[8] or of male domination. It is cause to wonder about the women in the Johannine community and the experience of the women in the early church.

Conclusion

Chapter 4 concludes back in Cana (2:1) with Jesus and an official who shows authentic Johannine faith when he trusts Jesus's word that his son will live (4:50). Like the mother of Jesus (2:4), this official is at first rebuffed by Jesus (4:48), but he too persists and his faith is rewarded. This Gentile official and the mother of Jesus serve as models of perfect Johannine faith, not in seeking signs, but in trusting the word. These two characters are like bookends enclosing a large section of the narrative: between the two Cana signs, the reader is introduced to others, both within and beyond Judaism, who display various faith responses to Jesus: complete faith in Jesus (John and the Samaritan woman: 3:29-30; 4:29), partial faith (Nicodemus and the Samaritan woman: 3:2; 4:19), no faith in Jesus ("the Jews" and the Samaritan woman: 2:20; 4:9).[9] The evangelist has crafted his narrative in this way to invite all hearers/readers into their own journey of faith, be they men or women, Jews, Samaritans, or Gentiles.

8. I do not consider that the episode of the woman accused of adultery was an original part of this Gospel; more will be said on this following John 8.

9. While the usual description of this section is "Cana to Cana," Smit argues that it would be more appropriate to speak of Galilee to Galilee, which highlights the Galilean/Judean dichotomy. Peter-Ben Smit, "Cana-to-Cana or Galilee-to-Galilee: A Note on the Structure of the Gospel of John," *ZNW* 98 (2007): 143–49.

The Feasts of the Jews

The next six chapters (John 5–10) form a distinct section of the Gospel generally called "the Feasts of the Jews." Across these chapters Jesus's ministry occurs within the contexts of the great Jewish festivals. In naming these festivals "of the Jews" (2:13; 5:1; 6:4; 7:2), the evangelist is speaking as someone from outside "the Jews" (οἱ Ἰουδαῖοι), someone who no longer considers himself, or his community, to be within this religious group, regardless of ethnicity. Even though the use of the term in this context appears neutral rather than hostile, there is a clear distancing of the evangelist (and community) from the Jewish and religious world of Jesus. "The Jews" are other than "us." This division may have come about through the initiative of the rabbis at Jamnia, as proposed by J. Louis Martyn,[1] but it may also be a division being created by this evangelist through the rhetoric of the Gospel, as argued by Adele Reinhartz, who states, "The gospel was not reacting to a forcible parting but rather attempting to produce one."[2] It is possible that the process of

1. J. Louis Martyn, *History and Theology in the Fourth Gospel* (New York: Harper and Row, 1968), 31–41.

2. Adele Reinhartz, "Story and History: John, Judaism, and the Historical Imagination," in *John and Judaism: A Contested Relationship in Context*, ed. R. Alan Culpepper and Paul N. Anderson, RBS 87 (Atlanta: SBL, 2017), 125. More recently, she wrote, "The gospel is advocating, at the very least, that Christ-confessors see themselves as separate from the *Ioudaioi*. This is not to say the Christ-confessors could not have been ethnically or genealogically Jewish, as were Jesus and the disciples. In undergoing the transformative process proposed and facilitated by the gospel, however, they become children of God and thereby cease being *Ioudaioi*." Adele Reinhartz, *Cast Out of the Covenant: Jews and Anti-Judaism in the Gospel of John* (Lanham, MD: Rowman & Littlefield, 2018), 87.

separating from each other was seen as necessary by both communities, as both were shaping and reshaping their identities within the Roman Empire following the Jewish War (66–70 CE). The process of separating would continue through the next two centuries.

In John 6, the setting is the springtime festival of Passover (6:4), a feast held in the first month of the Jewish liturgical calendar. This is the second of three Passovers in the Gospel (cf. 2:13; 13:1) and is the only one when Jesus is away from Jerusalem. The next festival in the liturgical calendar is the summer festival of First Fruits/Weeks or, within the Greek-speaking world, Pentecost, as it occurs fifty days after Passover. In my view this festival is the context for John 1:19–2:12, as previously discussed (pp. 58–60). The autumn festival of Sukkot (Booths/Tabernacles) covers John 7:1–10:21 (note 7:2). These three festivals are known as pilgrim festivals, as every male Jew was expected to celebrate these feasts in Jerusalem.[3] This section concludes with the winter festival of Hanukkah or Dedication (10:22). This was not a pilgrim festival, as it was introduced into the Jewish liturgical calendar quite late, following the victory of the Maccabees over Greek oppression and the rededication of the temple (164 BCE). John 5 begins this annual liturgical sequence with the weekly celebration of Sabbath (5:9).

These chapters have a pastoral purpose for this Christian community living toward the end of the first century CE. The Johannine community had its origins within Judaism, following a Jewish man, Jesus, and coming to understand him in the light of their Jewish Scriptures. The destruction of the temple by Rome in 70 CE thrust Judaism into crisis. With no temple, no sacrifice, and no need for a priesthood, how could the Jewish people remain the "holy nation" of God (Exod 19:6)?

Following the events of 70 CE, leadership of the Jewish community gradually shifted from the high priest and Sanhedrin to the great teachers of Torah. In the time of Jesus these teachers were known as the Pharisees; later they were known by the simpler title, "rabbi." These teachers shifted the focus of Judaism from sacrifice and temple to Torah and synagogue.

---

3. Because of regular menstruation, women were exempt from attending the festivals as an obligation, but they could choose to attend. The Mishnah states, "For every positive commandment dependent upon the time [of year], men are liable, and women are exempt. And for every positive commandment not dependent upon the time, men and women are equally liable. For every negative commandment, whether dependent upon the time or not dependent upon the time, men and women are equally liable" (m. Qidd. 1:7).

In this critical time, therefore, two groups, which had their origins in Second Temple Judaism, were both working to define themselves as the true heirs of their Jewish traditions. Over time these two groups became more clearly defined as Rabbinic Judaism and Christianity, but in the first century most "Christians" were Jews.[4]

In the decades after the destruction of the temple, the rabbis were focusing on Moses and the Torah, while some other Jews (and Gentiles) were focusing on Jesus as the one who embodies the teachings of Torah. According to the Gospel's rhetoric, these Jews were no longer considered "orthodox" in their beliefs and were no longer welcome in the synagogue community. This appears to be the situation of the Johannine community (see 9:22; 12:42; 16:2).

Without temple or synagogue, how could the members of this community celebrate the great saving acts of God in history? How could they encounter the liberating God of Passover, the gracious God of Tabernacles, and the faithful God of Dedication? In losing contact with Judaism, have they lost contact with the God of their ancestors?

Chapters 5–10 address the pain of these questions, and Wisdom Christology comes to the fore in Sophia's offer of bread,[5] light,[6] water,[7] and as the living hypostasis of Torah.[8] The God of the Festivals is still present among the community in Jesus/Sophia.

---

4. For many Christians this may come as a shock, but a recent book is well worth reading to clarify the status of religious affiliations in the first century. Paula Fredriksen, *When Christians Were Jews: The First Generation* (New Haven: Yale University Press, 2018).

5. "Instead of these things you gave your people food of angels, and without their toil you supplied them with bread from heaven [ἄρτον ἀπ᾽ οὐρανοῦ] ready to eat" (Wis 16:20).

6. "[She] became a shelter to them by day, and a starry flame through the night" (Wis 10:17).

7. "You gave them abundant water unexpectedly" (Wis 11:7).

8. The being of Sophia is called a hypostasis: "For your 'being' [ὑπόστασίς] manifested your sweetness toward your children" (Wis 16:21). Baruch identifies Wisdom with Torah: "She is the book of the commandments of God, the law that endures forever" (Bar 4:1; see also Sir 24:23).

John 5:1-47

Sophia Embodies the Law[1]

"Come my friend to meet the bride;
Let us welcome the presence of the Sabbath."[2]

John 5 begins a section exploring the great Jewish festivals. The festival in this chapter is not named, which allows greater emphasis to be given to the weekly "festival" of Sabbath.[3] Within the Scriptures two explanations are given for the Sabbath: the day of rest recalls the time in Egypt and celebrates release from slavery (Deut 5:12-15); the

---

1. "All this is the book of the covenant of the Most High God, / the law that Moses commanded us." (Sir 24:23)

2. Hymn from the synagogue prayers to mark the beginning of Sabbath.

3. Michael Daise offers references to scholars who attempt to name the festival; in my opinion by not naming the festival, the focus is kept on the Sabbath. See Michael A. Daise, *Feasts in John: Jewish Festivals and Jesus' "Hour" in the Fourth Gospel*, WUNT 2.229 (Tübingen: Mohr Siebeck, 2007), 11–18, esp. 18. Although the Sabbath is a single day, it is associated with feasts and festivals; e.g., "It shall be the prince's duty to furnish the burnt offerings, cereal offerings, and drink offerings, at the feasts, the new moons, and the Sabbaths, all the appointed feasts of the house of Israel" (Ezek 45:17); also Amos 8:5; Hos 2:13; Isa 1:13; 2 Kgs 4:23. Jubilees explicitly names the Sabbath as a festival: "For great is the honor which the Lord has given to Israel that they should eat and drink and be satisfied on this festival day" (Jub. 50:10). Therefore, the Sabbath itself may be the feast—unnamed in verse 1, then revealed in verse 9.

day emulates the divine rest when God finished the work of creating (Exod 20:8-11). This chapter draws on Jewish theological teaching and understanding about God's Sabbath rest from work. I suggest the following structure for this chapter:[4]

5:1-9a	The healing
5:9b-16	Consequences
5:17-18	The two issues involved
5:19-20	Parable—Statement of principle
5:21-23	Sabbath exemptions for God—giving life and judging
5:24-26	The Son is granted life-giving power
5:27-29	The Son is given power to judge
5:30-40	Witnesses to support Jesus's claims
5:41-47	From defense to accusation

Jesus's healing on the Sabbath leads to conflict, and his response is to claim authority to work as his father works, making use of the everyday experience of children learning from their parents. This is the household pattern. It means that the language of "son" and "father" will dominate. But it is important to remember that the Sabbath is a particularly feminine festival. Not only is Sabbath welcomed as a bride, but the woman of the household takes on many of the tasks associated with the priestly tasks when the tabernacle was erected with the lighting of a continual lamp (Exod 27:21).[5] When Jerusalem was destroyed in 587 BCE and many people were exiled in Babylon, this was a time when Sabbath became an important celebration of identity,[6] and it was a celebration

---

4. I am indebted to the work of Martin Asiedu-Peprah who considers John 5 and John 9 to follow the process of a two-party juridical controversy, where the aim is to find a resolution so that a trial is not needed. Martin Asiedu-Peprah, *Johannine Sabbath Conflicts as Juridical Controversy*, WUNT 2/132 (Tübingen: Mohr Siebeck, 2001).

5. Sara Paasche-Orlow, "Tetzaveh: Finding Our Home in the Temple and the Temple in Our Home," in *The Women's Torah Commentary: New Insights from Women Rabbis on the 54 Weekly Torah Portions*, ed. Elyse Goldstein (Woodstock, VT: Jewish Lights, 2000), 160.

6. While the origins of the Sabbath are unclear, many look to the time in exile as the starting point for Israel's religious appropriation of this day. Andreas Schuel, "Sabbath," *NIDB* 5 (2009): 4; Eduard Lohse, "Σάββατον, Σαββατισμός, Παρασκευή," *TDNT* 7 (1971): 4–5.

within the domestic arena rather than a temple. This practice continued when the people returned and rebuilt the temple in Jerusalem. Sabbath remained a household celebration where the woman's role was essential. She had the responsibility for, and was entrusted with, the preparations to ensure that the proper food was prepared with respect to the food laws of the covenant people. Then, at nightfall, she was the one who initiated the Sabbath meal with her blessing and lighting the candles.[7] In this she was acting as the priests once did in lighting the candles in the tabernacle.

> In the second Temple period, when the rabbis began the transfer of the locus of holiness from the Temple to the synagogues, there was also a transfer of ritual to the home, particularly relating to food and eating. . . . The Shabbat meal echoes the Temple ritual with the candles burning, ritual washing, bread with salt, and wine. Jewish homes now serve as temples. The Shabbat dinner is something that for centuries has not been the domain of rabbis and men, but of women and families together. It is women who have traditionally lit candles and this invoked God's presence.[8]

The Healing (5:1-9a)

Archaeologists have excavated the area beside the northern wall where the second temple once stood and have discovered an ancient healing pool with five porticoes.[9] This is one of a number of geographical features in the Gospel indicating that the evangelist knew Jerusalem and its environs very well.[10] The "stirring" of the waters probably refers

---

7. The tradition of women lighting the candles was already established from the beginning of the Common Era. Millgram describes this practice. "One of the unique practices of that time was the sounding of six Shofar blasts to announce the ushering in of the Sabbath. The first sound of the Shofar was a signal for the farmers in the fields to stop work and to start for home; the second blast was for the merchants to close their shops; the third blast was for the housewives to kindle the Sabbath lights; and the last three blasts announced the actual arrival of the Sabbath." Abraham Ezra Millgram, *The Sabbath Anthology*, JPS Holiday Anthologies (Philadelphia: The Jewish Publication Society, 2018), 228.

8. Paasche-Orlow, "Tetzaveh," 162–63.

9. James F. Strange, "Beth-Zatha," *ABD* 1 (1992): 700.

10. The pool mentioned in John 5 has various names in the manuscript tradition—Bethzatha, Bethsaida, and Bethesda. Because of the healing traditions associated with this location I favor Bethesda, from the Hebrew Beth Hesed, "house of mercy." "The Copper Scroll discovered at Qumran contains a reference to a pool at

5:1After this there was a festival of the Jews, and Jesus went up to Jerusalem. 2Now in Jerusalem by the Sheep Gate there is a pool, called in Hebrew Beth-zatha, which has five porticoes. 3In these lay many invalids—blind, lame, and paralyzed. 5One man was there who had been ill for thirty-eight years. 6When Jesus saw him lying there and knew that he had been there a long time, he said to him, "Do you want to be made well?" 7The sick man answered him, "Sir, I have no one to put me into the pool when the water is stirred up; and while I am making my way, someone else steps down ahead of me." 8Jesus said to him, "Stand up, take your mat and walk." 9aAt once the man was made well, and he took up his mat and began to walk.

to the bubbles that would surface with an influx of water and to the occasional bubbling when gasses would seep through the limestone rocks. This bubbling activity gave rise to legends appearing in some later manuscripts of an angel stirring the pool at different times. According to Deuteronomy 2:14, God commanded the Israelites to cross into the land of the Canaanites, but they refused and were punished by wandering without hope in the wilderness for thirty-eight years until that entire generation perished.[11] In stating that the man's illness had lasted for thirty-eight years the suggestion is that his time of living without hope of a cure is about to end.

Jesus asks the question, "Do you want to become healthy/sound?" The man's response is similar to Nicodemus's as he points out to Jesus the impossibility of his getting into the pool in time. Jesus then effects

---

Betheshdathayim, which the minority of the Committee interpreted as corroborating the reading Βηθεσδά"; see Bruce M. Metzger, *A Textual Commentary on the Greek New Testament: A Companion Volume to the United Bible Societies' Greek New Testament*, 4th rev. ed. (London: United Bible Societies, 1994), 178–79. For others supporting "Bethesda," see Craig S. Keener, *The Gospel of John: A Commentary*, 2 vols. (Peabody, MA: Hendrickson, 2003), 1:636.

11. "And the length of time we had traveled from Kadesh-barnea until we crossed the Wadi Zered was thirty-eight years, until the entire generation of warriors had perished from the camp, as the LORD had sworn concerning them" (Deut 2:14). The story of Israel's disobedience begins in Deut 1:19. Even when the people repent and acknowledge, "We have sinned against the LORD" (1:41), God's response is to say, "I am not in the midst of you" (1:42). This episode provides a possible background for 5:5; see Jean Zumstein, *L'Évangile selon Saint Jean (1–12)*, CNT 4a 2nd ser. (Genève: Labor et Fides, 2014), 181.

the cure by his word of command, "Rise, take your mat and walk" (v. 8). The man is immediately restored to health and walks away carrying his mat. The narrative so far has read as a "good news" account of a healing. With great artistry, the evangelist now shocks the reader with the "bad news"—"Now that day was a sabbath" (v. 9b).

The Consequences (5:9b-16)

The "Jews," not previously mentioned in this scene, now challenge the man for breaking the Sabbath by carrying his mattress. By the time of the Mishnah in the early third century CE, there were thirty-nine forms of "work" prohibited on the Sabbath. Even in first-century Judaism, the Book of Jubilees and the Dead Sea Scrolls list numerous forms of prohibited "work."[12] In carrying his mat the man has broken the Sabbath. "Thus says the LORD: For the sake of your lives, take care that you do not bear a burden on the sabbath day or bring it in by the gates of Jerusalem. And do not carry a burden out of your houses on the sabbath or do any work, but keep the sabbath day holy, as I commanded your ancestors" (Jer 17:21-22). The man shifts responsibility onto Jesus, declaring that someone had healed him and told him to do this. Unless it was a matter of life or death,[13] healing was also prohibited on the Sabbath. Now, the "Jews" have two causes for concern: someone has healed unnecessarily on the Sabbath and has told another to break the Sabbath by carrying goods.

The drama continues when Jesus encounters the man in the nearby temple and shifts the encounter to a new level. "Do not sin anymore, so that nothing worse happens to you" (v. 14). This is a puzzling statement. It cannot mean that Jesus is expressing a theology that physical illness is a manifestation of sin; this view is explicitly rejected by Jesus in 9:3-4. The man has been healed. This action is past. Now Jesus looks to the man's future and points out that there is worse than physical paralysis, and that is a moral paralysis caused when sin destroys one's relationship with God.[14] Such was the fate of the exodus generation

---

12. Jub. 50:6-13; 4QD (The Damascus Document) 10:14–11:18.

13. The Mishnah, although a later witness, expresses this understanding clearly: "And any matter of doubt as to danger to life overrides the prohibitions of the Sabbath" (m. Yom. 8:6).

14. In this interpretation I am in agreement with Zumstein, *L'Évangile selon Saint Jean (1–12)*, 181–83.

⁹ᵇNow that day was a sabbath. ¹⁰So the Jews said to the man who had been cured, "It is the sabbath; it is not lawful for you to carry your mat." ¹¹But he answered them, "The man who made me well said to me, 'Take up your mat and walk.'" ¹²They asked him, "Who is the man who said to you, 'Take it up and walk'?" ¹³Now the man who had been healed did not know who it was, for Jesus had disappeared in the crowd that was there. ¹⁴Later Jesus found him in the temple and said to him, "See, you have been made well! Do not sin any more, so that nothing worse happens to you." ¹⁵The man went away and told the Jews that it was Jesus who had made him well. ¹⁶Therefore the Jews started persecuting Jesus, because he was doing such things on the sabbath.

whose disobedience led to their wandering in the wilderness without God's presence for thirty-eight years. The man is encouraged not only to begin a new physical life restored to health but, more important, to begin a new moral life in right relationship with God.

The man is now able to identify Jesus as the one who healed him, and this begins the persecution of Jesus for breaking the Sabbath by healing the man and then telling him to walk with his mat. The Gospel now shifts from a narrative about a healing to a dialogue that some liken to a courtroom drama where the defendant (Jesus) justifies his actions to his accusers (the Jews).[15]

The Two Issues Involved (5:17-18)

Jesus begins his defense by drawing attention to the fact that God continues to work on the Sabbath, and because of his unique relationship as Son, his Sabbath work is justified. Jesus's claim that God continues work on the Sabbath is based in Jewish theology, which acknowledges the fact that God continues to create life, because children are born even on the Sabbath, and that God must continue to work as judge, since people die on the Sabbath and come before God in judgment.[16] These are the two

15. Many scholars write about the following confrontation as a "trial." Asiedu-Peprah considers it simply a two-party juridical controversy, in the hope of avoiding a trial. Only when there is no satisfactory conclusion need the issue go forward to a formal trial before a third party; in the Gospel narrative, this happens before Pilate. See Asiedu-Peprah, *Johannine Sabbath Conflicts*, 1–24.

16. Asiedu-Peprah, *Johannine Sabbath Conflicts*, 77; Georg Bertram, "ἔργον," *TDNT* 2 (1964): esp. 639–40.

¹⁷But Jesus answered them, "My Father is still working, and I also am working." ¹⁸For this reason the Jews were seeking all the more to kill him, because he was not only breaking the sabbath, but was also calling God his own Father, thereby making himself equal to God.

Sabbath exemptions for God—granting life and judging. In healing the man and then admonishing him to sin no more, Jesus has acted with the Sabbath authority of God.

Jesus's accusers understand his reasoning and the Sabbath exemptions from work he is claiming. Because they do not recognize his relationship with God, they consider his words blasphemous and think he is claiming to be "equal [ἴσον] to God" (v. 18). Jesus clarifies his relationship with God and further explains why he can work as he does, by means of a short parable.

A Parable—Statement of Principle (5:19-20)

The parable (vv. 19-20a) describes a typical household pattern of a son working as an apprentice to his father. In his work, the son does not act independently of his loving father's authority and guidance. Charles Dodd was among the first to identify these verses as a parable, which can be missed when the words "father" and "son" are capitalized as in the NRSV translation.[17] "When the evangelist speaks of a father who, because he loves his son, shows him everything that he himself does, and of a son who, instead of acting on his own initiative, watches his father at work and does exactly as he does, he is describing in the simplest and most realistic terms a perfectly familiar situation in everyday life."[18] When the parable ends it is allegorized with "the father and son of the parable becoming God the Father and Christ the Son,"[19] with the Son now declaring that even greater works will be shown (v. 20). In spite of the intimate union of Father and Son, the Gospel never collapses the

17. The genre of "parable" would be clearer if these verses were written in lowercase "son" and "father." It draws on the social experience of any child learning from a parent.

18. Charles H. Dodd, "A Hidden Parable in the Fourth Gospel," in *More New Testament Studies* (Manchester: Manchester University Press, 1968), 38–39.

19. Dodd, "A Hidden Parable in the Fourth Gospel," 31–32.

John 5:19-20

¹⁹Jesus said to them, "Very truly, I tell you, the Son can do nothing on his own, but only what he sees the Father doing; for whatever the Father does, the Son does likewise. ²⁰The Father loves the Son and shows him all that he himself is doing; and he will show him greater works than these, so that you will be astonished."

distinction between them.[20] The distinction is there when Jesus speaks of the Father as the one who sent him (v. 23) and that the Son can only do what "he sees the Father doing" (v. 19). The distinction in union is best expressed in terms such as mutuality or reciprocity within the Father-Son relationship. Dorothy Lee's contribution maintains that the terms "father" and "son" are symbolic, verbal icons, rather than ontological terms.[21] T. E. Pollard expresses this very carefully:

> Everywhere in John from the first verse of the prologue the unity of the Father and Son is never the undifferentiated unity of identity. It is a unity which permits distinctions. Always the relation between the Father and the Son is the paradoxical relation of distinction-in-unity.[22]

The Sabbath Exemptions for God—Giving Life and Judging (5:21-23)

Jesus's response to his opponents follows a careful logic. He begins by naming the central issue, that God still works on the Sabbath (v. 17), and then, through a parable, he clarifies his right to work on the Sabbath, not because he is "equal to God," but rather, as Son, he has been authorized by his Father in this work (vv. 19-20). He then reminds his opponents of their own law that recognizes God's ongoing work in the human events of birth and death, which do not cease with the Sabbath. The two issues here, of giving life and of judgment, must not be subsumed into one "end-time" event. Here, the expression "raises the dead" is

20. Painter maintains the unity and distinction by speaking of ontological equality and functional subordination. See John Painter, "Tradition, History and Interpretation in John 10," in *The Shepherd Discourse of John 10 and Its Context*, ed. Johannes Beutler and Robert Fortna, SNTSMS 67 (Cambridge: Cambridge University Press, 1991), 69.

21. See the excursus by Dorothy Lee, "The Iconic Father," at the end of this chapter.

22. T. E. Pollard, "The Father-Son and God-Believer Relationships according to St. John: A Brief Study of John's Use of Prepositions," in *L'Évangile de Jean: Sources, rédaction, théologie*, ed. M. de Jonge, BETL 44 (Gembloux: Duculot, 1977), 367.

²¹"Indeed, just as the Father raises the dead and gives them life, so also the Son gives life to whomever he wishes. ²²The Father judges no one but has given all judgment to the Son, ²³so that all may honor the Son just as they honor the Father. Anyone who does not honor the Son does not honor the Father who sent him."

used metaphorically as a way of describing "the human condition apart from the Logos."²³ The giving of life is a present reality, not something still to come, as evidenced by the use of the present tense:²⁴ "just as the Father raises the dead and gives them life, so also the Son gives life to whomever he wishes" (v. 21). Jean Zumstein writes, "The resurrection is not primarily an act of resuscitation, but the transmission *here and now* of the fullness of life as God desires."²⁵

The Son Is Granted Life-Giving Power (5:24-26)

Once again, the use of present-tense verbs indicates that the eternity life the Son offers is a present reality. "Anyone who hears my word and believes him who sent me *has* eternal life [ζωὴν αἰώνιον]" (v. 24).²⁶ The Son's purpose in coming into the world is to give life, not physical life, but eternity life (3:16), life in abundance (10:10). "His [Jesus's] coming to reveal God in history has made it possible for man [*sic*] to move from the sphere of death into that of life and to achieve his true existence, the life that he was intended to lead."²⁷ Those who do not have this quality of life are said to be "dead" even though they exist. This same sense of "the dead" as those spiritually dead recurs in verse 25: "The hour is coming,

23. For a discussion of "raising the dead" as a metaphor for belief, see Xavier Léon-Dufour, *Lecture de l'Évangile selon Jean*, 4 vols., Parole de Dieu (Paris: Seuil, 1988, 1990, 1993, 1996), 2:49–50.

24. This is also the position taken by Jörg Frey in his work on Johannine eschatology; see Jörg Frey, *Die johanneische Eschatologie: Die eschatologische Verkündigung in den johanneischen Texten*, vol. 3, WUNT 117 (Tübingen: Mohr Siebeck, 2000), 375.

25. Zumstein, *L'Évangile selon Saint Jean (1–12)*, 190.

26. "Similarly, eternal life is no longer an indefinite heavenly life which would follow earthly life, but the fullness of life as God desires which is received here and now by faith in the revealer." See Zumstein, *L'Évangile selon Saint Jean (1–12)*, 192.

27. Rudolph Schnackenburg, *The Gospel according to St John*, trans. K. Smyth et al., 3 vols., HTCNT (London: Burns & Oates, 1968–1982), 2:99.

John 5:24-26

[24]"Very truly, I tell you, anyone who hears my word and believes him who sent me has eternal life, and does not come under judgment, but has passed from death to life.

[25]"Very truly, I tell you, the hour is coming, and is now here, when the dead will hear the voice of the Son of God, and those who hear will live. [26]For just as the Father has life in himself, so he has granted the Son also to have life in himself."

and is now here, when the dead will hear the voice of the Son of God, and those who hear will live." The present reality is emphasized by the phrase "and is now here." The Father, who has life in himself, has granted the Son life in himself,[28] and so the Son, now present in history, is able to give life to those previously "spiritually dead" (v. 26).[29] While Aristotelean philosophy and patriarchal cultures saw only the male father as the giver of life, the book of Wisdom counters this distorted view:

> If riches are a desirable possession in life,
> what is richer than wisdom, the active cause [ἐργαζομένης] of all things?
> And if understanding is effective,
> who more than she is fashioner [τεχνῖτις] of what exists? (Wis 8:5-6)

The expression "and is now here" has a twofold temporal sense. It refers to the narrative time of Jesus and the possibility of those who hear his voice and believe receiving his gift of life. But the expression is also the proleptic experience of the post-Easter community who now, as it hears the Gospel narrative, has the same opportunity to believe and come to life.

The Son Is Given Power to Judge (5:27-29)

Just as raising the "dead" and giving them life is a present reality, so too is judgment. Judgment is being made here and now by the stance one takes toward Jesus. The word Jesus speaks is already judging each person, or, in a sense, each person brings judgment on themselves by

---

28. Von Wahlde discusses the background to the phrase "life in himself" and shows its association with Wis 15:16-17. His article adds further evidence of the influence of the book of Wisdom in the anthropology and eschatology of the Fourth Gospel. See Urban C. von Wahlde, "He Has Given to the Son to Have Life in Himself (John 5,26)," *Bib* 85 (2004): 409–12.

29. On the use of the title Son of God within a Father-Son relationship, see Francis J. Moloney, "The Johannine Son of God," *Salesianum* 38 (1976): esp. 73–77.

²⁷"and he has given him authority to execute judgment, because he is the Son of Man. ²⁸Do not be astonished at this; for the hour is coming when all who are in their graves will hear his voice ²⁹and will come out—those who have done good, to the resurrection of life, and those who have done evil, to the resurrection of condemnation."

their choice of belief or unbelief in Jesus. While judgment is already being made, the Fourth Gospel, in keeping with Jewish and early Christian tradition,[30] does not reject an end-time manifestation of that judgment. Where traditional eschatology required the end-time judgment as a way to reverse the fate of the just and grant them the reward of life with God, this is not the eschatology of John. There is no need for a final judgment or reversal of fate since those who believe in Jesus already come into eternity life in the present, but, as Zumstein says, "This does not exonerate them from physical death in this world as it moves toward its end."[31] Similarly those who do not accept Jesus bring judgment on themselves and remain in a state of spiritual death.

Echoing Isaiah 26:19 (LXX), verses 28-29 address the future for those who have died. On the last day, all those "in the tombs," who have passed from this earthly existence and continue to exist in either eternity life or deadliness, will come forth; i.e., their state of life or death will be made manifest. The good will come forth "to the resurrection of life." The term "life" qualifies the type of resurrection existence for the good. Conversely, evildoers will come forth "to the resurrection of condemnation/ judgment." The judgment they brought on themselves in their earthly existence will be manifest. The term "judgment" (κρίσεως) qualifies their experience of resurrection.

These verses speak of a fully realized eschatology of eternity life or judgment experienced in the present through the choices people make in response to Jesus's words, while allowing for an end-time bodily resurrection (vv. 28-29),[32] which will manifest the consequence of those choices.

30. See Rom 2:6-10; 2 Cor 5:10; Acts 17:31; 1 Pet 4:5; 2 Tim 4:1 for evidence of a Christian tradition of eschatological judgment.

31. Zumstein, *L'Évangile selon Saint Jean (1–12)*, 195.

32. Bodily resurrection from the dead may be assumed by the expression "in the tombs." According to Frey, the evangelist drew on traditional Jewish views of an end-time resurrection to appeal to his opponents. Since they had this belief, they may be able to understand that Jesus is simply claiming to bring into the present the

Witnesses to Support Jesus's Claims (5:30-40)

The juridical nature of this conflict comes to the fore in verses 31-40 as, in the manner of a legal case, Jesus calls on a series of witnesses ("on my behalf") in support of his claims. This accords with the Jewish law that requires "two or three" witnesses (Deut 19:15). His first witness is John. Earlier in the narrative, some of the Jerusalemites sought out John (1:19), and so Jesus can presume that John's testimony will be acceptable. John's description as a "lamp [ὁ λύχνος] burning and shining" may allude to messianic expectations, as Psalm 132 speaks of God preparing "a lamp for my anointed one" (LXX 131:17; ἡτοίμασα λύχνον τῷ χριστῷ μου).

Jesus next points to his "works" as testifying or bearing witness that he has been sent and therefore authorized by his Father, just as signs and wonders bore witness to Moses as one sent and authorized by God (Exod 7:3). Apart from this cure in John 5, there was mention earlier of the "signs" Jesus did in Jerusalem (2:23).

A third witness is the Father, but his accusers have not heard his voice (φωνή) or seen his image (εἶδος). In this accusation Jesus echoes the words spoken by Moses to the Israelites in the wilderness: "Then the LORD spoke to you out of the fire. You heard the sound of words but saw no form [likeness]; there was only a voice [sound]" (LXX: φωνὴν ῥημάτων ὑμεῖς ἠκούσατε καὶ ὁμοίωμα οὐκ εἴδετε, ἀλλ᾽ ἢ φωνήν; Deut 4:12). The obduracy of the wilderness generation now continues in the Jerusalem authorities.[33]

The final witness is the testimony of Israel's own Scriptures. Read through the lens of Christian faith, the Scriptures reach their fullness in Jesus.[34] Throughout the Gospel the evangelist explicitly cites numerous passages, sometimes introducing these with the formula, "as it is written" (e.g., 6:31, 45; 10:34; 12:15), and in the second "half" of the Gospel with a formula denoting the fulfillment of the Scriptures (12:38; 13:18; 15:25;

---

end-time expectation of God's raising the dead and exercising judgment. He continues: "The use of the tradition in Jn 5,28f. shows, however, that the stress on present eschatology does not exclude the expectation of a future eschatological act in which the present spiritual decision will come to its physical consequences." See Jörg Frey, "Eschatology in the Johannine Circle," in *Theology and Christology in the Fourth Gospel: Essays by the Members of the SNTS Johannine Writings Seminar*, ed. Gilbert Van Belle, Jan G. van der Watt, and P. Maritz (Leuven: Peeters, 2005), 78–79.

33. Zumstein, *L'Évangile selon Saint Jean (1–12)*, 200.

34. Recall the prologue's comparison of the gift of the law through Moses and a fuller gift that came through Jesus Christ (1:16-17).

³⁰"I can do nothing on my own. As I hear, I judge; and my judgment is just, because I seek to do not my own will but the will of him who sent me.

³¹"If I testify about myself, my testimony is not true. ³²There is another who testifies on my behalf, and I know that his testimony to me is true. ³³You sent messengers to John, and he testified to the truth. ³⁴Not that I accept such human testimony, but I say these things so that you may be saved. ³⁵He was a burning and shining lamp, and you were willing to rejoice for a while in his light. ³⁶But I have a testimony greater than John's. The works that the Father has given me to complete, the very works that I am doing, testify on my behalf that the Father has sent me. ³⁷And the Father who sent me has himself testified on my behalf. You have never heard his voice or seen his form, ³⁸and you do not have his word abiding in you, because you do not believe him whom he has sent.

³⁹"You search the scriptures because you think that in them you have eternal life; and it is they that testify on my behalf. ⁴⁰Yet you refuse to come to me to have life."

19:24, 36).[35] In their refusal to believe in Jesus, they are refusing to accept the witness of their own Scriptures and thus lose the very thing they are seeking: eternity life, which he alone, as Son, can give (see vv. 24-25).

From Defense to Accusation (5:41-47)

The legal controversy continues with Jesus shifting from defendant to prosecutor as he accuses his opponents of seeking human honor (δόξα) rather than seeking the glory (δόξα) of God.[36] Here Jesus draws on the double sense of the word δόξα, which means honor or glory in a simple

---

35. Two major studies have been done on the use of the OT citations in the Gospel and their introductory formulas: Andreas Obermann, *Die christologische Erfüllung der Schrift im Johannesevangelium*, WUNT 83 (Tübingen: Mohr Siebeck, 1996), and Ruth Sheridan, *Retelling Scripture: 'The Jews' and the Scriptural Citations in John 1:19–12:15*, BibInt 110 (Leiden: Brill, 2012).

36. Asiedu-Peprah writes: "The act of accusing one's accusers is an integral part of the accused person's defence in a bilateral juridical contest. It has a dual function. Firstly, it seeks to prove to the accusers why they are in the wrong and to put them on the defensive. Secondly, it facilitates an explicit comparison between the different behaviours of the two disputants in order to establish who is in the right and who is in the wrong so as to hasten the resolution of the conflict." Asiedu-Peprah, *Johannine Sabbath Conflicts*, 110.

John 5:41-47

⁴¹"I do not accept glory from human beings. ⁴²But I know that you do not have the love of God in you. ⁴³I have come in my Father's name, and you do not accept me; if another comes in his own name, you will accept him. ⁴⁴How can you believe when you accept glory from one another and do not seek the glory that comes from the one who alone is God? ⁴⁵Do not think that I will accuse you before the Father; your accuser is Moses, on whom you have set your hope. ⁴⁶If you believed Moses, you would believe me, for he wrote about me. ⁴⁷But if you do not believe what he wrote, how will you believe what I say?"

human sense. He accuses his opponents of seeking this human δόξα. But the word has a deeper theological sense through its use in the OT to refer to the revelation of God's δόξα, particularly the glory revealed to Moses and the people at Sinai (Exod 16:7, 10; 24:16, 17).[37] From the Gospel's perspective Jesus is now the locus of the revelation of God's glory as the prologue stated: "And the Word became flesh and lived among us, and we have seen his glory [δόξαν], the glory [δόξαν] as of a father's only son, the fullness of a gift which is true" (1:14; author's translation).

The episode concludes with the figure of Moses, remembered as the great covenant maker and law giver (1:17; 7:19). By the first century, Moses was also honored as the writer of Israel's Scriptures. The Book of Jubilees makes frequent mention of Moses as the one commanded by God to "incline thine heart to every word which I shall speak to thee on this mount, and write them in a book" (Jub. 1:5, similarly 1:7). This writing is to cover from the beginning of creation until the final age when God comes to dwell with the people for eternity (Jub. 1:26-27). In their attempt to make meaning of Jesus's life, death, and rising, the early believers turned to the Scriptures of Israel and saw this writing

---

37. In the LXX the term δόξα is used to translate the Hebrew כבוד (*kābôd*), a word that is associated with the weightiness that gives a person importance or honor. When used of God, the term, while associated with the visible storm cloud, refers to the invisible essence of God. The cloud appears necessary to veil the radiance of God's presence. As used in the LXX, δόξα takes on a distinct meaning quite different from its use in secular Greek literature. In the secular sense it usually means "opinion," while in the LXX is comes closer to the sense of *kābôd*, meaning the divine revelation of God's essential nature in the created world. The Gospel asserts that this revelation of God in the world is now made visible in the "flesh" of Jesus (1:14). See Gerhard von Rad and Gerhard Kittel, "δόξα," *TDNT* 2 (1964): esp. 238–46.

testifying to Jesus and interpreting him.[38] When Philip found Nathanael he said, "We have found him about whom Moses in the law and also the prophets wrote" (John 1:45).

Not only is Jesus the subject of the Law and the Prophets, but, as Sophia, Jesus embodies the law as Sirach celebrates, when following the lavish description of Sophia, Sirach states:

> All this is the book of the covenant of the Most High God,
> the law that Moses commanded us
> as an inheritance for the congregations of Jacob. (Sir 24:23)

Similarly, Baruch identifies Wisdom with the law:

> She is the book of the commandments of God,
> the law that endures forever. (Bar 4:1)[39]

The evangelist, when stating that Moses wrote about Jesus, is making a general statement about Jesus and the Scriptures but, even more specifically, making the claim that Jesus/Sophia *is* the life-giving Torah of Israel. In restoring life for the crippled man, Jesus/Sophia has not disregarded the Sabbath law but demonstrated that the Sabbath celebrates God's creative activity, and this once-crippled man can now fully participate in life.

Conclusion

At the heart of this controversy is the Jewish legal issue of work on the Sabbath. In the final verses, Jesus appeals to the great law-giver Moses and claims that Moses wrote about him (v. 46). This claim continues the Johannine view that the Mosaic gift of the law has now reached its perfection in Jesus (1:16). These verses, of course, are based in the faith of the postresurrection Christian community.

Behind this narrative of a Sabbath controversy between Jesus and the Jewish leaders of his time can be glimpsed a late first-century context where a young Christian community is seeking its own identity and practice, over against the synagogue of its time. While holding firm that believers already possess eternity life, they must also come to terms with the

---

38. Scripture witnesses to Jesus in that it functions to *interpret* Jesus, to make sense of Jesus to his audience in order to lead them to belief. Sheridan, *Retelling Scripture*, 30.

39. In a lavish poem praising Wisdom (Bar 3:9–4:4) various terms are used interchangeably: understanding (φρόνησις, 3:9, 14, 28), wisdom (σοφία, 3:12, 23), comprehension (σύνεσις, 3:14), knowledge (ἐπιστήμης, 3:20, 27, 36).

reality of physical death. This chapter holds both present and future within a theology of Jesus's Sabbath authority as the Son, authorized to give life and bring people to judgment *now* in the choice made for or against him, with the consequences of this choice to be revealed in the future.

The Iconic "Father" of Jesus[40]

I take as my starting point the view that the term "Father" is a symbol rather than a literal description of divine essence, in line with contemporary feminist theological thinking that sees exclusively male imagery for God as idolatrous.[41] The Christian tradition has tended to equivocate on the gender of God. The iconography, both verbal and pictorial, has been overwhelmingly male, creating the impression that the God of Israel is a male deity. Yet, the scriptural tradition, at its most reasonable, knows that God cannot be confined to the specificity of one gender, despite the weight of its theological representation. In a homily on the Song of Songs, Gregory of Nyssa argues that no human label can adhere to the innermost being of God, including gender: "For this reason, every name we turn up is of the same adequacy for purposes of pointing to the unutterable Nature, since neither 'male' nor 'female' defiles the meaning of the inviolate Nature" (Homily 7).[42] Here is an example of the tradition acknowledging the fundamentally symbolic nature of its own theology.

Symbolism is not ornamental language decorating the plain truth; symbols bear within them the transcendent reality to which they point.[43] They are deeply enmeshed in human experience; they contain cognitive content, and they are vehicles for transcendence rather than mere signposts on the way. At the same time, symbolism by its very nature is

---

40. This short excursus is a synopsis of two longer studies. See Dorothy A. Lee, "Beyond Suspicion? The Fatherhood of God in the Fourth Gospel," *Pacifica* 8 (1995): 140–54; Dorothy A. Lee, "The Symbol of Divine Fatherhood," *Semeia* 85 (1999): 177–87.

41. Elizabeth A. Johnson, *She Who Is: The Mystery of God in Feminist Theological Discourse* (New York: Crossroad, 1992), 33–41.

42. Richard A. Norris Jr., *Gregory of Nyssa: Homilies on the Song of Songs; Translated with Introduction and Notes*, WGRW (Atlanta: SBL, 2013).

43. Sandra M. Schneiders, "Symbolism and the Sacramental Principle in the Fourth Gospel," in *Segni E Sacramenti Nel Vangelo Di Giovanni*, ed. Pius-Ramon Tragan, Studia Anselmiana 67 (Rome: Editrice Anselmiana, 1977), 223; Craig Koester, *Symbolism in the Fourth Gospel: Meaning, Mystery, Community* (Minneapolis: Fortress, 1995), 4–15; Dorothy A. Lee, *The Symbolic Narratives of the Fourth Gospel: The Interplay of Form and Meaning*, JSNTSup 95 (Sheffield: JSOT Press, 1994), 29–33.

elusive and nonspecific, giving rise to a "surplus of meaning." The same multivalence means that symbols do not attempt to capture essence in a definitive way, but, like icons, they open windows on the eternal.[44]

What this means for divine fatherhood in the Fourth Gospel is that, as verbal icon, "Father" is neither an optional picture of God to be arbitrarily discarded nor a photograph of an ontic reality that cannot be touched by human hands. The father symbol is a "core symbol" in the Fourth Gospel,[45] primarily an expression of the relationship between God and Jesus,[46] and its theological manifestation is the incarnation. In Johannine terms, the symbol is both divinely revealed yet also grounded in human experience. The one who lies in the Father's embrace (1:18) is gathered into flesh; God takes shape in human form, created from clay, subject to death, mortal, vulnerable—radiant with deity, yes, but radiant also with the promise of flesh renewed, refined, immortal.[47]

This iconic framework shapes the Johannine understanding of fatherhood. C. H. Dodd has argued persuasively that the underlying imagery of father and son in the Fourth Gospel is that of a son apprenticed to his father.[48] Both father and son are at work on the same task, the son learning by imitating his father and not initiating his own independent work: "The Father is still working, and I also am working" (5:17); "the Son can do nothing on his own, but only what he sees the Father doing" (5:19b). This key christological text draws out the symbol pervading the Fourth Gospel's understanding of the Father-Son relationship, emphasizing the way in which, for John, divine revelation and human experience coalesce.

While the "father" is a core and pervading symbol across the entire narrative, in a number of ways the "fatherhood" of God in the Fourth Gospel deconstructs notions of patriarchy in ways that are surprising in a first-century CE text. First, the Johannine Father-symbol occurs in narrative contexts that are concerned with the surrender of power. The Johannine language

---

44. Dorothy A. Lee, "Touching the Sacred Text: The Bible as Icon in Feminist Reading," *Pacifica* 11 (1998): 249–64.

45. Koester, *Symbolism in the Fourth Gospel*, 4–8.

46. Paul Meyer, " 'The Father': The Presentation of God in the Fourth Gospel," in *Exploring the Gospel of John: In Honour of D. Moody Smith*, ed. R. Alan Culpepper and Carl Clifton Black (Louisville: Westminster John Knox, 1996), 255–73.

47. Dorothy A. Lee, *Flesh and Glory: Symbolism, Gender and Theology in the Gospel of John* (New York: Crossroad, 2002), 49.

48. Dodd, "A Hidden Parable," 30–40.

of "sending" is focused on mission and clusters particularly around the Father-Son image: God is frequently described by the Johannine Jesus as "the Father [or the one] who sent me" (5:36-37; 6:44, 57; 8:16, 18; 10:36; 11:41-42; 12:49; 14:24). As Son, Jesus is the one who is "sent" (ἀπεσταλμένος). Yet the sending of the Son by the Father does not protect either the messenger or the sender from harm. Motivated by love for the world (3:14-17), the Father is open to the vulnerability of love and the possibility of love received or love rejected (1:11). In life and in death the Son symbolizes and incarnates the gift to the world of God's own self (1:1).

The Fourth Gospel also speaks of the Father handing everything over to the Son (3:35; 5:22; 13:3; 16:15): for example, in the divine, sabbatical authority of giving life and judging (5:16-17, 21-27). Unlike the Roman-Hellenistic *paterfamilias*, who holds the power of life and death over members of the household, the power of the Johannine Father is handed over to the Son (5:21-22) and the believing community (15:5; 16:25-27). Authority is not held on to in the Fourth Gospel. The Father of the Johannine Jesus does not scheme to retain and increase power; on the contrary, power is given away again and again.

The second indication that divine fatherhood deconstructs patriarchal symbolism is the intimacy between the Johannine Jesus and God. The basis of the Father-Son relationship is the love each bears the other (3:35; 5:20; 10:17; 14:31; 15:9; 17:23, 26)—a love expressed in intimate and mutual terms rather than through duty and fear. This relationship is inclusive of others, unlike in the ancient world where patronage structures are predicated on elitism and hierarchy. In the Johannine symbolic world, creation is drawn into the relationships between Father and Son: the intimacy that exists within the being of God opens itself to other. All are invited to share the same love, the same "filiation" that the Johannine Jesus possesses.[49] The imagery of "abiding," as the narrative moves toward the passion and the full revelation of the glory, unfolds the same pattern of love, mutuality, and community (6:56; 8:31; 14:10, 17, 23; 15:1-17).[50]

The Johannine understanding of divine fatherhood thus involves a two-way movement. On the one hand, God's

---

49. Schneiders, "Symbolism and the Sacramental Principle in the Fourth Gospel," 228–32.

50. Fernando F. Segovia, *The Farewell of the Word: The Johannine Call to Abide* (Minneapolis: Fortress, 1991), 123–67; Dorothy A. Lee, "Abiding in the Fourth Gospel: A Case-Study in Feminist Biblical Theology," *Pacifica* 10 (1997): 123–36.

fatherhood, symbolically portrayed in the Father-Son relationship, is an outward movement of giving away power, surrendering selfhood as autonomous and self-sufficient. Such vulnerability places God on the side of the vulnerable, the outcast, and the powerless. On the other hand, divine fatherhood draws others into the filial relationship between God and Jesus, so that the Father-Son relationship becomes the fundamental icon of God's relations with the world. The Word spoken in love into the world inscribes a power of self-giving love into the structure of the universe.

God, in God's self, is beyond gender categories, is beyond names and representations, and would be utterly unknowable without God's condescending self-revelation in ways accessible to human apprehension. Even then, the language used to speak of this revelation is necessarily metaphorical due to the limitation of language to express adequately the divine reality. The God we speak of always "is" and "is not" communicable. In becoming flesh, the Divine has allowed a specific particularity, Jesus, to be the means of God's presence in history. The male Jesus is an icon of the divine Word, and the Father in this Gospel is an icon of the life-giving, self-surrendering God who invites all to be embraced as children (1:13). The fatherhood of God functions in the text to articulate the experience of being drawn into participation in God's own life mediated through Jesus and the Spirit. A father-son relationship becomes a symbol for the believer's post-Easter experience of life in Jesus. Ultimately, the challenge to the reader is not so much to see divinity in terms of fatherhood but to revision fatherhood in the light of the Gospel. The Johannine symbolism is both iconoclastic and iconographic: in writing the new, it demythologizes the old.

Dorothy A. Lee

John 6:1-71

Sophia Nourishes Her Children

Instead of these things you gave your people food of angels,
and without their toil you supplied them with bread from heaven ready to eat,
providing every pleasure and suited to every taste.
For your essence [ὑπόστασίς] manifested your sweetness toward your children;[1]
and it, ministering to the desire of the one who took it,
was changed to suit everyone's liking. (Wis 16:20-21; author's translation)

John 6 is a particularly complex chapter, drawing on the Jewish celebration of Passover and also the Jewish appropriation of the manna as a symbol of Wisdom and Torah. A trap for Christians is to move too quickly into reading the long discourse on the "Bread of Life" (vv. 25-59) as a reflection on the Eucharist, instead of following the development of the argument across these verses—from manna, to

---

1. LXX: ἡ μὲν γὰρ ὑπόστασίς σου τὴν σὴν πρὸς τέκνα ἐνεφάνιζεν γλυκύτητα. The term ἡ ὑπόστασίς (*hypostasis*) attempts to name God's inner being. Liddell translates it as "essence" and Köster describes it as an abstract term for God's "counsel." See Henry G. Liddell, "ὑπόστασις," in *A Lexicon: Abridged from Liddell and Scott's Greek-English Lexicon* (Oak Harbor, WA: Logos Research Systems, 1996), 847, and Helmut Köster, "'Υπόστασις," *TDNT* 8 (1972): 581–82. It is a feminine-gendered word and could be an alternative for God's wisdom.

nourishment through Wisdom/Torah, to nourishment by Jesus's teaching, to nourishment by Eucharist. It is like a symphony gradually unfolding across a number of movements. In his teaching Jesus personifies divine Wisdom offering guidance and nourishment to her children and the gift of eternity life.

The chapter develops in the following way:

6:1-4   A transition from Jerusalem to Galilee; Jesus depicted like Moses.

6:5-15   The account of the feeding of a multitude leading to the crowd's decision that Jesus is the one who is to come; Jesus's awareness that they wish to make him king, and his flight from that place.

6:16-21   The sea crossing and the revelation of Jesus as "I AM."

6:22-24   A second transition bringing all the characters together.

6:25-59   The discourse on the bread from heaven.

6:60-71   A crisis is created by the word of Jesus.

Jesus Like Moses (6:1-4)

The opening verses shift the geography from Jerusalem to Galilee and establish that it is the springtime festival of Passover. This is the second of three Passovers depicted in John and the only one where Jesus is not in Jerusalem. As Passover is one of the three major pilgrim festivals (Exod 34:22-23), Jewish men were expected to celebrate the festival in Jerusalem, with the sacrificing of the lamb in the temple followed by the Passover meal. It is possible that this Passover in Galilee is the second Passover prescribed for those who were unable to celebrate the festival at the proper time.[2] The normal Passover was held "in the first month, on the fourteenth day of the month, at twilight, in the wilderness of Sinai" (Num 9:4-5). But some people were unable to celebrate, and these complained to Moses. For these, and for others unable to keep the festival in the first month, provision was made for celebrating the following month (Num

---

2. For detailed arguments supporting the view that this feeding occurs during the second Passover, see Michael A. Daise, *Feasts in John: Jewish Festivals and Jesus' "Hour" in the Fourth Gospel*, WUNT 2:229 (Tübingen: Mohr Siebeck, 2007), 118–52.

6:1After this Jesus went to the other side of the Sea of Galilee, also called the Sea of Tiberias. 2A large crowd kept following him, because they saw the signs that he was doing for the sick. 3Jesus went up the mountain and sat down there with his disciples. 4Now the Passover, the festival of the Jews, was near.

9:10-12). Jesus may have fulfilled his religious obligation and attended the normal Passover in Jerusalem and then, one month later, been in Galilee, by the Sea of Tiberius,[3] at the time of the second Passover.

In Galilee, away from the Jerusalem temple, the key Passover symbol is the unleavened bread. Jesus's actions in crossing the Sea of Tiberias with a crowd following, going up a mountain and there sitting down, in the pose of a teacher with his student-disciples, connects this episode with the memory of Moses as the great leader and teacher of Israel, who received the revelation of the law on a mountain. The description of the crowd, who follow because they have seen the signs, is also reminiscent of the Israelites who believed and followed Moses because of the signs he produced (Exod 4:1-9, 30-31).

Feeding the Crowd (6:5-15)

The feeding of the multitude occurs six times in the Gospel tradition, twice in the Gospels of Mark and Matthew (Mark 6:30-44; 8:1-10; Matt 14:13-21; 15:32-39), and once each in Luke (Luke 9:10-17) and John (6:5-15). The second feeding in Mark and Matthew is a feeding on the Gentile side of the Sea of Galilee and most likely is a repetition for theological purposes rather than one with a historical basis.

When comparing the versions of the feeding of the five thousand, the Fourth Gospel has some significant differences. In the Synoptic Gospels, it is the disciples who initiate the action by speaking of the need to send the crowd away to get something to eat. In the Fourth Gospel,

3. In 20 CE, a new capital city of the Galilean region was built and named in honor of the emperor at that time. Daly-Denton comments, "Whatever the Evangelist's reason for adding 'of Tiberias,' for us today it underscores the hubris of the imperial claim to ownership of the entire (known) world's natural resources, in this case, a lake whose waters teemed with potential for tribute and tax revenue." See Margaret Daly-Denton, *John: An Earth Bible Commentary; Supposing Him to Be the Gardener*, Earth Bible Commentary (London: Bloomsbury T&T Clark, 2017), 105.

⁵When he looked up and saw a large crowd coming toward him, Jesus said to Philip, "Where are we to buy bread for these people to eat?" ⁶He said this to test him, for he himself knew what he was going to do. ⁷Philip answered him, "Six months' wages would not buy enough bread for each of them to get a little." ⁸One of his disciples, Andrew, Simon Peter's brother, said to him, ⁹"There is a boy here who has five barley loaves and two fish. But what are they among so many people?" ¹⁰Jesus said, "Make the people sit down." Now there was a great deal of grass in the place; so they sat down, about five thousand in all. ¹¹Then Jesus took the loaves, and when he had given thanks, he distributed them to those who were seated; so also the fish, as much as they wanted. ¹²When they were satisfied, he told his disciples, "Gather up the fragments left over, so that nothing may be lost." ¹³So they gathered them up, and from the fragments of the five barley loaves, left by those who had eaten, they filled twelve baskets. ¹⁴When the people saw the sign that he had done, they began to say, "This is indeed the prophet who is to come into the world." ¹⁵When Jesus realized that they were about to come and take him by force to make him king, he withdrew again to the mountain by himself.

Jesus initiates the action with his rhetorical question to Philip, "Where are we to buy bread for these people to eat?" (v. 5). The Fourth Gospel is unique in speaking of five *barley* loaves. According to Jewish law, the barley could not be used for ordinary eating until it had been offered on the second day within the first Passover liturgy (Lev 23:9-14). That barley loaves are now available further supports the view that this feeding, when barley can be used, must be the second Passover, celebrated a month after the "waving of the sheaf [Heb. *'Omer*]" of the firstfruits during the normal Passover festival (Lev 23:9-11, 14).[4]

When Jesus takes the loaves, in the Synoptic accounts on the Jewish side of the lake (Mark 6:30-44; Matt 14:13-21), he blesses and breaks the loaves and then gives them to the disciples to distribute to the crowd. A prayer of blessing over the bread would be the norm in ordinary Jewish family meals. Mark speaks of Jesus "giving thanks" (Mark 8:6) over the bread in the second feeding account, in a Gentile context. In the Fourth Gospel, with its one feeding account, Jesus offers a prayer of

---

4. The barley loaves and the link with the waving of the firstfruits also occur in a feeding miracle performed by the prophet Elisha (2 Kings 4:42-44). For more on the barley and the waving of the 'Omer, see Daise, *Feasts in John*, 105–18.

thanksgiving (εὐχαριστήσας), and then he himself distributes the bread (v. 11). These actions of Jesus anticipate the later eucharistic practice of a community who gathers for the Lord's Supper (1 Cor 11:20) and at this supper understand that it is Christ who is the host at *his* table (1 Cor 10:21).[5] When all have eaten, Jesus commands the disciples, "Gather up the fragments left over, so that nothing may perish[6] [συναγάγετε τὰ περισσεύσαντα κλάσματα, ἵνα μή τι ἀπόληται]" (6:12). Here also, the text may reflect later eucharistic practice where the verb συνάγω is used to speak of gathering the community for Eucharist (Did. 9.4; 1 Clem. 34.7 and Ign. Pol. 4.2),[7] and the *Didache* uses the term κλάσμα for the eucharistic fragments.[8]

The twelve baskets of fragments on this Jewish side of the lake allude to the future eschatological Israel, now reunited as one group of twelve tribes.[9] In this Jewish context, and with a view to the following discourse, the five loaves may well reflect the Torah—the five books of Moses—which provides nourishment to the children of Israel.

There were expectations that in the messianic end times there would be a new miracle of the manna. This is expressed in a Jewish text written about the same time as the Fourth Gospel:

> And it shall come to pass when all is accomplished that was to come to pass in those parts, that the Messiah shall then begin to be revealed. . . . And it shall come to pass at that self-same time that the treasury of manna shall again descend from on high, and they will eat of it in those years, because these are they who have come to the consummation of time. (2 Bar 29:3, 8)

5. "There is no doubt that, for Paul and the Corinthians, the risen Lord Jesus Christ, with his saving power, was personally present at the Eucharist as the host of the ritual." See Peter Lampe, "The Eucharist: Identifying with Christ on the Cross," *Int* 48 (1994): 42–43.

6. While the verb ἀπόλλυμι can mean "to be lost," in the following discourse much is made of the contrast between the manna that perished, along with Israel's ancestors who ate it, and the bread Jesus offers, which is for eternity life (6:27, 48-51).

7. Francis J. Moloney, *John*, SP 4 (Collegeville, MN: Liturgical Press, 1998), 198.

8. περὶ δὲ τοῦ κλάσμος (Did. 9:3); τὸ κλάσμα (Did. 9:4). See also the discussion by Johannes Behm, "κλάω, κλάσις, κλάσμα," *TDNT* 3 (1965): 726–43.

9. So also Andrew T. Lincoln, *The Gospel according to Saint John*, BNTC (London: Continuum, 2005), 213; Jean Zumstein, *L'Évangile selon Saint Jean (1–12)*, CNT 4a 2nd ser. (Genève: Labor et Fides, 2014), 213. Both Lincoln and Zumstein note the later reference to "the twelve" (6:67, 70), which Zumstein sees as an incarnation of the eschatological Israel. Recall that in John 4, Judeans and Samaritans have come together, so according to the narrative, the once-divided people are now one.

The crowd has seen the sign and understood that the abundant bread announces the arrival of this messianic time. Associated with the messianic times was an expectation that a "prophet like Moses" would appear fulfilling the promise of Deuteronomy 18:15-18; such expectation lies behind the people's attempt to make Jesus a king (6:15).[10]

The Works of Sophia Displayed[11] (6:16-21)

The sea crossing continues the Mosaic exodus theme present in the miraculous feeding. When a storm arises, a normal occurrence on the Sea of Galilee as it is surrounded by high hills and deep valleys, Jesus comes to the disciples "walking on [ἐπὶ] the sea."[12] The description of this sea crossing has echoes of Psalm 107:23-30 in its description of the disciples' going "down to the sea," their distress in the strong wind and rough seas, and their arrival at their "desired haven." The psalmist records that in this the deeds of the I AM are revealed, both in the storm and when the sailors cry to the I AM who delivers them:

> Some *went down to the sea* in ships,
>   doing business on the mighty waters;
> they saw the deeds of the I AM [Heb: יהוה],
>   wondrous works in the deep.
> For [God] commanded and raised the *stormy wind*,
>   which lifted up the waves of the sea.
> They mounted up to heaven, they went down to the depths;
>   their courage melted away in their calamity; . . .
> Then they cried to the I AM in their trouble,
>   and he brought them out from their distress;
> he made the storm be still,
>   and the waves of the sea were hushed.

---

10. There were traditions in Judaism predating the Fourth Gospel that depicted Moses as both prophet and king. These traditions are evident in the writing of Philo. For details of these traditions, see the study by Wayne A. Meeks, *The Prophet-King: Moses Traditions and the Johannine Christology*, NovTSup 14 (Leiden: Brill, 1967).

11. "It is your will that works of your wisdom [τῆς σοφίας σου ἔργα] should not be without effect; / therefore people trust their lives even to the smallest piece of wood, / and passing through the billows on a raft they come safely to land" (Wis 14:5).

12. "On the sea," ἐπὶ τῆς θαλάσσης: the more common meaning of ἐπί with the genitive is "on" or "upon," although it could also be translated "by the sea." The Mosaic-exodus theme of the bread miracle and the revelatory formula "I AM" suggests a miraculous manifestation of Jesus walking "on" the sea, rather than the more prosaic "beside" the sea.

16When evening came, his disciples went down to the sea, 17got into a boat, and started across the sea to Capernaum. It was now dark, and Jesus had not yet come to them. 18The sea became rough because a strong wind was blowing. 19When they had rowed about three or four miles, they saw Jesus walking on the sea and coming near the boat, and they were terrified. 20But he said to them, "It is I; do not be afraid." 21Then they wanted to take him into the boat, and immediately the boat reached the land toward which they were going.

> Then they were glad because they had quiet,
> and he brought them to their desired haven. (Ps 107:23-30)

For landlocked people, a large body of water known for terrifying storms can seem as threatening as the primeval sea.[13] The OT sings out God's praises for exercising divine authority over the power of the sea and creating order (Ps 65:7; 77:19; 89:9-10; Isa 43:16; 51:10, 15; Job 38:16). When Jesus identifies himself to his terrified disciples as I AM (ἐγώ εἰμι), he reveals himself as the manifestation of Israel's God whose divine name "I am, who I am" (Exod 3:14) was first revealed to Moses. Jesus does not demonstrate or legitimize human mastery of the sea. In this Gospel he does not speak a word of command to the winds or the waves (cf. Matt 8:26; Mark 4:39; Luke 8:25); rather, he acts as divine Sophia displaying her works and bringing those who trust their lives to a small piece of wood safely to land (Wis 14:5). The sea crossing functions as a divine epiphany for the disciples, correcting the crowd's notion of Jesus as "the prophet-king" in the style of Moses. It is as the Lord, the God of Israel, that Jesus comes across the waters, and with his presence the disciples safely reach their destination (v. 21).[14]

Transition (6:22-24)

With the sea crossing, there is now a separation between Jesus and the crowd; verses 22-24 bring together Jesus, the disciples, and the crowd

---

13. Daly-Denton, *John: An Earth Bible Commentary*, 112–13.

14. For similar imperatives using "Fear not" and "I am," see Gen 26:24; Isa 41:10; and LXX Jer 26:28; 49:11; 51:12. *Ego Eimi* as a revelatory formula can be found in Gen 26:24; Isa 43:25; 45:19; 51:12, as well as the revelation of the divine name to Moses (Exod 3:14). As Zumstein states, "It is not simply a formula of identification, but a theophany" (Zumstein, *L'Évangile selon Saint Jean [1–12]*, 217).

²²The next day the crowd that had stayed on the other side of the sea saw that there had been only one boat there. They also saw that Jesus had not got into the boat with his disciples, but that his disciples had gone away alone. ²³Then some boats from Tiberias came near the place where they had eaten the bread after the Lord had given thanks. ²⁴So when the crowd saw that neither Jesus nor his disciples were there, they themselves got into the boats and went to Capernaum looking for Jesus.

who had eaten the bread. The title "the Lord" (v. 23) is rare within the Johannine narrative, and the phrase "after the Lord had given thanks" is missing from some manuscripts but present in the earliest manuscripts. This phrase reflects the post-Easter eucharistic language of the community where there is one loaf (ἄρτος) and not the five loaves of the feeding miracle. Within the feeding there were five loaves (v. 11); this passage speaks of one loaf (v. 23).

The Bread of Life Discourse (6:25-59)

A structure I suggest for this rich theological passage is a parallel arrangement with an introduction (vv. 25-34) and conclusion (vv. 58-59). The entire discussion takes places in Capernaum (vv. 24, 59) which provides a geographical frame around the passage. The first part, verses 35-47, may be called "sapiential" as in this part, even while speaking of "bread," the verses repeatedly speak of "coming to Jesus" (vv. 35, 37, 44, 45) and "believing" (35, 36, 40, 47) in him, just as Wisdom invites her disciples to come to her and be nourished by her teaching.

> Come to me [Sophia], you who desire me,
>   and eat your fill of my fruits.
> For the memory of me is sweeter than honey,
>   and the possession of me sweeter than the honeycomb. (Sir 24:19-20)

There is no mention in the first part of the discourse of "eating" the bread. The sapiential theme continues into the second part even when the theme of "eating" the bread is introduced (vv. 49, 50, 51b). Within the wisdom literature the theme of eating of Wisdom's food, and being nourished by her bread and wine, is a metaphorical way of believing in and accepting her teaching: "Come, eat of my bread and drink of the wine I have mixed. Lay aside immaturity, and live, and walk in the way of insight"

(Prov 9:5-6). With the mention of "flesh" in 51c, the metaphor of eating from Wisdom's banquet leads into the sacramental language of eating the "flesh" and drinking the "blood" of Jesus in 51c, 53, 54, 55, 56, 57. These themes will be further developed in the discussion of each section.

Introduction (25-34): "ancestors ate . . . the bread from heaven."	
Part 1. Sapiential	**Part 2. Sapiential/Eucharistic**
35-40: I am the bread of life	48-51: I am the bread of life.
41-42: Murmuring by "the Jews"	52: Dispute by "the Jews"
43-47: I will raise him/her up on the last day; whoever believes has eternal life	53-57: I will raise her/him up on the last day; whoever eats and drinks has eternal life.
Conclusion (58-59): "The bread which came down from heaven . . . your ancestors ate."	

Introduction to the Discourse (6:25-34)

The introduction to the discourse takes the form of a dialogue be-tween Jesus and the crowd (v. 22, 24). At this point there is openness and even the respectful titles "Rabbi" (v. 25) and "Sir" or "Master" (κύριε). The "crowd" will become "the Jews" when their attitude changes to complaint (v. 41). One of the major themes developed in the discourse appears in Jesus's first response in the contrast between the "food that perishes [ἀπολλυμένην]" and the "food that continues into eternity life [μένουσαν εἰς ζωὴν αἰώνιον]" (v. 27). The food that perishes offers mul-tiple possible meanings. It may refer to ordinary food such as the bread that the crowd had eaten the day before. Such food does not last. There may also be an allusion to the manna that lasted only for one day, and those who collected more than they needed found that "it bred worms and became foul" (Exod 16:20). The food that continues into eternity life looks beyond the present miraculous feeding to a future gift of "the human-one."[15] The narrative has already introduced the figure of "the human-one" as a source of divine revelation (1:51), one who will be lifted up/exalted (3:13-14), one who has been authorized by the Father

---

15. See excursus on "Son of Man" at p. 50.

John 6:25-34

²⁵When they found him on the other side of the sea, they said to him, "Rabbi, when did you come here?" ²⁶Jesus answered them, "Very truly, I tell you, you are looking for me, not because you saw signs, but because you ate your fill of the loaves. ²⁷Do not work for the food that perishes, but for the food that endures for eternal life, which the Son of Man will give you. For it is on him that God the Father has set his seal." ²⁸Then they said to him, "What must we do to perform the works of God?" ²⁹Jesus answered them, "This is the work of God, that you believe in him whom he has sent." ³⁰So they said

to dispense life, and in whom judgment occurs through the choices individuals make in response to him (5:27). Once again his authority is emphasized through the image of a "seal," which was a formal mark placed on a message to signify its authenticity and authority as coming from the sender.[16] Jesus comes with credentials from God attesting to his unique authority.

The crowd's question about "doing the works of God" reflects a Jewish attitude of obedience to the law.[17] As Jan G. van der Watt notes, Jesus's response makes a dramatic change to their traditional views. "Works" becomes a single "work," "to believe in him whom [God] has sent" (v. 29). The singular work of God is the act of faith in Jesus; it "is a matter of opening up to Jesus and his revelation and to accept him and it in full behaviour."[18]

Jesus's reply that they believe in him elicits the challenge from the crowd asking for a sign as the basis for their belief. The "signs and wonders" (Exod 7:3; Deut 4:34) Moses performed for the Israelites proved his credentials and justified their belief in him. Can Jesus also produce credentials? At this point the crowd provides Jesus with an example of

---

16. Moloney, *John*, 209.

17. This phrase (ἐργαζώμεθα τὰ ἔργα τοῦ θεοῦ) is found elsewhere in the LXX (for instance Hab 1:5), Jewish literature (1 QS 4:4; 1 QH 5:36; Damascus Rule, 1:1; 2:14; 13:7), and the New Testament (Matt 6:3; Mark 2:24; 10:17). See Jan G. van der Watt, "The Gospel of John's Perception of Ethical Behaviour," *In die Skriflig* 45 (2011): 434.

18. Van der Watt, "The Gospel of John's Perception of Ethical Behaviour," 436. Van der Watt continues to note there is no conflict between "faith" and "works." He cites Raymond Brown to say that salvation is "not a question of works, as if faith did not matter; nor is it a question of faith without works. Rather, having faith is a work; indeed, it is the all-important work of God." See Raymond E. Brown, *The Gospel according to John*, 2 vols., AB 29–29A (New York: Doubleday, 1966, 1970), 1:265.

to him, "What sign are you going to give us then, so that we may see it and believe you? What work are you performing? [31]Our ancestors ate the manna in the wilderness; as it is written, 'He gave them bread from heaven to eat.'" [32]Then Jesus said to them, "Very truly, I tell you, it was not Moses who gave you the bread from heaven, but it is my Father who gives you the true bread from heaven. [33]For the bread of God is that which comes down from heaven and gives life to the world." [34]They said to him, "Sir, give us this bread always."

an acceptable sign, which was the provision of manna in the wilderness, along with a Scripture citation, "He gave them bread from heaven to eat," where, in their minds, "he" refers to Moses.[19] If this is the same group present at the feeding miracle who considered Jesus might be the "prophet like Moses" ushering in the messianic time, then they may have in mind the sign of abundant manna as prophesied by 2 Baruch (29:3, 8; cited above). As well as the association of the manna with the abundant bread of the preceding day, the manna miracle fell one month after the first Passover, i.e., on the day of the second concessional Passover for those who missed the regular date.[20]

The text given to Jesus by the crowd, "he gave them bread from heaven to eat [ἄρτον ἐκ τοῦ οὐρανοῦ ἔδωκεν αὐτοῖς φαγεῖν]" (v. 31), has no exact correspondence with any known biblical text. There are several possible sources,[21] and the Johannine text may be a conflation of them all.[22] Across the rest of the discourse (vv. 32-58) Jesus expounds on this text in the manner of an "expository sermon, set in the synagogue at Capernaum

---

19. Maarten J. Menken, *Old Testament Quotations in the Fourth Gospel: Studies in Textual Form*, CBET 15 (Kampen: Kok Pharos, 1996), 51; Ruth Sheridan, *Retelling Scripture: 'The Jews' and the Scriptural Citations in John 1:19–12:15*, BibInt 110 (Leiden: Brill, 2012), 139.

20. Brown, *The Gospel According to John*, 1:265; Daise, *Feasts in John*, 142.

21. Ps 78:24 (LXX Ps 77): "he rained down on them manna to eat [φαγεῖν], and gave them the grain of heaven [καὶ ἄρτον οὐρανοῦ ἔδωκεν αὐτοῖς]"; Exod 16:4: "I am going to rain bread from heaven for you [ἐγὼ ὕω ὑμῖν ἄρτους ἐκ τοῦ οὐρανοῦ]"; Wis 16:20: "Instead of these things you gave your people food of angels, and without their toil you supplied them from heaven with bread ready to eat [ἀνθ᾽ ὧν ἀγγέλων τροφὴν ἐψώμισας τὸν λαόν σου καὶ ἕτοιμον ἄρτον ἀπ᾽ οὐρανοῦ παρέσχες αὐτοῖς ἀκοπιάτως]."

22. For a recent discussion of these three texts, see Sheridan, *Retelling Scripture*, 146–54.

(John 6:59), which successively explicates each portion of the biblical text and, in so doing, elaborates the meaning of the signs."[23]

In reply Jesus corrects the crowd by stating that it was not Moses but "my Father" who provided bread for the ancestors, and Jesus brings this provision of bread into the present, "my Father who gives you the true bread from heaven" (6:32).[24] Up until this point the term "bread" (ἄρτος) has meant literal food, whether the bread supplied by Jesus the day before or the manna provided to the ancestors; Jesus now begins to use the term "bread" in a symbolic sense to speak of himself. He is the "true bread . . . which comes down from heaven and gives life to the world" (vv. 32-33; cf. 1:10; 3:16; 5:21). The crowd then responds with words similar to those of the Samaritan woman (4:15), "Sir/Master, give us this bread always" (v. 34). This request leads into the discourse where Jesus offers further clarification on the "bread" being offered to them by his Father.

Manna, Word, and Wisdom within Jewish Traditions

By late Second Temple Judaism, the manna episode in Exodus 16 had undergone various interpretive traditions found in such writings as the book of Wisdom[25] and Philo.[26] These may be summarized as follows:

1. Within the earlier Hebrew text the manna is understood as a test to see if the Israelites will obey God's word (Exod 16:4; Deut 8:3); in this way the manna from heaven is understood to be a preparation for receiving the Torah from heaven.[27]

23. Craig Koester, *Symbolism in the Fourth Gospel: Meaning, Mystery, Community* (Minneapolis: Fortress, 1995), 95. The understanding that the discourse may have been patterned on a synagogue sermon was first developed by Peder Borgen, *Bread from Heaven: An Exegetical Study of the Concept of Manna in the Gospel of John and the Writings of Philo*, NovTSup 10 (Leiden: Brill, 1965), 59–98.

24. "John 6:32, therefore, emphasizes that God gives the bread from heaven in the eschatological present"; see Borgen, *Bread from Heaven*, 168.

25. The book of Wisdom, written in Greek, is thought to have been written in Alexandria during a time of Jewish oppression in 38 CE. For more on this dating, see Jozsef Zsengéller, "'The Taste of Paradise': Interpretation of Exodus and Manna in the Book of Wisdom," in *Studies in the Book of Wisdom*, ed. Géza G. Xeravits and J. Zsengéller, JSJS 142 (Boston: Brill, 2010), 198, n. 4.

26. I am omitting the traditions found in the targums due to difficulties in dating these Aramaic rewritings of the Scriptures.

27. "Using this heavenly origin [of the manna] the author of the Book of Wisdom . . . forms a typological milieu for what is coming in the desert of Sinai: Word from the heaven." See Zsengéller, "The Taste of Paradise," 208.

2. The giver of the manna shifts from God to Moses,[28] possibly influenced by the other wonders and "gifts" ascribed to Moses, such as producing water from the rock (Exod 17:1-17).

3. As manna nourished the wilderness generations, so all future generations continue to be nourished by the Word of God and, in the sapiential writings, by Wisdom.[29] This leads to an identification found in Philo among the manna, the Word, and Wisdom.[30]

4. The bread *coming from* heaven (Exod 16:4, ἄρτους ἐκ τοῦ οὐρανοῦ) morphs into the bread *of* heaven or heavenly bread (Ps 78:24, ἄρτον οὐρανοῦ; LXX 77:24).[31]

5. Understood as bread *of* heaven it is perceived to be the bread on which the angels feed, which is not the same as human food.[32] Where the Hebrew text of Psalm 78:24-25 reads "bread of the mighty or strong ones" (לחם אבירים), the LXX translates this as "bread of angels" (ἄρτον ἀγγέλων)—a description that is then continued in the book of Wisdom (Wis 16:20: ἀγγέλων τροφὴν) and Pseudo-Philo.[33]

6. The manna, as the bread of heaven and angelic food, is a food that provides immortality and is called *ambrosia* (Wis 19:21: ἀμβροσίας τροφῆς), which in Hellenistic writings is the food of the gods, enabling them to be immortal.[34]

---

28. Menken, *Old Testament Quotations*, 48, and the discussion on 54.

29. "What manna signified for the desert generation, the Word now signifies for the present one." See Angela Passaro, "The Serpent and the Manna or the Saving Word: Exegesis of Wis 16," in *Deuterocanonical and Cognate Literature Yearbook 2005: The Book of Wisdom in Modern Research*, ed. Angelo Passaro and Giuseppe Bellia (Berlin: de Gruyter, 2005), 183–84.

30. Philo writes: "That the food of the soul is not earthly but heavenly, we shall find abundant evidence in the Sacred Word. 'Behold I rain upon you bread out of heaven' (Exod 16:4). You see that the soul is fed not with things of earth that decay, but with such words as God should have poured out like rain" (*Leg All* 3.162). See further discussion in Zsengéller, "The Taste of Paradise," 211–13; Edwin D. Freed, *Old Testament Quotations in the Gospel of John*, NovTSup 11 (Leiden: Brill, 1965), 12.

31. Tobias Nicklas, " 'Food of Angels' (Wis 16:20)," in *Studies in the Book of Wisdom*, ed. Géza G. Xeravits and J. Zsengéller, JSJS 14 (Boston: Brill, 2010), 92.

32. Nicklas, "Food of Angels," 84. In this article Nicklas examines those biblical and intertestamental passages where angels are offered human food.

33. "But know that you have eaten the bread of angels for forty years" (*LAB* 19.5a). Nicklas, "Food of Angels," 95. The *Liber Antiquitatum Biblicarum* (*LAB*) is dated to the first century CE with differences of opinion whether it was before or after the destruction of the temple.

34. Zsengéller, "The Taste of Paradise," 215–16; also Nicklas, "Food of Angels," 94.

7. In the eschatological age of the Messiah, once again manna will rain down from heaven (2 Bar 29:6-8) for those who have arrived at the consummation of time to eat from it. Those living in this eschatological time no longer eat normal food but heavenly food, the food of Paradise.[35]

Within the scriptural traditions of the Old Testament, manna is presented not only as a sign of God's care and nourishment[36] but also as a means of testing the Israelites to see if they will listen to and obey God's word. Thus when the manna is first described to Moses we read: "I am going to rain bread from heaven for you, and each day the people shall go out and gather enough for that day. In that way I will test them, whether they will follow my instruction [תורתי] or not" (Exod 16:4). A similar interpretation of the manna is given in Deuteronomy: "He humbled you by letting you hunger, then by feeding you with manna, with which neither you nor your ancestors were acquainted, in order to make you understand that one does not live by bread alone, but by every word [מוצא] that comes from the mouth of the LORD" (Deut 8:3; similarly 8:16).

This tradition of connecting the manna, eaten by the wilderness generation, with the Word of God, available to all generations, led into a prophetic tradition of being nourished by the word of God. "Your words were found, and I ate them, and your words [דברך] became to me a joy" (Jer 15:16).[37] "The time is surely coming, says the Lord GOD, when I will send a famine on the land; not a famine of bread, or a thirst for water, but of hearing the words of the LORD [דברי יהוה]" (Amos 8:11).

The theme of being nourished by God's word is further developed in the later wisdom literature with traditions of Wisdom's banquet.

> Wisdom has built her house;
> she has hewn her seven pillars.
> She has slaughtered her animals, she has mixed her wine,
> she has also set her table.
> She has sent out her servant-girls, she calls
> from the highest places in the town,

---

35. Zsengéller, "The Taste of Paradise," 212–13.

36. "I pitied your groanings and gave you manna for food; you ate the bread of angels" (2 Esd 1:19).

37. Similarly Ezekiel eats the scroll of a book (Ezek 3:3); Isaiah offers food without money and wine without cost to those who will listen (Isa 55:1-3).

"You that are simple, turn in here!"
   To those without sense she says,
"Come, eat of my bread
   and drink of the wine I have mixed.
Lay aside immaturity, and live,
   and walk in the way of insight." (Prov 9:1-6)

The nourishment that Wisdom offers is later identified with her own being. "Those who eat *of me* will hunger for more, and those who drink *of me* will thirst for more" (Sir 24:21).

Wisdom's invitation to her disciples to eat and drink at her table is a metaphorical way of inviting them to listen to and follow her teaching, and in the book of Sirach Wisdom is eventually enshrined in Torah. "All this is the book of the covenant of the Most High God, the law that Moses commanded us as an inheritance for the congregations of Jacob" (Sir 24:23).[38] These verses provide a brief sample of texts indicating a Jewish metaphorical interpretation of the manna, now continued in Israel through choosing the way of *Sophia* and following the teachings of Torah. By late Second Temple Judaism, through Wisdom enshrined in Torah, God continued to nourish Israel as once God fed the ancestors on manna.

The biblical tradition of equating the manna with the word of God continues in the first-century writing of Philo, an Alexandrian Jew who lived "from about 15 BCE to about 50 CE."[39] What is an implicit identification of manna, Wisdom, and word within Israel's Scriptures, Philo makes explicit:

When they sought what it is that nourishes the soul [ψυχήν] (for, Moses says, "they knew not what it was") (Exod xvi.15), they became learners and found it to be a saying [ῥῆμα] of God, that is the Divine Word [λόγον θεῖον], from which all kinds of instruction and wisdom [σοφία] flows in a perpetual stream. This is the heavenly nourishment, and it is indicated as such in the sacred records, when the First Cause in his own person says, "Lo, it is I that am raining upon you bread out of heaven [ἄρτους

---

38. Baruch makes a similar identification of Wisdom and Torah: "He found the whole way to knowledge, and gave her to his servant Jacob and to Israel, whom he loved. Afterward she appeared on earth and lived with humankind. She is the book of the commandments of God, the law that endures forever. All who hold her fast will live, and those who forsake her will die" (Bar 3:36–4:1).

39. Peder Borgen, *The Gospel of John: More Light from Philo, Paul and Archaeology; The Scriptures, Tradition, Exposition, Settings, Meaning*, NovTSup 154 (Leiden: Brill, 2014), 44.

ἐκ τοῦ οὐρανοῦ]" (Exod xvi. 4); for in very deed God drops from above the ethereal wisdom [σοφίαν]. (*De Fuga* 137)[40]

A few lines later Philo offers this interpretation of Exodus 16:15:

"This is the bread which the Lord has given them to eat" (Exod xvi. 15). Tell me, then, of what kind the bread is. "This saying [ῥῆμα]," he [Moses] says, "which the Lord ordained" (Exod xvi. 16). This divine ordinance fills the soul. (*De Fuga* 139)

Here, Philo is explicitly linking the manna with the Word (ῥῆμα) of God. In answer to the question, "What then is the bread?" Philo responds that it is "the saying [ῥῆμα]," he says, "which the Lord ordained."

Where usually the words "This is the saying which the Lord has appointed" are read as an introduction to the following instructions about the *omer* (Exod 16:16), Philo refers these words back as an answer to the question, "What is this bread?"[41] Thus, prior to the Johannine writings, there were interpretive traditions within Judaism identifying the manna with the Word or Wisdom of God.

Within the book of Wisdom a further element is added, that Wisdom is able to nourish her disciples with immortality, a gift to humans intended from the beginning, since "God did not make death" (Wis 1:13).

In the book of Wisdom, the manna tradition is interpreted as the "bread of heaven" or "food of the angels," i.e., the food of the immortal ones (Wis 16:20). Later this is called *ambrosia* (Wis 19:21),[42] reflecting the Hellenistic notion that the gods were immortal because they fed on ambrosia, which

---

40. Alena Nye-Knutson, "Hidden Bread and Revealed Word: Manna Traditions in Targums Neophyti 1 and Ps-Jonathan," in *Israel in the Wilderness: Interpretations of the Biblical Narratives in Jewish and Christian Traditions*, ed. Kenneth E. Pomykala, TBN 10 (Leiden: Brill, 2008), 222. The translation follows Philo, "De Fuga et Inventione," in *Philo with an English Translation*, ed. F. H. Colson and G. H. Whitaker (London: William Heinemann, 1958).

41. Nye-Knutson, "Hidden Bread and Revealed Word," 222. Nye-Knutson continues: "Amazingly, this is in fact precisely how the Septuagint divides the text. Verse 15 concludes with, '"What is this?" for they knew not what it was, and Moses said to them.' Verse 16 then begins, 'This is the bread which the Lord has given you to eat. This is the word (*rema*!) which the Lord has appointed.' Philo was in fact simply quoting the Septuagint, not offering an independent interpretation" (222).

42. See the arguments by Nicklas linking the elements of the *ambrosia* of Wis 19:21 with the elements of the manna, particularly its characteristics as "crystalline" and "easily melting"; Nicklas, "Food of Angels," 94.

prevented their atoms from dissipating, thus giving them immortality,[43] but in Greek thought, this food, *ambrosia*, was reserved for the gods alone. According to the book of Wisdom, "God created us for incorruption, and made us in the image of [God's] own eternity" (Wis 2:23), so that the righteous only "seemed to have died" (Wis 3:2), since "righteousness is immortal [ἀθάνατός]" (Wis 1:15). In Solomon's great prayer for Wisdom he proclaims, "because of her, I shall have immortality [ἀθανασίαν]" (Wis 8:13), because those who choose her, receive her own "immortal [ἄφθαρτόν] spirit" (Wis 12:1). According to the book of Wisdom, this food of immortality is now available as Wisdom's gift to her children.

> Instead of these things you gave your people food of angels [ἀγγέλων τροφὴν],
> and without their toil you supplied them from heaven with bread [ἄρτον ἀπ' οὐρανοῦ] ready to eat,
> providing every pleasure and suited to every taste.
> For your essence manifested your sweetness toward your children;
> and the bread, ministering to the desire of the one who took it,
> was changed to suit everyone's liking. (Wis 16:20-21)

In summary, the manna, the food of the angels, also called *ambrosia* (ἀμβροσίας τροφῆς, Wis 19:21), was considered incorruptible and also enabled incorruptibility. We find that this tradition continued into the first century CE as Philo states, "the manna" is "the word of God, the heavenly incorruptible food of the soul."[44] Jozsef Zsengéller sums up the manna tradition in these words: "As we have seen the heavenly origin or heavenly form of the manna, its nature as the food of the angels or *ambrosia*, its connection with Wisdom and immortality becomes a common sense in the period after the writing of the Book of Wisdom."[45]

Sophia/Logos Feeds Her Children[46] (6:35-57)

The following structure will help the reader follow the rhetorical shifts in this passage, part 1 vv. 35-47; part 2 vv. 48-57:

---

43. James M. Reese, *The Book of Wisdom, Song of Songs*, OTM 20 (Wilmington, DE: Michael Glazier, 1983), 42.

44. Τὸ μάννα . . . τὸν θεῖον λόγον, τὴν οὐράνιον ψυχῆς . . . ἄφθαρτον τροφήν. *Quis Rerum Divinarum Heres*, LCL vol. 4 (1958), 79.

45. Zsengéller, "The Taste of Paradise," 215.

46. "It is not the production of crops that feeds humankind but that your word sustains those who trust in you" (Wis 16:26).

³⁵Jesus said to them, "I am the bread of life. Whoever comes to me will never be hungry, and whoever believes in me will never be thirsty. ³⁶But I said to you that you have seen me and yet do not believe. ³⁷Everything that the Father gives me will come to me, and anyone who comes to me I will never drive away; ³⁸for I have come down from heaven, not to do my own will, but the will of him who sent me. ³⁹And this is the will of him who sent me, that I should lose nothing of all that he has given me, but raise it up on the last day. ⁴⁰This is indeed the will of my Father, that all who see the Son and believe in him may have eternal life; and I will raise them up on the last day."

⁴¹Then the Jews began to complain about him because he said, "I am the bread that came down from heaven." ⁴²They were saying, "Is not this Jesus, the son of Joseph, whose father and mother we know? How can he now say, 'I have come down from heaven'?" ⁴³Jesus answered them, "Do not com-

	Part 1. Sapiential		**Part 2. Sapiential/Eucharistic**
A	³⁵Jesus said to them, "*I am the bread of life.* Whoever *comes to me* will never be hungry, and whoever *believes* in me will never be thirsty. ³⁶But I said to you that you have seen me and yet do not believe. ³⁷Everything that the Father gives me will *come to me*, and anyone who *comes to me* I will never drive away; ³⁸*for I have come down from heaven*, not to do my own will, but the will of him who sent me. ³⁹And this is the will of him who sent me, that I should lose nothing of all that he has given me, but *raise it up on the last day.* ⁴⁰This is indeed the will of my Father, that all who see the Son and *believe* in him may have eternal life [ζωὴν αἰώνιον]; and I will *raise them up on the last day.*"	**A'**	⁴⁸*I am the bread of life.* ⁴⁹Your ancestors ate [ἔφαγον] the manna in the wilderness, and they died. ⁵⁰This is the bread that *comes down from heaven,* so that one may eat [φάγη] of it and not die. ⁵¹I am the *living bread that came down from heaven.* Whoever eats [φάγη] of this bread will live forever [ζήσει εἰς τὸν αἰῶνα]; and the bread that I will give for the life of the world is my flesh [σάρξ]."

plain among yourselves. ⁴⁴No one can come to me unless drawn by the Father who sent me; and I will raise that person up on the last day. ⁴⁵It is written in the prophets, 'And they shall all be taught by God.' Everyone who has heard and learned from the Father comes to me. ⁴⁶Not that anyone has seen the Father except the one who is from God; he has seen the Father. ⁴⁷Very truly, I tell you, whoever believes has eternal life. ⁴⁸I am the bread of life. ⁴⁹Your ancestors ate the manna in the wilderness, and they died. ⁵⁰This is the bread that comes down from heaven, so that one may eat of it and not die. ⁵¹I am the living bread that came down from heaven. Whoever eats of this bread will live forever; and the bread that I will give for the life of the world is my flesh."

⁵²The Jews then disputed among themselves, saying, "How can this man

B	Dispute	B'	Dispute
	⁴¹Then the Jews began to complain ['Εγόγγυζον] about him because he said, "I am the bread that came down from heaven." ⁴²They were saying, "Is not this Jesus, the son of Joseph, whose father and mother we know? *How* can he now say, 'I have come down from heaven'?"		⁵²The Jews then disputed ['Εμάχοντο] among themselves, saying, "*How* can this man give us his flesh to eat [φαγεῖν]?"
C	⁴³Jesus answered them, "Do not complain [γογγύζετε] among yourselves. ⁴⁴No one can *come to me* unless drawn by the Father who sent me; and *I will raise that person up on the last day.* ⁴⁵It is written in the prophets, 'And they shall all be taught by God.' Everyone who has heard and learned from the Father *comes to me.* ⁴⁶Not that anyone has seen the Father except the one who is from God; he has seen the Father. ⁴⁷Very truly, I tell you, *whoever believes has eternal life* [ζωὴν αἰώνιον].	C'	**Eucharistic** ⁵³So Jesus said to them, "Very truly, I tell you, unless you eat [φάγητε] the flesh of the Son of Man and drink his blood, you have no life in you. ⁵⁴Those who eat [τρώγων] my flesh and drink my blood have eternal life [ζωὴν αἰώνιον], and *I will raise them up on the last day;* ⁵⁵for my flesh is true food and my blood is true drink. ⁵⁶Those who eat [τρώγων] my flesh and drink my blood abide in me, and I in them. ⁵⁷Just as the living Father sent me, and I live because of the Father, so whoever eats [τρώγων] me will live because of me.

give us his flesh to eat?" [53]So Jesus said to them, "Very truly, I tell you, unless you eat the flesh of the Son of Man and drink his blood, you have no life in you. [54]Those who eat my flesh and drink my blood have eternal life, and I will raise them up on the last day; [55]for my flesh is true food and my blood is true drink. [56]Those who eat my flesh and drink my blood abide in me, and I in them. [57]Just as the living Father sent me, and I live because of the Father, so whoever eats me will live because of me.

I am the bread of life (6:35-40). The crowd had given Jesus a text of Scripture when asking him to perform a sign, "He gave them bread from heaven to eat" (v. 31). Jesus corrected their thinking that Moses was the provider of this bread and turned their attention to "my Father" and spoke of himself as the "bread" come down from heaven. The first section of the discourse develops this theme of Jesus as the "bread of life" and the one "come down from heaven." These statements need to be read in the light of the manna and wisdom traditions described above. Speaking as divine Wisdom inviting her disciples, Jesus invites the crowd to come to him in the manner of *Sophia*: "those who eat *of me* will hunger for more, and those who drink *of me* will thirst for more" (Sir 24:21). But the revelation of Jesus surpasses the promises of Wisdom, for "Whoever comes to me will never be hungry, and whoever believes in me will never be thirsty" (John 6:35). Coming to Jesus means to believe in him. Jesus's whole purpose in coming from the Father, as once the manna came down from heaven, is to make available a new quality of life, called in this Gospel "eternity life," ζωὴν αἰώνιον (see John 3:16). *Sophia* identified herself as food to nourish her children; similarly, Jesus reveals himself as "the bread of life." In line with Jewish traditions that the "bread of heaven" is *ambrosia*, offering eternity life to those who eat of it, Jesus also offers eternity life to those believing in him. Jesus then takes the wisdom tradition further to speak of resurrection on the last day. The eternity life offered now by Jesus will also be embodied through end-time resurrection. Israel's eschatological expectations are drawn into the present with believers experiencing a quality of eternity life *now*; the use of the present tense "may have [ἔχῃ] eternity life" means that "eternal life is no longer the future life of the coming aeon."[47]

Jozsef Zsengéller offers a helpful way of holding the tension between the "now" of eternity life and a "future" resurrection. He notes the word

47. Borgen, *Bread from Heaven,* 168.

"taste," γεῦσις, is used throughout Wisdom 16 (vv. 2, 3, 20). This Greek word, found only in Wisdom 16, means to taste something with the sense of trying it.[48] "Consequently what [a person] can receive on [sic] this world is not immortality itself, it is not the world to come itself, but it is the taste of paradise. . . . [T]hose who are led by God's wisdom will experience already here in this world the taste of the coming world, the taste of paradise."[49] Jesus offers eternity life now, with the promise of the full embodied experience of eternity life to come.

Sophia's words rejected (6:41-42). The listeners, who are now called "the Jews," complain.[50] The verb used (γογγύζω) is the same as that used in the manna accounts of Exodus 16 to describe the "murmuring" of the Israelites in the wilderness (Exod 16:7, 8; also Num 14:27, 36; 16:11; 17:5). Like their ancestors who "murmured" in the wilderness, "the Jews" cannot accept Jesus's words that he has "come down from heaven" (6:38) because in their perception his origins lie in Galilee, not in heaven (6:42).

All shall be taught (6:43-47).

A   [43]Jesus answered them, "Do not complain [γογγύζετε] among yourselves.

[44]No one can *come to me* unless drawn by the Father who sent me;

B   and *I will raise that person up on the last day.*

C   [45]It is written in the prophets, 'And they shall all be taught by God.'

A   Everyone who has heard and learned from the Father *comes to me.*

[46]Not that anyone has seen the Father except the one who is from God; he has seen the Father.

B   [47]Very truly, I tell you, *whoever believes has eternity life* [ζωὴν αἰώνιον]."

48. Henry G. Liddell, "γεύω," in *A Lexicon.*
49. Zsengéller, "The Taste of Paradise," 216.
50. Until this point, Jesus's interlocutors have been called "the crowd," but now that they move to a stance of opposition, shown in their complaint and refusal to believe Jesus's words, the narrator names them "the Jews." This narrative strategy needs to be interpreted cautiously as part of the narrative and not a statement about the historicity of this scene. See comments on "Characters Called 'the Jews'" and "'The Jews' in the Reception of the Gospel" in the author's introduction (p. lxxi).

There is a parallelism between verses 43-44 and verses 45c-47. Both units speak of "coming" to Jesus and the role of the Father in initiating this possibility. Verse 44 gives the promise of "resurrection" on the last day, while verse 47 names the current experience of eternity life. The "hinge" linking both small units is the quotation from the Scriptures, "And they shall all be taught by God."

The high degree of verbal similarity leads most scholars to conclude that the evangelist is here citing Isaiah 54:13: "All your children shall be taught by the LORD" (LXX: καὶ πάντας τοὺς υἱούς σου διδακτοὺς θεοῦ). In the Gospel there is the striking omission of the term "your sons," τοὺς υἱούς σου. Within the context of Deutero-Isaiah, "your children" refers to the children of Zion when they return following the exile. By omitting this phrase, the Gospel offers a universal possibility—"all [πάντες] shall be taught." "In the person of Jesus, all people have the chance to hear and learn of the Father, including Jesus' interlocutors in the Bread of Life discourse."[51] The expression "to be taught by God" seems to have had a technical sense of hearing and following the Torah.[52] According to Rudolph Schnackenburg, "In Judaism it was believed that learning the Torah was being instructed by God himself, and a perfect, inwardly active divine instruction was looked forward to as one of the blessings of the eschatological time."[53] The Scripture citation explains the Father's role in drawing believers to Jesus. An inner openness to the Father's instruction through the Scriptures has the possibility of leading to Jesus. That "the Jews" in this passage are murmuring against Jesus shows that, from the Johannine community's perspective, they have not really been taught by God.

51. Sheridan, *Retelling Scripture*, 169. Sheridan has a very helpful summary of the work of Maarten Menken, Bruce Schuchard, and Andreas Obermann on this passage. See Menken, *Old Testament Quotations*; Bruce G. Schuchard, *Scripture within Scripture: The Interrelationship of Form and Function in the Explicit Old Testament Citations in the Gospel of John*, SBLDS 133 (Atlanta: Scholars Press, 1992); Andreas Obermann, *Die christologische Erfüllung der Schrift im Johannesevangelium*, WUNT 83 (Tübingen: Mohr Siebeck, 1996).

52. The Book of Jubilees 1:4 gives an account of Moses on the mountain being taught everything by God. "And Moses was on the Mount forty days and forty nights, and God taught him the earlier and the later history of the division of all the days of the law and of the testimony." The Psalms of Solomon uses the expression διδακτὸς ὑπὸ θεοῦ (Pss. Sol. 17:32).

53. Rudolph Schnackenburg, *The Gospel according to St John*, trans. K. Smyth et al., 3 vols., HTCNT (London: Burns & Oates, 1968–1982), 2:51. Schnackenburg also notes places where the same expression occurs in writings from the Dead Sea Scrolls.

Nourished by the bread of Sophia (6:48-51). Even though Wisdom is not explicitly named, the strength of the *Sophia* imagery in the prologue (1:1-18) coupled with the continuation of the implicit allusions to the wisdom literature, especially in John 3 and 6, sustains her presence across the narrative. Once the wisdom "hermeneutical key" has been unlocked, she cannot be silenced. In this section, Jesus repeats much of what he taught in verses 35-40. He repeats his claim to the "the bread of life" (v. 48) that has "come down from heaven" (v. 50). These two phrases respond to the words of the crowd in verse 30, "he gave them bread from heaven to eat." Now, the third aspect of this citation is developed, "to eat." Still speaking metaphorically within the wisdom tradition of eating and drinking what she offers, Jesus speaks of eating *his* bread, which is his own being. The wisdom tradition has prepared the way for this identification between Jesus and the nourishment that he offers those who come to him and believe in him. Wisdom had said, "Those who eat *of me* will hunger for more, and those who drink *of me* will thirst for more" (Sir 24:21). Using their own allusion to the manna, Jesus compares the bread he offers that provides life forever (εἰς τὸν αἰῶνα, v. 51b) and the manna that sustained life only temporarily, "your ancestors . . . died" (v. 49). This section echoes his earlier teaching, "Do not work for the food that perishes, but for the food that endures for eternal life" (v. 27).

Throughout the discourse, from 6:25 to 6:51b, the language has been metaphorical, drawing on Jewish traditions of the manna and Wisdom, to speak of the teaching that Jesus is offering and the consequences for those who can believe in him. At verse 51c, with the mention of the word "flesh [σάρξ]," we move beyond Jewish metaphorical language to the sacramental language of the later Christian community.

Sophia is not recognized (6:52). Once again "the Jews" respond negatively to Jesus's words by quarrelling among themselves, and in words similar to those of Nicodemus, they ask, "How is it possible [Πῶς δύναται] for this man to give us his flesh to eat?"[54] In one sense they are correct. In the historical time of the setting for this exchange, it is not possible. The concluding section of the discourse provides an answer to this question.

"Because of her, I shall have immortality" (Wis 8:13) (6:53-57). It is important to take note of the verbs used across this exchange and the time indicated by these verbs. In verse 51c Jesus speaks of a *future* gift of bread—"and the bread that I *will give* [δώσω] for the life of the world

---

54. Author's translation.

is my flesh [σάρξ]." The response of "the Jews" in verse 52 brings this statement into the present, thus making it impossible: "How *can* this man give us his flesh to eat?" Replying to this question in verse 53 Jesus speaks of eating the "flesh of the *Son of Man* and drinking his blood." The use of "the human-one" (υἱὸς ἀνθρώπου) title points to the future.[55]

As flesh refers to that aspect of the human person that is transient and, in common with all material substances, will undergo decay and death, so blood refers to the inner life force of the human person.[56] In both Leviticus and Deuteronomy "blood" is equated with "life." "For the life [נפש; LXX: ψυχή] of the flesh [בשׂר; LXX: σαρκὸς] is in the blood" (Lev 17:11; similarly Deut 12:23). Thus, when Jesus speaks of eating the flesh and drinking the blood of the human-one, it can only mean to participate in the future action of Jesus, in both his death *and* his resurrection to new life. While verse 53 speaks of this as a possibility using the subjunctive mood (φάγητε), verse 54 speaks of a future *reality*, "those who eat," τρώγων. When speaking of a future real eating, the verb changes from ἐσθίω to τρώγω (vv. 54, 56, 57, 58c). There is a more material, even crude sense of eating associated with the verb τρώγω, which can be translated as gnaw, munch, or chew. Raymond Brown explains the change of the verb as "John's attempt to emphasize the realism of the Eucharistic flesh and blood."[57]

The change of verb to a more materialistic, as against metaphoric, eating as well as the shift to the future indicates that at this point the future eucharistic celebrations of the community are in mind. It is in the community's Eucharist that future followers of Jesus can encounter Jesus and can give expression to their faith in him as once the disciples and the crowds had opportunities to express belief beside the Sea of Tiberias. Eucharist makes possible the mutual indwelling of Jesus and the believer: "Those who eat my flesh and drink my blood abide in me, and I in them," ἐν ἐμοὶ μένει κἀγὼ ἐν αὐτῷ (v. 56). By participating in the Eucharist believers receive as gift the "bread of heaven," a taste of paradise, enabling them to participate now in eternity life, in and through Jesus's own death and rising, with the promise of this fullness in a future bodily resurrection.

Conclusion (6:58-59)

In the introduction to the discourse, the crowd asked Jesus for a sign and said, "Our ancestors ate the manna in the wilderness; as it is writ-

---

55. See excursus on Son of Man (p. 50).
56. S. David Sperling, "Blood," *ABD* 1 (1992):761.
57. Brown, *The Gospel According to John*, 1:283.

John 6:58-59

[58]This is the bread that came down from heaven, not like that which your ancestors ate, and they died. But the one who eats this bread will live forever." [59]He said these things while he was teaching in the synagogue at Capernaum.

ten, 'He gave them bread from heaven to eat' " (v. 31). Throughout the discourse Jesus has corrected their understanding about who really gave the "bread from heaven," and against contemporary Jewish associations of the manna with Wisdom and Torah, Jesus claimed to offer a superior wisdom and teaching, a "true" (v. 32) revelation of God, which, because of his relationship with the Father, only he could offer. In the first part of the discourse the language of eating bread was used in a metaphorical manner similar to the crowd's own Jewish traditions, to invite his listeners to faith in his teaching. Then, with the introduction of the word "flesh" (v. 51c), the discourse shifts to the future time of the Johannine community, when Jesus has passed through death into resurrection life and offers those who believe in him the opportunity to participate with him in this eternity life. The eucharistic bread of the community offers a "taste" of paradise now and a promise of a future, embodied experience of eternity life in him.

The Response (6:60-71)

Throughout the discourse (vv. 25-59) the reader has "overheard" the responses of the crowd, sometimes positive (vv. 28, 34) but becoming increasingly perplexed (vv. 42, 52). When the discourse concludes, attention focuses on the disciples. Using the verb "to complain," which was used of "the Jews" (γογγύζω, v. 41), indicates that some of his disciples are now siding with those among the crowd who cannot accept his teaching. Some find his teaching "hard," σκληρός, and walk away; Jesus also speaks of one, Judas, who was to betray him (v. 71). Between these examples of failed discipleship, Peter makes his threefold affirmation of faith, "Lord . . . you have the words of eternity life" (v. 68); "you are the Holy One of God" (v. 69). The title Lord (κύριος) is the LXX translation of "Adonai," which is the Hebrew circumlocution for the name of God, YHWH (יהוה). By using this title, Peter affirms his faith in Jesus's self-revelation when he crossed the sea as "I AM" (6:20). By his declaration that it is the word of Jesus that brings eternity life, Peter affirms Jesus's teaching in the Bread of Life discourse that Jesus, not the manna

⁶⁰When many of his disciples heard it, they said, "This teaching is difficult; who can accept it?" ⁶¹But Jesus, being aware that his disciples were complaining about it, said to them, "Does this offend you? ⁶²Then what if you were to see the Son of Man ascending to where he was before? ⁶³It is the spirit that gives life; the flesh is useless. The words that I have spoken to you are spirit and life. ⁶⁴But among you there are some who do not believe." For Jesus knew from the first who were the ones that did not believe, and who was the one that would betray him. ⁶⁵And he said, "For this reason I have told you that no one can come to me unless it is granted by the Father."

⁶⁶Because of this many of his disciples turned back and no longer went about with him. ⁶⁷So Jesus asked the twelve, "Do you also wish to go away?" ⁶⁸Simon Peter answered him, "Lord, to whom can we go? You have the words of eternal life. ⁶⁹We have come to believe and know that you are the Holy One of God." ⁷⁰Jesus answered them, "Did I not choose you, the twelve? Yet one of you is a devil." ⁷¹He was speaking of Judas son of Simon Iscariot, for he, though one of the twelve, was going to betray him.

or Torah, is the sole source of eternity life. By naming Jesus as "the Holy One of God," Peter acknowledges that Jesus, Wisdom enfleshed, is the true bread from heaven whose origins are in God.[58] Peter's words thus sum up the teaching across this entire chapter. Portraying Peter as the spokesperson for the disciples is unusual for this Gospel. Unlike in the Synoptic Gospels, where he takes the lead role, in the Fourth Gospel, it is the Beloved Disciple who is primary (see, e.g., 13:24, where the Beloved Disciple is closest to Jesus, and 20:8, where this disciple outruns Peter to the empty tomb and is first to believe). Female figures like the Samaritan woman (4:4-42), Martha and Mary (11:1–12:11), and Mary Magdalene (20:1-2, 11-18) play stronger parts in this Gospel than does Peter.

Conclusion

As Jews of all generations celebrated the ongoing liberation from slavery that Passover signified and the everlasting nourishment of the manna

---

58. The title "the Holy One" usually designates God, particularly in Isaiah, with the title "the Holy One of Israel" (e.g., Isa 41:14, 16, 20; 43:3, 14), but in Sirach the Holy One is identified as Wisdom: "Those who serve her [Wisdom] minister to the Holy One; the Lord loves those who love her" (Sir 4:14).

now available in Torah, a Johannine community was able to see in their eucharistic table meals the presence of their exalted and risen One. In their gatherings they could continue to hear the words of Sophia-Jesus and express their faith by eating the eucharistic bread of life and being drawn into communion (v. 56).

> Come to me [Sophia], you who desire me,
>> and eat your fill of my fruits.
> For the memory of me is sweeter than honey,
>> and the possession of me sweeter than the honeycomb. (Sir 24:19-20)

The Twelve

It is appropriate that "the twelve" be mentioned here, and only here, in the Fourth Gospel. This entire chapter draws on the exodus experience of ancient Israel, where, following their escape from Egypt, they come to Mount Sinai and for the first time as a people enter into a solemn covenant with the God who had carried them on eagles' wings (Exod 19:4). In this covenant ceremony Moses builds an altar and sets up twelve pillars, "corresponding to the twelve tribes of Israel" (Exod 24:4). The number twelve continues to have this symbolic function in the New Testament.

The symbolism is particularly clear in Mark's presentation of the Last Supper. Prior to the meal, Jesus is speaking with disciples (14:12, 13, 14, 16), and then following the meal he goes with his disciples to Gethsemane (14:32). It is only when they gather for the meal that the Twelve are mentioned (14:17, 20), and as the "cup of wine" is called "the blood of the covenant" the number "twelve" should be read symbolically referring back to the Sinai covenant with the twelve tribes. It ought not be interpreted literally, as if Jesus sent away some of the disciples for a short time and restricted the covenant meal to just twelve, then rejoined the total group of disciples in Gethsemane. This does not make narrative sense.

While in the Synoptic Gospels the Twelve are called and sent as apostles (Mark 3:13-19; 6:7-13; Matt 10:1-11; Luke 6:12-16; 9:1-6), they do not have such a function in John. The only mention of the Twelve is at 6:67, 70, 71, and 20:24, where Thomas is identified as one of the Twelve. The Johannine pattern of call and missioning differs from that of the Synoptics; the Samaritan woman (4:4-42) and Mary Magdalene (20:1-2, 11-18) exemplify those who believe and bring others to faith in Jesus on the basis of their word.

Women and the Eucharist[59]

Any discussion of Eucharist is immediately painful for many women in those Christian denominations that prevent women from full ministerial participation in their baptismal priesthood. This is an injustice to the women who have a vocation to such service and an injustice to the entire community who are being malnourished because of a prejudice that cannot be legitimized by biblical texts.

With the exception of Jesus, no one is named a priest in the New Testament.[60] Within the New Testament Eucharist is usually termed the Lord's Supper, where the Risen Christ is the celebrant at the table, and the prayer leader is never identified. It is only in the next century that the language around Eucharist shifts from table meal to sacrifice, and with this change, borrowed from the Roman cultic practice, the table becomes an altar and the celebrant is called a priest. Borrowing also from the Roman practice of status in society and the ability to change from one "order" to another "order," the rite of changing to a different "order" within the church was called "ordination."[61] It is also wrong to say that women were never "ordained" as there are liturgies describing the ordination of women into various roles within the church.[62]

The difficulty lies not in the New Testament evidence where women were known to be disciples (Mark 15:40-41; Matt 27:55-56), evangelists (John 4:29; 20:17), deacons (Rom 16:1-2), leaders of house churches,[63] apostles,[64] missionary

---

59. For a fuller presentation on this topic, please see https://ytu.edu.au/wp-content/uploads/The-time-is-now-paper1-Mary-Coloe.pdf.

60. In the Epistle to the Hebrews Christ is named "high priest" in a metaphorical sense in that he is compared to "a priest arising according to the order of Melchizedek, rather than one according to the order of Aaron" (Heb 7:11, 15, 17).

61. The first ritual of ordination is found in *The Apostolic Tradition* of Hippolytus, dated to around 215 CE. See Kenan Osborne, *Priesthood: A History of Ordained Ministry in the Roman Catholic Church* (Mahwah, NJ: Paulist Press, 1988), 117.

62. See my article cited above for details.

63. Nympha, Col 4:15; Apphia, Phlm 1:2; Mary, Acts 12:12. Lydia was the first European convert, and her home provided the first welcome to Paul and his Gospel (Acts 16:14-15).

64. Paul commends Junia, calling her "outstanding among the apostles" (Rom 16:7). Mary Magdalene was given the title Apostle to the Apostles in the church; this title, which became quite common in the twelfth century, appears to date back to Hippolytus, bishop of Rome (c. 170–235 CE) in his Commentary on the Canticle of Canticles (*In Cant.* 25.6). Likewise, the Samaritan woman (4:4-42) was called an apostle at least as early as Origen (185–ca. 251) and continues until now to be acclaimed "equal to the apostles" in Byzantine tradition (see excursus "A Woman's Witness," p. 126). There is

teachers,[65] and prophets (Luke 2:36-38; Acts 21:9; 1 Cor 11:5). The difficulty comes in part from Aristotelian philosophy based on incorrect physiology where women were thought to have no part in procreation, other than carrying the fetus created solely by the male sperm, and so were therefore innately inferior to men, considered less than human.[66] It was not until 1827 that Karl Ernst Von Baer identified and described the female ovum using a microscope and thus proved that women also participated in procreation. As the early Christians moved into the Greco-Roman culture Aristotle's view became the dominant factor, even overriding New Testament evidence about women's roles, the historical experience of women in liturgical leadership,[67] and the evidence of many epigraphs

---

some confusion about who is the subject of this epithet "apostle to the apostles." In the Commentary at 25.3 Hippolytus names Martha and Mary but then the text continues: "I will not let you go" to fly up "I am going to my father. Carry upwards a new sacrifice, indeed carry Eve upwards, she desires no longer to be tempted, but rather to hold to the tree of the life. See her holding fast to the feet Christ." This description of a woman clinging to the feet of Christ, and the words "I am going to my father" best describe the encounter with Mary Magdalene in John 20 rather than Martha and Mary of Bethany, unless Hippolytus merges into one character Mary of Bethany and Mary the Magdalene. See Yancy Warren Smith, "Hippolytus' Commentary on the Song of Songs in Social and Critical Context" (Thesis, Abilene Christian University, 2009), 351, https://repository.tcu.edu/bitstream/handle/116099117/4192/SmithY .pdf?sequence=1. Now published as Yancy Warren Smith, *The Mystery of Anointing: Hippolytus' Commentary on the Song of Songs in Social and Critical Context*, Gorgias Studies in Early Christianity and Patristics 62 (Piscataway, NJ: Gorgias, 2015).

65. Priscilla was a travelling missionary like Paul (Acts 18:2, 19; 1 Cor 16:18; 2 Tim 4:19; Rom 16:3).

66. "And a woman is as it were an infertile [or impotent] male." Aristotle, *On the Genesis of the Creatures* 1.20.

67. Widows had a role in receiving penitents who, according to Tertullian, were required "to prostrate themselves before the widows and the presbyters" (*De Pudicitia* 17.7). Translation taken from Sr. Prudence Allen, *The Concept of Woman: The Aristotelian Revolution, 750 B.C.* (Grand Rapids, MI: Eerdmans, 1985), 97. In addition to widows, virgins, and women deacons, an abbess was also "ordained" in a ritual laying on of hands. As head of her community, the abbess heard confession, absolved from sin, gave penances, and reconciled members back into the community. As part of her ordination ritual a religious mitre was placed on her head, and she received from the bishop a staff as a sign of office. A description of these rituals is given in Gary Macy, *The Hidden History of Women's Ordination: Female Clergy in the Medieval West* (New York: Oxford University Press, 2008), 81.

naming women as *presbytera*, *diakonos*, and even *episkopa*.[68]

The very clear Johannine theology of Jesus embodying Sophia could, and should, remove gender issues from consideration of eucharistic leadership. If gender is to be significant, then surely only women who know the experience of bearing, birthing, and nurturing a child can say with any realism, "This is my body, given for you." Only women can act *in persona Sophia/Christi*.

Deacon Sophia of Jerusalem

In 1903 on Mount Olives, Jerusalem, the following large slab of stone was discovered and later moved to the Franciscan museum near St. Anne's Church on the Via Dolorosa. The discovery was published in a brief notice in 1904, with the title "Épitaphe de la diaconesse Sophie"[69] where the Greek clearly calls Sophia a deacon (ΔΙΑΚΟΝΟΣ). The date on the inscriptions states Sophia's death as the twenty-first of March. The year is indicated with the Greek abbreviation for "indiction" (INΔ). This form of calculating years was introduced by Emperor Diocletian and continued by Constantine beginning with the year 312 CE, where an indiction covered a period of fifteen years. INΔ IA means "indiction 11" which could be as early as 323.

68. There are several books now available that provide primary sources such as ancient liturgical prayers and inscriptions from tombs and other monuments where women are named with the title *presbyteros*, "presbyter/priest"; *diakonos*, "deacon/deaconess"; and *episkopos*, "overseer/bishop." Macy's book, *The Hidden History of Women's Ordination*, provides liturgical evidence and examines the changes in the priesthood up until the twelfth century. Ute E. Eisen, *Women Officeholders in Early Christianity: Epigraphical and Literary Studies* (Collegeville, MN: Liturgical Press, 2000), examines the evidence from the New Testament and patristic writings in the early centuries. Kevin Madigan and Carolyn Osiek, *Ordained Women in the Early Church: A Documentary History* (Baltimore: John Hopkins University Press, 2005) list sixty-one inscriptions of ordained women in the East and four in the West covering the first six centuries. And Miriam Therese Winter, *Out of the Depths: The Story of Ludmila Javorova Ordained Roman Catholic Priest* (New York: Crossroad, 2001), describes the experience of a woman ordained in 1970 for the underground church of Czechoslovakia.

69. L. C., "Épitaphe de la diaconesse Sophie," *RB* 1 (1904): 260–62. The reference to the deacon Phoebe is Rom 16:1-2.

The inscription reads:

Photo and translation by Mary L. Coloe

Here lies the servant
and bride of Christ
Sophia the deacon the
Second Phoebe, [who] fell asleep
in peace on the 21st of the month
March, indiction 11.
Lord God . . . .

John 7:1-52; 8:12-59

Sophia's Homecoming: Tabernacles 1

A holy people and blameless race
wisdom delivered from a nation of oppressors.
[S]he guided them along a marvelous way,
and became a shelter to them by day,
and a starry flame through the night.
When they were thirsty, they called upon you,
and water was given them out of flinty rock. (Wis 10:15, 17; 11:4)

Water, Light, Worship

In the book of Sirach Sophia is told to make her dwelling in Jerusalem (Sir 24:8) and so she says, "In the holy tent [ἐν σκηνῇ ἁγίᾳ] I ministered before him, and so I was established in Zion" (Sir 24:10). The Festival of Tabernacles, which is given more narrative space than any other festival, is like Sophia's homecoming. But here in Jerusalem she meets again with the Jerusalemites (7:25) who opposed Jesus's earlier healing at the pool of Bethesda (John 5) since it was a Sabbath (5:9). Consequently Jesus/Sophia resumes a conflict about the Jewish law with those who do not recognize the words of Sirach—that *she* is "the book of the covenant . . . the law that Moses commanded" (Sir 24:23). Accordingly, at issue in this festival is the identity of Jesus/Sophia.

As part of the argument continued from John 5 two great male ancestors of Israel are brought into the debate: first Moses, the giver of the law (7:19), and then Abraham (8:39). In John 5 Jesus had argued that he was able to work on the Sabbath because God continued to work on the Sabbath—"My Father is still working, and I also am working" (5:17). In the earlier conflict Jesus claimed his authority had come from God to do as God does on the Sabbath. This is the issue in John 7: from where does Jesus get his authority (7:15)? Then in John 8 the question of "fatherhood" is raised. While Jesus has claimed his authority from "my Father" (7:26-27), his accusers do not accept that this is God and claim their identity from "our father Abraham" (8:39). With the book of Sirach in mind, these chapters during the Festival of Tabernacles need to be read through the insight that Jesus/Sophia embodies "the law that Moses commanded." Then, in the hostile debate in John 8, it is important to note that his opposition comes not from "the Jews" so much as from his former disciples (8:31) who now disassociate themselves from him. At the end of John 6 we heard of some of his disciples who found Jesus's teaching too difficult to accept (6:66). Could these be his interlocutors in John 8, former followers who have now turned back to being followers of the Mosaic law? The issues raised in chapters 7 and 8 continue in John 9:1–10:21, in the same festival setting. Jesus's words within the feast are then witnessed to as Sophia "ministers in the holy tent" (Sir 24:10) giving sight to one born blind (9:1–10:21).

Jewish Background[1]

Following the springtime festival of Passover, the next festival within the Jewish liturgical year is the summer Festival of Weeks (*Shavu'oth*), held fifty days after Passover and thus known as Pentecost in the Greek-speaking world.[2] In this current section of the Gospel, John 5–10, the next festival encountered is Sukkot, also known as Booths or Tabernacles.[3] This festival comes early in autumn in the northern hemisphere when the summer crops of grapes, olives, and nuts are harvested. The feast began on the fifteenth day of Tishri, shortly after the Day of Atone-

---

1. A helpful guide to this festival is Ronald L. Eisenberg, *Jewish Traditions: A JPS Guide* (Philadelphia: Jewish Publication Society, 2008), 227–43.

2. I argued earlier that this festival provides the key background for understanding John 1:19–2:13.

3. Heb: סֻכָּה; Gk: σκηνή.

ment (the tenth day of Tishri), and lasted for seven days, with the addition of a special eighth day of observance. During these days, the people slept and ate within a specially constructed booth originally made of myrtle, willow, and palm branches (Neh 8:13-18).

The origins of the festival lie in a joyful harvest festival gathering in the summer fruits, particularly the grapes; for this reason it was also called the "festival of ingathering" (Exod 23:16; 34:22), which is considered to be the earliest name for the feast. In an agricultural economy, women would have been involved in this critical harvesting time, either in the outdoor gathering of the crops or the indoor preserving of the harvest.[4] In time this festival took on a religious meaning celebrating the time when Israel lived in temporary shelters during the forty years in the wilderness after the exodus. As a memorial of this time, the festival recalled God's gracious gifts of water and guidance in a pillar of cloud by day and fire by night. In the book of Wisdom, it is Sophia who is the source of these gifts (Wis 10:15, 17; 11:4).

The Mishnah provides the following description of the rituals of this feast.[5] Each morning of the festival a water libation ceremony was conducted.[6] A procession of priests, Levites, and people filed down to the Pool of Siloam to draw a flagon of water that was carried with great solemnity back to the temple. When the procession passed through the Water Gate the *shofar* (a ram's horn) was blown (m. Sukkah 4:9). By the end of the first century CE, the Water Gate was identified as the south gate of the eschatological temple in Ezekiel's vision (chap. 47).[7] Through this gate the waters flowed from the Divine Presence out into

---

4. Carol L. Meyers, "Everyday Life: Women in the Period of the Hebrew Bible," in *The Women's Bible Commentary*, ed. Carol A. Newsom and Sharon H. Ringe (Louisville: Westminster John Knox, 1992), 251–59.

5. In using the Mishnah (second century CE) as a source for understanding Jewish liturgy in the first century, scholars assume that the Mishnah preserves older traditions predating the destruction of the temple. See Gale A. Yee, *Jewish Feasts and the Gospel of John* (Wilmington, DE: Michael Glazier, 1989), 74; Jeffrey Rubenstein, *The History of Sukkot in the Second Temple and Rabbinic Periods*, BJS (Atlanta: Scholars Press, 1995), 103–6. Rubenstein concludes (106) that the Mishnah Tractate *Sukkah* probably comprises an early source, "perhaps composed soon after the destruction" of the temple.

6. This was known as the *Simchat Beit ha-She'evah* (Rejoicing of the house of water drawing). The ceremony was based on Isa 12:3, "With joy you will draw water from the wells of salvation." Eisenberg, *Jewish Traditions*, 228.

7. Germaine Bienaimé, *Moïse et le don de l'eau dans la tradition juive ancienne: Targum et Midrash*, AnBib 98 (Rome: Biblical Institute Press, 1984), 202.

the desert lands bringing life and healing. During the procession the pilgrims sang the *Hallel* (Pss 113–118) and carried a bouquet of myrtle, willow, and palm branches (the *lulab*) in the right hand and a citron, representing the harvest produce, in the left.[8] The *lulab* was waved aloft at particular verses in the psalms (m. Sukkah 4:5). On reaching the altar, the priests and Levites circled the altar, and then the priest, chosen to carry the golden water flagon, ascended the ramp of the altar to perform the libation of water and wine. On the altar were two silver bowls, one for water and one for the wine.[9] These bowls had a spout, allowing the libations to flow onto the altar then down into the deep reservoirs below the temple (m. Sukkah 4:9). On the seventh day, they circled the altar seven times (m. Sukkah 4:5).[10]

In postexilic times, the feast developed an eschatological motif, looking ahead to the end time when all the nations would gather to worship in Jerusalem (Zech 14:16-19; Isa 2:2-4; 56:6-8). In later times, Zechariah 14 was one of the readings from the Prophets that was read on the first day of the festival.[11]

The Zechariah text indicates a further aspect of this feast in its connection with prayers for the autumn rains. Jewish mythology held that all the waters of creation lay beneath the temple; here was the great abyss of the primeval waters of creation. The water poured on the altar was thought to flow down through a channel into the waters of the abyss, stirring up these waters and thus by a kind of sympathetic magic ensuring the autumn rains. As Frédéric Manns states, "The union of this water with the lower water ensured the fertility of the earth."[12]

---

8. Yee, *Jewish Feasts*, 74. George MacRae, "The Meaning and Evolution of the Feast of Tabernacles," *CBQ* 22 (1960): 272. MacRae briefly discusses the use of the *lulab* symbol on tombs and its association with immortality for Christians.

9. Bowls are mentioned in Zech 14:20 but without explanation. The Mishnah explains their importance for Tabernacles. MacRae supposes that the wine libation harks back to the early offering of the fruits of the grape when this was simply a harvest festival (MacRae, "The Meaning and Evolution of the Feast of Tabernacles," 273).

10. A more detailed description of this ceremony can be found in Rubenstein, *The History of Sukkot*, 117–31.

11. Yee, *Jewish Feasts*, 73; Hayim H. Donin, ed. *Sukkot*, Popular Judaica Library (Jerusalem: Keter Books, 1974), 81.

12. Frédéric Manns, *Le Symbole Eau-Esprit dans le Judaïsme Ancien*, SBFA 19 (Jerusalem: Franciscan Printing Press, 1983), 228. Manns continues (229): "This union of the upper and lower waters symbolized in the rite reproduces the order of creation before the separation of the waters, when the Spirit hovered over the Deep. The fecundity and fertility of the earth depends on this union of the waters."

Along with this eschatological perspective were messianic expectations. The libation ceremony drew on traditions of Miriam and Moses as well givers (Num 21:16-18), where, in later traditions, the well became a symbol for the gift of Torah.[13] In recalling Moses, and the gift of water in the wilderness, the people looked forward to a new Moses-like figure. "The Targums on Gen 49:10 play on the digging of the scribes to promise a future Messiah who digs from the well of the Torah, as a final 'giving of water' from the Torah, the well of God."[14]

Water is an ambivalent symbol. It can signify life (Isa 41:18; 43:20; Joel 3:8) but also annihilation (Exod 14:26). For countless women and girls through history and in our own time, it means a daily trudge, often dangerous, crossing miles to find a distant well. Then to carry back jerrycans of water, hopefully of good quality, so the family can live another day. The chore takes hours. While it means life for the family, for the water-bearers it is a shackle keeping them impoverished through lack of time for education or for profitable employment. UNICEF estimates that "worldwide, women and girls spend an estimated 200 million hours—every day—collecting water. It's a colossal waste of their valuable time."[15] In the Festival of Tabernacles water is associated with fertility and life; in the Gospel it will re-appear to mark birth and death (19:34).

In addition to the water libation ceremony, and probably having a similar meaning in relation to the autumn rains, was a daily willow procession described in m. Sukkah 4:3, 5-7. Men collected willow branches from a nearby town, Moṣa, then processed to the temple where they circled the altar then placed the branches beside the altar so that their "tops bent over the altar" (m. Sukkah 4:5). This ritual required that the ordinary men of Israel were permitted inside the court of the priests where the altar was situated; usually this area was prohibited to non-priests. This ritual was permitted even on the Sabbath. As in the water

13. The Damascus document from Qumran states: "And they dug the well: *Num 21:18* 'A well which the princes dug, which the nobles of the people delved with the staff.' The well is the law" (CD 6.3-4). Translations of the Scrolls come from Florentino Garcia Martinez and Eibert J. C. Tigchelaar, *The Dead Sea Scrolls Study Edition (Translations)*, 2 vols. (Leiden: Brill, 1997–1998). See the excursus at pp. 232–33 for legends of Miriam's Well.

14. Francis J. Moloney, "Narrative and Discourse at the Feast of Tabernacles," in *Word, Theology and Community in John*, ed. John Painter, R. Alan Culpepper, and Fernando F. Segovia (St. Louis, MO: Chalice, 2002), 157.

15. UNICEF, "This Girl Spends Eight Hours a Day Doing Something That Takes Us Seconds," https://www.unicef.org.au/blog/stories/november-2016/this-girl-spends-eight-hours-a-day-doing-something.

libation ceremony, on the seventh day the altar was circled seven times, and, according to one rabbi, Yohanan b. Beroka, on this day they would "gather the branches and beat them on the altar" (m. Sukkah 4:6). The circumambulation of the altar and the use of willow suggest that this ritual was directed to producing rain. The prayer offered while circling the altar was from Psalm 118:25, "O Lord, deliver us, O Lord, deliver us." This prayer too "is a most appropriate plea for rain. Without rain crops wither, animals die and people suffer. Prayers for rain were essentially prayers for survival, for 'deliverance.'"[16]

A third aspect of this feast occurred each night in the court of the women.[17] Four huge menorahs fitted out with wicks made from "the worn-out undergarments and girdles of the priests" (m. Sukkah 5:3) illumined the entire temple area. Under them the celebrants danced a torch dance to the accompaniment of flute playing, and the Levites chanted the Psalms of Ascent (120–134), one each on the fifteen steps that led down from the court of the Israelites to the court of the women.[18] According to the Mishnah, "there was not a courtyard in Jerusalem that did not reflect the light of the *Beth hashe'ubah* [i.e., House of the Water Drawing]" (m. Sukkah 5:3).

After the exile, another more somber ritual was added to these joyous celebrations of water and light. In this ritual the priests would gather in the outer courts of the temple facing east toward the sun rising over the

---

16. Rubenstein, *The History of Sukkot*, 117. Rubenstein provides details of this ritual as well as references to pre-70 sources supporting the accuracy of the description in the Mishnah (Rubenstein, *The History of Sukkot*, 105–17).

17. The temple was laid out with three courts with each one raised higher than the preceding one, leading up to the holy of holies. The largest court inside the East Gate was called the court of the women or the treasury. This led into the court of Israel, only permitted for Jewish men, followed by the court of the priests. The court of the women was not exclusively for women, but it named the extent of women's place within the temple, and surrounding this court was a raised gallery only for women. It is estimated that this was 230 square feet. For further details of this ritual, see Rubenstein, *The History of Sukkot*, 131–45.

18. "The pious men and wonder workers would dance before them with flaming torches in their hand, and they would sing before them songs and praises. And the Levites beyond counting played on harps, lyres, cymbals, trumpets, and [other] musical instruments, standing, as they played on the fifteen steps which go down from the Israelites' Court to the Court of the Women" (m. Sukkah 5:4). The Mishnah notes that on this occasion the women observing from the upper balcony would be in a higher position than the men.

Mount of Olives. In this position their backs were to the holy of holies. At the moment of sunrise they turned round to the west with their backs to the rising sun and facing the temple they said,

> Our fathers who were in this place turned with their backs toward the temple of the Lord and their faces toward the east, and they worshipped the sun toward the east (Ezek 8:16). "But as to us, our eyes are to the Lord." (m. Sukkah 5:4)

The book of Ezekiel (8:16) recalls a time, just prior to the exile, when some Israelites turned away from God to worship foreign idols. The morning ritual by the priests recalled this apostasy and in words and actions repudiated it. These were the four rituals carried out each day of the festival.

At some point prior to New Testament times, an eighth day was added; the first mention of this additional feast day is found in Leviticus 23:36.[19] This day seems to have been added to bring the festival to its conclusion, and, since this was the final pilgrim festival of the year, the day also brought the cycle of feasts to a conclusion. On this eighth day the water, light, and worship rituals ceased, and it was a day of solemn rest and sacrifice. According to the LXX, Psalm 28 (29) was sung on this day.[20]

In John 7–8 the rituals of this feast involving water, light, and an affirmation of faith in God are given a new interpretation in the person of Jesus/Sophia. Messianic and eschatological hopes also lie behind the many questions asked about Jesus's identity across these chapters. The logic of the conflicts in these chapters only makes sense in the context of this Feast of Tabernacles as it was joyfully celebrated in first-century Judaism.[21]

Narrative Structure

An atmosphere of growing hostility pervades chapters 7 and 8. The threat of death introduces and concludes this section: "He did not wish to go about in Judea because the Jews were looking for an opportunity to kill him" (7:1); and then in 8:59, "So they picked up stones to throw at

---

19. The Book of Jubilees also records this additional "eighth" day (Jub. 32:27-29).

20. In the LXX, although not in the Hebrew version, Psalm 28 (29) has the heading "A psalm of David at the conclusion of Tabernacles" (Ψαλμὸς τῷ Δαυιδ, ἐξοδίου σκηνῆς); see MacRae, "The Meaning and Evolution of the Feast of Tabernacles," 258.

21. See further Moloney, "Narrative," 154–72.

him, but Jesus hid himself and went out of the temple." The introduction
(7:1-13) gives the reader background information about geography (v.
1), the time of the year (v. 2), the request by the brothers to go to Judea
(vv. 3-5), another time frame governing Jesus's actions (vv. 6-9), and then
Jesus's decision to attend the feast (vv. 10-13). This is the first time Jesus
is back in Jerusalem following his conflict about the healing of the man
at the pool of Bethesda on the Sabbath (5:1-9); conflict about the law and
Jesus's interpretation of the law continues across this festival.

The first discussion between Jesus and his audience occurs "about
the middle of the festival" (7:14). In this initial discussion the origin of
Jesus's teaching is questioned. In his argument Jesus appeals to the great
teacher of Jewish law, Moses (7:19).[22] As Tabernacles recalls God's care
during the wilderness wanderings, Moses is a key figure for the feast.
There are also hopes for a new "prophet like Moses" (Deut 18:18) who
would once again provide the gift of a "well" of Torah.

The discussion then moves away from Jesus's teaching authority to
the question of his identity (7:25-36). Each time this question is raised
the audience searches for an answer in terms of Jesus's origins. The participants in the story are limited in their perception and fail to accept
Jesus's claims of a divine origin in the One who sent him and to whom
he is going (7:28, 33).

The discussion is interrupted by another reference to time—"the last
day of the festival, the great day" (7:37). On this day, and within a feast
that has had daily water libations, Jesus proclaims a new source of living
water. In this proclamation Jesus identifies with one of the major liturgical symbols of the feast—living water (7:38).

At the center of the section (7:40-52) is a *schism* (7:43) based on a twofold questioning of Jesus's identity. For some he is "the prophet" (7:40);
for others, "the Christ" (7:41). But some, who attribute his origins to Galilee, reject these two titles; he is neither the Christ (7:41, 42) nor a prophet
(7:52). In refusing to accept Jesus's divine origins, they are blinded to
his true identity.

---

22. Jewish tradition has it that during the festival seven biblical figures are invited
as guests into the *sukkah*; these guests were all wanderers, not having a fixed abode.
Moses was the guest invited on the fourth day, which would be the middle of the
feast. See Eisenberg, *Jewish Traditions*, 236; Donin, *Sukkot*, 43. This tradition was not
recorded until later centuries, so it cannot be certain that it was occurring pre-70 CE.

The section continues in 8:12[23] with Jesus's second affirmation of his identity, using another major symbol of the Feast of Tabernacles, "I am the light of the world." The two self-revelatory statements of Jesus as living water and light bracket and bring into sharp relief the refusal of the participants to accept his claims. The discussion of Jesus's identity continues (8:13-30), and again the issue of identity is raised in terms of Jesus's origins and destiny.

The final section (8:31-58) brings the person of Abraham into the discussion and leads to Jesus's definitive nonpredicated statement of identity, "I am" (ἐγὼ εἰμί, 8:58). Jewish tradition remembers Abraham as the first to celebrate Tabernacles. "And he [Abraham] built booths for himself and for his servants on that festival. And he first observed the feast of booths on earth" (Jub. 16:30). The discussions begin with Moses and conclude with Abraham, enabling two great Jewish forebears associated with Tabernacles to bear witness to Jesus's claims.

Schematically, the structure can be shown thus:

Introduction 7:1-13 Where can Jesus/Sophia be found

Moses 7:14-24 The issue of origins—"you have a demon"

7:25-36 Who is Jesus? His origins and destiny

7:37-39 Jesus's first reply—LIVING WATER

7:40-52 Jesus's identity—Schism

8:12 Jesus's second reply—LIGHT OF THE WORLD

8:13-30 Who is Jesus? His origins and destiny

Abraham 8:31-58 The issue of origins—"You are from your father the devil"

Conclusion 8:59 "They took up stones to throw at him; he went out of the temple."

---

23. Along with the majority of scholars, I consider that the episode of the woman taken in adultery (7:53–8:11) is not part of the narrative of Tabernacles. It can be described as a non-Johannine interpolation that is part of the Gospel tradition even though there is uncertainty about which Gospel it belongs to. Because this passage has now found "a home" in the Fourth Gospel, I will discuss this at the conclusion of the discussion of Tabernacles. This placement will enable narrative continuity across 7:1–10:21.

As the structure shows, the central issue at Tabernacles is Jesus's identity. Who is he? The reader knows the answer, since the prologue (1:1-18) declared that Jesus is the tabernacling presence of God—"the word became flesh and tabernacled [ἐσκήνωσεν] among us" (1:14). But throughout this feast various groups are challenged to recognize him. Against the background of a daily affirmation of faith in Israel's God, will Jesus's contemporaries come to faith, or will they, like their ancestors, "turn their backs" on him?

Where Can Jesus/Sophia Be Found? (7:1-13)[24]

The introductory verses establish one of the great ironies of this festival known as the "Feast of Ingathering" (Exod 23:16; 34:22). Throughout the feast, rather than "ingathering," many of the characters will in fact separate from Jesus. In this short introduction Jesus's brothers and sisters are not aligned with Jesus.[25] Even the crowd is divided in its opinion of him, with some considering he is a "good man," while others think that he is a deceiver. At first, Jesus decides to remain in Galilee rather than travel to Jerusalem. In making this decision he is following a different "timetable" than the liturgical or seasonal timetable of his contemporaries; he states, "My time has not yet come" (v. 6).[26] Jerusalem is a source of danger to him with "the Jews" seeking to kill him (7:2, 11).[27] Later in the

---

24. "But where shall wisdom be found?" (Job 28:12).

25. This is the second occurrence of Jesus's brothers and sisters (οἱ ἀδελφοί). Following the first sign at Cana, they were mentioned accompanying Jesus, his mother, and his disciples to Capernaum (2:12). The masculine plural ἀδελφοί is an inclusive generic term meaning both brothers and sisters; see Henry G. Liddell, "ἀδελφός," in *A Lexicon: Abridged from Liddell and Scott's Greek-English Lexicon* (Oak Harbor, WA: Logos Research Systems, 1996). Within the Catholic tradition, the "brothers and sisters" are not considered to be blood brothers and sisters but perhaps stepbrothers/sisters or even cousins; see Raymond E. Brown, *The Gospel according to John*, 2 vols., AB 29–29a (New York: Doubleday, 1966, 1970), 1:112. John P. Meier (*A Marginal Jew: Rethinking the Historical Jesus*, vol. 1: The Roots of the Problem and the Person, ABRL [New York: Doubleday, 1991], 318–32) argues, however, that the brothers and sisters of Jesus were true siblings.

26. This expression is equivalent to the words spoken to his mother at Cana referring to his "hour" (cf. 2:4).

27. The first mention of "the Jews" seeking to kill Jesus occurred within the Sabbath healing (5:18). This threat is voiced repeatedly within the celebration of Tabernacles (7:1, 19, 20, 25; 8:22, 37, 40).

7:1After this Jesus went about in Galilee. He did not wish to go about in Judea because the Jews were looking for an opportunity to kill him. 2Now the Jewish festival of Booths was near. 3So his brothers said to him, "Leave here and go to Judea so that your disciples also may see the works you are doing; 4for no one who wants to be widely known acts in secret. If you do these things, show yourself to the world." 5(For not even his brothers believed in him.) 6Jesus said to them, "My time has not yet come, but your time is always here. 7The world cannot hate you, but it hates me because I testify against it that its works are evil. 8Go to the festival yourselves. I am not going to this festival, for my time has not yet fully come." 9After saying this, he remained in Galilee.

10But after his brothers had gone to the festival, then he also went, not publicly but as it were in secret. 11The Jews were looking for him at the festival and saying, "Where is he?" 12And there was considerable complaining about him among the crowds. While some were saying, "He is a good man," others were saying, "No, he is deceiving the crowd." 13Yet no one would speak openly about him for fear of the Jews.

Gospel narrative, events will happen that bring Jesus to recognize that his "hour" has come—but that lies in the future.

Moses and the Issue of Origins—"You Have a Demon" (7:14-24)

With no explanation, Jesus eventually travels to Jerusalem "about the middle of the festival" and teaches in the temple. His teaching leads some of "the Jews" to wonder about the origins of his learning (v. 15). In this discussion there are two groups of participants, who are all Jews but are divided on their attitude to Jesus. There are "the Jews," apparently the ones present at the Sabbath healing in Jerusalem, who have already decided to kill Jesus for his apparent blasphemy (5:18; 7:1, 11, 13, 15).[28] Also present is another group of Jews called the crowd (ὁ ὄχλος), whose members are divided in their opinion but not threatening death (7:12, 20).[29] Since Jesus was not part of a scribal school his teaching is a cause

---

28. Calling God "my Father" (5:17) seemed to the Torah-abiding Jews in Jerusalem to be blasphemy, and their law condemned a blasphemer to death (Lev 24:16).

29. See the author's introduction for comments on the Johannine use of the term "the Jews" as a rhetorical device rather than a historical description (p. lxxi). Remember, all the characters in the Gospel, including Jesus and his disciples, are Jews. So

¹⁴About the middle of the festival Jesus went up into the temple and began to teach. ¹⁵The Jews were astonished at it, saying, "How does this man have such learning, when he has never been taught?" ¹⁶Then Jesus answered them, "My teaching is not mine but his who sent me. ¹⁷Anyone who resolves to do the will of God will know whether the teaching is from God or whether I am speaking on my own. ¹⁸Those who speak on their own seek their own glory; but the one who seeks the glory of him who sent him is true, and there is nothing false in him.

¹⁹"Did not Moses give you the law? Yet none of you keeps the law. Why are you looking for an opportunity to kill me?" ²⁰The crowd answered, "You have a demon! Who is trying to kill you?" ²¹Jesus answered them, "I performed one work, and all of you are astonished. ²²Moses gave you circumcision (it is, of course, not from Moses, but from the patriarchs), and you circumcise a man on the sabbath. ²³If a man receives circumcision on the sabbath in order that the law of Moses may not be broken, are you angry with me because I healed a man's whole body on the sabbath? ²⁴Do not judge by appearances, but judge with right judgment."

of wonder.[30] Within the scribal schools authority was based on two credentials: first, the teaching had to be grounded in the Scriptures, and second, it must be possible to trace the line of argument back to a great teacher of the law. "In Judaism a teacher acquires his knowledge at the school of some other Rabbi; he belongs to an unbroken line of tradition which goes back to Moses."[31] Jesus traces his teaching authority back to the One who sent him (vv. 16-18). Jesus also appeals to the Scriptures (vv. 19-23) accusing the crowd of breaking the Mosaic law by wanting to kill him. The crowd, as distinct from "the Jews," appears not to know about a plot to kill him and accuses him of being possessed by a demon (v. 20). In reply, Jesus refers to the earlier episode known to "the Jews" concerning his healing on the Sabbath (5:1-9). The Mosaic law allows Sabbath regulations to be set aside for circumcision: "And all things required for circumcision do they perform on the Sabbath" (m. Sukkah 18:3). Using a

---

far, the narrative has shown two notable exceptions: the Samaritan woman and the royal official in John 4.

30. See further Chris Keith, *Jesus' Literacy: Scribal Culture and the Teacher from Galilee*, Library of Historical Jesus Studies 8, LNTS 413 (New York: T&T Clark, 2011), 147–55.

31. Severino Pancaro, *The Law in the Fourth Gospel: The Torah and the Gospel, Moses and Jesus, Judaism and Christianity according to John*, NovTSup 42 (Leiden: Brill, 1975), 82.

rabbinic form of argumentation, from a lesser to a greater,[32] Jesus claims he is therefore able to set aside the Sabbath law to heal a whole person. Circumcision draws a person into the fullness of covenanted life, which takes precedence over Sabbath restrictions; Jesus's healing gives a person fullness of human life (ὅλον ἄνθρωπον, 7:23), and so his actions also have precedence over the Sabbath.[33] The discussion about the Sabbath and the appeal to "the one who sent" him (v. 16) attempt to answer the initial query about the origin of his teaching.

Who Is Jesus? (vv. 25-36)

These verses address the crucial question raised within the feast celebrating God's gifts to Israel in their wilderness experience. As they rejoice in the gifts of God's presence in the cloud (Exod 13:21) and tabernacle (Exod 40:34), God's sustenance and care in the gifts of water (Exod 17) and manna (Exod 16), and God's covenant with them in the Torah (Exod 24), they are challenged to recognize in Jesus a new gift of a loving God (cf. 3:16; 4:10). The issue of Jesus's identity is discussed in terms of where he has come from and where he is going. Limited by their "this-worldly" perceptions, the people of Jerusalem think they know Jesus's origins. In reply to their clear statement, "We know where this man is from" (v. 27), I read Jesus's response with a degree of sarcasm that undermines the truth of their statement: "You know me, and you know where I am from" (v. 28). In fact, the people of Jerusalem should know where Jesus comes from for he told them clearly after the Sabbath healing, "The Father has sent me" (5:36); "I have come in my Father's name" (5:43). In rejecting the words of Jesus, they reject not only him but also the One who sent him. In the context of Tabernacles and its daily ritual and affirmation of faith in Israel's one true God, the Jerusalemites are blind to the identity of Jesus and so repeat the act of their fathers who rejected God and turned to the sun (m. Sukkah 5:4). There continues to be division among the participants in this scene; some, the Jerusalemites, the Pharisees, and the chief priests, wish to arrest Jesus, while others in the crowd believe in him (v. 31).

---

32. Frédéric Manns, *L'Evangile de Jean à la lumière du Judaïsme*, SBFA 33 (Jerusalem: Franciscan Printing Press, 1991), 314. See pp. 307–19 for a detailed description of rabbinic exegesis.

33. Francis J. Moloney, *John*, SP 4 (Collegeville, MN: Liturgical Press, 1998), 244.

25Now some of the people of Jerusalem were saying, "Is not this the man whom they are trying to kill? 26And here he is, speaking openly, but they say nothing to him! Can it be that the authorities really know that this is the Messiah? 27Yet we know where this man is from; but when the Messiah comes, no one will know where he is from." 28Then Jesus cried out as he was teaching in the temple, "You know me, and you know where I am from. I have not come on my own. But the one who sent me is true, and you do not know him. 29I know him, because I am from him, and he sent me." 30Then they tried to arrest him, but no one laid hands on him, because his hour had not yet come. 31Yet many in the crowd believed in him and were saying, "When the Messiah comes, will he do more signs than this man has done?"

32The Pharisees heard the crowd muttering such things about him, and the chief priests and Pharisees sent temple police to arrest him. 33Jesus then said, "I will be with you a little while longer, and then I am going to him who sent me. 34You will search for me, but you will not find me; and where I am, you cannot come." 35The Jews said to one another, "Where does this man intend to go that we will not find him? Does he intend to go to the Dispersion among the Greeks and teach the Greeks? 36What does he mean by saying, 'You will search for me and you will not find me' and 'Where I am, you cannot come'?"

Jesus's Reply—Living Water (vv. 37-39)

The preceding section posed a series of questions concerning Jesus's identity:

Some of the Jerusalemites: "Is not this the man whom they are trying to kill?" (v. 25)

"Can it be that the authorities really know that this is the Messiah?" (v. 26)

The crowd: "When the Messiah comes, will he do more signs than this man has done?" (v. 31)

The Jews: "Where does this man intend to go that we will not find him?" (v. 35)

In verses 37-39 Jesus gives his first reply to these questions by referring to one of the major rituals of the feast, the water libation. But these three verses present possibly the greatest challenge for translators and interpreters. Scholars have differing views on almost every aspect.

John 7:37-39

³⁷On the last day of the festival, the great day, while Jesus was standing there, he cried out, "Let anyone who is thirsty come to me, ³⁸and let the one who believes in me drink. As the scripture has said, 'Out of the believer's heart shall flow rivers of living water.'" ³⁹Now he said this about the Spirit, which believers in him were to receive; for as yet there was no Spirit, because Jesus was not yet glorified.

- How should these verses be punctuated? Should the main period be after the word "me," as in some early manuscript traditions, or after the word "drink," as in other early manuscript traditions?

- The Scripture citation simply states "out of his heart [κοιλίας] shall flow rivers of living water."³⁴ Whose "heart" is meant; the believer's or Jesus's? And how is κοιλίας to be translated—as heart, womb, or belly? Since the same word was used in speaking with Nicodemus, where it clearly referred to a mother's womb (τὴν κοιλίαν τῆς μητρὸς), in the following discussion I will use "womb" rather than "heart."

- What day is meant by "the last day"? Is it day seven when the altar is circled seven times before the water libation, or is it the additional eighth day when this ceremony has ceased?

- To what Scripture passage does Jesus refer?

In this commentary it is not possible to explore the complex debates on each of these issues, but it is important to know that there is no consensus or even majority opinion among scholars. In what follows I offer my perspective with footnotes directing the reader to further discussion.

The difficulty lies in the fact that the ancient manuscripts have different ways of punctuating verses 37-38. One form of punctuation has the major stop after "drink." This leads to the following translation:

Translation A.   "If any one thirst, let him come to me and drink. The one who believes in me, as the scripture has said, 'Out of his heart [κοιλία] shall flow rivers of living water'" (vv. 37b-38). "Now this he said about the Spirit, which

---

34. "From his belly/womb shall flow rivers of living water." The term κοιλία is the Greek translation of בֶטֶן whose primary meaning is "womb" or "uterus." Johannes Behm, "κοιλία," *TDNT* 3 (1965): 786–89.

> those who believed in him were to receive; for as yet the Spirit had not been given, because Jesus was not yet glorified" (v. 39).[35]

This translation, which I support, suggests that "his" refers to the believer, and so the κοιλία of the believer will be a source of living water.

Other manuscripts place the major stop after "me," leading to the following:

Translation B.   If any one thirst, let him come to me; and let whoever believes in me drink, as the Scripture has said, "Out of his heart shall flow rivers of living water" (vv. 37b-38).[36]

This translation suggests that "his" refers to Jesus and so the κοιλία of Jesus will be a source of living water.

Modern scholars are divided on the question of whose κολία is being referred to, the believer's or Jesus's, and editors of different editions of the Bible frequently give one translation in the main text with a footnote to the alternative.

Since the manuscript tradition alone cannot resolve this, then the translator and interpreter must look to other factors to try to make sense of these verses. I take the following position, based on my theological understanding of the Gospel and the artistry of the evangelist in his use of symbolism.

The statement in 7:37-38 is very similar to the earlier dialogue with the Samaritan woman, where Jesus promised that the believer would never thirst, and indeed within the believer there would arise a "spring of water" (4:13-14). While 4:14 spoke of a spring of water *within* the believer (ἐν αὐτῷ), 7:38 speaks of water flowing *out of* the believer (ἐκ τῆς κοιλίας αὐτοῦ). Earlier I argued that a key text behind the Johannine image of living water in the encounter with the Samaritan woman was Ezekiel 47. In John 7:38 the depiction of the eschatological temple from

---

35. This translation is favored by scholars such as Charles K. Barrett, John H. Bernard, Robert H. Lightfoot, Barnabas Lindars, and Xavier Léon-Dufour and is supported by the second-century papyrus 𝔓[66] and the fourth-century Codex Sinaiticus. Additionally, this has the strongest support among the early Eastern patristics.

36. This translation is followed by scholars such as Francis J. Moloney, Raymond E. Brown, Rudolph Bultmann, Charles H. Dodd, Edwyn Hoskyns, and Marie-Émile Boismard.

Ezekiel continues to influence the interpretation of Jesus's words.[37] In Ezekiel's vision the actual source of the water is not seen; the waters are simply flowing from beneath the threshold of the sanctuary (Ezek 47:1). The waters have their source in the divine Presence, and the temple is the point of intersection between heaven and earth and thus the locus of the divine Presence on earth. In presenting a case for the water flowing from the κοιλία of the believer, there is no suggestion that the believer is an independent source. The believer possesses living water only because he or she has already "come to me" (v. 37; cf. 4:14).[38]

It is important to read verse 38 in the light of verse 39; "Now this he said about the Spirit, which those who believed in him were to receive; for as yet the Spirit had not been given, because Jesus was not yet glorified." Jesus is referring to a future time when believers will be the recipients of the Spirit. In the present narrative time, Jesus is the source of living water, able to invite others to come to him, but the passage indicates a future time when he will not be present, but believers, gifted with the Spirit, will themselves be such sources of living water.

The discussion above, on the punctuation and on the identity of the referent in the biblical text, Jesus or the believer, is important for the interpretation of the scriptural citation and for identifying the text to which Jesus refers. It is also important to note that Jesus's words are proclaimed on "the last day" of the feast. The time indicator forms an essential part of the context of his words and is critical for their interpretation.

On the Last Day, the Great Day (7:37)

The celebration of Tabernacles lasted for seven days (Deut 16:13) with the addition of an eighth day of solemn assembly similar to the Sabbath (Lev 23:34-36). If the expression is a reference to a specific day of the festival, does it mean the seventh, *Hoshanna Rabbah*, or the eighth, *Shemini Atzeret*?[39] Both are possible. The image of water in verses 37 and 38 sug-

---

37. There are many different views on what passage of Scripture is referred to in 7:38. I will discuss this issue below and present arguments in support of Ezek 47.

38. "Jesus gives life-giving water, so that everyone, who, through faith, shares in this water, will become a source of living water (7:38)." See Andreas Obermann, *Die christologische Erfüllung der Schrift im Johannesevangelium*, WUNT 83 (Tübingen: Mohr Siebeck, 1996), 356.

39. For a survey of opinions on whether it is the seventh or eighth day, see Barnabas Lindars, *The Gospel of John*, NCB (London: Oliphants, 1972), 297–98.

gests the seventh day when the participants process with the water libation seven times around the altar.[40] According to the Mishnah, the water
and light ceremonies did not continue into the eighth day (m. Sukkah 4:1).

Alternatively, the eighth day, a special sabbatical day (Lev 23:36), may
have provided the vacuum in which Jesus's offer of water and light
would have been more keenly appreciated. The eighth day of the feast
had particular significance as it "was the last festival day in the Jewish
calendar and is called 'the last good day' (m. Sukk. 4:8)."[41] On this day
special prayers for rain were said, which continued until the first day
of Passover (m. Ta'an. 1:2). On this eighth day an extended prayer for
rain was offered.[42]

A third possibility is that the expression has its full meaning beyond
the actual feast in the "hour" of Jesus.[43] The text of verses 37 and 38 supports this interpretation and its eschatological thrust, without becoming
totally divorced from its meaning within the feast. Within the Gospel
"the last day" has been mentioned in the Bread of Life discourse (6:39, 40,
44, 54) and will occur again in 11:24 and 12:48. The next time the reader
hears of a "great" day is the Passover-Sabbath day after the crucifixion
(19:31). During this Sabbath, "while it was still dark" and so, according
to Jewish reckoning, not yet over, Mary Magdalene discovers the empty
tomb (20:1). The "great" day in the Johannine Gospel is the day of Jesus's
resurrection, which is the *eighth* day, with a promise that the believer
will share this resurrection experience. Because of these textual links to
the resurrection of the believer and Jesus, the "last day, the great day"
has a particular Johannine eschatological perspective that continues in
the next two verses. Verse 38 looks to a future time when rivers of living water "shall flow" from the womb (κολία) of Sophia-Jesus (19:34),
giving birth to children of God, who, with the bestowal of the Spirit,
will become ongoing sources of living water. Verse 39 makes the future
reference quite explicit in mentioning the Spirit who has "not yet" been
given, because Jesus has "not yet" been glorified.

The arguments so far have reached beyond the narrative time to the time
of the Johannine community to find a meaning for the phrase "on the last

---

40. Brown, *The Gospel according to John*, 1:327.

41. Leon Morris, *The Gospel according to John*, rev. ed., NICNT (Grand Rapids: Eerdmans, 1995), 373 n. 79.

42. The prayers for rain were delayed until the eighth day so that the rain would
not fall during the actual festival because of the obligation to dwell in the temporary
shelter (*sukkah*). Eisenberg, *Jewish Traditions*, 240.

43. Zane Hodges, "Rivers of Living Water—John 7:37-39," *BSac* 136 (1979): 247.

day, the great day" (v. 37). Within the actual feast, the narrative time that best expresses the Johannine meaning of Jesus's words on "the last day of the feast" is the eighth day. In the stark absence of water rituals and light, Jesus announces that the water has *not* dried up and the light has *not* been extinguished. Jesus is a source of water for the thirsty (v. 37) and light for those in darkness (8:12). In asserting the eighth day as most appropriate, I point to a key Johannine theme that has been developing throughout the narrative—the paradox of presence in absence. For a Christian community living at the end of the first century when the temple has been destroyed and they no longer have access to synagogue worship, how can God be present to them? In the absence of a physical temple, Jesus/Sophia provides a new temple where God may be encountered and worshiped (2:21; 4:21). In the absence of water rituals and temple candelabras, Jesus/Sophia provides water and light. The significance of the eighth day is also reflected in the post-Easter stories. The eighth day, which is also the first day of the Jewish week, is the day when Jesus breathes the gift of the Spirit onto the community of disciples (20:19-22), fulfilling the words of 7:39. On the next "eighth" day Jesus comes to Thomas who, in the absence of Jesus, cannot believe. On this "eighth" day Jesus announces a blessing to all who come to faith without seeing his presence. Within this Gospel the eighth day juxtaposes presence and absence and invites all to experience the eschatological blessings of the eighth day.

What Is the Scripture Passage Cited by Jesus?

Commentators who accept a christological reading of verses 37 and 38 suggest Isaiah 12:3; Zechariah 13:1; Ezekiel 47:1; Exodus 17:5-6; Numbers 20:7-16; and Psalm 78:15-16 as the Scripture passage cited by Jesus. Those favoring the alternative interpretation I have adopted suggest Zechariah 14:8; Proverbs 4:23; 5:15; Sirach 24:30-33; and others.[44] To this list can also be added Isaiah 58:11 and Proverbs 18:4. The obvious lack of agreement in identifying the text leads to great differences in interpretation. Since there is no exact parallel to Jesus's words in either the Hebrew or Greek versions of the OT, it is possible that a targumic text lies behind Jesus's words, or that he was not quoting exactly but simply alluding to a text (or texts) from the scriptural tradition.

The Greek expression ποταμοὶ ἐκ τῆς κοιλίας αὐτοῦ ῥεύσουσιν ὕδατος ζῶντος (v. 38) arises from a distinctly Aramaic idiom, which indicates

---

44. Juan B. Cortés, "Yet Another Look at Jn 7,37-38," *CBQ* 29 (1967): 85.

that, if Jesus is quoting a text exactly, it will be from the targums.[45] Alternatively, Pierre Grelot suggests that the expression is not a single verse of Scripture but a combination of two texts following rabbinic exegetical principles.[46] A clue to what Scripture is in mind can be found within the Mishnah. The tractate Šeqalim has the following explanation for why one of the temple gates is called the Water Gate: "For through it they take the flask of water used in the water offering on the Festival [of Tabernacles]. R. Eliezer b. Jacob says, 'Through it *the waters trickle forth* and in time to come they will *issue out from under the threshold of the house*' (Ez. 47:1-5)" (m. Šeqal. 6:3; italics in original.). A third-century rabbinic commentary on Exodus, the Tosefta, elaborates further on this:[47]

> Whence is the name "Water Gate"? It is so called because through it they take the flask of water used for the libation at the Feast. R. Eliezer b. Jacob says of it: "The waters are dripping," intimating that water oozing out and rising, as if from this flask, will in future days come forth from under the threshold of the temple; and so it says, When the man went forth eastward with the line in his hand, he measured a thousand cubits, and caused me to pass through the waters. (t. Sukkah 3:3)[48]

In the Tosefta, the ritual of the water libation is first linked with the waters from the temple (Ezek 47) and then Zechariah 14.[49] The witness of

---

45. Pierre Grelot, "Jean, VII, 38: Eau du rocher ou source du Temple?," *RB* 70 (1963): 43; Bienaimé, *Moïse et le don de l'eau*, 283. Menken accepts the Aramaism but disputes that this necessitates a targumic citation. Maarten J. J. Menken, *Old Testament Quotations in the Fourth Gospel: Studies in Textual Form*, CBET 15 (Kampen: Kok Pharos, 1996), 199.

46. Grelot, "Jean, VII, 38," 47–48. Sheridan considers that "the matrix of John's thought in 7:37b-39 lay in a combination of the Ezekiel-temple tradition and the wilderness-wandering narrative retold in Ps 77"; see Ruth Sheridan, *Retelling Scripture: 'The Jews' and the Scriptural Citations in John 1:19–12:15*, BibInt 110 (Leiden: Brill, 2012), 192.

47. This rabbinic text is also discussed by Grelot ("Jean, VII, 38," 46); Bienaimé, *Moïse et le don de l'eau*, 202; Bruce Grigsby, " 'If Any Man Thirsts . . . ': Observations on the Rabbinic Background of John 7:37-39," *Bib* 67 (1986): 105–8.

48. Quotation from A. W. Greenup, *Sukkah, Mishna and Tosefta: With Introduction, Translation and Short Notes*, Translations of Early Documents, ser. 3, Rabbinic Texts (New York: Macmillan, 1925), 73–74.

49. The cautionary comments made about the Mishnah and its reliability for knowing the rituals in the first century apply even more so to the Tosefta, which is a commentary on the Mishnah from ca. 200–300 CE. For further analysis of the relationship between the Mishnah and Tosefta, see Jacob Neusner, *The Classics of Judaism: A Textbook and Reader* (Louisville: Westminster John Knox, 1995), 19, 53.

a first-century rabbi who had known the temple prior to its destruction in 70 CE identifies the Water Gate through which the libation ceremony passed with the South Gate of Ezekiel's temple vision.[50]

The clearest text indicated by both the Mishnah (m. Šeqal. 6:3) and the Tosefta (t. Sukkah 3:3) is Ezekiel 47, the vision of the eschatological temple, which in Jewish tradition was associated with Zechariah 14:8. The waters of Ezekiel's temple are "living" in the sense that they are moving and also in the sense that they give life (Ezek 47:9). The image of life-giving waters flowing from the side of the eschatological temple provides a most appropriate scriptural text for Jesus to allude to, given a daily liturgical procession through Ezekiel's "South Gate" (Ezek 47:2), even if there is not exact verbal parallelism.[51] The eschatological temple vision is also consistent with Johannine symbolism (1:14; 2:19) and suits the physical context within the temple and the time reference to "the last day." It must also be noted that the waters in Zechariah's text flow from Jerusalem (14:8), the city, while Ezekiel's text, by naming the temple as the water source (Ezek 47:1), has more in common with the Gospel symbolism. In the Johannine text, temple imagery is applied to Jesus (2:21) so that when he says, "come to me and drink," he is able to offer water because he is the new temple and source of living waters.

In his analysis of the significance of the rituals of Sukkot for the Second Temple period, Jeffrey Rubenstein argues that the meaning of the libation ceremony must be found in the ancient myths about the temple and its "foundation stone" resting directly above, and therefore giving access to, the primordial flood waters of the deep (*tehom*). "The libation descended through channels beneath the altar, stimulated the waters, and set in motion a process which led to the refertilization of nature."[52] The very focus of this festival is the temple and its abundant life-giving waters that the cult actualizes through its rituals. In this context, the temple therefore provides the most likely image of a source of water. But can this temple imagery be applied to the believer?

---

50. Grelot, "Jean, VII, 38," 38. Bienaimé, *Moïse et le don de l'eau*, 202.

51. Hooke comments that, after the temple *logion* in chapter 2, there is a similar reference to an unspecified word of Scripture, testifying to future postresurrection events; Samuel H. Hooke, " 'The Spirit Was Not Yet,' " *NTS* 9 (1962–1963): 377. It is also possible, as I noted above, that the text quoted in the Gospel came from a targumic tradition rather than from the MT or the LXX.

52. Jeffrey Rubenstein, "Sukkot, Eschatology and Zechariah 14," *RB* 103 (1996): 83.

The first-time reader of verses 37-39, who has only what has been read so far as an interpretive guide, would certainly be puzzled by this citation. The alert reader has already been led to understand Jesus as the tabernacle (1:14) and temple (2:21) and as one who supplants Jacob in the gift of living water (4:7-15). Given the dynamic interplay of these images, the reader would expect the stream of living water to come from the side of *Jesus*, but that is not what the text says. The third-person pronoun "his" (αὐτοῦ, v. 38), rather than the first (my), sounds a jarring note that is not immediately comprehensible. Verse 39 confirms that the text cannot be deciphered accurately in the present time, as there is a "not yet" time and a future gift to which the text refers, "For the Spirit had not yet been given" (v. 39). In narrative time, the words "Out of *his* heart shall flow rivers of living water" (v. 38) can only be a promise, not fully clear, of something still to happen. The proleptic nature of the verses transfers to the believer imagery that rightly applies only to Jesus during the historical time of his ministry, hence the masculine singular αὐτου (his). In his flesh (1:14) and body (2:21) he is the divine Presence dwelling with us and the source of living water. The text proclaims that there will come a future time when, through the gift of the Spirit to the believer, such images will also apply to the believer. The future, postresurrection time forcefully interrupts the narrative, bringing the eschatological "last day" into the present moment in Jesus's words. Here, the first-time reader needs to allow the narrative to unfold, even if all is not clear. A second-time reading through the lens of "the hour" adds meaning and depth to these puzzling verses.[53]

The Spirit Who Was Not Yet

There is a strong scriptural tradition linking water and the Spirit, stretching back to creation and forward to the end time (Gen 1:3; Ezek 36:25-26; Isa 44:3; Joel 3:1).[54] The liturgy of Tabernacles also makes this association of water and Spirit, for according to rabbinic traditions, the place where the candelabra were set up was called the "House of Draw-

---

53. A second-time reader will know that "the Johannine community experienced Jesus as the one who birthed new life in them, but when he had handed over the Spirit to them, they, too, became the source of living water, of birth to new life for others." See Barbara E. Reid, "John 7:37-39," *Int* 63 (2009): 395.

54. Brown, *The Gospel according to John*, 1:324.

ing" because "from there they draw the Holy Spirit."[55] Garry Burge comments that "rivers of water" (v. 38) would be the "perfect metaphor for the abundance of the divine Spirit in the Messianic age."[56] In Isaiah 44, Spirit and water are eschatological gifts promising life to the exiles: "For I will pour water on the thirsty land, and streams on the dry ground; I will pour my spirit upon your descendants, and my blessing on your offspring" (Isa 44:3). In the Johannine narrative, the Spirit has already been given to Jesus (1:32) but is not yet a power in the life of the believers. The Spirit will only be released upon the community in the hour of Jesus's glorification (19:30; 20:22).

In summary, my understanding of these verses is that on the last day, the eighth day of the festival, in the absence of the water libation rituals, Jesus speaks of himself as a source of water, much as he had promised to the Samaritan woman. Then, recalling the passage from Ezekiel 47 describing a stream of water flowing from the threshold of the temple bringing abundant life to the arid land, Jesus speaks of a future time, in his absence, when believers will also be sources of living water, through the future gift of the Spirit. This passage, therefore, is suggesting that, even when Jesus has returned to his previous glory, there will still be a temple presence able to provide abundant water; believers endowed with the Spirit will continue to be living temples of God's presence. The promise is given here, in chapter 7, and will be resolved in the "hour."

Jesus's Identity—Schism (vv. 40-52)

The response to Jesus's proclamation and invitation is schism within the crowd and among the Jewish leaders. The crowd, who had not heard the description of Jesus as the tabernacle (1:14) and temple (2:21), probably heard in his words echoes of the miracle in the wilderness when Moses produced water from the side of the rock (Num 20:9-11; cf. Exod 17:6), because the participants at the feast are celebrating the wilderness

---

55. Garry H. Burge, *The Anointed Community: The Holy Spirit in the Johannine Community* (Grand Rapids: Eerdmans, 1987), 92. Burge cites the Jerusalem Talmud (y. Sukkah 55a): "Why was the place called the place of drawing? Because there the Holy Spirit was drawn by virtue of the saying [Isa 12:3]: with joy you shall draw water out of the wells of salvation."

56. Burge, *The Anointed Community*, 92.

John 7:40-52

⁴⁰When they heard these words, some in the crowd said, "This is really the prophet." ⁴¹Others said, "This is the Messiah." But some asked, "Surely the Messiah does not come from Galilee, does he? ⁴²Has not the scripture said that the Messiah is descended from David and comes from Bethlehem, the village where David lived?" ⁴³So there was a division in the crowd because of him. ⁴⁴Some of them wanted to arrest him, but no one laid hands on him.

⁴⁵Then the temple police went back to the chief priests and Pharisees, who asked them, "Why did you not arrest him?" ⁴⁶The police answered, "Never has anyone spoken like this!" ⁴⁷Then the Pharisees replied, "Surely you have not been deceived too, have you? ⁴⁸Has any one of the authorities or of the Pharisees believed in him? ⁴⁹But this crowd, which does not know the law—they are accursed." ⁵⁰Nicodemus, who had gone to Jesus before, and who was one of them, asked, ⁵¹"Our law does not judge people without first giving them a hearing to find out what they are doing, does it?" ⁵²They replied, "Surely you are not also from Galilee, are you? Search and you will see that no prophet is to arise from Galilee."

wanderings and remembering all the Mosaic gifts.⁵⁷ For these listeners, Jesus is the expected prophet like Moses repeating his wonders:⁵⁸ "This is really the prophet" (v. 40). Others, given the messianic hopes expressed in Zechariah 9–14 and the liturgy of Tabernacles, perceive that these longings have now been fulfilled: "This is the Messiah" (v. 41). While others in the crowd, who fix on Galilee as the place of Jesus's origins, deny these assertions, pointing to the Scriptures to support their blindness: "The Messiah is descended from David and comes from Bethlehem" (v. 42). Even the Jewish leaders are divided. The temple police sent earlier to arrest him were amazed by his words, and Nicodemus reenters the narrative to speak up on Jesus's behalf. The chief priests and Pharisees erroneously claim scriptural authority to say, "no prophet is to arise from Galilee" (v. 52).⁵⁹ A feast anticipating the eschatological gathering

57. There are two descriptions of Moses striking the rock and producing a flow of water; of these two, Bienaimé argues that Exod 17:6 best aligns with John 7:37 (Bienaimé, *Moïse et le don de l'eau*, 285). See also Grelot, "Jean, VII, 38," 48. Sheridan and Menken consider that it is possible that the wilderness rock has been conflated with the "Foundation Stone" of the temple, resting above the waters of creation. See Sheridan, *Retelling Scripture*, 192; Menken, *Old Testament Quotations*, 203.

58. Marie-Émile Boismard, *Moses or Jesus: An Essay in Johannine Christology*, trans. B. T. Viviano (Minneapolis: Fortress, 1993), 6–10; Brown, *The Gospel according to John*, 1:329.

59. This claim overlooks that Jonah was from Gathhepher in Galilee (2 Kgs 14:25).

of the nations has brought about division among the people of Israel (v. 43); some are prepared to see him as a "prophet" or even the "Messiah" while the leaders are blind to his identity.

Jesus's Second Reply—I Am the Light (8:12)

Faced with the confusion and denial of his listeners, Jesus makes a second self-disclosure, again in terms of the symbols of Tabernacles. "On the last day . . . the great day" (7:37), when the lights in the temple court-yard have been extinguished, Jesus offers a new guiding light, not just for Israel, but for the entire world: "I am the light of the world" (8:12).[60] In the wilderness the people of Israel had followed a pillar of cloud by day and a pillar of fire by night.[61] In the book of Exodus, the cloud is the manifestation of YHWH's glory/presence (Exod 13:21; 14:24; 16:10; 19:9, 16; 24:15). The fire/cloud settled on the tabernacle, and the people were guided to journey or rest according to its movements (Exod 40:34-38; Num 9:15, 17). Later, when the temple was built and the tabernacle placed within it, the glory cloud of God filled the temple (1 Kgs 8:4-11). By late Second Temple Judaism, Sophia is attributed as the source of light and guidance during the wilderness: she is "a starry flame through the night" (Wis 10:17). Jesus now offers a light surpassing the wilderness cloud, for Jesus embodies Sophia and has already been described as a light that the darkness could not extinguish (cf. 1:5).

I Am Woman

When Jesus says, "I am the light of the world" (8:12), he affirms the glory of Sophia, "For she is a reflection of eternal light, a spotless mirror of the working of God. . . . Compared with the light she is found to be superior, for it is succeeded by the night, but against wisdom evil does not prevail" (Wis 7:26, 29-30). From his examination of the "I am" statements across the Fourth Gospel, Martin Scott asserts: "The ἐγώ εἰμι sayings were shown to be thoroughly *rooted*

---

60. As Tabernacles was celebrated at the full moon during the autumnal equinox, the "world" was lit by the sun during the day and by the radiance of the moon by night. See Håkan Ulfgard, *Feast and Future: Revelation 7:9-17 and the Feast of Tabernacles* (Stockholm: Almqvist & Wiksell, 1989), 115.

61. The pillar of cloud/fire was one of three Mosaic gifts associated with Tabernacles that looked to a second redeemer to fulfill their promise. These gifts were the manna, the well, and the cloud. See Bienaimé, *Moïse et le don de l'eau*, 210–11.

John 8:12

12Again Jesus spoke to them, saying, "I am the light of the world. Whoever follows me will never walk in darkness but will have the light of life."

in Sophia speculation more than merely touched by it."62

The only explicit "I am" statement made by Wisdom is Sirach 24:18, which is in the main text of Joseph Ziegler's critical edition of the Göttingen Septuagint but found as a textual note in Alfred Rahlfs's edition and usually placed as a footnote in current English translation. This verse reads, "I am the mother [ἐγὼ μήτηρ] of beautiful love, of fear, of knowledge, and of holy hope; being eternal, I am given to all my children, to those who are named by him" (Sir 24:18).63

In her investigation of the "I Am" sayings, Satoko Yamaguchi points out that these express relational claims and would not have been heard exclusively as a male image.64 One very early relational commitment is that made with Abraham: "*I am* El Shaddai [אני־אל שדי]; walk before me, and be blameless. And I will make my covenant between me and you, and will make you exceedingly numerous" (Gen 17:1-2). The covenant is then repeated to Jacob, "*I am* El-Shaddai: be fruitful and multiply; a nation and a company of nations shall come from you, and kings shall spring from you" (Gen 35:11). Here God is named as El-Shaddai, which is "certainly an early name in Israelite literature, since it occurs in three early poems: the Testament of Jacob (Gen. 49:25), the Balaam oracles, and Psalm 68—all of which date from the tenth century BCE at the latest."65 While scholars have not reached consensus about the etymology of Shaddai, a strong case is made by David Biale that

62. Martin Scott, *Sophia and the Johannine Jesus*, JSNTSup 71 (Sheffield: JSOT Press, 1992), 169; italics in the original.

63. In this verse the simple "I am" (ἐγώ) is used, rather than the emphatic I am (ἐγώ εἰμι).

64. Satoko Yamaguchi, "'I Am' Sayings and Women in Context," in *A Feminist Companion to John*, vol. 2, ed. Amy-Jill Levine with Marianne Blickenstaff, FCNTECW 5 (London: Sheffield Academic, 2003), 47.

65. David Biale, "The God with Breasts: El Shaddai in the Bible," *HR* 21 (1982): 243–44.

its ancient origins refer to "God of the Breasts."[66] Such meaning is suggested by the fertility blessing Jacob gives to Joseph naming God as Shaddai (שדי) and calling down blessings of the breasts (שדים) and the womb (רחם).

> by the God of your father,
> who will help you,
> By Shaddai [שדי] who will
> bless you
> with blessings of heaven above,
> blessings of the deep that
> lies beneath,
> blessings of the breasts
> [שדים] and of the womb.
> (Gen 49:25)

Biale also notes that of the five passages in Genesis where Shaddai occurs "four are fertility blessings using the 'be fruitful and multiply' formula of Genesis 1 and 9 or varying it slightly."[67]

From this can be concluded that a very early use of the "I am" expression involved the memory of ancient fertility blessings by a God named as "God of the Breasts" (El-Shaddai). And so, when Sophia says "I am," she embraces an ancient memory of a female divinity known for her abundant blessings of fertility.

Who Is Jesus?—His Origins and Destiny (8:13-30)

Jesus's second self-disclosure does not resolve the schism. There is still the possibility of arrest (v. 20) and belief (v. 30). Following the appeal of Nicodemus to give Jesus a proper hearing (7:51), verses 8:13-30 take on a forensic tone as the Pharisees require a witness to support Jesus's testimony (v. 13).[68] The discussion of Jesus's origins in chapter 8 recalls words and themes from a similar discussion in chapter 7, but now Jesus identifies the one who sent him as "my Father" (vv. 18, 19). The union of Jesus and the Father who sent him is forcefully expressed in the triple

---

66. Biale suggests it may be borrowed from Egypt "where *shdi* is a verb meaning 'to suckle.' Here, it is not even necessary to tinker with the suffix, since it is identical to the Hebrew. In this case, El Shaddai might be better rendered as 'El who suckles' or El of 'the suckling.'" Biale, "The God with Breasts," 249.

67. Biale, "The God with Breasts," 247. He discusses Gen 17:1; 28:3; 35:9-12; 48:3-4. The blessing of Joseph quoted above, while departing from the form "be fruitful and multiply," then asks for "blessings of the breasts and of the womb" (Gen 49:25).

68. Although Bibles make a chapter break after 7:52 and also include the pericope of the "Woman caught in adultery," the original text would have had no such breaks, with 7:52 continuing with Jesus's self-identification as the light of the world and the Pharisees' accusation about self-witness. E.g., Codex Sinaiticus reads: "They answered and said to him: Are you also from Galilee? Search and see that no prophet arises out of Galilee. Again therefore Jesus spoke to them, saying: I am the Light of the world."

John 8:13-30

¹³Then the Pharisees said to him, "You are testifying on your own behalf; your testimony is not valid." ¹⁴Jesus answered, "Even if I testify on my own behalf, my testimony is valid because I know where I have come from and where I am going, but you do not know where I come from or where I am going. ¹⁵You judge by human standards; I judge no one. ¹⁶Yet even if I do judge, my judgment is valid; for it is not I alone who judge, but I and the Father who sent me. ¹⁷In your law it is written that the testimony of two witnesses is valid. ¹⁸I testify on my own behalf, and the Father who sent me testifies on my behalf." ¹⁹Then they said to him, "Where is your Father?" Jesus answered, "You know neither me nor my Father. If you knew me, you would know my Father also." ²⁰He spoke these words while he was teaching in the treasury of the temple, but no one arrested him, because his hour had not yet come.

²¹Again he said to them, "I am going away, and you will search for me, but you will die in your sin. Where I am

use of the absolute "I am [ἐγώ εἰμι]" (vv. 18, 24, 28). Unlike verse 12, these three verses have no predicate to "I am."[69] Jesus's first witness is none other than Israel's ἐγώ εἰμι, which is the LXX translation of the divine name, YHWH. "I Am [ἐγώ εἰμι], the one witnessing to myself, and the Father who sent me bears witness to me" (v. 18). But Jesus's opponents fail to recognize both Jesus and his Father. Then, speaking of his future "hour," Jesus discloses that he is going away, meaning, he is returning to his Father through his death, but they remain confused. In the face of their confusion, Jesus speaks a second time about the "lifting up" of "the human-one" (ὁ υἱὸς τοῦ ἀνθρώπου; cf. 1:51), which has the double sense of being lifted up in the crucifixion and in exaltation (v. 28).[70]

Within the feast, during the procession with the willow branches, the supplicants would pray, "*ani wehu* [literally I and He] come to our aid."[71] The Hebrew phrase *ani wehu* was used as an oblique way of referring to

69. Many scholars trace the Johannine unpredicated use of "I am" to the self-revelatory formula of Deutero-Isaiah (41:4; 43:10, 25; 45:18; 46:4; 51:12; 52:6). For more on this see Philip Harner, *The "I Am" of the Fourth Gospel: A Study in Johannine Usage and Thought*, FBBS (Philadelphia: Fortress, 1970), 6.

70. Gerd Lüdemann, "ὑψόω," *EDNT* 3 (1993): 410; Georg Bertram, "ὑψόω," *TDNT* 8 (1972): 602–20.

71. Harner, *The "I Am" of the Fourth Gospel*, 18–21; Frederic Manns, *Jewish Prayer in the Time of Jesus*, SBFA 22 (Jerusalem: Franciscan Printing Press, 1994), 214; Ulfgard, *Feast and Future*, 111, n. 466.

going, you cannot come." [22]Then the Jews said, "Is he going to kill himself? Is that what he means by saying, 'Where I am going, you cannot come'?" [23]He said to them, "You are from below, I am from above; you are of this world, I am not of this world. [24]I told you that you would die in your sins, for you will die in your sins unless you believe that I am he." [25]They said to him, "Who are you?" Jesus said to them, "Why do I speak to you at all? [26]I have much to say about you and much to condemn; but the one who sent me is true, and I declare to the world what I have heard from him." [27]They did not understand that he was speaking to them about the Father. [28]So Jesus said, "When you have lifted up the Son of Man, then you will realize that I am he, and that I do nothing on my own, but I speak these things as the Father instructed me. [29]And the one who sent me is with me; he has not left me alone, for I always do what is pleasing to him." [30]As he was saying these things, many believed in him.

YHWH and thus avoiding saying the sacred name. Having celebrated the feast and heard the daily recitation of *ani wehu*, Jesus's use of the phrase "I Am" as a term of self-designation would have been both striking and offensive to his opponents.

Abraham: The Issue of Origins (8:31-58)

Corresponding to the focus on Moses the law giver in 7:14-24, which opened the disputes at Tabernacles, verses 8:31-58 close the discussions by referring to another of Israel's ancestors associated with the feast, Abraham, who was remembered as the first to celebrate Tabernacles (Jub. 16:30). This section is dominated by references to the figure of Abraham (vv. 33, 37, 39 [3x], 40, 52, 53, 56, 57, 58).

The passage presents in highly condensed form key aspects of Johannine theology. First is the late Second Temple cosmological understanding of this world (*kosmos*) being held captive by a power of evil named as Satan, the devil, Belial, and, later in the Gospel of John, the "ruler of this world" (12:31; 14:30; 16:11).[72] In John's Gospel the word

---

72. On Jewish understanding of the cosmic power of evil in the first century, see Loren T. Stuckenbruck, "'Protect Them from the Evil One' (John 17:15): Light from the Dead Sea Scrolls," in *John, Qumran, and the Dead Sea Scrolls: Sixty Years of Discovery and Debate*, ed. Mary L. Coloe and Tom Thatcher, EJL 32 (Atlanta: SBL, 2011), esp. 145–59. Also, Adele Reinhartz who speaks of a "cosmological" tale telling the story

John 8:31-58

³¹Then Jesus said to the Jews who had believed in him, "If you continue in my word, you are truly my disciples; ³²and you will know the truth, and the truth will make you free." ³³They answered him, "We are descendants of Abraham and have never been slaves to anyone. What do you mean by saying, 'You will be made free'?"

³⁴Jesus answered them, "Very truly, I tell you, everyone who commits sin is a slave to sin. ³⁵The slave does not have a permanent place in the household; the son has a place there forever. ³⁶So if the Son makes you free, you will be free indeed. ³⁷I know that you are descendants of Abraham; yet you look for an opportunity to kill me, because there is no place in you for my word. ³⁸I declare what I have seen in the Father's presence; as for you, you should do what you have heard from the Father."

³⁹They answered him, "Abraham is our father." Jesus said to them, "If you were Abraham's children, you would be doing what Abraham did, ⁴⁰but now you are trying to kill me, a man who has told you the truth that I heard from God. This is not what Abraham did. ⁴¹You are indeed doing what your father does." They said to him, "We are not illegitimate children; we have one father, God himself." ⁴²Jesus said to them, "If God were your Father, you would love me, for I came from God and now I am here. I did not come on my own, but he sent me. ⁴³Why do you not understand what I say? It is because you cannot accept my word. ⁴⁴You are from your father the devil, and you choose to do your father's desires. He was a murderer from the beginning and does not stand in the truth, because there is no truth in him. When he lies, he speaks according to

kosmos is polyvalent and used with multiple meanings, which can be determined only by examining the context. As Sandra Schneiders states: " 'World' is not an 'objective' thing but an imaginative construction of reality."[73] She describes four different uses of the term *kosmos*. First, it refers to the entire created universe (John 1:1-3). Second, it is the context in which we live, "humanity's natural home." Then, at times it is used to refer to humanity, the object of God's love (3:16). Only the fourth use of the term has a negative sense, as there are times when "world" refers to a realm that is evil due to the free moral choices of human beings, influenced by Satan.[74]

---

of the Eternal Word coming into this world to do battle with a power of evil before returning to the Father. See Paula Fredriksen and Adele Reinhartz, eds., *Jesus, Judaism and Christian Anti-Judaism: Reading the New Testament after the Holocaust* (Louisville: Westminster John Knox, 2002), esp. 101–2, 104–10.

73. Sandra M. Schneiders, "The Word in the World," *Pacifica* 23 (2010): 254.

74. Ibid., 256–57.

his own nature, for he is a liar and the father of lies. [45]But because I tell the truth, you do not believe me. [46]Which of you convicts me of sin? If I tell the truth, why do you not believe me? [47]Whoever is from God hears the words of God. The reason you do not hear them is that you are not from God."

[48]The Jews answered him, "Are we not right in saying that you are a Samaritan and have a demon?" [49]Jesus answered, "I do not have a demon; but I honor my Father, and you dishonor me. [50]Yet I do not seek my own glory; there is one who seeks it and he is the judge. [51]Very truly, I tell you, whoever keeps my word will never see death." [52]The Jews said to him, "Now we know that you have a demon. Abraham died, and so did the prophets; yet you say, 'Whoever keeps my word will never taste death.' [53]Are you greater than our father Abraham, who died? The prophets also died. Who do you claim to be?" [54]Jesus answered, "If I glorify myself, my glory is nothing. It is my Father who glorifies me, he of whom you say, 'He is our God,' [55]though you do not know him. But I know him; if I would say that I do not know him, I would be a liar like you. But I do know him and I keep his word. [56]Your ancestor Abraham rejoiced that he would see my day; he saw it and was glad." [57]Then the Jews said to him, "You are not yet fifty years old, and have you seen Abraham?" [58]Jesus said to them, "Very truly, I tell you, before Abraham was, I am."

Because of this fourth way of thinking, all humans could be described as being under the dominion of evil and thus "children of the devil."[75] According to the Fourth Gospel, through faith in Jesus, the Son, humans can be drawn into his filiation and so be liberated from a state of "slavery" to the Evil One. Jesus begins by promising such liberation to those who believed in him (v. 31);[76] "the truth will make you free" (v. 32). This statement leads his opponents to speak of Abraham and to describe themselves as Abraham's seed (v. 33), meaning his rightful children through Sarah, rather than his children through the slave girl Hagar.[77]

75. Keck argues that in the Fourth Gospel Christology, anthropology, and soteriology are correlated. To this I would add cosmology. This passage in chap. 8 shows how these perspectives "reinforce one another." See Leander E. Keck, "Derivation as Destiny: 'Of-ness' in Johannine Christology, Anthropology, and Soteriology," in *Exploring the Gospel of John: In Honor of D. Moody Smith*, ed. R. Alan Culpepper and C. Clifton Black (Louisville: Westminster John Knox, 1996), 279–83.

76. Throughout this vitriolic argument, it is essential to keep in mind that Jesus is speaking with those who used to believe in him, but have now turned away.

77. According to Zumstein the figures of Isaac and Ishmael continue into the contrasts between the son and slave within the household. See Jean Zumstein, *L'Évangile selon Saint Jean (1–12)*, CNT 4a 2nd ser. (Genève: Labor et Fides, 2014), 298.

Both women were the founding mothers of nations. Susan Niditch comments, "It is, moreover, the women who are the critical ancestors for the
proper continuation of the Israelites."[78] Jesus then clarifies that he is not
speaking of physical descent but spiritual—"Those committing sin are
slaves to sin" (v. 34). The following verse (v. 35) I consider to be a parable
where Jesus draws on the daily experience within a household to make
the distinction between sons and slaves: "The slave does not have a permanent place in the household; the son has a place there forever."[79] Only
sons remain within the household, even when they marry; daughters join
the household of their husband's father.[80] Slaves, on the other hand, can
be bought, sold, or given as a gift, or, if they gain sufficient wealth, they
can purchase their own freedom.[81] So only sons remain forever within
the household. Jesus draws the conclusion from this parable that only he,
as son in his Father's household, can truly liberate.[82] While "the Jews" in
this scene can claim physical descent from Abraham they fail to accept
Jesus and, by doing so, fail to become part of his Father's household,
thereby failing to become children of God.

The following verse has been a problem to translators. The NRSV
has, "I declare what I have seen in the Father's presence; as for you,
you should do what you have heard from the Father" (v. 38). The RSV
has, "I speak of what I have seen with *my* Father, and you do what
you have heard from *your* father" (italics added). Apart from different
manuscript versions where some have the verb "to see" while others
have "to hear" in the second clause, there is the problem of "the Father."

---

78. Susan Niditch, "Genesis," in *Women's Bible Commentary: Expanded Edition with
Apocrypha*, ed. Carol A. Newsom and Sharon H. Ringe (Louisville: Westminster John
Knox, 1998), 19.

79. For a discussion of this verse as a possible Johannine parable, see Charles H.
Dodd, *Historical Tradition in the Fourth Gospel* (New York: Cambridge University
Press, 1963), 379–82; Charles H. Dodd, "Behind a Johannine Dialogue," in *More New
Testament Studies*, ed. Charles H. Dodd (Manchester: Manchester University Press,
1968), 41–57.

80. On the terminology "Father's house/hold" and recent challenges made to it
being understood as reflecting male-only power, I refer you to the excursus on the
father's house at 2:16 (p. 74), the first time the expression occurs.

81. For ancient references on slavery, see Craig S. Keener, *The Gospel of John: A Commentary*, 2 vols. (Peabody, MA: Hendrickson, 2003), 1:751.

82. Earlier in the Gospel Jesus spoke of the temple as his Father's house (τὸν οἶκον
τοῦ πατρός μου, 2:16). Later, the Gospel will draw on the double meaning of the Father's house to mean both the temple and household of the Father's indwelling
presence (John 14).

The NRSV translators understand that "the Father" is used in the same sense throughout this verse, meaning God, while the RSV translators understand that two "fathers" are being referred to, Jesus's "Father" in the first clause, and another "father" in the second.[83] Again, manuscripts vary on this. Some scholars argue that the conflict about "fathers" is not introduced until verses 41-44.[84] My position is that conflict has already been introduced. There are some among "the Jews" who believe in Jesus, but there are others who do not and who are looking for an opportunity to kill him (v. 37). In this situation of conflict it matters whose child you are. Are you, through Jesus, a liberated child of God, or are you a slave of another power? This conflict about one's paternity, and therefore one's identity, will continue in the following verses.

In response to Jesus's words about "your father," Jesus's opponents once again claim to be descendants of Abraham, a claim Jesus challenges because they do not do as Abraham did (v. 39). In chapter 5 Jesus had claimed to be a true son of the Father because he did only what he saw the Father doing: "for whatever the Father does, the Son does likewise" (5:19). Doing as one's father does is the true measure of lineage. In rejecting Jesus who spoke the truth, and in seeking to kill him (v. 40), these former believers in Jesus show that they are now children of another "father" (v. 41).[85] His opponents hear in these words an accusation that they are illegitimate and now claim to have only God as their father (v.

---

83. See the comment by Moloney (*John*, 278) that although the possessive pronouns *"my* Father" and *"your* father" are not found in the best manuscripts they balance the pronoun "I" (what *I* have seen) and "you" (what *you* have heard). The personal pronouns are present in Codex Sinaiticus but not Vaticanus, $\mathfrak{P}^{66, 75}$. Among others who read v. 38 describing two contrasting "fathers" are Charles K. Barrett, *The Gospel according to St John*, 2nd ed. (London: SPCK, 1978), 347; Rudolph Schnackenburg, *The Gospel according to St John*, trans. K. Smyth et al., 3 vols., HTCNT (London: Burns & Oates, 1968–1982), 2:208–11; Andrew T. Lincoln, *The Gospel according to Saint John*, BNTC (London: Continuum, 2005), 262. Byrne states, "Though not explicit at this point, it seems necessary to understand that by 'father' here, Jesus already has in mind the devil"; see Brendan Byrne, *Life Abounding: A Reading of John's Gospel* (Collegeville, MN: Liturgical Press, 2014), 152.

84. This is the position taken by Brown, *The Gospel according to John*, 1:356; Bruce M. Metzger, *A Textual Commentary on the Greek New Testament: A Companion Volume to the United Bible Societies' Greek New Testament*, 4th rev. ed. (London: United Bible Societies, 1994), 192.

85. As Reinhartz states, "In the black-and-white world of Johannine rhetoric, if the Jews are not the children of God, then they must be children of the devil." See Fredriksen and Reinhartz, *Jesus, Judaism and Christian Anti-Judaism*, 109.

41). In response Jesus now identifies his opponents as children of the devil, described as a murderer and a liar, because of their actions toward him (vv. 42-47).

Verses 42-47 contain some of the harshest words in the Christian Scriptures about "the Jews," and it is essential that the term be understood in its narrative and post-70 CE historical contexts. Within the narrative, this dialogue takes place between Jesus and some of the Ἰουδαῖοι *who had believed in him* (v. 31). Already some disciples have chosen to leave him (6:66); within the festival some of the crowd believed in him (7:31); but now, these former believers have turned against him, accusing him of being a Samaritan and having a demon (v. 48). Friends have become enemies in this encounter.[86] Historically, the conflict is best understood as a struggle between two groups trying to establish their own self-identity in the aftermath of the destruction of Jerusalem. The Gospel records the vitriolic rhetoric this conflict triggered; research shows that similarly harsh rhetoric was being employed in the synagogue against those perceived as heretics.[87] The following comment by James Dunn succinctly states the necessary caution with which readers today must approach this text:

> To hear John's polemic with first-century ears requires us to compare it with the factional polemic within Second Temple Judaism, or indeed the factional polemic within earliest Christianity. . . . Even Jesus is recalled as rebuking Peter as Satan (Mark 8:33 / Matt 16:23). Such identification with Satan of those with opposing views seems to have been characteristic of both Jewish and Christian polemic of the time. The "diabolizing" of "the Jews" in John 8 (8:44—"You are from your father the devil"), which we quite properly find so offensive when judged by today's standards of disagreement and polemic, was evidently a standard topos in the ancient Jewish/Christian rhetoric of vilification.[88]

---

86. The Johannine letters provide evidence of the harsh language used when believers turn away from the Johannine community. There are those "who went out from us," who are linked with the antichrists (1 John 2:18); these are called "liars" (2:22) and deceivers (2 John 7).

87. More will be said about the rhetoric of the synagogue in the discussion of John 9.

88. James D. G. Dunn, "The Embarrassment of History: Reflections on the Problem of 'Anti-Judaism' in the Fourth Gospel," in *Anti-Judaism and the Fourth Gospel*, ed. Reimund Bieringer, Didier Pollefeyt, and Frederique Vandecasteele-Vanneuville (Louisville: Westminster John Knox, 2001), 51–52. Note also, that Jesus's opponents accuse him twice of being possessed by a demon (7:20; 8:48). Further discussion of Jewish-Christian rhetoric can be found in Claudia Setzer, *Jewish Responses to Early*

Therefore I reiterate that the term οἱ Ἰουδαῖοι in the Johannine Gospel must be read as a rhetorical strategy in this emergence of a Christian identity, rather than as a description of members of Second Temple Judaism. Christians today have a moral responsibility to accurately portray the Jewishness of Jesus, his mother, and all his disciples and to stand up against neo-Nazi racist words or actions against the Jews of our time. There is no religious justification for anti-Jewish vilification or violence. There is no place in synagogues, mosques, or churches for slaughter in the name of any "religious" or social agenda.

What is it that Abraham *did* (v. 39) that "the Jews" are not doing? "Abraham rejoiced that he would see my day" (v. 56). The action of rejoicing in the day of Jesus is what "the Jews" fail to do. Frequently Abraham is described as a man of faithful obedience, but in this feast, it is not Abraham's faith or obedience that is commended by Jesus but his joy (8:56). The book of Jubilees and the celebration of Tabernacles provide a likely context for this unusual emphasis on joy.[89] In the Book of Jubilees, Abraham's joy in this feast is striking:

> He built an altar there to the Lord who delivered him and who made him rejoice in the land of his sojourn. And he celebrated a feast of rejoicing in this month. (Jub. 16:20)

> He observed this feast seven days, rejoicing with all his heart. (16:25)

> And he blessed and rejoiced and called the name of this festival "the festival of the Lord" a joy acceptable to God Most High. (16:27)

The cause of Abraham's joy lies in the future that he is permitted to see:[90] "for he knew and perceived that from him there would be a righteous planting for eternal generations and a holy seed from him" (Jub. 16:26).

Christians: History and Polemic, 30–150 C.E. (Minneapolis: Fortress, 1994); Martin Hengel and Charles K. Barrett, *Conflicts and Challenges in Early Christianity* (Harrisburg, PA: Trinity Press International, 1999); Fredriksen and Reinhartz, *Jesus, Judaism and Christian Anti-Judaism*; and Irvin J. Borowsky, ed. *Defining New Christian/Jewish Dialogue* (New York: Crossroad, 2004).

89. In celebrating the Feast of Tabernacles, the Israelites are specifically commanded to celebrate it with joy. "And you shall take on the first day the fruit of goodly trees, branches of palm trees, and boughs of leafy trees, and willows of the brook; and you shall rejoice before the Lord your God seven days" (Lev 23:40; also Deut 16:14).

90. "Early Jewish tradition held that Abraham had been privileged with a disclosure of the secrets of the ages to come, especially the messianic age." See Francis J.

Abraham's perception enables Jesus to say, "Your ancestor Abraham rejoiced that he would see my day; he saw it and was glad" (John 8:56). In failing to rejoice in Jesus, as Abraham did, "the Jews" reveal that they are not true children of Abraham. In this confrontation where "the Jews" call on Abraham to add legitimacy to their argument (v. 33), Jesus shows that their claim is not true. The post-70 Christian readers of this dispute may at this point be thinking that the narrative is going to reveal that *they* are the true children of Abraham because they have responded positively to Jesus. But there is more!

Abraham as a Witness to Jesus's Origins

It is not just a question of the identity of the son/daughter; also at stake is the question of the identity of the father. "The Jews" insist that their father is Abraham (v. 33, 39) and even God (v. 41), a claim Jesus challenges by pointing to what they *do* to him (v. 40) and showing that in fact they cannot have their origins in either Abraham or God. By contrast, Jesus does the will of his Father. He speaks what he has seen and heard with his Father (v. 38, 40). Jesus is a true son, and his Father is none other than the one "the Jews" claim as their God (v. 54). There is a contrast established between "our/your father Abraham" (vv. 53, 56) and "my Father"/God (vv. 49, 54). The sonship Jesus claims goes far beyond the sonship of belonging to the "seed" of Abraham; his is a divine filiation, as stated in the prologue (1:18), and a filiation promised to all women and men who would believe in him (1:12). The promise made that believers would become "children"[91] of God, far transcends "the Jews'" claim to be children of Abraham.

In a number of debates Jesus has been challenged by comparison with one of Israel's patriarchs: the Samaritan woman asked, "Are you greater than our father Jacob?" (4:12); at Passover, the crowd asks implicit questions comparing Jesus and Moses when asking for a sign such as the one Moses gave, "He gave them bread from heaven" (6:31); now, in Tabernacles "the Jews" ask, "Are you greater than our father Abraham,

---

Moloney, *Signs and Shadows: Reading John 5–12* (Minneapolis: Fortress, 1996), 112. This reference has further Jewish sources on Abraham's foreknowledge.

91. Personal and familial language has been used across the Gospel to speak of a close and loving relationship between Jesus and God, and believers and God. It is metaphorical rather than ontological, coming from "the will of God," rather than being "born of blood, or the will of the flesh" (1:13).

who died?" (8:53). In each case, Jesus responds, "I am [ἐγώ εἰμι]" (4:26; 6:35; 8:58). The ancestors died as "the Jews" acknowledge, but Jesus speaks with the eternity life of divine Sophia, and so ἐγώ εἰμι transcends mortal life. She revealed herself to Abraham, saying, "I am Shaddai" (Gen 17:1), to Jacob (Gen 35:11), and to Moses, where she affirmed her identity before introducing Moses to her new name: "I appeared to Abraham, Isaac, and Jacob as El Shaddai, but by my name 'YHWH' [יהוה] I did not make myself known to them" (Exod 6:3). Although the patriarchs Moses and Abraham are drawn into Jesus's conflict during Tabernacles, these patriarchs first knew the feminine face of God as El Shaddai, while their descendants cannot see in Jesus divine Sophia.

Throughout the encounters at Tabernacles a critical issue has been the identity of Jesus. His opponents accuse him of leading the people astray (7:47) and of being possessed by a demon (8:48). Even those inclined to accept him do so within the limitations of their own expectations: he is the prophet (7:40), the Christ (7:41). There is a failure to see the answer to the question asked, "Are you greater than our father Abraham?" (8:53). Jesus is indeed greater than Israel's patriarchs. He is the incarnate *logos*, "the only Son who is in the bosom of the Father" (1:18; author's translation). As son and not slave, he continues forever (v. 35), within a relationship that transcends all time, as was stated in the prologue (1:1). His concluding "I Am" affirms his identity with Israel's God whom he calls Father (8:54) and who is the El Shaddai of Israel's patriarchs (Exod 3:6).

Conclusion (8:59)

On the Temple Mount, the place that recalled the obedience of Abraham and his sacrifice, and during a feast that remembered Abraham's perception and joy, Jesus confronts the children of Abraham with their disobedience and true paternity, disclosed in their seeking to kill the "only son" of the Father.[92] The Father of Jesus is the one "the Jews" claim as their God (8:41, 54) and whom, every morning during the Feast of Tabernacles, they profess to worship. The challenge to believe that Jesus is "I Am" speaks precisely to this ritual profession of faith carried out

92. Johannine irony pervades this exchange as Abraham's faith was demonstrated in his willingness to sacrifice his only son, but now these former believers in Jesus are threatening to kill the "only son" of God (1:18; 3:16, 18). Furthermore, Jewish lineage is claimed through the mother, and so more accurately they should be claiming to be children of Sarah, rather than use the male-centered language of Σπέρμα Ἀβραάμ (8:33).

John 8:59

[59]So they picked up stones to throw at him, but Jesus hid himself and went out of the temple.

each morning during the feast. Will the Israel of Jesus's day repeat the sins of their fathers or accept a new manifestation of God's tabernacling presence? Will they move beyond their identification with "our father Abraham" (vv. 33, 39) to perceive in Jesus the one Abraham "rejoiced to see" (v. 56) and their true Father (v. 41) whom Jesus reveals (1:18; 8:58)? The concluding verse answers this question.

The words Jesus has spoken across chapters 7 and 8 will be verified in the next scene when he encounters one who has always lived in darkness.

Life-Giving Waters from the Womb of Sophia

Out of his womb shall flow rivers of living water [ποταμοὶ ἐκ τῆς κοιλίας αὐτοῦ ῥεύσουσιν ὕδατος ζῶντος]. (7:38)

Within the context of the festival and its rituals, the symbolism of "rivers of living water" draws on Jesus's identity as the temple (2:22). But symbols are polyvalent as the temple is the place were Sophia was established. The festival is called the Festival of Tabernacles (ἡ σκηνοπηγία), and in the book of Sirach Wisdom is commanded to dwell within the tabernacle (σκηνῇ).

> Then the Creator of all things gave me a commandment, and the one who created me assigned a place for my tent [σκηνήν],

and said,—"Make your dwelling [κατασκήνωσον] in Jacob, and in Israel receive your inheritance."
From eternity, in the beginning, God created me, and for eternity I shall not cease to exist.
In the holy tabernacle [σκηνῇ ἁγίᾳ] I ministered before him, and so I was established in Zion. (Sir 24:8-10; author's translation)

During Tabernacles Jesus speaks as divine Sophia when issuing the invitation to "come to me . . . and drink" (7:38). Most Bibles then describe "rivers of living water" flowing from the "heart," but the Greek word κοιλία can be translated belly, heart, or "(frequently), 'mother's womb' (Gen 25:24; Deut 28:4, 11;

Job 1:21; 3:11; Ruth 1:11)."[93] The term κοιλία was used earlier in the discussion with Nicodemus to refer to the mother's womb (3:4), and so it would be more consistent to again speak of the waters issuing from a "womb," rather than "heart," which is usually written as καρδία and not used here to express the evangelist's meaning. The close association of water and womb (7:38) strongly suggests birth; similarly water and spirit together allude to the act of creation (Gen 1:3) and were used in the dialogue with Nicodemus to compare two types of birth (3:5). In this text there is a melding of genders where once again the male Jesus is personified as *Sophia*, Wisdom. The inner "womb" of Sophia-Jesus is a current source of the life-giving waters of birth.[94] The image will be repeated at the cross when blood and water will flow from his pierced side (19:34) and the Spirit is breathed down to those gathered at the cross.

The tabernacle/tent (σκηνή) is the rightful home of *Sophia*.

From her home *Sophia* issues her invitation to share of her bounty—"Come to me, you who desire me, and eat your fill of my produce. Those who eat me will hunger for more, and those who drink me will thirst for more" (Sir 24:19, 21; also Prov 9:1-6). Those who live according to Israel's law will be welcomed by Wisdom as a young bride, and she will feed them with "the bread of learning" and give them "the water of wisdom to drink" (Sir 15:2-3). In the Fourth Gospel, Jesus incarnates *Sophia* to dwell (ἐσκήνωσεν; 1:14) among us, as *Sophia* was once commanded to make her dwelling (κατασκήνωσον) in Jacob. Jesus has claimed the temple as his "Father's house" (2:16) and throughout this feast acts as the rightful son of his Father in offering a permanent place within the Father's house/hold to those who believe in him (8:31-36). As *Sophia*, Jesus invites those who thirst to come and drink (7:37) and promises that believers will themselves become as *Sophia*, sources of water (7:38).

93. Behm, "κοιλία," 786. See also Reid, "John 7:37-39," 395; and Dorothy A. Lee, *Flesh and Glory: Symbolism, Gender and Theology in the Gospel of John* (New York: Crossroad, 2002), 149.

94. Ben Witherington states: "One needs to be aware that in ancient Near Eastern literature the word 'water' can be and is used as a *terminus technicus*, or at least a well-known circumlocution, for matters involving procreation, childbearing, child-bearing capacity, or the act of giving birth itself. Sometimes water is a circumlocution for semen, for amniotic fluid, or for the process of birth itself from the breaking of the waters to the actual delivery." Ben Witherington III, "The Waters of Birth: John 3.5 and 1 John 5.6-8," *NTS* 35 (1989): 156.

A late tradition found in the Wisdom of Solomon attributes to Wisdom the marvels of the exodus. It was *Sophia* who "guided them along a marvelous way, and became a shelter to them by day, and a starry flame through the night" (Wis 10:17). When they thirsted for water in the wilderness, they called on *Sophia* and she gave them abundant water (Wis 11:4). Within this festival commemorating the exodus journey, *Sophia* offers herself as water for the thirsty and light in the darkness. In depicting Jesus against the background of Israel's wisdom traditions, the evangelist portrays Jesus in a manner where there is a blurring of genders, with consequences for the depiction of God. Jesus acts as Son to his Father (1:18) but also as *Sophia*. "Gender boundaries are overcome in his person. And because Jesus is one with his Father . . . the Father's characterization is also affected. Consequently, the Johannine God-Father must also be viewed in female terms."[95] This blurring of gender boundaries will continue across the narrative and will be particularly evident in "the hour."

Miriam's Well

In Jewish tradition there is a midrash extolling Miriam as the one who provided water from a well to the people as they journeyed through the wilderness that then dried up at her death. The manna is linked with Moses, but water and a traveling well with Miriam.[96] According to the legend, a well was one of ten things created on the eve of the first Sabbath at twilight[97] and entrusted to worthy recipients in desperate need of water in the wilderness. Jacob is linked to a traveling well[98] as is Miriam, who "received the well on behalf of the children of Israel who were wandering in the desert after their escape from Egypt.

95. Ingrid Rosa Kitzberger, "Transcending Gender Boundaries in John," in *A Feminist Companion to John*, vol. 1, ed. Amy-Jill Levine with Marianne Blickenstaff, FCNTECW 4 (London: Sheffield Academic, 2003), 193. See also the reflection by Dorothy Lee, "The Iconic 'Father' of Jesus," pp. 156–57 in this volume.

96. Roger Le Déaut, "Miryam, soeur de Moïse, et Marie, mère du Messie," *Bib* 45 (1964): 209–13.

97. *Pirque Avot* 6:6.

98. *Pirque R. El.* 35. Jerome H. Neyrey, "Jacob Traditions and the Interpretation of John 4:10-26," *CBQ* 41 (1979): 421–24.

According to the legend, she was able to call forth the water with her beautiful voice."[99]

In her first appearances, Miriam is the unnamed older sister of Moses; she manages to preserve his life when he is hidden in the Nile (Exod 2:4, 7-9). When the people escaped from the Egyptians, Moses sings a song (Exod 15:1-18), then his sister is named, "the prophet Miriam" (Exod 15:20).[100] She leads the women and they sing with tambourines and dancing (15:21). It is Miriam who "leads the Israelites in their first service of worship as a free people."[101] Where Moses sings as an individual, "*I* will sing," Miriam's song uses a plural form. Miriam goes out with all the women to sing and dance. While the English reads, "And Miriam sang to them," the Greek and Hebrew verbs present her "taking the lead" (ἐξάρχω) with the women responding as a chorus, and the verb form of "sing" is plural (ושיר).[102]

> Let *us* sing to the LORD,
> for he has triumphed gloriously;
> horse and rider he has thrown into the sea. (author's translation)

When they enter into the wilderness, folklore describes a rolling rock-well accompanying the people. It is only with the death of Miriam (Num 20:1) that there was "no water for the congregation" (Num 20:2). This led to the belief that it was Miriam who was the cause of water during their forty years wandering.[103] The linking of Miriam's death with the cessation of water has led Christianne Méroz to ask: "But who then had been able to comprehend that it was through the mediation of his prophet Miriam that God was present in the midst of his people like a gushing spring?"[104]

---

99. Penina V. Adelman, "A Drink from Miriam's Cup: Invention of Tradition among Jewish Women," *JFSR* 10 (1994): 151–66. For more details about the legends of Miriam's well, see Penina V. Adelman, *Miriam's Well: Rituals for Jewish Women around the Year* (New York: Biblio Press, 1986), 69–71.

100. The OT gives evidence of a number of women who prophesy: Deborah (Jud 4:4), Huldah (2 Kgs 22:14), Noadiah (Neh 6:14), and an unnamed woman (Isa 8:3). Ezekiel criticizes the "daughters of your people" who prophesy falsely (Ezek 13:17), and Joel looks to a time when "your sons and your daughters will prophesy" (Joel 2:28).

101. Moshe Reiss, "Miriam Rediscovered," *JBQ* 38 (2010): 184.

102. Miriam's singing in an antiphonal manner is similar to the women in 1 Sam 18:7. See the comment on Exod 15:21 in J. H. Hertz, ed., *Pentateuch and Haftorahs: Hebrew Text English Translation and Commentary*, 2nd ed. (London: Soncino, 1960), 273.

103. b. Ta'an. 9a.

104. Christianne Méroz, *Three Women of Hope: Miriam, Hannah, Huldah*, trans. Dennis Wienk (Eugene, OR: Wipf and Stock, 2014), 14.

John 9:1–10:21

Sophia Ministers in the Tabernacle

In the holy tent [σκηνῇ ἁγίᾳ] I ministered before him. (Sir 24:10)

Afterward she [Wisdom] appeared on earth
 and lived with humankind.
She is the book of the commandments of God,
 the law that endures forever. (Bar 3:37–4:1)

The story of the man born blind[1] in John 9 is both engaging literature and rich theology. We meet a series of characters who interact with one another: Jesus and the disciples, Jesus and the man born blind, the neighbors, the parents, the Pharisees, "the Jews." In all these interactions there is a play on blindness and sight, as the one born in darkness shows the greatest insight, while the learned are bewildered and "in the dark." Once again there is the comparison between Jesus and Moses, and through it all run the motifs of the Feast of Tabernacles:

---

1. People with disabilities advocate identifying the person first, not their disability, e.g., "the man born blind" or "a man suffering from blindness," rather than "the blind man."

water, light, Siloam, and true worship. At the conclusion of the episode, Jesus confronts the Jewish leaders and accuses them of "blindness." Then, as part of this dispute, he employs a "parable" (παροιμία)[2] of sheep and shepherds to condemn false leadership. As in the previous discussions within this Feast of Ingathering, "the Jews" end up in a state of division with some accusing Jesus of demonic possession (10:20), while others refute this charge (10:21).[3]

It is particularly significant that this episode is about blindness and not some other form of disability or illness, as in the OT "blindness is portrayed as an unmitigated evil."[4] Blindness is also used in a metaphorical sense to speak of the wickedness of Israel and its foes.[5] Physical and metaphorical blindness will be addressed in this passage, set against the background of Tabernacles and Sophia/Jesus's declaration to be "the light of the world" (8:12).

This passage has been a source of much discussion about both the Gospel and the Johannine community due to the hypothesis of J. Louis Martyn, who saw in this episode evidence for understanding the Gospel as a "two-level" drama.[6] On one level, it presents a narrative about the historical figure Jesus, dealing with his contemporary world around 30 CE; but the Gospel also has in view its audience, the Johannine community, reading/hearing this Gospel as they deal with their situation vis-à-vis Judaism in the decades after the destruction of Jerusalem in 70 CE. More will be said on this.

Structurally the passage can be shown as follows:[7]

---

2. The Greek word παροιμία does not exactly translate as "parable" and is not the word used in the Synoptic Gospels (παραβολή). Hauk states that "παροιμία in Jn. means 'hidden, obscure speech' which stands in need of interpretation." See Friedrich Hauck, "παροιμία" *TDNT* 5 (1967): 856. This will be discussed further below.

3. See comments on characters called "the Jews" and the Jews in the reception of the Gospel in the author's introduction (lxxi).

4. Mary Ann Beavis, "From the Margin to the Way: A Feminist Reading of the Story of Bartimaeus," *JFSR* 14 (1998): 24.

5. E.g., Isa 56:10; see Beavis, "From the Margin to the Way," 24.

6. J. Louis Martyn, *History and Theology in the Fourth Gospel* (New York: Harper and Row, 1968).

7. This structure follows the pattern in ancient drama of having only two characters on stage at the same time; I include the shepherd parable of 9:39–10:21 because a parable can be part of a juridical controversy as shown by Martin Asiedu-Peprah, *Johannine Sabbath Conflicts as Juridical Controversy*, WUNT 2/132 (Tübingen: Mohr Siebeck, 2001), 20, 151–83. Others see that the shepherd discourse "acts partly as a commentary on the narrative of John 9." See Dorothy A. Lee, *The Symbolic Narratives of*

Act 1: Jesus and the disciples, 9:1-5 (blindness, physical and moral)

Act 2: Jesus and the man born blind, 9:6-7

Act 3: The man born blind and his neighbors, 9:8-12

Act 4: The man who had been blind and the Pharisees, 9:13-17

Act 5: The parents and "the Jews," 9:18-23

Act 6: The man who had been blind and "the Jews," 9:24-34

Act 7: Jesus and the man who had been blind, 9:35-38

Act 8: Jesus and the Pharisees, 9:39–10:21 (blindness, moral and physical)

Act 1: Jesus and the Disciples (9:1-5)

The encounter with a man blind from birth raises for the disciples the question of moral responsibility for disability or illness. At its heart this is an issue of "theodicy"—is God just? Surely if people live good and upright lives will they not be rewarded with blessings of health and longevity, while a person who has been a sinner, or whose ancestors have been sinners, will be punished? This theology was countered by Ezekiel (18:20) at the time of the exile, who argued for personal responsibility, and the book of Job addressed this attitude at length. Ultimately, the question of God's justice led to the late development of a theology of some type of life after death where the righteous can receive the blessings that they did not experience in life.[8] Jesus's reply asserts that there is no moral or divine underlying cause for this blindness, but through this affliction "the works of God" will be revealed.[9] In John 6, the crowd

---

the Fourth Gospel: The Interplay of Form and Meaning, JSNTSup 95 (Sheffield: JSOT Press, 1994), 163; also Charles H. Dodd, *The Interpretation of the Fourth Gospel* (Cambridge: Cambridge University Press, 1953), 156. The motif of the man born blind opens in 9:1 and concludes the entire pericope in 10:21 with the question that looks back to Jesus's actions: "Can a demon open the eyes of the blind?"

8. See the Nicodemus episode in John 3 where I discussed two approaches to Jewish eschatology.

9. Marianne Meye Thompson (*John: A Commentary*, NTL [Louisville: Westminster John Knox, 2015], 206, n. 236) explains that ἵνα need not mean purpose (so that the works of God might be revealed) but simply a result (with the result that the works of God might be revealed). Similarly, Lee, *Symbolic Narratives*, 166, n. 1. All life experiences have the possibility of being revelatory. Daniel B. Wallace (*Greek Grammar beyond the Basics: An Exegetical Syntax of the New Testament* [Grand Rapids: Zondervan,

John 9:1-5

⁹⁻¹As he walked along, he saw a man blind from birth. ²His disciples asked him, "Rabbi, who sinned, this man or his parents, that he was born blind?" ³Jesus answered, "Neither this man nor his parents sinned; he was born blind so that God's works might be revealed in him. ⁴We must work the works of him who sent me while it is day; night is coming when no one can work. ⁵As long as I am in the world, I am the light of the world."

in Galilee had asked Jesus about doing "the works of God," which Jewish thinking equated with obedience to the law, but Jesus spoke of one "work" (ἔργον): "to believe in him whom [God] has sent" (6:29). By the end of this episode such belief will be revealed. The use of the plural "we must" (ἡμᾶς δεῖ, v. 4a) is strange,[10] but C. H. Dodd suggests that a proverbial wisdom saying, already within the tradition, may have been reshaped by the evangelist in this dialogue.[11] Mention of "night" and that Jesus's time in the world is limited adds an ominous tone, only slightly relieved by his self-revelatory statement, "I am the light of the world" (v. 5; cf. 8:12). With the decision of "the Jews" to kill Jesus already made (7:1), and the reference to his being "lifted up" (8:28), the future passion of Jesus is already impinging on the narrative.

Act 2: Jesus and the Man Born Blind (9:6-7)

The actual healing is described briefly. Jesus uses spittle to make clay, then spreads this on the man's eyes.[12] The mention of the pool of Siloam

---

1996], 473) gives John 9:2 as his example of the ἵνα conjunction used to indicate a consequence.

10. The statement "we must work the works of him who sent me" (v. 4), although strange, appears in the early manuscripts, rather than "I must."

11. Charles H. Dodd, *Historical Tradition in the Fourth Gospel* (New York: Cambridge University Press, 1963), 186, 188. Dodd cites Rabbi Tarphon (ca. 100 CE): "The day is short and there is much work to be done; the workers are lazy and the reward is great and the Master of the house is urgent." The use of "we" may also hint "at the future inclusion of disciples in Jesus's mission." See Brendan Byrne, *Life Abounding: A Reading of John's Gospel* (Collegeville, MN: Liturgical Press, 2014), 161. Similarly, Jean Zumstein, *L'Évangile selon Saint Jean (1–12)*, CNT 4a 2nd ser. (Genève: Labor et Fides, 2014), 318.

12. Spittle was commonly used for healing purposes. For ancient references to its use, see Craig S. Keener, *The Gospel of John: A Commentary*, 2 vols. (Peabody, MA:

John 9:6-7

⁶When he had said this, he spat on the ground and made mud with the saliva and spread the mud on the man's eyes, ⁷saying to him, "Go, wash in the pool of Siloam" (which means Sent). Then he went and washed and came back able to see.

is a reminder that this healing takes place in the context of the Festival of Tabernacles. Each morning of this festival priests and Levites led the celebrants to the pool of Siloam to gather water for the daily libation ceremony in the temple. The evangelist's explanation that Siloam means "sent" makes the christological identification between the waters of Siloam and Jesus, the Sent One of God.[13] The Hebrew name for the pool is *Shiloaḥ* (שלח; see Isa 8:6), whose consonants are the same as *šālaḥ* (שלח), "to send." The evangelist has stretched the etymology of Siloam to make the christological link. The healing occurs not through the waters of Siloam but through Jesus, the Sent One of God, who is able to provide life-giving waters (7:37-39). In the ancient world only a divinely sanctioned person could heal blindness, which was considered incurable through available medical practices.[14]

Disability studies challenge the perception of differences as a problem to be solved or cured. They ask questions when reading the healing

---

Hendrickson, 2003), 1:779–81. Recently, Daniel Frayer-Griggs ("Spittle, Clay, and Creation in John 9:6 and Some Dead Sea Scrolls," *JBL* 132 [2013]: 670) has revived the interpretation of Irenaeus that links Jesus's action with the creation of Adam in Genesis. He finds numerous parallels in the Dead Sea Scrolls linking the act of creation with clay and spittle: "Given the numerous creation motifs in ch. 9 and throughout John's Gospel, interpreters of 9:6 would do well to pay closer attention to the role of both spittle and clay in the creation of humankind as attested to by the Dead Sea Scrolls and ancient Near Eastern creation stories surveyed above, for in these texts the view that John 9:6 is sounding subtle notes of creation—an interpretation that traces its exegetical lineage back to Irenaeus—may find its confirmation." James Alison also links this episode with the statement in 5:17 of God's continual working and considers that in this action Jesus "brings creation to its proper fulfillment, making people whole on the Sabbath." See James Alison, *Raising Abel: The Recovery of the Eschatological Imagination* (New York: Crossroad, 1996), 72–73.

13. Up until this point Jesus has consistently claimed to be acting according to the authority and the will of the One who sent him. See 4:34; 5:23, 24, 30, 37; 6:38, 39, 44; 7:16, 18, 28, 33; 8:16, 18, 26, 29; 9:4.

14. Beavis, "From the Margin to the Way," 28.

narratives of Jesus such as: Is this to be celebrated as a sign of divine power or lamented that he does not act in a way to bring acceptance of some form of disability? Is the "whole" body more Godlike than one that has some impairment? Such was the attitude in ancient Israel where the blind and the lame were not permitted within the temple (2 Sam 5:8b).[15] They would be an affront to God's holy perfection.

Jesus finds the man outside the temple enclosure, as Jewish law demanded (Lev 21:17-23).[16] It seems that he would have passed by but his disciples drew attention to the man asking about sin. Jesus's response is more than a cure, an eradication of a physical disability. In his social setting this man was excluded from social prayer. His blindness was not simply a biological problem but a cause of social exclusion. Jesus's actions remove such a social obstacle. "Jesus as a prophet engaged in faith healing treats disability as any other socially made obstacle."[17] He acts as liberator as much as healer.

Act 3: The Man Who Had Been Blind and His Neighbors (9:8-12)

The evangelist now begins a series of descriptions of the impact the healing has on the man's neighbors, on the Pharisees, on his parents, and on the man himself. This healing will cause division. First, the neighbors are divided whether this really is the one they knew as a blind beggar. In response to their questions, the man continually affirms "I am" (ἐγώ εἰμι; v. 9). Without knowing his healer by sight, the man is already moving towards identification with Jesus who has just claimed to be "I Am" (ἐγώ εἰμι) (8:58). The neighbors' bewilderment provided an opportunity for the man to describe what happened to him, in a similar way to the woman of Samaria in John 4, as he is now evangelizing his neighbors.

---

15. For a discussion on this prohibition, see Saul M. Olyan, " 'Anyone Blind or Lame Shall Not Enter the House': On the Interpretation of Second Samuel 5:8b," *CBQ* 60 (1998): 218–27.

16. Although this law was about only priests, there were similar laws about sacrificial animals having no imperfections (Lev 22:17-25; Deut 15:21; 17:1); the passage in 2 Sam 5:8 appears to extend such prohibitions to any worshiper.

17. David Mitchell and Sharon Snyder, " 'Jesus Thrown Everything Off Balance': Disability and Redemption in Biblical Literature," in *This Abled Body: Rethinking Disabilities in Biblical Studies*, ed. Hector Avalos, Sarah J. Melcher, and Jeremy Schipper, SemeiaSt 55 (Atlanta: SBL, 2007), 179.

⁸The neighbors and those who had seen him before as a beggar began to ask, "Is this not the man who used to sit and beg?" ⁹Some were saying, "It is he." Others were saying, "No, but it is someone like him." He kept saying, "I am the man." ¹⁰But they kept asking him, "Then how were your eyes opened?" ¹¹He answered, "The man called Jesus made mud, spread it on my eyes, and said to me, 'Go to Siloam and wash.' Then I went and washed and received my sight." ¹²They said to him, "Where is he?" He said, "I do not know."

Act 4: The Man Who Had Been Blind and the Pharisees (9:13-17)

Next, the neighbors, who have heard in his description of the healing a possible infringement of the law, take the man to the Pharisees. As in John 5, the evangelist has held back information from the reader/listener and only now we hear, "Now it was a sabbath day" (9:14; cf. 5:9). In performing this healing Jesus has "made clay," an action prohibited on the Sabbath, and told the man to break the Sabbath also by washing his eyes.[18]

Questions from the Pharisees provide a further occasion for the man to report the facts about what happened to him. This leads to a schism (σχίσμα, v. 16) among the Pharisees, with some recognizing an infringement of the Sabbath, and so denying that Jesus has come from God, while others are aware that a sinner could not do such signs. Turning to the man who had been blind, they ask his opinion. Once again it is the man who was formerly blind who "sees" clearly and considers Jesus to be a prophet. This gradual perception of Jesus's identity has some similarities to that of the Samaritan woman, who shifted from hostility to polite respect to thinking of Jesus as a prophet (4:19).

---

18. The Mishnah lists thirty-nine breaches of the Sabbath, among which are: "he who sews, ploughs, reaps, binds sheaves, threshes, winnows, selects [fit from unfit produce or crops], grinds, sifts, *kneads*, bakes" (m. Šabb. 7:2; italics added). Although the act of making clay is not mentioned, in using water and dust Jesus has "kneaded" this mixture to make a salve. In washing this salve from his eyes, the man has also broken the Sabbath. "He who takes out wine enough to mix a cup; milk enough for a gulp; honey enough to put on a sore; oil enough to anoint a small limb; *water enough to rub off an eye salve*; and of all other liquids, a quarter *log*; and of all slops [refuse], a quarter *log*" (m. Šabb. 8:1). It is not certain which of these prohibitions were in effect in Jesus's day, as the Mishnah was not given final form until the early third century CE.

John 9:13-17

¹³They brought to the Pharisees the man who had formerly been blind. ¹⁴Now it was a sabbath day when Jesus made the mud and opened his eyes. ¹⁵Then the Pharisees also began to ask him how he had received his sight. He said to them, "He put mud on my eyes. Then I washed, and now I see." ¹⁶Some of the Pharisees said, "This man is not from God, for he does not observe the sabbath." But others said, "How can a man who is a sinner perform such signs?" And they were divided. ¹⁷So they said again to the blind man, "What do you say about him? It was your eyes he opened." He said, "He is a prophet."

Act 5: The Parents and "the Jews" (9:18-23)

Until this point, the man's neighbors, and even the Pharisees, seem more bewildered than hostile about what has happened. A change occurs in verse 18 when a group, presumably some of the Pharisees, now called "the Jews," do not believe that he had really been blind from birth. The ones who can verify this are the man's parents, who now join the discussion. They answer with the facts: this is our son; he was born blind. Beyond that they claim ignorance. The narrator's comment in verse 22 informs the reader that the parents' words are more than simple ignorance but are the result of fear of their interrogators, "the Jews." They do not want to get involved and deflect the questions twice with the statement, "he is of age; ask him" (v. 21, 23). The narrative describes a situation where "anyone who confessed Jesus to be the Messiah would be put out of the synagogue [ἀποσυνάγωγος]" (v. 22).[19] Daniel Boyarin offers a more nuanced approach to understanding what might lie behind this verse's claim that believers could be put "out of the synagogue."

> On the one hand there was sufficient pressure from Gentile Christianity in Asia Minor to stimulate Jewish hostility, even perhaps, to the point of cursing, but also that there was sufficient pressure on Gentile Christian identity to produce the need for clearer articulation of separation

---

19. See the author's introduction (li), where I discussed this verse and other ἀποσυνάγωγος passages (12:42; 16:2), recommending caution about accepting such statements as a description of historical fact; certainly it would be anachronistic to read this as a description of the time of the historical Jesus. For a recent evaluation of the historical accuracy of this verse, see Edward W. Klink III, "Expulsion from the Synagogue? Rethinking a Johannine Anachronism," *TynBul* 59 (2008): 99–118.

[18]The Jews did not believe that he had been blind and had received his sight until they called the parents of the man who had received his sight [19]and asked them, "Is this your son, who you say was born blind? How then does he now see?" [20]His parents answered, "We know that this is our son, and that he was born blind; [21]but we do not know how it is that now he sees, nor do we know who opened his eyes. Ask him; he is of age. He will speak for himself." [22]His parents said this because they were afraid of the Jews; for the Jews had already agreed that anyone who confessed Jesus to be the Messiah would be put out of the synagogue. [23]Therefore his parents said, "He is of age; ask him."

> from Judaism. . . . Hence orthodoxy/heresy came to function as a
> boundary marker, because the boundaries had indeed been blurred.[20]

Whether historically there was such an action of casting out believers from the synagogue or not, this phrase forms part of the polemic to set up distinctions between the Johannine community and post-70 Judaism. Since the Jewish authorities have identified Jesus as "possessed by a demon" (7:20; 8:48, 52), claims that this man was "the Christ" could only be thought of as heretical. The parents' fear is understandable, even as it throws into relief their son's persistent affirmation of Jesus.

Act 6: The Man Who Had Been Blind and "the Jews" (9:24-34)

Because the parents have been unable to satisfy "the Jews" they once again question the man who formerly had been blind, placing him under oath, "Give glory to God" (v. 24).[21] They then state what they know—that "this man [Jesus] is a sinner." In spite of the many recitations of the facts of what happened and the facts about the man who had been blind, they claim as fact something the Gospel has shown to be wrong. In John 5, by the pool of Bethesda, near the temple, and throughout John 7 and 8 Jesus has consistently testified that he has been authorized and sent by God.

---

20. Daniel Boyarin, *Border Lines: The Partition of Judaeo-Christianity* (Philadelphia: University of Pennsylvania Press, 2004), 73.

21. A similar oath form can be found in the OT; e.g., "Then Joshua said to Achan, 'My son, give glory to the LORD God of Israel and make confession to him'" (Josh 7:19; similarly, 1 Chr 30:6-9; Jer 13:16).

24So for the second time they called the man who had been blind, and they said to him, "Give glory to God! We know that this man is a sinner." 25He answered, "I do not know whether he is a sinner. One thing I do know, that though I was blind, now I see." 26They said to him, "What did he do to you? How did he open your eyes?" 27He answered them, "I have told you already, and you would not listen. Why do you want to hear it again? Do you also want to become his disciples?" 28Then they reviled him, saying, "You are his disciple, but we are disciples of Moses. 29We know that God has spoken to Moses, but as for this man, we do not know where he comes from." 30The man answered, "Here is an astonishing thing! You do not know where he comes from, and yet he opened my eyes. 31We know that God does not listen to sinners, but he does listen to one who worships him and obeys his will. 32Never since the world began has it been heard that anyone opened the eyes of a person born blind. 33If this man were not from God, he could do nothing." 34They answered him, "You were born entirely in sins, and are you trying to teach us?" And they drove him out.

The man replies accurately about what he knows and what he doesn't know—he knows he was once blind, but he does not know that Jesus is a sinner. In the manner of a hostile prosecutor, "the Jews" ask again for the man to tell them what happened, perhaps hoping to confuse him and to trip him up in some inaccuracy. The man now replies that he has told them and they refused to listen. With wonderful irony he asks if they want to hear his account again, so that they too could become disciples of Jesus. This leads to a clarification of the key issue. One can be a disciple of Jesus *or* one can be a disciple of Moses. Not both.[22] Not only is this an issue for the participants in this episode, but this is the

---

22. In making the sharp distinction between Moses and Jesus, there is the danger of interpreting John in a supersessionist manner, i.e., as if Judaism has been replaced by Christian faith. This is not the perspective of this commentary, and in my opinion such supersessionist views gravely overlook the Jewish nature of this narrative. The Fourth Gospel can make sense only when it is read from within a deep knowledge and appreciation of first-century Judaism. The Catholic position on the continuation of God's covenant with Israel was summed up by Philip A. Cunningham (*Seeking Shalom: The Journey to Right Relationship between Catholics and Jews* [Grand Rapids: Eerdmans, 2015], 180), citing Pope John Paul II: "The Holy Father has stated this permanent reality of the Jewish people in a remarkable theological formula, in his allocution to the Jewish community of West Germany at Mainz, on November 17th, 1980: 'The people of God of the Old Covenant, *which has never been revoked.'*"

issue facing believers in the Johannine community. As both nascent rabbinic Judaism and early Christianity shape their traditions and form their identities following the destruction of Jerusalem, distinctions are beginning to be made: Moses *or* Jesus, the gift of the law *or* the gift of becoming "children of God" (1:17), with both groups looking back to the same Scriptures and both claiming to be the "true" Israel and the true descendants of Abraham.[23] While the Gospel describes the issues in clear opposing terms "Moses" or "Jesus," in fact such clarity was not obvious for some centuries. The Gospel reflects an early stage in a long process of separation and, through its polemic, tries to be a catalyst in such separation.[24] As Judith Lieu comments,

> The texts do not simply reflect a "history" going on independently of them, they are themselves part of the process by which Judaism or Christianity came into being. For it was through literature that the ideas were formulated, a self-understanding shaped and articulated, and then mediated to and appropriated by others, and through literature that people and ideas were included or excluded. What the texts were doing is sometimes as, if not more, important than what they were saying.[25]

"The Jews" claim certainty with regard to Moses, probably based on the "signs and wonders" that Moses performed, but uncertainty with regard to Jesus's origins. In reply the man who formerly was blind points to the sign of his healing as testimony that Jesus must be from God. "If this man were not from God, he could do nothing" (v. 33). "The Jews" then return to the theology expressed by the disciples at the beginning of this episode—since this man was born blind, he must have been born in sin, the sins of either his parents or other ancestors. Their action, "they drove him out [ἔξω]," clearly reflects the rhetoric of verse 22 and the possibility of being "thrown out of the synagogue."

---

23. Christianity's claim to be the "true" Israel can already be found in the Pauline writings such as Rom 9:6-8; Gal 3:6-7, 29. In John this is the issue in the discussion of Abraham's children in 8:39-47.

24. In this confrontation between the Pharisees and the man who had been blind, the Pharisees emphasize the "we"-"you" distinctiveness by using personal pronouns, which in Greek are not really necessary. Beth M. Stovell (*Mapping Metaphorical Discourse in the Fourth Gospel: John's Eternal King*, ed. Stanley E. Porter, LBS 5 [Leiden: Brill, 2012], 226) comments, "The Pharisees' repeated use of 1st person plural redundant pronouns to refer to themselves leave both Jesus and the man born blind out of this collective and contrast the Pharisees' perspective to the healed man and Jesus (e.g., 9:28)."

25. Judith M. Lieu, *Neither Jew Nor Greek? Constructing Early Christianity*, SNTW (Edinburgh: T&T Clark, 2002), 2–3.

Act 7: Jesus and the Man Who Had Been "Blind" (9:35-38)

The final encounter between Jesus and the man recalls one of the daily rituals of the Festival of Tabernacles, when the priests refuted the false worship of the past.[26] Each morning the priests would stand facing the rising sun, with their backs to the temple; then, at the moment of sunrise they would turn and profess their faith in God (m. Sukkah 5:4). Jesus asks, "Do you believe in the Son of Man?"

In the prologue, the evangelist introduced Jesus as having his origins in God's eternity (1:1) and then becoming flesh to dwell among "us" (1:14). This is the underlying paradox, the mystery of who Jesus is, that in his *humanity*, God is revealed. Within the Gospel narrative, this incarnational theology and paradox is expressed in the title ὁ υἱὸς τοῦ ἀνθρώπου, "the human-one."[27] Jesus, one who is fully human, enters into the vulnerability of all humankind and will experience death. While the title clearly emphasizes the humanity of Jesus, this humanity can never be divorced from the divine *Logos*. When Jesus asks, "Do you believe in the Son of Man?" it is as if he is asking, "Can you see in me, this human one before you, the revelation of God's glory? Can you believe that here, in me, you encounter the God of this festival, the God who provided Israel with water and light, the God whom Israel worships?"

The man's response expresses ignorance of who Jesus is speaking about and yet a willingness to believe. Jesus then reveals himself, and the man confesses his belief with the title "Lord" and worships him.[28]

---

26. "And he brought me into the inner court of the house of the LORD; there, at the entrance of the temple of the LORD, between the porch and the altar, were about twenty-five men, with their backs to the temple of the LORD, and their faces toward the east, prostrating themselves to the sun toward the east" (Ezek 8:16).

27. On the title ὁ υἱὸς τοῦ ἀνθρώπου, "the human-one," see excursus (p. 50).

28. Some manuscripts omit the man's response in v. 38 and have Jesus continuing to speak. The verse is present in 𝔓⁶⁶, which is one of the earliest witnesses. In my view this act of worship accords with the style of the Gospel's Christology whereby the rituals of the feast—water, light, and now worship—are given a focus in the person of Jesus. The editorial committee of the UBS 4th edition included this verse with the following comment, "In view of the overwhelming preponderance of external attestation in favor of the longer text it appears that the omission, if not accidental, is to be regarded as editorial, made in the interest of unifying Jesus' teaching in verses 37 and 39." See Bruce M. Metzger, *A Textual Commentary on the Greek New Testament: A Companion Volume to the United Bible Societies' Greek New Testament*, 4th rev. ed. (London: United Bible Societies, 1994), 195. For a detailed appraisal of the textual evidence, see Martijn Steegen, "To Worship the Johannine 'Son of Man': John 9:38 as Refocusing on the Father," *Bib* 91 (2010): 534–54.

³⁵Jesus heard that they had driven him out, and when he found him, he said, "Do you believe in the Son of Man?" ³⁶He answered, "And who is he, sir? Tell me, so that I may believe in him."

³⁷Jesus said to him, "You have seen him, and the one speaking with you is he." ³⁸He said, "Lord, I believe." And he worshiped him.

This act of recognition and worship ironically mimics the actions of Israel's priests who every morning during the festival profess belief in the God of Israel and yet, throughout this feast, did not recognize God's tabernacling presence in Jesus (1:14). One blind from birth is the only one who really "sees." As Dorothy Lee states, "The man progresses from blindness to sight while the Pharisees move the in opposite direction."[29]

Act 8: Jesus and the Pharisees (9:39–10:21)[30]

The Structure

Structurally the passage begins with an introduction that identifies Jesus's opponents, linking what follows to the cure of the man born blind.[31] It also identifies them as spiritually blind. This theme is echoed in the conclusion, and the theme of a schism recurs during the Festival of

29. Lee, *Symbolic Narratives*, 162.

30. Some scholars consider that 9:39-41 brings the narrative of the man born blind to a conclusion, but I do not agree. With Dodd and Asiedu-Peprah, I propose that 9:39–10:21 continues the dispute about Jesus's authority to heal on the Sabbath. The narrative does not reach its conclusion until 10:19-21 where the theme of blindness and sight return. See Dodd, *The Interpretation of the Fourth Gospel*, 354–57; Asiedu-Peprah, *Johannine Sabbath Conflicts*, 119–20. A monograph that argues for the unity of this section is Karoline M. Lewis, *Rereading the "Shepherd Discourse": Restoring the Integrity of John 9:39–10:21*, StBibLit (New York: Lang, 2008). Along similar lines is the work of Stovell, *Mapping Metaphorical Discourse*, chap. 6. She argues on literary grounds for the unity of 9:39–10:21 and presents these verses as the discourse accompanying the "sign" of the healing miracle in John 9.

31. In this structure I follow the suggestion of Brown in noting that verses 7-18 elaborate on the gate, the shepherd, and the sheep who are introduced in vv. 1-6; see Raymond E. Brown, *The Gospel according to John*, 2 vols., AB 29–29a (New York: Doubleday, 1966, 1970), 1:391. Brown does not link 10:1-19 with 9:39-41. I consider the concluding verses of chapter 9 are an introduction to the following dialogue with the Pharisees that then concludes by returning back to the theme of blindness, thus linking this entire dialogue to the encounter with the man born blind in chap. 9.

³⁹Jesus said, "I came into this world for judgment so that those who do not see may see, and those who do see may become blind." ⁴⁰Some of the Pharisees near him heard this and said to him, "Surely we are not blind, are we?" ⁴¹Jesus said to them, "If you were blind, you would not have sin. But now that you say, 'We see,' your sin remains.

¹⁰:¹"Very truly, I tell you, anyone who does not enter the sheepfold by the gate but climbs in by another way is a thief and a bandit. ²The one who enters by the gate is the shepherd of the sheep. ³The gatekeeper opens the gate for him, and the sheep hear his voice. He calls his own sheep by name and leads them out. ⁴When he has brought out all his own, he goes ahead of them, and the sheep follow him because they know his voice. ⁵They will not follow a stranger, but they will run from him because they do not know the voice of strangers."

⁶Jesus used this figure of speech with them, but they did not understand what he was saying to them.

⁷So again Jesus said to them, "Very truly, I tell you, I am the gate for the sheep. ⁸All who came before me are thieves and bandits; but the sheep did not listen to them. ⁹I am the gate. Whoever enters by me will be saved, and will come in and go out and find pasture. ¹⁰The thief comes only to steal and kill and destroy. I came that they may have life, and have it abundantly.

¹¹"I am the good shepherd. The good shepherd lays down his life for the

Ingathering. This conclusion brings the disputes, the healing, and further dispute during Tabernacles to an unresolved conclusion. In a two-party dispute Jesus employs a parable as a means of trying to help his opponents find themselves and the error of their argument. A similar strategy was used in John 5 with the parable about the apprentice son (5:17). The parable is first stated (vv. 1-5) and then expanded upon (vv. 7-18), interrupted by a brief narrative comment (v. 6). This can be shown as follows.

Introduction 9:39-41

Parable   10:1-5 gate, the shepherd, sheep

   Narrative Comment 10:6

Exposition   10:7-10 the gate

              10:11-15 the shepherd

              10:16-18 the sheep

Conclusion   10:19-21

sheep. ¹²The hired hand, who is not the shepherd and does not own the sheep, sees the wolf coming and leaves the sheep and runs away—and the wolf snatches them and scatters them. ¹³The hired hand runs away because a hired hand does not care for the sheep. ¹⁴I am the good shepherd. I know my own and my own know me, ¹⁵just as the Father knows me and I know the Father. And I lay down my life for the sheep. ¹⁶I have other sheep that do not belong to this fold. I must bring them also, and they will listen to my voice. So there will be one flock, one shepherd. ¹⁷For this rea-son the Father loves me, because I lay down my life in order to take it up again. ¹⁸No one takes it from me, but I lay it down of my own accord. I have power to lay it down, and I have power to take it up again. I have received this command from my Father."

¹⁹Again the Jews were divided be-cause of these words. ²⁰Many of them were saying, "He has a demon and is out of his mind. Why listen to him?" ²¹Others were saying, "These are not the words of one who has a demon. Can a demon open the eyes of the blind?"

Introduction (9:39-41)

The narrative seems to shift away from the healing as Jesus speaks to the Pharisees (9:40). Following the destruction of Jerusalem, the Pharisees were one group working to exercise leadership within a shattered Jewish community. In the following dialogue, once again, we may "overhear" a struggle between the Johannine community and their Jewish contem-poraries. The healing shows the possibility of moving from blindness to sight physically and from blindness to the insight of faith.[32] One person has made these journeys; can the Pharisees be convinced about Jesus and make a similar journey? The healing narrative continues in the fol-lowing discussion.

Jesus described his role as bringing judgment (κρίμα; 9:39). Linguistically, the verb κρίνω has as its root meaning in the physical act to "sift" or to "part" as one might sift wheat from chaff. This leads to the sense of dividing or selecting, of making an assessment. And this has led to the word's use in a legal sense of "judging."[33] As one bring-ing judgment to the world, it is not that Jesus *acts* as a judge; rather,

32. The theme of spiritual "blindness" is quite common in the prophetic literature, especially in Isaiah, Jeremiah, and Ezekiel. On this, see Keener, *The Gospel of John*, 1:796.

33. Friedrich Büchsel, "κρίνω," *TDNT* 3 (1965): 921–22; similarly, Mathias Rissi, "κρίμα," *EDNT* 2 (1981): 317–18.

those who encounter him are required to make a decision, and, as has been the case throughout the Festival of Tabernacles (chaps. 7–9), decisions about Jesus bring about divisions (σχίσμα; 7:43; 9:16; 10:19). Some respond positively toward him, while others cannot accept his claims. Jesus describes the division he causes using the image of blindness or sight (9:39). The Pharisees accept that he is speaking about them and challenge him: surely, they, the leaders of Israel, could not be described as blind! Because they say, "we see," and yet have rejected him, the Sent One of God, Jesus, accuses them of sin. What is at stake here is that these leaders have seen the healing. They have questioned the man and his parents in order to know the facts about his blindness from birth, and yet they refuse to accept this extraordinary healing as a "sign" of Jesus's identity, even though they have accepted Moses's authority (cf. 5:16, 18, 39-40; 9:24, 29). Such refusal to "see" Jesus labels sin (9:41), not in the sense of a final judgment, but as part of a "rhetoric of persuasion," revealing to his opponents the seriousness of their situation if they continue to choose to reject him. With no break, his statement continues into a discourse where they are invited to see the truth of what he says.[34]

The shift from the festival to a parable about shepherding is not only because Jesus is speaking to the Pharisees, leaders among the Jews, but also because the name of the festival in Hebrew is "shelters" or Succoth (סכות). The first time this term occurs in the OT is when Jacob builds a house, a shelter, for his livestock, which includes sheep and cattle, and so names that place "Shelters" (סכת, Exod 33:17).[35]

Following the introductory verses about blindness and sight is a parable (παροιμία) involving the familiar pastoral scene of a sheepfold, describing a gate, a shepherd, and sheep, contrasting the actions of the shepherd with those of a thief, a bandit, and a stranger (10:1-5).[36] Three of

---

34. In this view I am in agreement with Asiedu-Peprah, *Johannine Sabbath Conflicts*, 154–55.

35. Thomas A. Golding, "The Imagery of Shepherding in the Bible, Part 2," *BSac* 163 (2006): 171–72.

36. There are differing opinions about whether to call 10:1-5 a proverb, a parable, or an allegory; along with Raymond Brown, Francis J. Moloney, Ruben Zimmermann, and others, I consider it to be parable. Asiedu-Peprah argues that within a two-party juridical controversy, a parable is a very usual form to be found within the argument; see Asiedu-Peprah, *Johannine Sabbath Conflicts*, 20. An insightful essay on Johannine figurative language is that of Ruben Zimmermann, "Imagery in John: Opening Up Paths into the Tangled Thicket of John's Figurative World," in *Imagery in the Gospel of John: Terms, Forms, Themes, and Theology of Johannine Figurative Language*, ed. Jörg

these terms are then elaborated on: gate (vv. 7-10), shepherd (vv. 11-15), and sheep (vv. 16-20). The passage then concludes with the theme of blindness and sight, noting that "the Jews were divided because of these words" (v. 19). The judgement (κρίνα) Jesus came to bring (9:39) has happened as his opponents have now been separated on the basis of their belief.[37]

A parable is a strategy that is used in disputes to help one's opponents recognize the point you are trying to make, with an example that may offer objectivity, e.g., Nathan's parable of the ewe lamb in his confrontation with David (2 Sam 12:1-14), or the parable of the apprentice son who only does what he has been instructed to do by his father (John 5:17). This strategy tries to convince one's opponent of the truth of one's claims.[38]

Within Israel's Scriptures the shepherd was a familiar image used for leaders, particularly in the light of David, who rose from being the young shepherd to the warrior-king. During the exile the prophet Ezekiel decried the rulers who had not been wise leaders with an extended metaphor of false shepherds. "You have not strengthened the weak, you have not healed the sick, you have not bound up the injured, you have not brought back the strayed, you have not sought the lost, but with force and harshness you have ruled them. So they were scattered, because there was no shepherd" (Ezek 34:4-5). Because Israel's leadership has failed the people, God will now be the true shepherd. "For thus says the Lord God: I myself will search for my sheep, and will seek them out. As shepherds seek out their flocks when they are among their scattered

---

Frey, Jan G. van der Watt, and Ruben Zimmermann, WUNT 200 (Tübingen: Mohr Siebeck, 2006), 1–43. Zimmermann considers vv. 1-5 a parable, noting that vv. 7-18 have been considered an "allegorical version" of the parable (24). He then discusses newer terms such as "image texts" and "figurative narratives." Robert Kysar's earlier study also offers helpful insights into how this passage (10:1-18) impacts on the reader. He concludes, "In terms of their function for the reader the images are poetic metaphors and as such they share much with the parables attributed to Jesus in the synoptic gospels." See Robert D. Kysar, "Johannine Metaphor—Meaning and Function: A Literary Case Study of John 10:1-8," *Semeia* 53 (1991): 101.

37. Two helpful articles by Thomas Golding describe the practice of shepherding in the ancient world and also its metaphorical use: Thomas A. Golding, "The Imagery of Shepherding in the Bible, Part 1," *BSac* 163 (2006): 18–28; and Golding, "The Imagery of Shepherding in the Bible, Part 2," *BSac* 163 (2006): 158–75.

38. "The use of a juridical parable constitutes a subtle means by which a party in the conflict uses a fictitious case in a bid to get the other party to unknowingly commit himself/herself and therefore to accept the truthfulness of the position of the party making use of the juridical parable." See Asiedu-Peprah, *Johannine Sabbath Conflicts*, 33.

sheep, so I will seek out my sheep. I will rescue them from all the places to which they have been scattered on a day of clouds and thick darkness. I will bring them out from the peoples and gather them from the countries, and will bring them into their own land" (Ezek 34:11-13). Jesus's words to the Pharisees, and the contrast he makes between the hireling and himself, evokes this passage and numerous others that speak of God as "the Shepherd of Israel."[39]

The shepherding role of women is often overlooked; however, two shepherdesses stand out in relation to Israel's experience of liberation from Egypt. First is Rachel, the shepherdess who meets and later marries Jacob/Israel (Gen 29). It is her son Joseph (Gen 30:24) who enables the household to find refuge in Egypt. Yosef Green considers that "of the four matriarchs, it is Rachel who has inspired the most creative response in art and literature."[40] Green continues, "Rachel . . . became in time the legendary shepherdess and mother of all Israel, rising up from her tomb to console her suffering children"[41] (see Matt 2:18). The memory of the shepherdess Rachel lives on in midrash (Tana de'bei Eliyahu). "The Hebrew letters in the name Rachel [rhl] are used to form the words 'Ruah El.' "[42] When the Babylonians force the captive Israelites into exile (587 BCE), they pass the tomb of Rachel and Jeremiah writes, "A voice is heard in Ramah, lamentation and bitter weeping. Rachel is weeping for her children" (Jer 31:15). The midrash then states, "Read not, 'Rachel, weeping for her children' but *Ruah El*—the spirit of God—weeping for her children. The Midrash here suggests that Rachel caused the spirit of God to join her in weeping for her children."[43]

A second shepherdess appears when there is a change of Egyptian leadership and the children of Israel are forced into slavery. Moses flees into Midian, and, sitting by a well, he encounters Zipporah, a Midianite woman, who, with her sisters, tends the flocks of their father Ruel (Exod 2:15-18). Moses marries Zipporah, and it is she who circumcises her son

---

39. There is no explicit citing of Scripture, but there are many passages in the Scriptures and later Jewish first-century writing that describe unfaithful leaders of Israel as bad shepherds; see, for example, Jer 23:1-18; Ezek 34; Zech 10:2-3; 1 En. 89:12-27. For further references in Jewish literature, see Francis J. Moloney, *John*, SP 4 (Collegeville, MN: Liturgical Press, 1998), 301.

40. Yosef Green, "Our Mother Rachel: Prima inter Pares," *JBQ* 33 (2005): 166.

41. Ibid., 167.

42. Ibid., 170.

43. Ibid.

and demonstrates to Moses the apotropaic (designed to avert evil) use of blood when Moses is threatened by YHWH (Exod 4:24-26). Later, it will be the apotropaic ritual of anointing the doors of their homes that will protect the Israelites during the Passover.[44]

The Parable and Comment (10:1-6)

The parable begins by setting up a contrast between two ways of entering the sheepfold: by the gate or by some other way. The means of entry determines the identity of the one entering as either a thief and a robber or the shepherd. If it is the shepherd, the gate is opened for him or her.[45] The gate (θύρα), and whether this is opened or not, reveals the identity of the person wanting to access the sheep. At the heart of the parable is the question of who has legitimate access to the sheep (i.e., the people of God?).[46] The second part of the parable offers a second way of identifying the legitimacy of the entrant. If it is the shepherd, the sheep recognize the voice and immediately follow.[47] If it is a stranger, the sheep scatter. What matters is the intimate mutual relationship.[48] The shepherd knows the sheep by name, and they know their shepherd, or, conversely, because they know the shepherd, they are identified as belonging to him or her.[49] By contrast, they will flee from the stranger. The narrative comment (v. 6) clarifies that the parable is directed to the Pharisees, but instead of responding to the parable by offering a comment on the behavior of the

---

44. Victor Hurowitz and Shamir Yonah, *Marbeh Ḥokmah: Studies in the Bible and the Ancient Near East in Loving Memory of Victor Avigdor Hurowitz* (Winona Lake, IN: Eisenbrauns, 2015), 129.

45. Women who had the task of caring for sheep include Rachel, who looked after Laban's sheep (Gen 29:6), and Zipporah, one of seven daughters tending their father's sheep (Exod 2:16-21), who became Moses's wife. Solomon sings of a Shulamite woman tending her vineyard and her flock (Song 1:5-8).

46. As in Ezek 34:30-31, the image of "sheep" is a reference to God's people.

47. In John, ἀκούειν, "to hear," with φωνῆς, "voice," has the sense of "obey." See Friedrich Blass, Albert Debrunner, and Robert W. Funk, *A Greek Grammar of the New Testament and Other Early Christian Literature* (Cambridge: Cambridge University Press, 1961), 95 §173.

48. Zumstein, *L'Évangile selon Saint Jean (1–12)*, 340, similarly, Asiedu-Peprah, *Johannine Sabbath Conflicts*, 159.

49. Zumstein comments that the metaphor establishes Jesus as the only one who has legitimate access to God's people and that only those who recognize him can be God's people (Zumstein, *L'Évangile selon Saint Jean [1–12]*, 342).

shepherd or the stranger, they remain silent. The narrator explains their silence as a lack of understanding.[50]

The Gate (10:7-10)

In the face of his opponents' silence, Jesus expands on the parable in a form named by Jean Zumstein as a *relecture*, rather than allegory. Zumsteim describes this as a literary technique where "a second text is created by the process of rereading the first text."[51] The second text presupposes the first and develops it further while offering further explanation and recontextualizing it.[52]

The image of the gate of/for the sheep has the double sense as the means of access into the sheep and the means for the sheep to leave the fold in search of pasture. As a means of protecting the flock, the shepherd will lie across the entrance to the sheepfold, so the shepherd *is* the gate.[53] The emphasis is on the uniqueness of Jesus. Further explanation comes by describing those "who came before me" as thieves and bandits. Who are meant by this statement? Rudolph Schnackenburg cautions against understanding this phrase as a reference to Israel's great figures such as Abraham or Moses, because for John, "they are men of God,"[54] and the narrative has shown that Jesus speaks of these figures positively as witnessing to him (1:45; 5:46; 8:56). "So it must have to do with people claiming leadership on false messianic or religious grounds. . . . [T]hose that come more readily to mind are the Pharisees, whose attitude towards the man born blind in chapter 9 exemplifies and illustrates cunning and violence."[55] While some may make leadership claims, they are seen to be false and not heeded, as exemplified by the healed man in John 9,

---

50. Interpreters are not as benign as the narrator. Brown (*The Gospel according to John*, 1:393) considers their silence as "an unwillingness to respond to the challenge."

51. This description comes from Lewis, *Rereading the "Shepherd Discourse*," 51. The process is described in Jean Zumstein, *Kreative Erinnerung: Relecture und Auslegung im Johannesevangelium*, ATANT (Zürich: TVZ, 2004), see esp. 24–30.

52. Zumstein, *Kreative Erinnerung*, 26.

53. This practice of the shepherd lying across the entrance to the sheepfold is described in E. F. F. Bishop, " 'Door of the Sheep': John 10:7-9," *ExpTim* 71 (1960): 307.

54. Rudolph Schnackenburg, *The Gospel according to St John*, trans. K. Smyth et al., 3 vols., HTCNT (London: Burns & Oates, 1968–1982), 2:291, similarly, Zumstein, *L'Évangile selon Saint Jean (1–12)*, 342. In a footnote, Schnackenburg criticizes the interpretations of Marcion and the Manichees who understand the phrase "before me" to refer to Israel's prophets (2:507, n. 61).

55. Schnackenburg, *The Gospel according to St John*, 2:291.

who would not accept the accusations made about Jesus, that he was a sinner (9:25, 30-33).

As the unique means of access, Jesus is the only one able to offer salvation, described as being able to "come in and go out and find pasture."[56] When speaking to Nicodemus Jesus described his mission as bringing salvation to the world (3:17). In that conversation salvation was described as a quality of God's own eternity life (ζωὴν αἰώνιον). Here, drawing on pastoral imagery, salvation is described as safety and pastures. Where the thief comes to steal, kill, and destroy (v.10), Jesus comes offering life abundantly (περισσὸν). "Abundantly" (περισσός) is a rare adverb in the NT.[57] The verb "to abound" (περισσεύειν) is used almost always to speak of a fullness present "in the age of salvation as compared with the old aeon. . . . To this extent περισσεύειν is an eschatological catchword."[58] The Gospel narrative, particularly the earlier Sabbath controversy in John 5, presented a distinctly Johannine view that, in the presence of Jesus, the eschatological moment is *now*. What Israel had hoped for the future is being brought into the present moment ("the hour is coming and now is," 4:23; 5:25); the eternity life expected at the end of time is now a present gift to those who are open to receive it. Expressions such as "eternity life" and "life in its fullness" (10:10) are what is meant by "salvation" in this Gospel.

The Shepherd (10:11-15)

The shepherd imagery, elaborated on in verses 11-15, provides a "mini" Gospel. In these verses Jesus declares his love unto death and that the extraordinary mutual intimacy between Jesus and the Father (1:1, 18) is the same mutual intimacy between shepherd and sheep. The theological impact of these verses will continue in the final discourse, chapters 13–17. Here, in chapter 10, is an intimation of how the Gospel will unfold. The verses contrast the Good Shepherd with the hireling who flees, allowing the sheep to be forcefully snatched and then left scattered. This is the plight of the sheep in Ezekiel's metaphor, prior to God's intervention.[59] In identifying himself as the "shepherd" Jesus draws on Israel's traditions

---

56. The expression to "go in and go out" is an OT idiom expressing total "freedom of movement and security." See Asiedu-Peprah, *Johannine Sabbath Conflicts*, 165.

57. It occurs at Matt 5:37, 47; Mark 6:51; Rom 3:1; 2 Cor 9:1; John 10:10.

58. Friedrich Hauck, "περισσεύω," *TDNT* 6 (1968): 59.

59. The verb σκορπίζω, "to scatter," is used seven times in this chapter (see also Ezek 34:5 [3x], 12 [2x]).

of a messianic royal shepherd. During the time of the exile God was portrayed as the shepherd of Israel (Jer 31:10; 13:17; 23:3; Isa 40:11; 49:9-10; Ezek 34). The image continued in the postexilic prophets confirming the notion of a future shepherd, like David, "I will set up over them one shepherd, my servant David, and he shall feed them: he shall feed them and be their shepherd" (Ezek 34:23; cf. Mic 5:2-4; Jer 3:4-6). This future Davidic shepherd will gather the scattered sheep together into one flock. "Thus says the Lord GOD: I will take the people of Israel from the nations among which they have gone, and will gather them from every quarter, and bring them to their own land. I will make them one nation in the land, on the mountains of Israel; and one king shall be king over them all. Never again shall they be two nations, and never again shall they be divided into two kingdoms. . . . My servant David shall be king over them; and they shall all have one shepherd" (Ezek 37:21-22, 24).[60] As Francis Moloney comments, "The introduction of the image of the good shepherd links Jesus with the traditions of a messianic shepherd of the People of God."[61]

There are no explicit references in the OT to an anointed one who dies for the people, but first-century Jewish exegetical methods have led Donald Juel and Jocelyn McWhirter to link "David, scorned, shamed, and insulted by his enemies in Psalms 22 and 69 with the Lord's anointed one scorned, shamed and insulted by his enemies in Ps. 80:38," a clearly recognized messianic psalm.[62] In Psalm 69:7 David cries out, "it is for your sake that I have borne reproach," indicating that his suffering is for others. Similar exegetical methods allow the fourth Servant Song of Isaiah 52:13–54:12 also to be read as a messianic prophecy, and early Christians related this Servant Song and the David psalms to the death of Jesus.[63] As the messianic Good Shepherd Jesus lays down his life for his sheep, fulfilling the testimony of Israel's Scriptures.

---

60. This theme of the reunification of Israel emerged in John 4 in the discussion between Jesus, from Judea, and a woman from Samaria.

61. Moloney, *John*, 304.

62. Jocelyn McWhirter, "Messianic Exegesis in the Fourth Gospel," in *Reading the Gospel of John's Christology as Jewish Messianism: Royal, Prophetic, and Divine Messiahs*, ed. Benjamin Reynolds and Gabriele Boccaccini, AJEC 106 (Leiden: Brill, 2018), 131; Donald Juel, *Messianic Exegesis: Christological Interpretation of the Old Testament in Early Christianity* (Philadelphia: Fortress, 1988), 109–11.

63. Ps 22:18/Mark 15:24; Ps 22:1/Mark 15:34; Ps 69:21/Mark 15:36; Isa 53:7/Acts 8:32; Pss 22:18; 69:21/John 19:23-25, 28-29. McWhirter ("Messianic Exegesis in the

The Sheep (10:16-18)

As Ezekiel announced, the messianic shepherd will bring together all the scattered sheep, uniting them under one royal shepherd. This theme is taken up in verses 16-18 with the mention of "other sheep" not belonging to the fold. These "other sheep" can mean both those within Israel who have not yet come to faith in Jesus and also those beyond Israel who need to be embraced into the fold, where they too can find "life in abundance."[64] In these verses we hear again of the shepherd's willingness to lay down his life for his sheep, and now further elements are added to this willing self-gift. Now we hear not only that Jesus is involved in his self-gift but that this gift also expresses the Father's love. Father and son are united in this action of love: "For God so loved the world that God gave the only Son" (3:16). Furthermore, the laying down of life is not an end in itself but points beyond death to the resurrection, when life will be taken up again.

Conclusion (10:19-21)

The parable and its elaboration were intended to convince Jesus's opponents of the truth of his words and thus invite them also to become "one of his fold." The response to his words repeats a familiar theme throughout the Festival of Tabernacles, that of division (σχίσμα).[65] The context remains the Festival of Tabernacles, known also as the Festival of Ingathering, and yet within this feast, even recalling the divine royal shepherd of Ezekiel 34, who gathers the scattered sheep together into one fold, there is division. There are some among God's people open to the words of Jesus and reassured of the truth of his claims by his sign of opening the eyes of the man who had been blind; but there are others

---

Fourth Gospel," 133) concludes, "Clearly, he [John] reads Pss 22:18; 69:21 as prophecies about a crucified messiah."

64. Throughout the OT the image of the "sheep" is consistently applied to the people of Israel in their relationship to God, their shepherd. To speak then of "other sheep" beyond the fold hints of those outside Israel. For this interpretation of the "other sheep" as including Gentiles, see Brown, *The Gospel according to John*, 1:396; Zumstein, *L'Évangile selon Saint Jean (1–12)*, 345; Frédéric Manns, *L'Evangile de Jean à la lumière du Judaïsme*, SBFA 33 (Jerusalem: Franciscan Printing Press, 1991), 225; Charles K. Barrett, *The Gospel according to St John*, 2nd ed. (London: SPCK, 1978), 376.

65. Although the word "division" (σχίσμα) is used only in 7:43 and 9:16, on other occasions the narrative shows a division within groups, e.g., 7:12, 31, 50-52; 9:9, 19.

who have witnessed the same deed but who consider Jesus to be possessed and manic (μαίνεται).[66] These refuse to listen and are "blind" in the presence of the Light of the world. The man born blind received the life-giving waters of the Sent One (Siloam) and came to physical sight and the insight of faith. The joyful Festival of Ingathering closes with these deep divisions unresolved.

It is important that when examining John 9:1–10:21 we keep the context of Tabernacles clearly in view along with its rituals, involving water from Siloam, blazing light in the darkness, and worship of Israel's God. The dialogues of chapters 7 and 8 provide the interpretive clues to relate Jesus to these rituals. I began the discussion of these chapters referring to Wisdom/Sophia as the one who guided the Israelites through their wilderness journey, providing shelter in the day, light in the darkness, and water (Wis 10:15, 17; 11:4). The festival of *Sukkot* (Shelters) recalls the wilderness journey and identifies Jesus/Sophia as the one offering water to the thirsty (7:37), as the light of the world (8:12), and as the preexistent I AM (8:58). The words of Sophia are then demonstrated in the episode with the man born blind, who moves from permanent darkness to light, through waters provided by the Sent One (9:7), and from ignorance of Jesus to acknowledgment and worship (9:38). But Wisdom's demonstration through the miracle concludes with some still blind (9:9-40), and so Wisdom attempts another common educative strategy by offering a parable (παροιμία, 10:6)[67] in the hope that this will lead some of the Pharisees to "sight."

By the end of the first century, when the temple no longer exists, and sacrifices have finished, the Jewish leaders turn to the law to find the replacement for all they have lost. In this situation, the author of 2 Baruch offers these words of consolation to Israel:

> The whole people answered and they said to me:
> " . . . For the shepherds of Israel have perished, and the lamps which gave light are extinguished, and the fountains from which we used to drink have withheld their streams. Now we have been left in the darkness and in the thick forest and in the aridness of the desert."

---

66. In the NT, the verb μαίνεσθαι is rare, being used "only to characterize the messengers of God with their unheard-of proclamation." Such divine revelation is considered by some to be the ravings of a lunatic, e.g., Festus's response to Paul—"you are mad" (Acts 26:24). The verb is thus an expression of unbelief toward a revelation of divine salvation. See Herbert Preisker, "μαίνομαι," *TDNT* 4 (1967): 361.

67. The parable (παροιμία) or wisdom saying is not found in the historical books or prophets but is typical of the wisdom literature, occurring in Prov 1:1; 26:7; Sir 6:35; 8:8; 18:29; 39:3; 47:17. Hauck, "παροιμία," 855.

And I answered and said to them:

"Shepherds and lanterns and fountains came from the Law and when we go away, the Law will abide. If you, therefore, look upon the Law and are intent upon wisdom, then the lamp will not be wanting and the shepherd will not give way and the fountain will not dry up." (2 Bar 77:11, 13-16)[68]

By late Second Temple Judaism the law had been identified as Wisdom (Sir 24:23; Bar 4:1). Around the same time as the author of 2 Baruch,[69] the Fourth Evangelist presents Jesus/Sophia, as the light (John 8:12; cf. Wis 10:17), the fountain (John 7:37; cf. Wis 11:6), and the good shepherd (John 10:11). Throughout this Festival of Tabernacles, Sophia has revealed and demonstrated her presence.

"Offer It Up"

There is a double meaning in the phrase, "the good shepherd lays down his life for the sheep" (10:11); quite literally the shepherd would lie down across the entrance to the sheepfold so that nothing could enter to harm the sheep and no sheep could leave. When the phrase is first used it could depict this pastoral practice and continue the parabolic genre. Later, "laying down life" clearly has the sense of death (10:17). The Gospel does not identify this self-gift of life as a "sacrifice." There is no mention of priest, of cult, or of victim. In the culture at that time a sacrifice was a bloody killing of an animal and/or non-animal produce, and offering it to a god. It did not yet have a spiritual, metaphorical sense that later tradition would employ to speak of an act of utmost generosity. So the terms "sacrifice" and "offer it up" were at first related to killing an animal, which was always carried out by a male. As Johanna Dewey writes, "Sacrifice is not a gender-neutral practice."[70] The cross, for those who lived in the years when crucifixion happened, could never be termed a "sacrifice." "For non-Christians and Christians alike, crucifixion had nothing to do with sacrifice. Crucifixion was the most shameful means of political execution, reserved for slaves and lower-class rebels. It had no connection to religious ritual."[71]

In the NT there are a few metaphorical references to Jesus's death in sacrificial terms (Rom 3:25; Eph 5:2; 1 John 2:2;

---

68. James H. Charlesworth, ed. *The Old Testament Pseudepigrapha*, 2 vols. (London: Darton, Longman & Todd, 1985), 1:647.

69. Moloney, *John*, 307.

70. Joanna Dewey, "Sacrifice No More," *BTB* 41 (2011): 69.

71. Ibid., 71.

4:10; Heb 2:17; 9:26; 10:12). An important thrust in the letter to the Hebrews is that Jesus's death was a once-and-for-all sacrifice ending the sacrificial system (9:26; 10:12). "For the author of Hebrews, blood sacrifice has come to an end."[72]

With the destruction of the Jewish temple animal sacrifices ceased, and the meaning of the temple cult was transferred to obedience to Torah within Judaism. The cult was spiritualized from bloody sacrifices to "steadfast love" (Hos 6:6). Similarly in Christianity the eucharistic meal was understood first as a communion in the Lord's Supper, but then later, under influence from the surrounding Roman cult, the focus shifted to speak of altar, sacrifice, and priest, and in this imagery the death of Jesus was perceived as a "sacrifice." Cyprian (c. 200–258), the bishop of Carthage, is "the first to refer to the body and blood of Christ as the object of sacrifice by Christian priests."[73]

This shift in theology led to Jesus's death being interpreted as a sacrifice, and then through his words, such as "lay down my life" (John 10:17), his death was understood as *self-sacrifice*, where he is both victim and priest.

Understanding Jesus as a self-sacrificing victim led to false asceticism and a false piety where one could be encouraged to endure suffering as a means of communion and identification with Jesus. For many women this is what they are encouraged to do as a way of enduring constant impoverishment, malnourishment, illiteracy, and domestic violence. "Offer it up" is the advice they are given. "Self-sacrifice for the sake of others is the highest value."[74]

The Gospel of John will overturn such false piety, as surely as Jesus overturned the tables in the temple and drove out the sacrificial animals (John 2:15). In John, Jesus does not die as a victim but as one who has been victorious over evil. "I have conquered the world" (16:33).[75]

---

72. Dewey, "Sacrifice No More," 72.

73. Nancy Jay, *Throughout Your Generations Forever* (Chicago, Il: CUP, 1992), 116.

74. Barbara E. Reid, *Taking up the Cross: New Testament Interpretations through Latina and Feminist Eyes* (Minneapolis: Augsburg, 2007), 19.

75. Here, the term κόσμος is being used in the fourth sense described by Sandra Schneiders: this world (κόσμος) being held captive by a power of evil named as Satan, the devil, Belial, and, later in the Gospel of John, the "ruler of this world" (12:31; 14:30; 16:11). See Sandra M. Schneiders, "The Word in the World," *Pacifica* 23 (2010): 254. See also the discussion of John 8:31-58.

John 7:53–8:11

In Search of a Home

Text Matters

The most ancient manuscripts of the Fourth Gospel (e.g., Sinaiticus and Vaticanus) lack 7:53–8:11; other authorities add the passage here or after John 7:36 or 21:25 or after Luke 21:38 or 24:53, with variations in the text; some mark the passage as doubtful. Eusebius, citing comments by Papias, writes "about a woman, accused in the Lord's presence of many sins, which is contained in the Gospel according to the Hebrews" (Eus., *Hist. eccl.* 3.39.16). Some scholars have accepted this as a reference to the woman accused of one sin, adultery. Others remain unconvinced.[1]

It would seem that this was a tradition about Jesus that existed independently of early manuscripts and yet was considered so important

---

1. See a more developed discussion of this in C. K. Barrett, *The Gospel according to St John*, 2nd ed. (London: SPCK, 1978), 589–90. An overview of the textual discussion can be found in Chris Keith, "Recent and Previous Research on the *Pericope Adulterae* (John 7.53–8.11)," *CurBR* 6 (2008): 377–404. A very detailed examination of the textual transmission can be found in Jennifer Wright Knust and Tommy Wasserman, *To Cast the First Stone: The Transmission of a Gospel Story* (Princeton: Princeton University Press, 2019).

⁵³Then each of them went home, ⁸:¹while Jesus went to the Mount of Olives. ²Early in the morning he came again to the temple. All the people came to him and he sat down and began to teach them. ³The scribes and the Pharisees brought a woman who had been caught in adultery; and making her stand before all of them, ⁴they said to him, "Teacher, this woman was caught in the very act of committing adultery. ⁵Now in the law Moses commanded us to stone such women. Now what do you say?" ⁶They said this to test him, so that they might have some charge to bring against him. Jesus bent down and wrote with his finger on the ground. ⁷When they kept on questioning him, he straightened up and said to them, "Let anyone among you who is without sin be the first to throw a stone at her." ⁸And once again he bent down and

that it survived and finally found its home after John 7:52.² Perhaps the fact that Jesus was threatened with stoning at the end of Tabernacles (8:59) was sufficient to link his experience with the story of a woman threatened with stoning. It is impossible to be fully certain of the pericope's reception history, hence Gail O'Day's assertion that the text is "a story without time or place, a story to be read on its own terms without sustained reference to its larger literary context."³ Because the passage clearly interrupts the narrative of the Feast of Tabernacles, I have chosen to discuss it here, following the Festival of Tabernacles.⁴

2. The earliest manuscript that places the pericope here is Codex Bezae. See Holly J. Toensing, "Divine Intervention or Divine Intrusion? Jesus and the Adulteress in John's Gospel," in *A Feminist Companion to John*, vol. 1, ed. Amy-Jill Levine with Marianne Blickenstaff, FCNTECW 4 (London: Sheffield Academic, 2003), 157, n. 1; Knust and Wasserman, *To Cast the First Stone*, 91. David C. Parker (*Manuscripts, Texts, Theology: Collected Papers 1977–2007* [Berlin: de Gruyter, 2009]) uses both the Greek and Latin palaeographic clues to find "evidence of a second-century text" (112).

3. Gail R. O'Day, "John," in *Women's Bible Commentary*, ed. Carol A. Newsom and Sharon H. Ringe, rev. and exp. ed. (Louisville: Westminster John Knox, 1998), 385.

4. While noting the interruption, there is a link with what has been happening in John 7, namely, the dispute about the law of Moses (7:19), which has continued since the Sabbath healing in John 5. Following a detailed examination of the textual tradition, Knust and Wasserman (*To Cast the First Stone*, 343) reach the following conclusion: "Our survey of the evidence has convinced us that the story was interpolated into a Greek copy of John in the West, probably during the first half of the third century, and with great care."

wrote on the ground. [9]When they heard it, they went away, one by one, beginning with the elders; and Jesus was left alone with the woman standing before him. [10]Jesus straightened up and said to her, "Woman, where are they? Has no one condemned you?" [11]She said, "No one, sir." And Jesus said, "Neither do I condemn you. Go your way, and from now on do not sin again."

Introduction (7:53–8:2)

The hill opposite the temple is called the Mount of Olives only in the Synoptic Gospels and only here in John. Similarly, the linking of "scribes and Pharisees" is common in the Synoptics but not in John, where "scribes" are mentioned only here.[5]

Who's on Trial? (8:3-6)

In bringing the woman to Jesus, citing the law of Moses and asking Jesus for his decision, the scribes and Pharisees are really placing Jesus on trial, seeking "some charge to bring against him" (v. 6). They have no need for his opinion to carry out the sentence as she "was caught in the very act of committing adultery" (v. 4).

For adultery to occur, the woman must be married or betrothed.[6] In that society it meant that she "belonged" to another man, and so the

5. There is much in this passage to question its historicity. Execution for adultery was not practiced in the time of Jesus. The characterization of the scribes and Pharisees as the representatives of the law sets in sharp relief Jesus and his stance to the law. Naming the scribes pits Jesus not only against those who teach the law but against those responsible for copying and writing the law. They are "the most educated of Torah authorities." See Chris Keith, "The Scribes and the Elders: Mirror Characterization of Jesus and His Opponents in the *Pericope Adulterae*," in *Character Studies in the Fourth Gospel: Narrative Approaches to Seventy Figures in John*, ed. Steven A. Hunt, D. Francois Tolmie, and Ruben Zimmermann, WUNT 314 (Tübingen: Mohr Siebeck, 2013), 405. Jesus counters their claim but shows, for the only time in the Gospels, that he too is grapho-literate.

6. In ancient Israel, as in other ancient Near East lands, betrothal was a formal, contractual arrangement made between the two fathers, with the marriage taking place a year or more later. From the time of this betrothal the woman was regarded as the lawful "wife," and a divorce was required to set the contract aside. Women were usually married on reaching puberty, while men could be thirty or more. In the Roman Empire, the Augustan law "set the minimum age of marriage at 12." Karen R. Keen, "Sexuality, Critical Issues," in *The Lexham Bible Dictionary*, ed. John D. Barry et al. (Bellingham, WA: Lexham Press, 2016).

offense is against his property rights. If the woman is single there is no adultery, even if the man is already married. If adultery has occurred, then both the man and the woman are condemned to death (Lev 20:10; Deut 22:24). Leviticus does not specify the form of death, but Deuteronomy 22:24 states, "you shall bring both of them to the gate of that town and stone them to death."[7] The laws are clearly androcentric,[8] in that they consider only the marital status of the woman and ignore the status of the man. In this episode, a further injustice is evident in that only one party, the woman, is paraded before Jesus and the crowd of people while the offending man is not. She stands, "Nameless, claimless still . . . Faceless, Shameless."[9]

Peter Phillips writes, "She has been standing there in the middle, dishevelled, embarrassed, alone, and we have ignored her all this time. The controversy of the text has blinded us to the controversy of the woman."[10] She has been objectified and described by her accusers as "a type" of woman who deserves to be stoned. Holly Toensing writes, "The scribes and Pharisees' use of τὰς τοιαύτας indicates that they do not see the woman as an individual but as a kind of woman—the kind that categorically deserves death."[11] Like an object to be stared at, they "stood her in the middle," στήσαντες αὐτὴν ἐν μέσῳ (v. 3), of the crowd.

---

7. While there are many references in the OT to stoning someone to death, in fact only six men are said to have been stoned to death, and no one for adultery (Lev 24:3; Num 15:36; Josh 7:25; 1 Kgs 12:18; 2 Chr 10:18; 1 Kgs 21:13; 2 Chr 24:21). Also, Roman law did not permit execution for adultery. Toensing discusses the laws around adultery and claims that "as execution became first a contested, then disavowed punishment for adultery during the Second Temple period, other punishments, also formulated from biblical texts, came to predominate"; Toensing, "Divine Intervention," 162, n. 10. The whole point of this confrontation is to "test" Jesus.

8. I use the term "androcentric" rather than "patriarchal" in the light of Carol L. Meyers's critique: "As a constructed model, it [patriarchy] is essentially an oversimplification and systematization of data used for comparative purposes. . . . And male control of female sexuality does not mean male control of adult women in every aspect of household or community life. In short, male dominance was real; but it was fragmentary, not hegemonic" (Carol L. Meyers, "Was Ancient Israel a Patriarchal Society?," *JBL* 133 [2014]: 26 and 27.

9. Taken from the song "Nameless" by Dr. Maeve Heaney, VDMF, on the CD *Strange Life: The Music of Doubtful Faithful* (Australia: Willow Publishing, 2020), and in an article in *Theological Studies* (forthcoming). This song was written to honor the interpretive work of Sandra Schneiders, particularly her work on John 4.

10. Peter Phillips, "The Adulterous Woman: Nameless, Partnerless, Defenseless," in Hunt, Tolmie, and Zimmermann, *Character Studies in the Fourth Gospel*, 411.

11. Toensing, "Divine Intervention," 162.

Unlike the heroic Susannah of Daniel 13, we hear nothing of her background, her family, or the circumstances of her experience. Was she the victim of a plot? of rape? Or is it enough that this "type of woman" be caught with a man? She must be guilty. She is "an implicit victim of the patriarchal system which dragged her into the middle of the scene."[12]

But Jesus has also been dragged from his teaching into this scene to be tested on his fidelity to the Mosaic law, and, as for the woman, the threat of stoning by the crowd is very real (8:9). "Jesus is seen as sharing the experience of being on trial together with the accused woman."[13] Phillips asks whether "the woman's experience in the present somehow prefigures Jesus's experience in the future. Does the arrest of the woman, the accusations, the humiliations of public display, the crowds looking on, her very silence, presage Jesus's own experience to come?"[14] In this scene, the woman is a "pawn" in a power play between Jesus and the scribes and Pharisees.

The Heart of the Matter (8:6b-8)[15]

Jesus's response is to write (κατέγραφεν), possibly accusations,[16] on the ground, apparently ignoring the accusers by bending forward (κύψας) from his sitting position. When they continue to challenge him, he straightens up, or perhaps stands up (ἀνέκυψεν), and gives his judgment—the one without sin may begin the punishment. His statement does not deny the Mosaic law but reminds them that all fall short of keeping the law, making forgiveness necessary. Even though some acts were considered capital offences, such as murder and adultery, this

---

12. Phillips, "The Adulterous Woman," 415.

13. Leticia Guardiola-Sáenz, "Border Crossing and Its Redemptive Power in John 7:53–8:11: A Cultural Reading of Jesus and *The Accused*," in *Transformative Encounters: Jesus and Women Re-Viewed*, ed. Ingrid R. Kitzberger, BibInt 43 (Leiden: Brill, 2000), 280.

14. Phillips, "The Adulterous Woman," 417.

15. I take the action of Jesus in writing on the ground (vv. 6c, 8) to be the narrative frame around this central section.

16. To set something in writing or engraving was primarily associated with formal, legal documents in the ancient world; Gottlob Schrenk, "Γράφω," *TDNT* 1 (1964): 742–43. But καταγράφω "also means 'write down an accusation'" (BDAG, 516). Although there is no indication what Jesus wrote, it could be that he was writing accusations or other "'kinds' of actions . . . also condemned by the Law" (Toensing, "Divine Intervention," 164). This writing may have led the accusers to realize that they were not sinless at this time.

was balanced by the command, "Thou shall not kill" (Exod 20:13), so that "those who harm others should be forgiven, and even murderers should be permitted to live, whether banished or as fugitives in exile. At any rate, retribution, if called for, should be left to the Almighty."[17] The sinless one may cast the first stone. Speaking stops and a silent pause follows, broken only by the sound of a finger moving over the ground. Will anyone respond?

Judgment (8:9-11)

Challenged by his statement, the accusers and the crowd gradually withdraw, leaving Jesus alone with the woman. For a second time Jesus straightens or stands to speak to the woman, according her the same respect that he showed earlier to the scribes and Pharisees (v. 7).[18] He asks where her accusers have gone: "Has no one condemned you?" His words emphasize the changed circumstances for the woman. The accusatory eyes have closed; the harsh voices have been silenced. His questions also draw her into speech. "No one, sir." The pericope then closes with Jesus's judgment: "Neither do I condemn you. Go your way." While the text we now have closes with "and sin no more," which contradicts the words Jesus has just spoken, these condemnatory words are not found in early versions of the scene, in the *Didascalia* (*Did. Apost.* 7.2.23, dated 200–250 CE)[19] and the *Apostolic Constitutions* (2.24). Barnabas Lindars proposes that the additional phrase "and sin no longer" was added when the passage eventually found a place in John, as it is identical with Jesus's words to the man whom he healed of paralysis in John 5:14.[20]

Conclusion

Who is the focus of this passage? It is usually titled "The Woman Caught in Adultery," as if she is the focal point. But she says little and

---

17. Richard H. Hiers, *Justice and Compassion in Biblical Law* (New York: Continuum, 2009), 82. See also the commendation of mercy and forgiveness in Sir 28:2-7.

18. O'Day, "John," 385.

19. The *Didascalia* reads: "Have the elders condemned thee, my daughter? She saith to him: Nay, Lord. And he said unto her: Go thy way: neither do I condemn thee" (*Did. apost.* 7). While clearly a reference to this story, it did not ascribe it to any particular Gospel.

20. Barnabas Lindars, *The Gospel of John*, NCB (London: Oliphants, 1972), 312.

generates no action. In fact, what does not happen to her has the greater impact than the threatened action. The ones who say the most are the scribes and Pharisees, who depart presumably because they recognize their own sinfulness. Structurally, the centre of the passage is verses 6b-8:

> Jesus bent down and wrote with his finger on the ground.
>> When they kept on questioning him, he straightened up and said to them, "Let anyone among you who is without sin be the first to throw a stone at her."
> And once again he bent down and wrote on the ground.

Within this chiasm, the focus is on the statement made by Jesus—"Let the one among you without sin throw [βαλέτω] the first stone"—followed by silence. This is a gnomic wisdom statement, challenging all readers of all time to be self-discerning and merciful.[21] The placement of this text in the *Didascalia* and *Apostolic Constitutions* as an admonition to the bishops in the community to be merciful toward sinners suggests why this passage was considered so important that it was circulated and preserved, even if its provenance was in doubt. Forgiveness and compassion have their place within the law. "The text identifies all the characters as in need of and receiving an invitation to new life. Jesus does offer grace and mercy to sinners in this story, but the offer is extended equally to scribes, Pharisees, and women."[22] The text is at home within the Gospel tradition.

---

21. βαλέτω is an aorist imperative that is translated into the present in English. This is called the gnomic aorist and "is used in proverbial sayings (γνῶμαι), to express what generally happens." Henry P. Nunn, *A Short Syntax of New Testament Greek* (Cambridge: Cambridge University Press, 1920), 70.

22. O'Day, "John," 385–86.

John 10:22-42

Sophia's Festival of Lights (Hanukkah)

²⁴*For wisdom is more mobile than any motion;*
because of her pureness she pervades and penetrates all things.
²⁵*For she is a breath of the power of God,*
and a pure emanation of the glory of the Almighty;
therefore nothing defiled gains entrance into her.
²⁶*For she is a reflection of eternal light,*
a spotless mirror of the working of God,
and an image of God's goodness. (Wis 7:24-26)

"It was winter" (10:22). With these words the evangelist sets the tone for this final Jewish festival. The sequence was introduced by the Sabbath festival, that weekly affirmation of the creativity of God (chap. 5). There followed the springtime festival of Passover (chap. 6) and the autumn feast of Tabernacles (7:1–10:21). These previous festivals have all related to the exodus and were pilgrim festivals requiring Jewish men to go to Jerusalem (Deut 16:16; Exod 23:14-17). Because of childbearing and raising responsibilities, women were free from all positive commandments and would not be expected to make the pilgrimage. While under no obligation, many women did attend the pilgrimage festivals, e.g., Hanna and Peninnah (1 Sam 1) and Mary (Luke 2:41). The Festival

²²At that time the festival of the Dedication took place in Jerusalem. It was winter, ²³and Jesus was walking in the temple, in the portico of Solomon. ²⁴So the Jews gathered around him and said to him, "How long will you keep us in suspense? If you are the Messiah, tell us plainly." ²⁵Jesus answered, "I have told you, and you do not believe. The works that I do in my Father's name testify to me; ²⁶but you do not believe, because you do not belong to my sheep. ²⁷My sheep hear my voice. I know them, and they follow me. ²⁸I give them eternal life, and they will never perish. No one will snatch them out of my hand. ²⁹What my Father has given me is greater than all else, and no one can snatch it out of the Father's hand. ³⁰The Father and I are one."

³¹The Jews took up stones again to stone him. ³²Jesus replied, "I have shown you many good works from the Father. For which of these are you going to stone me?" ³³The Jews answered, "It is not for a good work that we are going to stone you, but for blasphemy, because you, though only

of Dedication is different. As a religious festival, Hanukkah looks back to the liberation of the people from the tyranny of the Greek ruler Antiochus IV (175 BCE), under the leadership of the Maccabees. Its origins may "be rooted in the fact that pagan societies, from Babylon onward, marked the beginning of the winter solstice in middle to late December with a festival of lights, which, coincidentally enough, lasted for eight days."[1] In a Gospel that is sensitive to the symbolism of light and darkness,[2] the movement through the seasonal year suggests the coming to closure of Jesus's public ministry, a closure that will result in the departure of "the light of the world" (8:12). Within a festival celebrating the consecration of the temple after it had been desecrated by idolatry, Jesus's self-revelatory words that he is the consecrated One because of his intimate relationship with the Father are a final challenge and appeal to "the Jews." Where they sought the presence of God in the temple, Jesus is now the enfleshed dwelling place of God and locus of God's glory (1:14).[3] But they reject

1. Lee I. Levine, *Jerusalem: Portrait of the City in the Second Temple Period (538 B.C.E.–70 C.E.)* (Philadelphia: Jewish Publication Society, 2002), 83.

2. See excursus on light and darkness (pp. 26–27).

3. Recall from the earlier discussion of this verse, 1:14, the allusions to Sophia, who tabernacles in Jerusalem (Sir 24:8, 10) and who is "a pure emanation of the glory of the Almighty" (Wis 7:25), and Wisdom who will "guard me with her glory" (Wis 9:11).

a human being, are making yourself God." ³⁴Jesus answered, "Is it not written in your law, 'I said, you are gods'? ³⁵If those to whom the word of God came were called 'gods'—and the scripture cannot be annulled—³⁶can you say that the one whom the Father has sanctified and sent into the world is blaspheming because I said, 'I am God's Son'? ³⁷If I am not doing the works of my Father, then do not believe me. ³⁸But if I do them, even though you do not believe me, believe the works, so that you may know and understand that the Father is in me and I am in the Father." ³⁹Then they tried to arrest him again, but he escaped from their hands.

⁴⁰He went away again across the Jordan to the place where John had been baptizing earlier, and he remained there. ⁴¹Many came to him, and they were saying, "John performed no sign, but everything that John said about this man was true." ⁴²And many believed in him there.

his claims, and the consecrated glory of God must depart Israel's House of God, never to return.

The text can be broken into two sections: 10:22-31, where the dominant issue is Jesus's identity in relation to his followers, and 10:32-39, where the dominant issue is his relationship with God. Both sections end with Jesus's affirmations of his relationship with his Father, followed by "the Jews'" rejection of his claims. The final verses, 40-42, provide a conclusion as Jesus withdraws to the place where John had been baptizing and where Jesus's public ministry began.

The Central Issues

Throughout this section of the Gospel there has been an emphasis on showing a relationship between Jesus's identity and the primary symbols and rituals of Israel's festivals. During the Festival of Dedication the issue of identity and how the identity of Jesus is revealed in the symbols of this feast continue to be central.

Following a brief introduction (v. 22), the first section begins with the challenge, "How long will you keep us in suspense? If you are the Messiah, tell us plainly." Jesus's reply points to the witness of his works, then to his own "messianic" definition in terms of shepherd and life-giver, and finally to his unique relationship with his Father, "The Father and I are one" (v. 30). Considering this statement blasphemy, "the Jews" respond by taking up stones against him (v. 31).

The second section begins with Jesus's question and leads into the accusation "you, being human, make yourself divine" (v. 33).[4] Jesus's defense begins again by appealing to a witness, this time the testimony of the Scriptures: "Is it not written in your law, 'I said, you are gods'?" (v. 34; citing LXX Ps 81:6). Again he reveals his own identity as the sanctified or consecrated One and his role as the Sent One of the Father (v. 36). His conclusion to this section (vv. 32-37) rephrases the earlier conclusion in verse 30, "the Father is in me and I am in the Father" (v. 38). "The Jews" again respond by rejecting his words and by trying to arrest him. The passage concludes with Jesus's escape (v. 39b) and departure across the Jordan.

The final verses, 40-42, not only bring the narration of this feast to its end but also function as a conclusion to Jesus's entire ministry among "the Jews." Jesus's first appearance in the Gospel was in Bethany beyond the Jordan where John was baptizing (1:28-29). He now returns to that place. In chapters 1–10 Jesus has been engaged in a ministry to Israel, even to those no longer considered true Israelites by the Jews (the Samaritans) but who nevertheless claim Jacob as their father (chap. 4). He has come to his own, and his own have not received him (1:11). From chapter 11 onward the narrative moves into a story of death leading to glory (11:4).

The Festival of Dedication

Dedication is called in Hebrew *Hanukkah*, and Josephus refers to it as the Feast of Lights (*Ant.* 12.325).[5] It celebrates the rededication of the temple in 164 BCE by Judas Maccabeus.[6] In 175 BCE the Seleucid ruler Antiochus IV became ruler of Judea.[7] In order to consolidate his power he instigated a ruthless program of Hellenization, with some support by segments of the Jewish aristocracy and priesthood. He deposed the

---

4. The lack of the definite articles suggests the use of ἄνθρωπος and θεόν as adjectives: "you being human [ἄνθρωπος] make yourself divine [θεόν]" (v. 33).

5. See Gale A. Yee, *Jewish Feasts and the Gospel of John* (Wilmington, DE: Michael Glazier, 1989), 83–92; James C. vanderKam, "Dedication, Feast of," *ABD* 2 (1992): 123; Levine, *Jerusalem*, 78–86.

6. "Then Judas and his brothers said, 'See, our enemies are crushed; let us go up to cleanse the sanctuary and dedicate [ἐγκαινίσαι] it'" (2 Macc 10:36). The LXX and Fourth Gospel use ἐγκαινίζω with the sense of "renew."

7. "'Judaea' was the official title of much, if not all, of the country for most of this time. A related term, 'Yehud,' was used in the Persian and early Hellenistic eras. . . . Only in 135 C.E., in the aftermath of the Bar-Kokhba revolt, did Hadrian officially change the name to 'Syria Palaestina.'" Levine, *Jerusalem*, 3.

legitimate high priest and installed the high priest's brother, Joshua, who Hellenized his name to Jason (2 Macc 4:7-10). In support of Antiochus, Jason established a gymnasium in Jerusalem in which some Jews hid their covenantal sign of circumcision in order to compete naked in the athletic events (1 Macc 1:11-15). In effect, these Jews repudiated their heritage and revoked their identity as a covenant people. As Gale Yee says, "it was apostasy in the worst sense."[8]

Antiochus stripped the wealth of the temple treasury (1 Macc 1:20-28) and established himself as divine. He gave himself the title "Epiphanes," or "God Manifest," and decreed the worship of the Greek god Zeus as the national religion. On 25 Kislev (November–December) 167 BCE, the temple was defiled when a pagan altar was erected over the altar of burnt offerings in the temple, and sacrifices were offered to Zeus (1 Macc 1:59). A Jewish revolt was led by Judas Mattathias and his sons, who, using guerilla tactics from the hills of Modein, defeated the Greek forces in 164 BCE and established an independent Jewish kingdom.

Judas immediately set about the task of purifying the temple from all signs of pagan defilement (1 Macc 4:36-51; 2 Macc 10:1-6). On 25 Kislev 164 BCE the temple was rededicated and the first celebration of Hanukkah took place. There is no description of the rituals of Dedication in the Mishnah. According to the description in the book of Maccabees, the festival lasted for eight days and was patterned on the Feast of Tabernacles, since, as Israel's ancestors once dwelt in tents following the exodus, the Maccabean rebels also were homeless in the mountains (2 Macc 10:6). The lighting of the Hanukkah lamps plays an important part in the ritual, both in the temple and in private homes. The lamps are associated with the fire that was miraculously preserved when the temple was first destroyed (2 Macc 1:18-36).

Dedication thus celebrates a Jewish victory over foreign oppression and a victory over those sections within Judaism that conspired to destroy covenant faith. The apostasy of those Jews who sacrificed before the "desolating sacrilege" (1 Macc 1:54) threatened the very identity of the Jewish nation as a people belonging to God alone. In the light of this experience, when many succumbed to pagan influence and denied their faith, Dedication is both a celebration of victory and a reminder of failure. It is a summons to faith and an affirmation, "Never again!"[9] The

---

8. Yee, *Jewish Feasts*, 85.
9. Ibid., 88.

memory of Judas's victory gave to this feast a strong "messianic" outlook.[10] Judas was hailed as "the savior of Israel" (1 Macc 9:21), and when he died he was mourned with the refrain first sung by David over Saul and his son Jonathan, "How is the mighty fallen" (1 Macc 9:21; cf. 2 Sam 1:19). Against the nationalistic messianic hopes evoked by the memories and celebration of this Festival of Light,[11] the major issue remains clearly focused on the identity of Jesus, who has already identified himself as "the light of the world" (8:12; 9:5). Remembering the saving exploits of Judas Mattathias, "the Jews" ask at first if Jesus is "the Christ/Messiah." When Jesus answers openly in terms of his union with his Father (v. 30), he is then accused of being a second Antiochus Epiphanes, "you make yourself divine" (v. 33).

The Messianic Shepherd-Leader

In reply to the first query on his identity, "if you are the Christ tell us plainly" (v. 24), Jesus indicates his works (v. 25). Within late Second Temple Judaism, there were some who carried an expectation that when the Messiah appeared his authenticity would be demonstrated by signs and wonders.[12] Such an expectation lies behind the earlier statement,

10. In the first century it was celebrated like Tabernacles (2 Macc 10:6) but with a strong messianic theme; the feast declined after the failure of the Bar Kokhba revolt. See Étienne Nodet, "La Dédicace, les Maccabées et le Messie," *RB* 93 (1986): 373–75.

11. During the time of the Maccabean revolt, there is no evidence that Judas was given messianic status, but in the next century, there was a revival of messianism in Judea "in reaction to the non-Davidic kingship of the Hasmoneans and then to Roman rule." See John J. Collins, *Jewish Cult and Hellenistic Culture: Essays on the Jewish Encounter with Hellenism and Roman Rule* (Leiden: Brill, 2005), 80, also 62. The trajectory of ascribing "anointed" or "messianic" status to Judas continues in the Mishnah (m. Soṭah 8:1 A); Nodet, "La Dédicace, les Maccabées et le Messie," 366–67.

12. This expectation of messianic signs is not explicit within Israel's Scriptures but is clear in other first-century texts. "And it shall come to pass when all is accomplished that was to come to pass in those parts, that the Messiah shall then begin to be revealed. . . . The earth also shall yield its fruit ten thousandfold and on each vine there shall be a thousand branches, and each branch shall produce a thousand clusters, and each cluster produce a thousand grapes, and each grape produce a cot of wine. . . . And it shall come to pass at that self-same time that the treasury of manna shall again descend from on high, and they will eat of it in those years, because these are they who have come to the consummation of time" (2 Bar 29:3, 5, 8).

The so-called Messianic Apocalypse (4Q521) from Qumran also testifies to Messianic expectations:

"When the Christ appears, will he do more signs than this man has done?" (7:31).[13] Jesus does not respond in terms of "sign" expectations but speaks of his works (τὰ ἔργα). Signs and wonders direct attention to the wonder-worker; Jesus comes to complete the work (τὸ ἔργον) of his Father (4:34), and this *work* is manifest in the many *works* Jesus accomplishes. Jesus's works witness that he is authorized by his Father (5:36) and point beyond his own person to the one who sent him (5:19).

At a festival commemorating a military victory and looking to a future Messiah, Jesus speaks again of the only messianic model he will accept, that of the shepherd-leader who will ultimately lay down his life for his sheep (10:11).[14] The shepherd image, as a symbol of care and leadership, was first applied to God (Gen 48:15; 49:24; Ps 23:1; 80:1). True leaders and rulers of Israel were then called shepherds (2 Sam 5:2; 7:7), and the false leaders were depicted as false shepherds (Jer 23:1, 2; 50:6; Ezek 34:2, 5, 7-10). With the failure of these shepherds the promise was given that God would raise up true shepherds (Jer 23:4) and that God would be the shepherd of Israel (Ezek 34:12, 15). The promised Davidic king would be a shepherd (Ezek 34:23, 24), and even the Persian king Cyrus, who was responsible for the rebuilding of Jerusalem and its temple, was called shepherd (Isa 44:28). The evangelist has already announced that the shepherd-leader of Israel is now present in Jesus, and those

---

[1][for the heav]ens and the earth will listen to his anointed one [למשיחו],
[6]and his spirit will hover upon the poor, and he will renew the faithful with his strength.
[7]For he will honour the pious upon the throne of an eternal kingdom,
[8]freeing prisoners, giving sight to the blind, straightening out the twis[ted].
[11]And the Lord will perform marvelous acts such as have not existed, just as he sa[id]
[12]he will heal the badly wounded and will make the dead live, he will proclaim good news to the poor.
For further discussion, see Andrew B. Perrin, "From Qumran to Nazareth: Reflections on Jesus' Identity as Messiah in Light of Pre-Christian Messianic Texts among the Dead Sea Scrolls," *RelStTh* 27 (2008): 213–30.

13. John Ashton (*Understanding the Fourth Gospel* [Oxford: Clarendon, 1996], 273–78) discusses the place of miraculous signs associated with eschatological figures such as the "prophet like Moses" and Elijah. Within Israel's Scriptures there is no clear evidence that such signs and wonders were to accompany the Messiah, but from the comments in 7:31 it seems that this may have been a popular expectation with some.

14. On the kingship theme hinted at in the Gospel and its links with the shepherd image, see Adele Reinhartz, *The Word in the World: The Cosmological Tale in the Fourth Gospel*, SBLMS 45 (Atlanta: Scholars Press, 1992), 110–12.

who belong to him hear and follow his voice (10:3, 4, 27) and are given eternity life (10:28).

The discussion has now moved from an initial query about Jesus's messianic status to a redefining of the Messiah as the long-awaited Shepherd-Leader. Since Israel's primary Shepherd is God, Jesus can only claim to be the Shepherd-Leader and the giver of eternity life because of his union with God (1:1). The image of "the Father's hand" (v. 29) speaks of the power of God's hand displayed throughout Israel's history of salvation (cf. Exod 13:14; 15:6; Ps 118:15; Isa 48:13), but by the first century BCE God's salvific activity is reinterpreted and attributed to Wisdom. So it is the hand of Sophia that created the world (Wis 11:17), guided the ark of Noah (Wis 14:6), and enabled the escape from Egypt (Wis 16:15; 19:8). The Wisdom Christology of the prologue comes to the fore in Jesus's final words, "The Father and I are one" (v. 30). Recall from the discussion of the prologue that the Word (1:1-5) has the same characteristics of preexistent Sophia, through whom all things were created (Prov 8:22-31; Sir 24:3-5; Wis 7:22-27) and who is the life and light of all things (Prov 3:18; 8:35; Wis 6:12; 7:25-26); she dwells with God (Prov 8:27-30), and God intensely delights (שעשעים) in her (Prov 8:30). Like Wisdom/Sophia, who searched for and found a place to tabernacle (κατασκήνωσον) within Israel (Sir 24:8-10), so the "Word became flesh and tabernacled [ἐσκήνωσεν] among us" (1:14).

This is the first time in the *narrative* that the intimate union of God and the Word (1:1) is voiced explicitly as the union of Jesus and his Father (cf. 1:18), yet the Gospel never collapses the distinction between them.[15] The distinction is there when Jesus speaks of his Father as "greater" and as the one who gave him the sheep (10:29). The distinction in union is best expressed in terms such as loving mutuality or reciprocity. Jesus's response has gone far beyond the expectations of "the Jews'" initial query about his messianic status. His hearers do not believe what they have been told (v. 25) or the works they have seen (v. 26). They hear his claim of union with God as blasphemy and take up stones against him as they had done once before in the Feast of Tabernacles (8:59).

---

15. John Painter ("Tradition, History and Interpretation in John 10," in *The Shepherd Discourse of John 10 and Its Context*, ed. Johannes Beutler and Robert Fortna, SNTSMS 67 [Cambridge: Cambridge University Press, 1991], 69) maintains the unity and distinction by speaking of ontological equality and functional subordination.

The Consecrated and Sent One

The second section, while still a reply to the initial query, "If you are the Christ tell us plainly" (v. 24), continues to develop the theme of Jesus's identity, only now it is clarifying his relationship with God. "The Jews" state clearly their opposition to Jesus, "you, being human, make yourself divine" (v. 33), which to them is blasphemy, recalling the claims of Antiochus IV. This is the charge "the Jews" will later bring to Pilate demanding the death penalty, "We have a law, and by that law he ought to die, because he has *made himself* son of God" (19:7; RSV, emphasis added). To defend himself Jesus appeals to the witness of the Scriptures and quotes from LXX Psalm 81:6, "I said, you are gods" (v. 34).[16] It is not clear who are the "gods" being addressed: angels, members of God's heavenly court, Israel's judges,[17] those Israelites who were gathered at Sinai,[18] or if the psalm reflects Israel's early polytheism.[19] Here, Jesus is using an argument following a rabbinic principle of arguing from the lesser to the greater (*a minori ad maius*).[20] If the ones who *receive* the word of God can be called "gods," how much more should the one who *is* himself the Word (1:1) be able to call himself "Son of God." Augustine comments:

> If the word of God came to men, that they might be called gods, how can the very Word of God, who is with God, be otherwise than God? If by the word of God, men [and women] become gods, if by fellowship

16. LXX: ἐγὼ εἶπα Θεοί ἐστε καὶ υἱοὶ ὑψίστου πάντες; "I said, 'you are gods and all of you, children of the most high'" (82:6).

17. Bruce G. Schuchard (*Scripture within Scripture: The Interrelationship of Form and Function in the Explicit Old Testament Citations in the Gospel of John*, SBLDS 133 [Atlanta: Scholars Press, 1992], 66–67) contends that Israel's judges shared in the prerogatives given to Moses who was said to be like God (Exod 4:16; 7:1), therefore they too could be called "gods."

18. Later Jewish midrash claims that those who received God's word at Sinai were "gods" and shared the divine quality of immortality until they sinned and lost this. "R. Jose says: It was upon this condition that the Israelites stood up before Mount Sinai, on condition that the Angel of Death should have no power over them. For it is said: 'I said: Ye are godlike beings' (Ps. 82.6)." "Baḥodesh 9:80," in *Mekilta De-Rabbi Ishmael*, ed. Jacob Zallel Lauterbach (Dulles: Jewish Publication Society, 2004). See also, Marianne Meye Thompson, *John: A Commentary*, NTL (Louisville: Westminster John Knox, 2015), 235–36.

19. Michael S. Heiser, "Monotheism, Polytheism, Monolatry, or Henotheism? Toward an Assessment of Divine Plurality in the Hebrew Bible," *BBR* 18 (2008): 1–30.

20. Yee, *Jewish Feasts*, 91; Francis J. Moloney, *Signs and Shadows: Reading John 5–12* (Minneapolis: Fortress, 1996), 149; Frédéric Manns, *L'Evangile de Jean à la lumière du Judaïsme*, SBFA 33 (Jerusalem: Franciscan Printing Press, 1991), 313–14.

they become gods, can He by whom they have fellowship not be God? (Augustine, *Homilies on the Gospel of John*, Tract. 48.9)

An explicit link is made between the Feast of Hanukkah and Jesus's identity in verse 36 when Jesus speaks of himself as the "consecrated/ sanctified and sent" one (ἡγίασεν καὶ ἀπέστειλεν) of the Father. In the restoration program following the victory of the Maccabees, the same verb, ἀγιάζω, "consecrated," is used to describe the consecration of the temple courts (LXX: 1 Macc 4:48; 3 Macc 2:9, 16). The very word central to the celebration of Dedication is now applied to Jesus. The Mosaic tabernacle and the Solomonic temple had also been consecrated by God (Ps 45:4; 2 Chr 7:20; 30:8) and filled with God's glory (Exod 40:34-35; 2 Chr 7:3). As Wisdom was the tabernacling presence (Sir 24:8-18) and glory (Sir 24:2; Wis 7:25; 9:11) of God in the world, Jesus is now the tabernacling presence of God enfleshed and the new locus of God's glory (1:14).[21] As in the tabernacle and the temple, God's glory dwells in him, consecrating him as a new House of God (2:21).[22]

"The Jews" recognize as God the one whom Jesus calls "Father," as shown by their readiness to stone him for blasphemy. He then supports his claims by once again appealing to his works (v. 37; cf. v. 25). Because Jesus is son (1:18) he does the work of his Father (John 5:19). The works of the son give evidence of his paternity. This principle has run throughout the feasts of "the Jews." In the Sabbath controversy of chapter 5, Jesus had said that the son can do "only what he sees the Father doing" (5:19). The works Jesus has done in giving fuller life and forgiveness on the Sabbath (chap. 5), in giving bread to the multitude at Passover (chap. 6), and in giving light to a man born in darkness during Tabernacles (chap. 9) should be sufficient for his opponents to recognize in him the God of their festivals. They should by now know and understand that "the Father is in me and I am in the Father" (v. 36).

"The Jews" respond to Jesus's words by trying to arrest him, as they had done previously at the Feast of Tabernacles (7:32, 44; 8:20). Jesus then moves out of the temple, away from Jerusalem and to the east across the Jordan (10:40). This movement of one who is the consecrated dwelling-place of God's glory is ominous. During the Feast of Tabernacles Jesus

---

21. Jesus can rightfully be called the *Shekinah*, the Aramaic term from the targums to describe the numinous presence of God in the world. See the discussion of the *Shekinah* and targums (pp. 23–26).

22. See also the significance of the term "glory" in relation to the Aramaic word *Shekinah* in the excursus on the targums in the discussion of the prologue (1:1-18).

is within the temple (7:14). Following his initial confrontation with "the Jews" he moves outside (8:59). At the Festival of Dedication, Jesus walks in the colonnades around the perimeter of the temple courts (10:23). With the final refusal of "the Jews" to believe either his words or his works, Jesus permanently leaves the temple mount. He goes east, probably crossing the Mount of Olives and then across the Jordan. Jesus's movement from within the temple, to the colonnades, then eastward across the Jordan traces the path of God's glory when it left the Solomonic temple prior to its destruction by the Babylonians (Ezek 10:18-19; 11:23). In the Gospel, God's glory will next be manifested in the hour of Jesus's death and resurrection, prefigured in the next section of the Gospel in the raising of Lazarus.

From the perspective of the Johannine community, Jesus has celebrated the great festivals of his people and revealed, in his own person, the rich salvation offered in Israel's traditions and worship. In his coming, Israel's hopes have now been realized and their meaning given a new focus. "For John, the institutions of Judaism serve a definite divine purpose. . . . They function as living prophecies pointing to the eschatological salvation of Jesus. The coming of Jesus, therefore, witnesses not the casting aside of Judaism but the 'filling up to the top' of its various institutions."[23]

Conclusion

During the cycle of Israel's feasts, throughout chapters 5–10, Jesus has come up to Jerusalem in obedience to the requirements of Torah. He has offered life and judgment on the Sabbath, bread during Passover, light and water at Tabernacles, and his own consecrated presence, which is the presence of Israel's God, during Dedication. The narrative has shown that during this time with "his own" some have refused to see the glory of God now revealed in their midst in the person of Jesus, as witnessed by his words and works. Within the Feast of Dedication, Jesus twice affirms that, in his very person, Israel encounters the presence of his Father (10:30, 38). The God of Israel's festivals is embodied in their midst, no longer in symbols or rituals but in the flesh (σάρξ) of Jesus. The year's cycle of feasts comes to its dramatic climax in this revelation, "The Father and I are one" (v. 30; cf. v. 38), and some of "the Jews" give

---

23. Gerry Wheaton, *The Role of Jewish Feasts in John's Gospel*, SNTSMS 162 (Cambridge: Cambridge University Press, 2015), 185.

their definitive response, "they tried to arrest him" (v. 39). The words of the prologue are now fulfilled, "he came to his own, and his own did not receive him" (1:11). At a festival reaffirming their faith in Israel's God and repudiating idolatry, some have rejected Jesus and in so doing have rejected the Father. The glory of the God of Israel, revealed in Jesus, permanently leaves the temple building.

Jesus's experience parallels the experience of Sophia as recorded in 1 Enoch 42.[24] "Wisdom went out in order to dwell among the sons of men, but did not find a dwelling, wisdom returned to her place and took her seat in the midst of the angels."[25] Wisdom cannot find a home within humankind and so must return. The book of Wisdom similarly describes the experience of the righteous one at the hand of disbelievers:

> [H]e calls the last end of the righteous happy,
> and boasts that God is his father.
> Let us see if his words are true,
> and let us test what will happen at the end of his life. (Wis 2:16-17)

Such Second Temple writings provide an ominous background to the conflicts Jesus/Sophia has encountered across the narrative (John 1–10). The next volume will demonstrate how Wisdom is tested and returns to her place, where she existed with God "at the beginning of God's works" (Prov 8:22).

Women and the Cult

Across the narrative so far Jesus has been in the temple for Passover (2:13-22), Tabernacles (chaps. 7 and 8), and Dedication (10:22-42), and yet he has not been shown as a participant in any of the cultic rituals. On the contrary, during Passover he drove out the sacrificial animals and overturned the tables that enabled payment of the tax to support the temple (2:14); at Tabernacles he appropriated to himself the signs of the main rituals, water (7:37), light (8:12), and the recitation of "I am" (8:58). During Dedication he identified himself as the Consecrated One (10:36). In all these ways Jesus has

---

24. The dating of the Parables of Enoch is still contentious. A strong argument is presented that this section of Enoch was composed at the end of the first century, around the same time as the writing of John's Gospel. See Michael A. Knibb, "The Date of the Parables of Enoch: A Critical Review," *NTS* 25 (1979): 358.

25. John Ashton, "The Transformation of Wisdom: A Study of the Prologue of John's Gospel," *NTS* 32 (1986): 168–69.

shown that he lived out his words to the Samaritan woman: worship must be in spirit and truth and need no longer be in temples, "neither on this mountain nor in Jerusalem" (4:21). Jesus/Sophia is the presence of the God sought in the cult, if only this could be recognized.

The Jewish temple cult was exclusively male. Only some men could be priests and Levites; only the men could advance into the court of Israel; only men were obliged to attend the temple rituals. Women were kept on the boundaries by many man-made rules and architecture. Through the cult, and its sacrificial bloodletting, men sought communion with God, while the natural bloodletting of women was a pollution in their eyes.

Women know innately that they participate in the life-giving power of God and their bodies are all the temple they need. The very rhythm of their cycle is a constant sign of God's presence in their being. They need no external killing and bloodletting, as a woman's womb is sufficient holy space for God to occupy. Their holy of holies lies within, not without. Women do not need a temple or its cult to be in communion with God and to participate in God's being in creation.

Works Cited

Adelman, Penina V. "A Drink from Miriam's Cup: Invention of Tradition among Jewish Women." *JFSR* 10 (1994): 151–66.

———. *Miriam's Well: Rituals for Jewish Women around the Year*. New York: Biblio Press, 1986.

Akala, Adesola Joan. *The Son-Father Relationship and Christological Symbolism in the Gospel of John*. LNTS 505. London: Bloomsbury T&T Clark, 2014.

Aland, Kurt, and Barbara Aland. *The Text of the New Testament: An Introduction to the Critical Editions and to the Theory and Practice of Modern Textual Criticism*. Grand Rapids: Eerdmans, 1987.

Alexander, Philip. "Targum." *ABD* 6 (1992): 320–31.

Alison, James. *Raising Abel: The Recovery of the Eschatological Imagination*. New York: Crossroad, 1996.

Allen, Sr. Prudence. *The Concept of Woman: The Aristotelian Revolution, 750 B.C.–A.D. 1250*. Grand Rapids: Eerdmans, 1985.

Allison, Dale C., Jr. *Constructing Jesus: Memory, Imagination, and History*. Grand Rapids: Baker Academic, 2010.

Alter, Robert. *The Art of Biblical Narrative*. New York: Basic Books, 1981.

Anderson, Robert T. "Samaritans." *ABD* 7 (1996): 940–47.

Arndt, William. "γίνομαι." BDAG (2000): 197–99

Ashton, John. "The Identity and Function of the *Ioudaioi* in the Fourth Gospel." *NovT* 27 (1985): 40–75.

———. "The Transformation of Wisdom: A Study of the Prologue of John's Gospel." *NTS* 32 (1986): 161–86.

———. *Understanding the Fourth Gospel*. Oxford: Clarendon, 1996.

Asiedu-Peprah, Martin. *Johannine Sabbath Conflicts as Juridical Controversy*. WUNT 2/132. Tübingen: Mohr Siebeck, 2001.

"Baḥodesh 9:80." In *Mekilta De-Rabbi Ishmael*, edited by Jacob Zallel Lauterbach. Philadelphia: Jewish Publication Society, 2004.

Barker, Margaret. *The Gate of Heaven: The History and Symbolism of the Temple in Jerusalem*. London: SPCK, 1991.

Barrett, Charles K. *The Gospel according to St John*. 2nd ed. London: SPCK, 1978.

Bassler, Jouette M. "Mixed Signals: Nicodemus in the Fourth Gospel." *JBL* 108 (1989): 635–46.

Beasley-Murray, George R. *John*. WBC 36. Waco, TX: Word Books, 1987.

Beavis, Mary Ann. "From the Margin to the Way: A Feminist Reading of the Story of Bartimaeus." *JFSR* 14 (1998): 19–39.

Bechtel, Lyn M. "A Symbolic Level of Meaning: John 2.1-11." In *A Feminist Companion to the Hebrew Bible in the New Testament*, edited by Athalya Brenner, 241–55. FCB. Sheffield: Sheffield Academic, 1996.

Beck, David R. *The Discipleship Paradigm: Readers and Anonymous Characters in the Fourth Gospel*. BibInt 27. Leiden: Brill, 1997.

Behm, Johannes. "κλάω, κλάσις, κλάσμα." *TDNT* 3 (1965): 726–43.

———. "κοιλία." *TDNT* 3 (1965): 786–89.

Beirne, Margaret M. *Women and Men in the Fourth Gospel: A Genuine Discipleship of Equals*. JSNTSup 242. London: Sheffield Academic, 2003.

Ben Ezra, Daniel Stökl. *The Impact of Yom Kippur on Early Christianity: The Day of Atonement from Second Temple Judaism to the Fifth Century*. WUNT 163. Tübingen: Mohr Siebeck, 2003.

Bertram, Georg. "ἔργον." *TDNT* 2 (1964): 635–55.

———. "ὑψόω." *TDNT* 8 (1972): 606–13.

Betsworth, Sharon. *Children in Early Christian Narratives*. New York: Bloomsbury T&T Clark, 2015.

Biale, David. "The God with Breasts: El Shaddai in the Bible." *HR* 21 (1982): 240–56.

Bienaimé, Germaine. *Moïse et le don de l'eau dans la tradition juive ancienne: Targum et Midrash*. AnBib 98. Rome: Biblical Institute Press, 1984.

Bieringer, Reimund, Didier Pollefeyt, and Frederique Vandecasteele-Vanneuville, eds. *Anti-Judaism and the Fourth Gospel*. Louisville: Westminster John Knox, 2001.

Bird, Phyllis A. "Women: Old Testament." *ABD* 6 (1992): 951–57.

Bishop, E. F. F. " 'Door of the Sheep': John 10:7-9." *ExpTim* 71 (1960): 307–9.

Blass, Friedrich, Albert Debrunner, and Robert W. Funk. *A Greek Grammar of the New Testament and Other Early Christian Literature*. Cambridge: Cambridge University Press, 1961.

Blenkinsopp, Joseph. *Creation, Un-creation, Re-creation: A Discursive Commentary on Genesis 1–11*. London: T&T Clark, 2011.

Boismard, Marie-Émile. "L'ami de l'Époux (Jo., 111, 29)." In *A la recontre de Dieu: Mémorial Albert Gelin*, edited by A. Barucq, J. Duplacy, A. George, and H. de Lubac. Bibliothèque de la Faculté Catholique de Théologie de Lyon 8, 289–95. Le Puy: Xavier Mappus, 1961.

————. *Moses or Jesus: An Essay in Johannine Christology*. Translated by Benedict T. Viviano. Minneapolis: Fortress, 1993.

Borgen, Peder. *Bread from Heaven: An Exegetical Study of the Concept of Manna in the Gospel of John and the Writings of Philo*. NovTSup 10. Leiden: Brill, 1965.

————. *The Gospel of John: More Light from Philo, Paul and Archaeology; The Scriptures, Tradition, Exposition, Settings, Meaning*. NovTSup 154 Leiden: Brill, 2014.

Boring, M. Eugene. "Seven, Seventh, Seventy." *NIDB* 5 (2009): 197–99.

Bornhäuser, K. B. *Das Johannesevangelium: Eine Missionschrift für Israel*. Gütersloh: Bertelsmann, 1928.

Borowsky, Irvin J., ed. *Defining New Christian/Jewish Dialogue*. New York: Crossroad, 2004.

Boyarin, Daniel. *Border Lines: The Partition of Judaeo-Christianity*. Philadelphia: University of Pennsylvania Press, 2004.

————. "The Gospel of the Memra: Jewish Binitarianism and the Prologue to John." *HTR* 94 (2001): 243–84.

————. "The Ioudaioi in John and the Prehistory of Judaism." In *Pauline Conversations in Context: Essays in Honor of Calvin J. Roetzel*, edited by Janice Capel Anderson, Philip Sellew, and Claudia Setzer, 216–39. Sheffield: Sheffield Academic, 2002.

Bratcher, Robert G. "What Does 'Glory' Mean in Relation to Jesus? Translating *doxa* and *doxazo* in John." *BT* 42 (1991): 401–8.

Brown, Raymond E. *The Community of the Beloved Disciple: The Life, Loves, and Hates of an Individual Church in New Testament Times*. New York: Paulist Press, 1979.

————. *The Gospel according to John*. 2 vols. AB 29–29A. New York: Doubleday, 1966, 1970.

————. *An Introduction to the Gospel of John: Edited, Updated, Introduced and Concluded by Francis J. Moloney*. ABRL. New York: Doubleday, 2003.

Bruns, J. Edgar. "Use of Time in the Fourth Gospel." *NTS* 13 (1967): 285–90.

Büchsel, Friedrich. "Ἀντί." *TDNT* 1 (1964): 372–73.

————. "κρίνω." *TDNT* 3 (1965): 921–22.

————. "Μονογενής." *TDNT* 4 (1967): 737–38.

Bultmann, Rudolph. *The Gospel of John: A Commentary*. Translated by G. R. Beasley Murray et al. Oxford: Blackwell, 1971.

Burge, Garry H. *The Anointed Community: The Holy Spirit in the Johannine Community*. Grand Rapids: Eerdmans, 1987.

Byrne, Brendan. *Life Abounding: A Reading of John's Gospel*. Collegeville, MN: Liturgical Press, 2014.

Carson, Donald A. *The Gospel according to John*. Grand Rapids: Eerdmans, 1991.

Carter, Warren. "The Prologue and John's Gospel: Function, Symbol and the Definitive Word." *JSNT* 39 (1990): 35–58.

Cathcart, Kevin, Michael Maher, and Martin McNamara, eds. *Targum Neofiti 1: Genesis*. The Aramaic Bible 1A. Collegeville, MN: Liturgical Press, 1990.

————, eds. *Targum Pseudo-Jonathan: Genesis*. The Aramaic Bible 1B. Collegeville, MN: Liturgical Press, 1992.

Charlesworth, James H. "The Historical Jesus in the Fourth Gospel: A Paradigm Shift?" *JSHJ* 8 (2010): 3–46.

———, ed. *The Old Testament Pseudepigrapha*. 2 vols. London: Darton, Longman & Todd, 1985.

Chennattu, Rheka M. *Johannine Discipleship as a Covenant Relationship*. Peabody, MA: Hendrickson, 2006.

Chilton, Bruce, and Jacob Neusner, eds. *In Quest of the Historical Pharisees*. Waco, TX: Baylor University Press, 2007.

Christie, Douglas E. "The Insurmountable Darkness of Love: Contemplative Practice in a Time of Loss." *Cross Currents* 69 (2019): 105–27.

C. L. "Épitaphe de la diaconesse Sophie." *RB* 1 (1904): 260–62.

Cohen, Shaye J. D. *Boundaries, Varieties, Uncertainties*. Berkeley: University of California Press, 1999.

Collins, John J. *Jewish Cult and Hellenistic Culture: Essays on the Jewish Encounter with Hellenism and Roman Rule*. Leiden: Brill, 2005.

———. *Jewish Wisdom in the Hellenistic Age*. Edinburgh: T&T Clark, 1997.

Collins, Marilyn F. "The Hidden Vessels in Samaritan Traditions." *JSJ* 3 (1973): 97–116.

Collins, Raymond F. *These Things Have Been Written: Studies on the Fourth Gospel*. Louvain Theological and Pastoral Monographs 2. Louvain: Peeters, 1990.

Coloe, Mary L. " 'Behold the Lamb of God': John 1:29 and the Tamid Service." In *Rediscovering John: Essays on the Fourth Gospel in Honour of Frédéric Manns*, edited by L. Daniel Chrupcala, 337–50. SBFA 80. Milan: Editioni Terra Santa, 2013.

———. *Dwelling in the Household of God: Johannine Ecclesiology and Spirituality*. Collegeville, MN: Liturgical Press, 2007.

———. " 'The End Is Where We Start From': Afterlife in the Fourth Gospel." In *Living Hope—Eternal Death?! Conceptions of the Afterlife in Hellenism, Judaism and Christianity*, edited by Manfred Lang and Michael Labhan, 177–99. Leipzig: Evangelische Verlagsanstalt, 2007.

———. *God Dwells with Us: Temple Symbolism in the Fourth Gospel*. Collegeville, MN: Liturgical Press, 2001.

———. "The Johannine Pentecost: John 1:19–2:12." *ABR* 55 (2007): 41–56.

———. "The Mother of Jesus: A Woman Possessed." In *Character Studies in the Fourth Gospel: Narrative Approaches to Seventy Figures in John*, edited by Steven A. Hunt, D. Francois Tolmie, and Ruben Zimmermann, 202–13. WUNT 314. Tübingen: Mohr Siebeck, 2013.

———. "Response: The Beyond Beckons." In *What We Have Heard from the Beginning: The Past, Present and Future of Johannine Studies*, edited by Tom Thatcher, 211–14. Waco, TX: Baylor University Press, 2007.

———. "The Structure of the Johannine Prologue and Genesis 1." *ABR* 45 (1997): 40–55.

Coloe, Mary, and Tom Thatcher, eds. *John, Qumran, and the Dead Sea Scrolls: Sixty Years of Discovery and Debate*. EJL 32. Atlanta: SBL, 2011.

Connolly, R. Hugh. *Didascalia Apostolorum*. Oxford: Clarendon, 1929.

Conway, Colleen M. "Gender Matters in John." In *A Feminist Companion to John*, vol. 2, edited by Amy-Jill Levine with Marianne Blickenstaff, 79–103. FCNTECW 5. London: Sheffield Academic, 2003.

———. *Men and Women in the Fourth Gospel: Gender and Johannine Characterization*. SBLDS 167. Atlanta: SBL, 1999.

Corbo, Virgilio C. "Capharnaüm." *RB* 78 (1971): 588–91.

Cortés, Juan B. "Yet Another Look at Jn 7,37-38." *CBQ* 29 (1967): 75–86.

Culpepper, R. Alan, and Paul N. Anderson, eds. *John and Judaism: A Contested Relationship in Context*. RBS 87. Atlanta: SBL, 2017.

Culpepper, R. Alan. *Anatomy of the Fourth Gospel: A Study in Literary Design*. New Testament: FF. Philadelphia: Fortress 1983.

———. "Nicodemus: The Travail of New Birth." In *Character Studies in the Fourth Gospel: Narrative Approaches to Seventy Figures in John*, edited by Steven A. Hunt, D. Francois Tolmie, and Ruben Zimmermann, 249–59. WUNT 314. Tübingen: Mohr Siebeck, 2013.

Cunningham, Philip A. *Seeking Shalom: The Journey to Right Relationship between Catholics and Jews*. Grand Rapids: Eerdmans, 2015.

Daise, Michael A. *Feasts in John: Jewish Festivals and Jesus' "Hour" in the Fourth Gospel*. WUNT 2:229. Tübingen: Mohr Siebeck, 2007.

Daly-Denton, Margaret. *John: An Earth Bible Commentary; Supposing Him to Be the Gardener*. Earth Bible Commentary. London: Bloomsbury T&T Clark, 2017.

D'Angelo, Mary Rose. "Abba and 'Father': Imperial Theology and the Jesus Traditions." *JBL* (1992): 611–30.

de Jong, Henk Jan. "'The Jews' in the Gospel of John." In *Anti-Judaism and the Fourth Gospel*, edited by Reimund Bieringer, Didier Pollefeyt, and Frederique Vandecasteele-Vanneuville, 121–40. Louisville: Westminster John Knox, 2001.

De La Potterie, Ignace. "Οἶδα et γινώσκω: Les deux modes de la connaissance dans le quatrième évangile." *Bib* 40 (1959): 709–25.

Dewey, Joanna. "Sacrifice No More." *BTB* 41 (2011): 68–75.

Díez Macho, Alejandro. "Targum y Nuevo Testamento." In *Mélanges Eugène Tisserant*, 153–85. Vatican: Biblioteca apostolica vaticana, 1964.

Dimant, Devorah. "Between Qumran Sectarian and Non-Sectarian Texts: The Case of Belial and Mastema." In *The Dead Sea Scrolls and Contemporary Culture: Proceedings of the International Conference Held at the Israel Museum, Jerusalem (July 6–8, 2008)*, edited by Shani Tzoref, Lawrence H. Schiffman, and Adolfo Daniel Roitman, 235–56. Leiden: Brill, 2011.

Dodd, Charles H. "Behind a Johannine Dialogue." In *More New Testament Studies*, edited by Charles H. Dodd, 41–57. Manchester: Manchester University Press, 1968.

———. "A Hidden Parable in the Fourth Gospel." In *More New Testament Studies*, edited by Charles H. Dodd, 30–40. Manchester: Manchester University Press, 1968.

————. *Historical Tradition in the Fourth Gospel*. New York: Cambridge University Press, 1963.

————. *The Interpretation of the Fourth Gospel*. Cambridge: Cambridge University Press, 1970.

Donaldson, Terence L. *Jews and Anti-Judaism in the New Testament: Decision Points and Divergent Interpretations*. Waco, TX: Baylor University Press, 2010.

Donin, Hayim H., ed. *Sukkot*. Popular Judaica Library. Jerusalem: Keter Books, 1974.

Douglas, Sally. *Early Church Understandings of Jesus as the Female Divine: The Scandal of the Scandal of Particularity*. LNTS 557. London: Bloomsbury T&T Clark, 2016.

Duke, Paul. *Irony in the Fourth Gospel*. Atlanta: John Knox, 1985.

Dunn, James D. G. "The Embarrassment of History: Reflections on the Problem of 'Anti-Judaism' in the Fourth Gospel." In *Anti-Judaism and the Fourth Gospel*, edited by Reimund Bieringer, Didier Pollefeyt, and Frederique Vandecasteele-Vanneuville, 41–60. Louisville: Westminster John Knox, 2001.

————, ed. *Jews and Christians: The Parting of the Ways A.D. 70 to 135*. Grand Rapids: Eerdmans, 1999.

Dunne, John S. *The Homing Spirit: A Pilgrimage of the Mind, of the Heart, of the Soul*. New York: Crossroad, 1987.

Durand, Gilbert. *L'imagination symbolique*. Initiation philosophique. Paris: PUF, 1968.

Edersheim, Alfred. *The Temple: Its Ministry and Services*. Updated ed. Peabody, MA: Hendrickson, 1994.

Edwards, Matthew. *Pneuma and Realized Eschatology in the Book of Wisdom*. FRLANT 242. Göttingen: Vandenhoeck & Ruprecht, 2012.

Edwards, Ruth B. *Discovering John: Content, Interpretation, Reception*. DisBT. Grand Rapids: Eerdmans, 2015.

————. "ΧΑΡΙΝ ΑΝΤΙ ΧΑΡΙΤΟΣ (John 1:16): Grace and the Law in the Johannine Prologue." *JSNT* 32 (1988): 3–15.

Eisen, Ute E. *Women Officeholders in Early Christianity: Epigraphical and Literary Studies*. Collegeville, MN: Liturgical Press, 2000.

Eisenberg, Ronald L. *Jewish Traditions: A JPS Guide*. Philadelphia: Jewish Publication Society, 2008.

Estes, Douglas, and Ruth Sheridan. *How John Works: Storytelling in the Fourth Gospel*. SBLRBS 86. Atlanta: SBL, 2016.

Evans, Craig. *Word and Glory: On the Exegetical and Theological Background of John's Gospel*. JSNTSup 89. Sheffield: JSOT Press, 1993.

Fawcett, Thomas. *The Symbolic Language of Religion: An Introductory Study*. London: SCM, 1970.

Fehribach, Adeline. "The 'Birthing' Bridegroom: The Portrayal of Jesus in the Fourth Gospel." In *A Feminist Companion to John*, vol. 2, edited by Amy-Jill

Levine with Marianne Blickenstaff, 104–29. FCNTECW 5. London: Sheffield Academic, 2003.

———. *The Women in the Life of the Bridegroom: A Feminist Historical-Literary Analysis of the Female Characters in the Fourth Gospel*. Collegeville, MN: Liturgical Press, 1998.

Fohrer, Georg. "Σιών." *TDNT* 7 (1971): 292–319.

Ford, Josephine Massyngbaerde. *Redeemer—Friend and Mother: Salvation in Antiquity and in the Gospel of John*. Minneapolis: Fortress, 1997.

Frayer-Griggs, Daniel. "Spittle, Clay, and Creation in John 9:6 and Some Dead Sea Scrolls." *JBL* 132 (2013): 659–70.

Fredriksen, Paula. *When Christians Were Jews: The First Generation*. New Haven: Yale University Press, 2018.

Fredriksen, Paula, and Adele Reinhartz, eds. *Jesus, Judaism and Christian Anti-Judaism: Reading the New Testament after the Holocaust*. Louisville: Westminster John Knox, 2002.

Freed, Edwin D. *Old Testament Quotations in the Gospel of John*. NovTSup 11. Leiden: Brill, 1965.

Frey, Jörg. *Die johanneische Eschatologie: Die eschatologische Verkündigung in den johanneischen Texten*. Vol. 3. WUNT 117. Tübingen: Mohr Siebeck, 2000.

———. "Eschatology in the Johannine Circle." In *Theology and Christology in the Fourth Gospel: Essays by the Members of the SNTS Johannine Writings Seminar*, edited by Gilbert Van Belle, Jan G. van der Watt, and P. Maritz, 47–82. Leuven: Peeters, 2005.

———. *The Glory of the Crucified One: Christology and Theology in the Gospel of John*. Translated by Wayne Coppins and Christoph Heilig. BMSEC. Waco, TX: Baylor University Press, 2018.

Fullilove, William B. "Bethany beyond the Jordan." In *The Lexham Bible Dictionary*, edited by John D. Barry et al. Bellingham, WA: Lexham Press, 2016.

Furlong, Dean. *The Identity of John the Evangelist: Revision and Reinterpretation in Early Christian Sources*. Lanham, MD: Lexington/Fortress Academic, 2020.

García Martínez, Florentino, and Eibert J. C. Tigchelaar. *The Dead Sea Scrolls Study Edition (Translations)*. 2 vols. Leiden: Brill, 1997–1998.

Giblin, Marie J. "Dualism." In *Dictionary of Feminist Theologies*, edited by Letty M. Russell and J. Shannon Clarkson. Louisville: Westminster John Knox, 1996.

Glicksman, Andrew T. *Wisdom of Solomon 10: A Jewish Hellenistic Reinterpretation of Early Israelite History through Sapiential Lenses*. DCLS 9. Berlin: de Gruyter, 2011.

Goldenberg, David. "Racism, Color Symbolism, and Color Prejudice." In *The Origins of Racism in the West*, edited by Miriam Eliav-Feldon, Benjamin Isaac, and Joseph Ziegler, 88–108. Cambridge: Cambridge University Press, 2009.

Golding, Thomas A. "The Imagery of Shepherding in the Bible, Part 1." *BSac* 163 (2006): 18–28.

———. "The Imagery of Shepherding in the Bible, Part 2." *BSac* 163 (2006): 158–75.

Gordon, Julie K. "Yitro: We All Stood at Sinai." In *The Women's Torah Commentary: New Insights from Women Rabbis on the 54 Weekly Torah Portions*, edited by Elyse Goldstein. Woodstock, VT: Jewish Lights, 2000.

Gowan, Donald E. *Eschatology in the Old Testament*. Philadelphia: Fortress, 1986.

Green, Yosef. "Our Mother Rachel: Prima inter Pares." *JBQ* 33 (2005): 166–73.

Greenup, A. W. *Sukkah, Mishna and Tosefta: With Introduction, Translation and Short Notes*. Translations of Early Documents. Series 3. Rabbinic Texts. New York: Macmillan, 1925.

Grelot, Pierre. "Jean, VII, 38: Eau du rocher ou source du Temple?" *RB* 70 (1963): 43–51.

Grigsby, Bruce. " 'If Any Man Thirsts . . . ': Observations on the Rabbinic Background of John 7:37-39." *Bib* 67 (1986): 101–8.

Guardiola-Sáenz, Leticia. "Border Crossing and Its Redemptive Power in John 7:53–8:11: A Cultural Reading of Jesus and *The Accused*." In *Transformative Encounters: Jesus and Women Re-Viewed*, edited by Ingrid R. Kitzberger, 267–91. BibInt 43. Leiden: Brill, 2000.

Günther, Eva. *Wisdom as a Model for Jesus' Ministry: A Study on the "Lament over Jerusalem" in Matt 23:37-39 Par. Luke 13:34-35*. WUNT 2.513. Tübingen: Mohr Siebeck, 2020.

Hägerland, Tobias. "John's Gospel: A Two-Level Drama?" *JSNT* 25 (2003): 309–22.

Hakola, Raimo. *Identity Matters: John, the Jews and Jewishness*. NovTSup 18. Leiden: Brill, 2005.

Harner, Philip. *The "I Am" of the Fourth Gospel: A Study in Johannine Usage and Thought*. FBBS 26. Philadelphia: Fortress, 1970.

Harrington, Hannah K. "Clean and Unclean." *NIDB* 1 (2006): 681–89.

Hauck, Friedrich. "παροιμία." *TDNT* 5 (1967): 854–56.

———. "περισσεύω." *TDNT* 6 (1968): 58–63.

Hayward, C. T. R. *The Jewish Temple: A Non-Biblical Sourcebook*. London: Routledge, 1996.

Heiser, Michael S. "Monotheism, Polytheism, Monolatry, or Henotheism? Toward an Assessment of Divine Plurality in the Hebrew Bible." *BBR* 18 (2008): 1–30.

Hengel, Martin, and Charles K. Barrett. *Conflicts and Challenges in Early Christianity*. Harrisburg, PA: Trinity Press International, 1999.

Hertz, J. H., ed. *Pentateuch and Haftorahs: Hebrew Text English Translation and Commentary*. 2nd ed. London: Soncino, 1960.

Hiers, Richard H. *Justice and Compassion in Biblical Law*. New York: Continuum, 2009.

Hill, Charles E. *The Johannine Corpus in the Early Church*. Oxford: Oxford University Press, 2004.

Himmelfarb, Martha. "Afterlife and Resurrection." In *The Jewish Annotated New Testament*, edited by Amy-Jill Levine and Marc Zvi Brettler, 691–95. 2nd ed. Oxford: Oxford University Press, 2017.

Hodges, Zane. "Rivers of Living Water—John 7:37-39." *BSac* 136 (1979): 239–48.

Hoegen-Rohls, Christina. *Der nachösterliche Johannes: Die Abschiedsreden als hermeneutischer Schlüssel zum vierten Evangelium*. WUNT 2.84. Tübingen: Mohr Siebeck, 1996.

Holladay, William L., and Ludwig Köhler. "חיל." In *A Concise Hebrew and Aramaic Lexicon of the Old Testament*. Leiden: Brill, 2000.

Hooke, Samuel H. " 'The Spirit Was Not Yet.' " *NTS* 9 (1962–1963): 372–80.

Hunt, Steven A., D. Francois Tolmie, and Ruben Zimmerman, eds. *Character Studies in the Fourth Gospel: Narrative Approaches to Seventy Figures in John*. WUNT 314. Tübingen: Mohr Siebeck, 2013.

Hurowitz, Victor, and Shamir Yonah. *Marbeh Ḥokmah: Studies in the Bible and the Ancient Near East in Loving Memory of Victor Avigdor Hurowitz* [in English]. Winona Lake, IN: Eisenbrauns, 2015.

Hylen, Susan E. *Imperfect Believers: Ambiguous Characters in the Gospel of John*. Louisville: Westminster John Knox, 2009.

———. "Lamb." *NIDB* 3 (2008): 563.

Irarrázaval, Diego. "La otra globalización—anotación teológica." *Pasos* 77 (1998): 2–10.

Isherwood, Lisa, and Elizabeth Stuart. *Introducing Body Theology*. IFT 2. Sheffield: Sheffield Academic, 1998.

Jay, Nancy. *Throughout Your Generations Forever*. Chicago: CUP, 1992.

Jeremias, J. "νύμφη, νυμφίος." *TDNT* 4 (1967): 1099–1106.

Johnson, Elizabeth A. *Creation and the Cross: The Mercy of God for a Planet in Peril*. Maryknoll, NY: Orbis Books, 2018.

———. "Jesus, the Wisdom of God: A Biblical Basis for Non-Androcentric Christology." *ETL* 61 (1985): 261–94.

———. *She Who Is: The Mystery of God in Feminist Theological Discourse*. New York: Crossroad, 1992.

Jojko, Bernadeta. "Eternity and Time in the Gospel of John." *Verbum Vitae* 35 (2019): 245–78.

Jones, Larry Paul. *The Symbol of Water in the Gospel of John*. JSNTSup 145. Sheffield: Sheffield Academic, 1997.

Josephus, Flavius, and William Whiston. *The Works of Josephus: Complete and Unabridged*. Peabody, MA: Hendrickson, 1987.

Juel, Donald. *Messianic Exegesis: Christological Interpretation of the Old Testament in Early Christianity*. Philadelphia: Fortress, 1988.

Käsemann, Ernst. "The Structure and Purpose of the Prologue to John's Gospel." In *New Testament Questions of Today*, 138–67. London: SCM, 1969.

Keck, Leander E. "Derivation as Destiny: 'Of-ness' in Johannine Christology, Anthropology, and Soteriology." In *Exploring the Gospel of John: In Honor of D. Moody Smith*, edited by R. Alan Culpepper and C. Clifton Black, 274–88. Louisville: Westminster John Knox, 1996.

Keen, Karen R. "Sexuality, Critical Issues." In *The Lexham Bible Dictionary*, edited by John D. Barry et al. Bellingham, WA: Lexham Press, 2016.

Keener, Craig S. *The Gospel of John: A Commentary.* 2 vols. Peabody, MA: Hendrickson, 2003.

Keith, Chris. *Jesus' Literacy: Scribal Culture and the Teacher from Galilee.* Library of Historical Jesus Studies 8. LNTS 413. New York: T&T Clark, 2011.

———. "Recent and Previous Research on the *Pericope Adulterae* (John 7.53–8.11)." *CurBR* 6 (2008): 377–404.

———. "The Scribes and the Elders: Mirror Characterization of Jesus and His Opponents in the *Pericope Adulterae.*" In *Character Studies in the Fourth Gospel: Narrative Approaches to Seventy Figures in John,* edited by Steven A. Hunt, D. Francois Tolmie, and Ruben Zimmermann, 403–6. WUNT 314. Tübingen: Mohr Siebeck, 2013.

Kierspel, Lars. *'The Jews' and the World in the Fourth Gospel: Parallelism, Function and Context.* WUNT 2.20. Tübingen: Mohr Siebeck, 2006.

Kitzberger, Ingrid Rosa. "Transcending Gender Boundaries in John." In *A Feminist Companion to John,* vol. 1, edited by Amy-Jill Levine with Marianne Blickenstaff, 173–207. FCNTECW 4. London: Sheffield Academic, 2003.

Klink, Edward W., III. "Expulsion from the Synagogue? Rethinking a Johannine Anachronism." *TynBul* 59 (2008): 99–118.

———. *The Sheep of the Fold: The Audience and Origin of the Gospel of John.* SNTSMS 141. Cambridge: Cambridge University Press, 2007.

Kloppenborg, John S. "Isis and Sophia in the Book of Wisdom." *HTR* 75 (1982): 57–84.

Knibb, Michael A. "The Date of the Parables of Enoch: A Critical Review." *NTS* 25 (1979): 345–59.

Knust, Jennifer Wright, and Tommy Wasserman. *To Cast the First Stone: The Transmission of a Gospel Story.* Princeton: Princeton University Press, 2019.

Koester, Craig. "The Death of Jesus and the Human Condition: Exploring the Theology of John's Gospel." In *Life in Abundance: Studies of John's Gospel in Tribute to Raymond E. Brown,* edited by John R. Donahue, 141–57. Collegeville, MN: Liturgical Press, 2005.

———. *The Dwelling of God: The Tabernacle in the Old Testament, Intertestamental Jewish Literature, and the New Testament.* CBQMS 22. Washington, DC: Catholic Biblical Association of America, 1989.

———. "Messianic Exegesis and the Call of Nathanael (John 1.45-51)." *JSNT* 39 (1990): 23–34.

———. *Symbolism in the Fourth Gospel: Meaning, Mystery, Community.* Minneapolis: Fortress, 1995.

Kopas, Jane. "Jesus and Women: John's Gospel." *ThTo* 41 (1985): 201–5.

Köster, Helmut. "Ὑπόστασις." *TDNT* 8 (1972): 581–82.

Kysar, Robert D. "Johannine Metaphor—Meaning and Function: A Literary Case Study of John 10:1-8." *Semeia* 53 (1991): 81–111.

Labahn, Michale. "Between Tradition and Literary Art: The Miracle Tradition in the Fourth Gospel." *Bib* 80 (1999): 178–203.

LaCugna, Catherine Mowry. *God for Us: The Trinity and Christian Life*. San Francisco: HarperCollins, 1991.

Lampe, Peter. "The Eucharist: Identifying with Christ on the Cross." *Int* 48 (1994): 36–49.

Le Déaut, Roger. *The Message of the New Testament and the Aramaic Bible (Targum)*. SubBi 5. Rome: Biblical Institute Press, 1982.

———. "Miryam, soeur de Moïse, et Marie, mère du Messie." *Bib* 45 (1964): 198–219.

Leal, Juan. "El simbolismo histórico del IV Evangelio." *EstBíb* 19 (1960): 329–48.

Lee, Dorothy A. "Abiding in the Fourth Gospel: A Case-Study in Feminist Biblical Theology." *Pacifica* 10 (1997): 123–36.

———. "Abiding in the Fourth Gospel: A Case Study in Feminist Biblical Theology." In *A Feminist Companion to John*, vol. 2, edited by Amy-Jill Levine with Marianne Blickenstaff, 64–78. FCNTECW 5. London: Sheffield Academic, 2003.

———. "Beyond Suspicion? The Fatherhood of God in the Fourth Gospel." *Pacifica* 8 (1995): 140–54.

———. *Flesh and Glory: Symbolism, Gender and Theology in the Gospel of John*. New York: Crossroad, 2002.

———. "The Symbol of Divine Fatherhood." *Semeia* 85 (1999): 177–87.

———. *The Symbolic Narratives of the Fourth Gospel: The Interplay of Form and Meaning*. JSNTSup 95. Sheffield: JSOT Press, 1994.

———. "Touching the Sacred Text: The Bible as Icon in Feminist Reading." *Pacifica* 11 (1998): 249–64.

Léon-Dufour, Xavier. *Lecture de l'Évangile selon Jean*. Parole de Dieu. 4 vols. Paris: Seuil, 1988, 1990, 1993, 1996.

Levine, Etan. *The Aramaic Version of the Bible: Contents and Context*. Berlin: de Gruyter, 1988.

Levine, Lee I. *Jerusalem: Portrait of the City in the Second Temple Period (538 B.C.E.–70 C.E.)*. Philadelphia: JPS, 2002.

Lewis, Karoline M. *Rereading the "Shepherd Discourse": Restoring the Integrity of John 9:39–10:21*. StBibLit. New York: Lang, 2008.

Liddell, Henry G. "ὑπόστασις." In *A Lexicon: Abridged from Liddell and Scott's Greek-English Lexicon*. Oak Harbor, WA: Logos Research Systems, 1996.

———. "ἀδελφός." *A Lexicon: Abridged from Liddell and Scott's Greek-English Lexicon*. Oak Harbor, WA: Logos Research Systems, 1996.

———. "γεύω." In *A Lexicon: Abridged from Liddell and Scott's Greek-English Lexicon*. Oak Harbor, WA: Logos Research Systems, 1996.

Lieu, Judith M. "Anti-Judaism in the Fourth Gospel: Explanation and Hermeneutics." In *Anti-Judaism and the Fourth Gospel*, edited by Reimund Bieringer, Didier Pollefeyt, and Frederique Vandecasteele-Vanneuville, 101–17. Louisville: Westminster John Knox, 2001.

———. "Anti-Judaism, the Jews, and the Worlds of the Fourth Gospel." In *The Gospel of John and Christian Theology*, edited by Richard Bauckham and Carl Mosser, 168–82. Grand Rapids: Eerdmans, 2008.

————. "The Mother of the Son in the Fourth Gospel." *JBL* 117 (1998): 61–77.

————. *Neither Jew Nor Greek? Constructing Early Christianity*. SNTW. Edinburgh: T&T Clark, 2002.

————. "Scripture and the Feminine in John." In *A Feminist Companion to the Hebrew Bible in the New Testament*, edited by Athalya Brenner, 225–40. FCB. Sheffield: Sheffield Academic, 1996.

Lincoln, Andrew T. *The Gospel according to Saint John*. BNTC. London: Continuum, 2005.

Lindars, Barnabas. *The Gospel of John*. NCB. London: Oliphants, 1972.

Loader, William. "Wisdom and Logos Tradition in Judaism and John's Christology." In *Reading the Gospel of John's Christology as Jewish Messianism: Royal, Prophetic, and Divine Messiahs*, edited by Benjamin E. Reynolds and Gabriele Boccaccini, 303–34. AGJU 106. Leiden: Brill 2018.

Lohse, Eduard. "Σάββατον, Σαββατισμός, Παρασκευή." *TDNT* 7 (1971): 1–35.

Louw, Johannes P., and Eugene Albert Nida. *Greek-English Lexicon of the New Testament: Based on Semantic Domains*. Vol. 1. 2nd ed. New York: United Bible Societies, 1996.

————. "πατρίς." In *Greek-English Lexicon of the New Testament: Based on Semantic Domains*. New York: United Bible Societies, 1996.

Lovell, Beth M. *Mapping Metaphorical Discourse: John's Eternal King*. LBS 5. Leiden: Brill, 2012.

Lowe, Malcolm. "Who Were the ΙΟΥΔΑΙΟΙ?" *NovT* 18 (1976): 101–30.

Lüdemann, Gerd. "ὑψόω." *EDNT* 3 (1993): 410.

MacRae, George. "The Meaning and Evolution of the Feast of Tabernacles." *CBQ* 22 (1960): 251–76.

Macy, Gary. *The Hidden History of Women's Ordination: Female Clergy in the Medieval West*. New York: Oxford University Press, 2008.

Madigan, Kevin, and Carolyn Osiek. *Ordained Women in the Early Church: A Documentary History*. Baltimore: John Hopkins University Press, 2005.

Manns, Frédéric. *Jewish Prayer in the time of Jesus*. SBFA 22. Jerusalem: Franciscan Printing Press, 1994.

————. *L'Évangile de Jean à la lumière du Judaïsme*. SBFA 33. Jerusalem: Franciscan Printing Press, 1991.

————. *Le Symbole Eau-Esprit dans le Judaïsme Ancien*. SBFA 19. Jerusalem: Franciscan Printing Press, 1983.

Marcus, Joel. "*Birkat Ha-Minim* Revisited." *NTS* 55 (2009): 523–51.

Martyn, J. Louis. *History and Theology in the Fourth Gospel*. 2nd ed. Nashville: Abingdon, 1979.

————. *History and Theology in the Fourth Gospel*. New York: Harper and Row, 1968.

Maynard, Arthur H. "ΤΙ ΕΜΟΙ ΚΑΙ ΣΟΙ." *NTS* 31 (1985): 582–86.

McKnight, Scot. *Jesus and His Death: Historiography, the Historical Jesus, and Atonement Theory*. Waco, TX: Baylor University Press, 2005.

McLaren, James. "Corruption among the High Priesthood: A Matter of Perspective." In *A Wandering Galilean: Essays in Honour of Séan Freyne*, edited by Zuleika Rodgers with Margaret Daly-Denton and Anne Fitzpatrick McKinley, 141–57. JSJS 132. Leiden: Brill, 2009.

McNamara, Martin. *Targum and Testament: Aramaic Paraphrases of the Hebrew Bible; A Light on the New Testament*. Grand Rapids: Eerdmans, 1972.

———. *Targum Neofiti 1: Genesis*. The Aramaic Bible 1A. Edinburgh: T&T Clark, 1992.

McNamara, Martin, and Michael Maher. *Targum Neofiti 1: Exodus; Targum Pseudo-Jonathan: Exodus*. The Aramaic Bible 2. Edinburgh: T&T Clark, 1994.

McWhirter, Jocelyn. *The Bridegroom Messiah and the People of God: Marriage in the Fourth Gospel*. SNTSMS 138. Cambridge: Cambridge University Press, 2006.

———. "Messianic Exegesis in the Fourth Gospel." In *Reading the Gospel of John's Christology as Jewish Messianism: Royal, Prophetic, and Divine Messiahs*, edited by Benjamin Reynolds and Gabriele Boccaccini. AJEC 106. Leiden: Brill, 2018.

Meeks, Wayne A. *The Prophet-King: Moses Traditions and the Johannine Christology*. NovTSup 14. Leiden: Brill, 1967.

Meier, John P. *A Marginal Jew: Rethinking the Historical Jesus*. Vol. 2: *Mentor, Message, and Miracles*. ABRL. New York: Doubleday, 1994.

Melcher, Sarah J., Mikeal C. Parsons, and Amos Yong, eds. *The Bible and Disability: A Commentary*, Studies in Religion, Theology and Disability. Waco, TX: Baylor University Press, 2017.

Menken, Maarten J. J. *Old Testament Quotations in the Fourth Gospel: Studies in Textual Form*. CBET 15. Kampen: Kok Pharos, 1996.

Méroz, Christianne. *Three Women of Hope: Miriam, Hannah, Huldah*. Translated by Dennis Wienk. Eugene, OR: Wipf and Stock, 2014.

Metzger, Bruce M. *A Textual Commentary on the Greek New Testament: A Companion Volume to the United Bible Societies' Greek New Testament*. 4th rev. ed. London: United Bible Societies, 1994.

Meyer, Paul. "'The Father': The Presentation of God in the Fourth Gospel." In *Exploring the Gospel of John: In Honour of D. Moody Smith*, edited by R. Alan Culpepper and C. C. Black, 255–73. Louisville: Westminster John Knox, 1996.

Meyers, Carol L. "Everyday Life: Women in the Period of the Hebrew Bible." In *The Women's Bible Commentary*, edited by Carol A. Newsom and Sharon H. Ringe, 244–51. Louisville: Westminster John Knox, 1992.

———. "Material Remains and Social Relations: Women's Culture in Agrarian Households of the Iron Age." In *Symbiosis, Symbolism, and the Power of the Past: Canaan, Ancient Israel, and Their Neighbors from the Late Bronze Age through Roman Palaestina*, edited by William G. Dever and Seymour Gitin, 425–44. Winona Lake, IN: Eisenbrauns, 2003.

———. "Was Ancient Israel a Patriarchal Society?" *JBL* 133 (2014): 8–27.

Michaud, Jean-Paul. "Le signe de Cana dans son contexte johannique." *LTP* 18 (1962): 239–85.

Millgram, Abraham Ezra. *The Sabbath Anthology* [in English]. JPS Holiday Anthologies. Philadelphia: Jewish Publication Society, 2018.

Mitchell, David, and Sharon Snyder. " 'Jesus Thrown Everything Off Balance': Disability and Redemption in Biblical Literature." In *This Abled Body: Rethinking Disabilities in Biblical Studies*, edited by Hector Avalos, Sarah J. Melcher, and Jeremy Schipper. SemeiaSt 55. Atlanta: SBL, 2007.

Moloney, Francis J. *Belief in the Word: Reading John 1–4*. Minneapolis: Fortress, 1993.

———. "From Cana to Cana (Jn. 2:1–4:54) and the Fourth Evangelist's Concept of Correct (and Incorrect) Faith." *Salesianum* 40 (1978): 817–43.

———. "The Johannine Son of God." *Salesianum* 38 (1976): 71–86.

———. *The Johannine Son of Man*. 2nd rev. ed. Biblioteca di Scienze Religiose 14. Rome: LAS, 1978.

———. "The Johannine Son of Man Revisited." In *Theology and Christology in the Fourth Gospel*, edited by Gilbert Van Belle, Jan G. van der Watt, and P. Maritz, 177–202. BETL 184. Leuven: Peeters, 2005.

———. *John*. SP 4. Collegeville, MN: Liturgical Press, 1998.

———. "Narrative and Discourse at the Feast of Tabernacles." In *Word, Theology and Community in John*, edited by John Painter, R. Alan Culpepper, and Fernando F. Segovia, 154–72. St. Louis: Chalice, 2002.

———. "The *Parables of Enoch* and the Johannine Son of Man." In *Parables of Enoch: A Paradigm Shift*, edited by Darrell L. Bock and James H. Charlesworth, 269–93. JCTCRS 11. London: Bloomsbury, 2013.

———. *Signs and Shadows: Reading John 5–12*. Minneapolis: Fortress, 1996.

———. "When Is John Talking about Sacraments?" *ABR* 30 (1982): 10–33.

Montefiore, C. G., and H. Loewe. *A Rabbinic Anthology*. New York: Schocken Books, 1974.

Moore, George F. *Judaism in the First Centuries of the Christian Era: The Age of the Tannaim*. 3 vols. Cambridge, MA: Harvard University Press, 1927–1930.

Morris, Leon. *The Gospel according to John*. Rev. ed. NICNT. Grand Rapids: Eerdmans, 1995.

Motyer, Stephen. "Bridging the Gap: How Might the Fourth Gospel Help Us Cope with the Legacy of Christianity's Exclusive Claim over against Judaism?" In *The Gospel of John and Christian Theology*, edited by Richard Bauckham and Carl Mosser, 143–67. Grand Rapids: Eerdmans, 2008.

Murphy-O'Connor, Jerome. *The Holy Land: An Oxford Archaeological Guide from Earliest Times to 1700*. 5th ed. Oxford: Oxford University Press, 2008.

Mussner, Franz. *Die johanneische Sehweise und die Frage nach dem historischen Jesus*. QD 28. Freiburg: Herder, 1965.

Neusner, Jacob. *The Classics of Judaism: A Textbook and Reader*. Louisville: Westminster John Knox, 1995.

———. "Judaism in a Time of Crisis: Four Responses to the Destruction of the Second Temple." *Judaism* 21 (1972): 313–27.

———. "Money-Changers in the Temple: The Mishnah's Explanation." *NTS* 35 (1989): 287–90.

Neyrey, Jerome H. "Jacob Traditions and the Interpretation of John 4:10-26." *CBQ* 41 (1979): 419–37.

———. "What's Wrong with This Picture? John 4, Cultural Stereotypes of Women, and Public and Private Space." In *A Feminist Companion to John*, vol. 1, edited by Amy-Jill Levine with Marianne Blickenstaff, 98–125. FCNTECW 4. London: Sheffield Academic, 2003.

Nicklas, Tobias. " 'Food of Angels' (Wis 16:20)." In *Studies in the Book of Wisdom*, edited by Géza G. Xeravits and J. Zsengéller, 83–100. JSJS 14. Boston: Brill, 2010.

Nicol, Willem. *The Semeia in the Fourth Gospel: Tradition and Redaction*. NovTSup 32. Leiden: Brill, 1972.

Niditch, Susan. "Genesis." In *Women's Bible Commentary: Expanded Edition with Apocrypha*, edited by Carol A. Newsom and Sharon H. Ringe, 13–29. Louisville: Westminster John Knox, 1998.

Nodet, Étienne. "La Dédicace, les Maccabées et le Messie." *RB* 93 (1986): 321–75.

Norris, Richard A., Jr. *Gregory of Nyssa: Homilies on the Song of Songs; Translated with Introduction and Notes*. WGRW. Atlanta: SBL, 2013.

Nunn, Henry P. *A Short Syntax of New Testament Greek*. Cambridge: Cambridge University Press, 1920.

Nye-Knutson, Alena. "Hidden Bread and Revealed Word: Manna Traditions in Targums Neophyti 1 and Ps-Jonathan." In *Israel in the Wilderness: Interpretations of the Biblical Narratives in Jewish and Christian Traditions*, edited by Kenneth E. Pomykala, 201–25. TBN 10. Leiden: Brill, 2008.

Obermann, Andreas. *Die christologische Erfüllung der Schrift im Johannesevangelium.* WUNT 83. Tübingen: Mohr Siebeck, 1996.

O'Brien, Julia M., ed. *The Oxford Encyclopedia of the Bible and Gender Studies.* Vol. 1. Oxford: Oxford University Press, 2014.

O'Day, Gail R. "John." In *The Gospel of Luke; the Gospel of John*, edited by R. Alan Culpepper and Gail R. O'Day, 491–865. NIB 9. Nashville: Abingdon, 1995.

———. "John." In *Women's Bible Commentary*, edited by Carol A. Newsom and Sharon H. Ringe, 293–304. Rev. and exp. ed. Louisville: Westminster John Knox, 1998.

———. "John." In *Women's Bible Commentary: Revised and Updated*, edited by Carol A. Newsom, Sharon H. Ringe, and Jacqueline E. Lapsley, 517–30. 3rd ed. Louisville: Westminster John Knox, 2012.

Oepke, Albrecht. "Divine Sonship." *TDNT* 5 (1967): 652–54.

Okure, Teresa. *The Johannine Approach to Mission: A Contextual Study of John 4:1-42.* WUNT 2, Reihe 32. Tübingen: Mohr Siebeck, 1988.

O'Leary, Peter. *Thick and Dazzling Darkness: Religious Poetry in a Secular Age.* New York: Columbia University Press, 2017.

Olyan, Saul M. " 'Anyone Blind or Lame Shall Not Enter the House': On the Interpretation of Second Samuel 5:8b." *CBQ* 60 (1998): 218–27.

Osborne, Kenan. *Priesthood: A History of Ordained Ministry in the Roman Catholic Church*. Mahwah, NJ: Paulist Press, 1988.

Paasche-Orlow, Sara. "Tetzaveh: Finding Our Home in the Temple and the Temple in Our Home." In *The Women's Torah Commentary: New Insights from Women Rabbis on the 54 Weekly Torah Portions*, edited by Elyse Goldstein, 160–63. Woodstock, VT: Jewish Lights, 2000.

Painter, John. "Tradition, History and Interpretation in John 10." In *The Shepherd Discourse of John 10 and Its Context*, edited by Johannes Beutler and Robert Fortna, 53–74. SNTSMS 67. Cambridge: Cambridge University Press, 1991.

Pancaro, Severino. *The Law in the Fourth Gospel: The Torah and the Gospel, Moses and Jesus, Judaism and Christianity according to John*. NovTSup 42. Leiden: Brill, 1975.

Park, In-Hee. "Women and Q: Metonymy of the *Basileia* of God." *JFSR* 35 (2019): 41–54.

Parker, David C. *Manuscripts, Texts, Theology: Collected Papers 1977–2007* [in English]. Berlin: de Gruyter, 2009.

Passaro, Angela. "The Serpent and the Manna or the Saving Word: Exegesis of Wis 16." In *Deuterocanonical and Cognate Literature Yearbook 2005: The Book of Wisdom in Modern Research*, edited by Angelo Passaro and Giuseppe Bellia, 179–93. Berlin: de Gruyter, 2005.

Peacore, Linda D. *The Role of Women's Experience in Feminist Theologies of Atonement*. PrTMS 131. Eugene, OR: Pickwick, 2010.

Perkins, Pheme. *Gnosticism and the New Testament*. Minneapolis: Fortress, 1993.

Perrin, Andrew B. "From Qumran to Nazareth: Reflections on Jesus' Identity as Messiah in Light of Pre-Christian Messianic Texts among the Dead Sea Scrolls." *RelStTh* 27 (2008): 213–30.

Phillips, Peter. "The Adulterous Woman: Nameless, Partnerless, Defenseless." In *Character Studies in the Fourth Gospel: Narrative Approaches to Seventy Figures in John*, edited by Steven A. Hunt, D. Francois Tolmie, and Ruben Zimmermann, 407–20. WUNT 314. Tübingen: Mohr Siebeck, 2013.

Philo. "De Fuga et Inventione." In *Philo with an English Translation*, edited by F. H. Colson and G. H. Whitaker. London: William Heinemann, 1958.

Plaskow, Judith. "Standing again at Sinai: Jewish Memory from a Feminist Perspective." *Tikkum* 2 (1986): 28–34.

———. *Standing again at Sinai: Judaism from a Feminist Perspective*. New York: HarperCollins, 1990.

Poe, Gary R. "Light to Darkness: From Gnosis to Agape in the Apophatic Imagery of Gregory of Nyssa." *Baptist History and Heritage* 53 (2018): 57–67.

Pollard, T. E. "The Father-Son and God-Believer Relationships according to St John: A Brief Study of John's Use of Prepositions." In *L'Évangile de Jean: Sources, rédaction, théologie*, edited by Marinus de Jonge, 363–69. BETL 44. Gembloux: Duculot, 1977.

Preisker, Herbert. "μαίνομαι." *TDNT* 4 (1967): 360–61.

Redman, Judith C. S. "Eyewitness Testimony and the Characters in the Fourth Gospel." In *Characters and Characterization in the Gospel of John*, edited by Christopher W. Skinner and Mark Goodacre. LNTS 461. London: Bloomsbury, 2013.

Reese, James M. *The Book of Wisdom, Song of Songs*. OTM 20. Wilmington, DE: Michael Glazier, 1983.

Reicke, Bo. "πρός." *TNDT* 6 (1968): 720–25.

Reid, Barbara E. "Birthed from the Side of Jesus (John 19:34)." In *Finding a Woman's Place: Essays in Honor of Carolyn Osiek, R.S.C.J.*, edited by David L. Balch and Jason T. Lamoreaux, 191–214. Eugene, OR: Pickwick, 2011.

———. "John 7:37-39." *Int* 63 (2009): 394–96.

———. *Taking up the Cross: New Testament Interpretations through Latina and Feminist Eyes*. Minneapolis: Augsburg, 2007.

———. *Wisdom's Feast: An Invitation to Feminist Interpretation of the Scriptures*. Grand Rapids: Eerdmans, 2016.

Reid, Barbara E., and Shelly Matthews. *Luke 1–9*. WCS 43A. Collegeville, MN: Liturgical Press, 2021.

Reinhartz, Adele. *Befriending the Beloved Disciple: A Jewish Reading of the Gospel of John*. New York: Continuum, 2001.

———. "The 'Bride' in John 3:29: A Feminist Perspective." In *The Lost Coin: Parables of Women, Work and Wisdom*, edited by Mary Ann Beavis, 230–41. BibSem 86. London: Sheffield Academic, 2002.

———. *Cast Out of the Covenant: Jews and Anti-Judaism in the Gospel of John*. Lanham, MD: Lexington Books 2018.

———. "From Narrative to History: The Resurrection of Mary and Martha." In *A Feminist Companion to the Hebrew Bible in the New Testament*, edited by Athalya Brenner, 197–224. Sheffield: Sheffield Academic, 1996.

———. "The Gospel of John." In *Searching the Scriptures*, vol. 2: *A Feminist Commentary*, edited by Elisabeth Schüssler Fiorenza, 561–600. New York: Crossroad, 1994.

———. "'Jews' and Jews in the Fourth Gospel." In *Anti-Judaism and the Fourth Gospel*, edited by Reimund Bieringer, Didier Pollefeyt, and Frederique Vandecasteele-Vanneuville, 213–27. Louisville: Westminster John Knox, 2001.

———. "A Nice Jewish Girl Reads the Gospel of John." *Semeia* 77 (1997): 177–93.

———. "Story and History: John, Judaism, and the Historical Imagination." In *John and Judaism: A Contested Relationship in Context*, edited by R. Alan Culpepper and Paul N. Anderson, 113–26. RBS 87. Atlanta: SBL, 2017.

———. *"Why Ask My Name?" Anonymity and Identity in Biblical Narrative*. New York: Oxford University Press, 1998.

———. "Women in the Johannine Community: An Exercise in Historical Imagination." In *A Feminist Companion to John*, vol. 2, edited by Amy-Jill Levine with Marianne Blickenstaff, 14–33. FCNTECW 5. London: Sheffield Academic, 2003.

————. *The Word in the World: The Cosmological Tale in the Fourth Gospel*. SBLMS 45. Atlanta: Scholars Press, 1992.

Reiss, Moshe. "Miriam Rediscovered." *JBQ* 38 (2010): 183–90.

Rengstorf, Karl Heinrich, and Friedrich Büchsel. "γεννάω." *TDNT* 1 (1964): 665–75.

————. "Ἑπτά, Ἑπτάκις, Ἑπτακισχίλιοι, Ἕβδομος, Ἑβδομήκοντα, Ἑβδομηκοντάκις." *TDNT* 2 (1964): 627–35.

Ricoeur, Paul. *Interpretation Theory: Discourse and the Surplus of Meaning*. Fort Worth: Texas Christian University Press, 1976.

————. *The Symbolism of Evil*. Translated by Emerson Buchanan. Boston: Beacon, 1967.

Ringe, Sharon H. "An Approach to a Critical, Feminist, Theological Reading of the Bible." In *A Feminist Companion to Reading the Bible: Approaches, Methods and Strategies*, edited by Athalya Brenner and Carole Fontaine, 156–63. Sheffield: Sheffield Academic, 1997.

————. *Wisdom's Friends: Community and Christology in the Fourth Gospel*. Louisville: Westminster John Knox, 1999.

Rissi, Mathias. "κρίμα." *EDNT* 2 (1981): 317–18.

Ronning, John. *The Jewish Targums and John's Logos Theology*. Grand Rapids: Baker Academic, 2010.

Rosenberg, Stephen G. "The Jewish Temple at Elephantine." *NEA* 67 (2004): 4–13.

————. "Two Jewish Temples in Antiquity in Egypt." *BAIAS* 19–20 (2001–2002): 182–84.

Roth, Cecil. "The Historical Implications of the Jewish Coinage of the First Revolt." *IEJ* 12 (1962): 33–46.

Rowe, Eric, and Jerome H. Neyrey. "Christ and Time Part Three: 'Telling Time' in the Fourth Gospel." *BTB* 402 (2010): 79–92.

Rubenstein, Jeffrey. *The History of Sukkot in the Second Temple and Rabbinic Periods*. BJS. Atlanta: Scholars Press, 1995.

————. "Sukkot, Eschatology and Zechariah 14." *RB* 103 (1996): 161–95.

Ruether, Rosemary Radford. "The Future of Feminist Theology in the Academy." *JAAR* 53 (1985): 703–13.

Rushton, Kathleen P. "The (Pro)creative Parables of Labour and Childbirth (John 3:1-10 and 16:21-22)." In *The Lost Coin: Parables of Women, Work, and Wisdom*, edited by Mary Ann Beavis, 206–29. BibSem 86. Sheffield: Sheffield Academic, 2002.

Russell, Letty M. *Church in the Round: Feminist Interpretation of the Church*. Louisville: Westminster John Knox, 1993.

Russell, Letty M., and J. Shannon Clarkson. *Dictionary of Feminist Theologies*. Louisville: Westminster John Knox, 1996.

Sanders, Ed P. *Jesus and Judaism*. Philadelphia: Fortress, 1985.

————, ed. *Jewish and Christian Self-Definition: The Shaping of Christianity in the Second and Third Centuries*. Vol. 1. London: SCM, 1980.

Schiffman, Lawrence H. "Pharisees." In *Jewish Annotated New Testament*, edited by Amy-Jill Levine and Marc Zvi Brettler, 619–22. 2nd ed. Oxford: Oxford University Press, 2017.

Schmidt, Karl L. "Βασιλικός." *TDNT* 1 (1964): 591–93.

Schnackenburg, Rudolph. *The Gospel according to St John*. Translated by K. Smyth et al. HTCNT. 3 vols. London: Burns & Oates, 1968–1982.

Schneiders, Sandra M. *Beyond Patching: Faith and Feminism in the Catholic Church*. New York: Paulist Press, 1990.

———. "Feminist Ideology Criticism and Biblical Hermeneutics." *BTB* 19 (1989): 3–10.

———. "The Lamb of God and the Forgiveness of Sin(s) in the Fourth Gospel." *CBQ* 73 (2011): 1–29.

———. "The Resurrection (of the Body) in the Fourth Gospel: A Key to Johannine Spirituality." In *Life in Abundance: Studies of John's Gospel in Tribute to Raymond E. Brown*, edited by John R. Donahue, 168–98. Collegeville, MN: Liturgical Press, 2005.

———. *The Revelatory Text: Interpreting the New Testament as Sacred Scripture*. 2nd ed. Collegeville, MN: Liturgical Press, 1999.

———. "Scripture and Spirituality." In *Christian Spirituality: Origins to the Twelfth Century*, edited by Bernard McGinn and John Meyendorff. World Spirituality: An Encyclopedic History of the Religious Quest. New York: Crossroad, 1985.

———. "Symbolism and the Sacramental Principle in the Fourth Gospel." In *Segni e sacramenti nel vangelo di Giovanni*, 221–35. Rome: Editrice Anselmiana, 1977.

———. "The Word in the World." *Pacifica* 23 (2010): 247–66.

———. *Written That You May Believe: Encountering Jesus in the Fourth Gospel*. Rev. and exp. ed. New York: Crossroad, 2003.

Schrenk, Gottlob. "Γράφω." *TDNT* 1 (1964): 742–73.

Schuchard, Bruce G. *Scripture within Scripture: The Interrelationship of Form and Function in the Explicit Old Testament Citations in the Gospel of John*. SBLDS 133. Atlanta: Scholars Press, 1992.

Schuel, Andreas. "Sabbath." *NIDB* 5 (2009): 3–10.

Schüssler Fiorenza, Elisabeth. "Between Movement and Academy: Feminist Biblical Studies in the Twentieth Century." In *Feminist Biblical Studies in the Twentieth Century: Scholarship and Movement; The Contemporary Period*, edited by Elisabeth Schüssler Fiorenza, 1–17. Bible and Women: An Encyclopedia of Exegesis and Cultural History 9.1. Atlanta: SBL, 2014.

———, ed. *Feminist Biblical Studies in the Twentieth Century: Scholarship and Movement; The Contemporary Period*. Bible and Women: An Encyclopedia of Exegesis and Cultural History 9.1. Atlanta: SBL, 2014.

———. *In Memory of Her: A Feminist Theological Reconstruction of Christian Origins*. New York: Crossroad, 1983.

————. *Jesus: Miriam's Child, Sophia's Prophet; Critical Issues in Feminist Christology.* 2nd ed. London: Bloomsbury T&T Clark, 2015.

————. *Wisdom Ways: Introducing Feminist Biblical Interpretation.* Maryknoll, NY: Orbis Books, 2005.

Schwartz, Joshua. "Jubilees, Bethel and the Temple of Jacob." *HUCA* 56 (1985): 63–85.

Schweizer, Eduard, and Friedrich Baumgärtel. "Σάρξ, Σαρκικός, Σάρκινος." *TDNT* 7 (1971): 98–151.

Scott, J. Julius, Jr. *Jewish Backgrounds of the New Testament.* Grand Rapids: Baker Books, 1995.

Scott, Martin. *Sophia and the Johannine Jesus.* JSNTSup 71. Sheffield: JSOT Press, 1992.

Segovia, Fernando F. *The Farewell of the Word: The Johannine Call to Abide.* Minneapolis: Fortress, 1991.

————, ed. *What Is John?* Vol. 1: *Readers and Readings of the Fourth Gospel.* SBLSymS 3. Atlanta: Scholars Press, 1996.

————, ed. *What Is John?* Vol. 2: *Literary and Social Readings of the Fourth Gospel.* SBLSymS 7. Atlanta: Scholars Press, 1998.

Setzer, Claudia. *Jewish Responses to Early Christians: History and Polemic, 30–150 C.E.* Minneapolis: Fortress, 1994.

Sheridan, Ruth. "Issues in the Translation of οἱ Ἰουδαῖοι in the Fourth Gospel." *JBL* 132 (2013): 671–95.

————. *Retelling Scripture: 'The Jews' and the Scriptural Citations in John 1:19–12:15.* BibInt 110. Leiden: Brill, 2012.

Skinner, Christopher W., ed. *Characters and Characterization in the Gospel of John.* LNTS 461. London: Bloomsbury, 2013.

Smit, Peter-Ben. "Cana-to-Cana or Galilee-to-Galilee: A Note on the Structure of the Gospel of John." *ZNW* 98 (2007): 143–49.

Smith, Yancy Warren. "Hippolytus' Commentary on the Song of Songs in Social and Critical Context." Thesis, Abilene Christian University, 2009. https://repository.tcu.edu/bitstream/handle/116099117/4192/SmithY.pdf?sequence=1.

Sperling, S. David. "Blood." *ABD* 1 (1992): 761–63.

Stapfer, Edmond. *Palestine in the Time of Christ.* Translated by A. H. Holmden. New York: Armstrong and Son, 1885.

Steegen, Martijn. "To Worship the Johannine 'Son of Man': John 9:38 as Refocusing on the Father." *Bib* 91 (2010): 534–54.

Stovell, Beth M. *Mapping Metaphorical Discourse in the Fourth Gospel: John's Eternal King.* LBS 5. Leiden: Brill, 2012.

Strange, James F. "Beth-Zatha." *ABD* 1 (1992): 700–701.

Stuckenbruck, Loren T. " 'Protect Them from the Evil One' (John 17:15): Light from the Dead Sea Scrolls." In *John, Qumran, and the Dead Sea Scrolls: Sixty Years of Discovery and Debate*, edited by Mary L. Coloe and Tom Thatcher. EJL 32. Atlanta: SBL, 2011.

Tannen, Deborah. *Gender and Discourse.* New York: Oxford University Press, 1996.

Thatcher, Tom, and Stephen D. Moore, eds. *Anatomies of Narrative Criticism: The Past, Present, and Futures of the Fourth Gospel as Literature.* SBLRBS 55. Atlanta: SBL, 2008.

"Theophylacti." In *Patrologiæ cursus completus,* edited by Jacques-Paul Migne, 1864–. http://books.google.com/books?id=mL7UAAAAMAAJ.

Thompson, Marianne Meye. *The God of the Gospel of John.* Grand Rapids: Eerdmans, 2001.

———. *John: A Commentary.* NTL. Louisville: Westminster John Knox, 2015.

Toensing, Holly J. "Divine Intervention or Divine Intrusion? Jesus and the Adulteress in John's Gospel." In *A Feminist Companion to John*, vol. 1, edited by Amy-Jill Levine with Marianne Blickenstaff, 159–72. FCNTECW 4. London: Sheffield Academic, 2003.

Trigg, Joseph W. *Origen.* Edited by Carol Harrison. ECF. New York: Routledge, 1998.

Ulfgard, Håkan. *Feast and Future: Revelation 7:9-17 and the Feast of Tabernacles.* Stockholm: Almqvist & Wiksell, 1989.

UNICEF. "This Girl Spends Eight Hours a Day Doing Something that Takes Us Seconds." https://www.unicef.org.au/blog/stories/november-2016/this -girl-spends-eight-hours-a-day-doing-something.

Unterman, A. "Shekinah." *Encyclopedia Judaica* 14 (1971): 1350–52.

van Belle, Gilbert. "The Faith of the Galileans: The Parenthesis in Jn 4,44." *ETL* 74 (1998): 27–44.

vanderKam, James C. "Dedication, Feast of." *ABD* 2 (1992): 123.

———. "Weeks, Festival of." *ABD* 6 (1992): 895–97.

van der Watt, Jan G. "The Gospel of John's Perception of Ethical Behaviour." *In die Skriflig* 45 (2011): 431–47.

van Selms, A. "The Best Man and Bride: From Sumer to St. John." *JNES* 9 (1950): 65–70.

Vermes, Géza A. "The Son of Man Debate Revisited (1960–2012)." In *Parables of Enoch: A Paradigm Shift*, edited by Darrell L. Bock and James H. Charlesworth, 3–17. JCTCRS 11. London: Bloomsbury T&T Clark, 2013.

Visotsky, Burton L. "Methodological Considerations on the Study of John's Interaction with First-Century Judaism." In *Life in Abundance: Studies of John's Gospel in Tribute to Raymond E. Brown*, edited by John R. Donahue, 91–107. Collegeville, MN: Liturgical Press, 2005.

von Rad, Gerhard. *Wisdom in Israel.* London: SCM, 1972.

von Rad, Gerhard, and Gerhard Kittel. "δόξα." *TDNT* 2 (1964): 233–55.

von Wahlde, Urban C. "He Has Given to the Son to Have Life in Himself (John 5,26)." *Bib* 85 (2004): 409–12.

———. "The Johannine Jews: A Critical Survey." *NTS* 28 (1982): 33–60.

Walker, Norman. "The Reckoning of Hours in the Fourth Gospel." *NovT* 41 (1960): 69–73.

Wallace, Daniel B. *Greek Grammar beyond the Basics: An Exegetical Syntax of the New Testament.* Grand Rapids: Zondervan, 1996.

Westcott, Brooke Foss. *The Gospel according to St John: With Introduction and Notes.* London: John Murray, 1890.

Wheaton, Gerry. *The Role of Jewish Feasts in John's Gospel.* SNTSMS 162. Cambridge: Cambridge University Press, 2015.

Williams, Ritva H. "The Mother of Jesus at Cana: A Social-Science Interpretation of John 2:1-12." *CBQ* 59 (1997): 679–92.

Wilson, Stephen. *Related Strangers: Jews and Christians, 70–170 CE.* Minneapolis: Fortress, 1995.

Winstead, Melton B. "Capernaum." In *The Lexham Bible Dictionary,* edited by John D. Barry et al. Bellingham, WA: Lexham Press, 2016.

Winston, David. *The Wisdom of Solomon.* AB 43. New York: Doubleday, 1979.

Winter, Miriam Therese. *Out of the Depths: The Story of Ludmila Javorova Ordained Roman Catholic Priest.* New York: Crossroad, 2001.

Witherington, Ben, III. *John's Wisdom: A Commentary on the Fourth Gospel.* Louisville: Westminster John Knox, 1995.

———. "The Waters of Birth: John 3.5 and 1 John 5.6-8." *NTS* 35 (1989): 155–60.

Wrigley-Carr, Robyn. "Darkness and Light in Evelyn Underhill." *Journal of Spiritual Formation and Soul Care* 12 (2019): 135–51.

Yamaguchi, Satoko. "'I Am' Sayings and Women in Context." In *A Feminist Companion to John,* vol. 2, edited by Amy-Jill Levine with Marianne Blickenstaff, 34–63. FCNTECW 5. London: Sheffield Academic, 2003.

———. *Mary and Martha: Women in the World of Jesus.* Maryknoll, NY: Orbis Books, 2002.

Yee, Gale A. *Jewish Feasts and the Gospel of John.* Wilmington, DE: Michael Glazier, 1989.

Zimmermann, Ruben. "Are There Parables in John? It Is Time to Revisit the Question." *JSHJ* 9 (2011): 266.

———. "Imagery in John: Opening Up Paths into the Tangled Thicket of John's Figurative World." In *Imagery in the Gospel of John: Terms, Forms, Themes, and Theology of Johannine Figurative Language,* edited by Jörg Frey, Jan G. van der Watt, and Ruben Zimmermann, 1–43. WUNT 200. Tübingen: Mohr Siebeck, 2006.

———. "'The Jews': Unreliable Figures or Unreliable Narration?" In *Character Studies in the Fourth Gospel: Narrative Approaches to Seventy Figures in John,* edited by Steven A. Hunt, D. Francois Tolmie, and Ruben Zimmermann, 70–109. WUNT 314. Tübingen: Mohr Siebeck, 2013.

Zsengéller, Jozsef. "'The Taste of Paradise': Interpretation of Exodus and Manna in the Book of Wisdom." In *Studies in the Book of Wisdom,* edited by Géza G. Xeravits and J. Zsengéller, 197–216. JSJS 142. Boston: Brill, 2010.

Zumstein, Jean. *Kreative Erinnerung: Relecture und Auslegung im Johannesevangelium.* ATANT. Zürich: TVZ, 2004.

———. *L'Évangile selon Saint Jean (1–12).* CNT 4a 2nd ser. Genève: Labor et Fides, 2014.

Author

Mary L. Coloe, PBVM, is a professor of New Testament within the University of Divinity in Melbourne, Australia. She has published books, essays, and articles on John for academics and nonprofessionals, some of which are listed at http://marycoloe.org.au/homepage/. For her revised dissertation, *God Dwells with Us: Temple Symbolism in the Fourth Gospel* (Liturgical Press, 2001), she was awarded a large Australian Research Grant, resulting in *Dwelling in the Household of God: Johannine Ecclesiology and Spirituality* (Liturgical Press, 2007). Mary was appointed for six years to an international dialogue between the Catholic Church and the Church/Disciples of Christ and has been outspoken on the need for justice in relation to women's place in the Catholic Church.

Volume Editor

Mary Ann Beavis, editor of this volume, is professor emerita of religion and culture at St. Thomas More College in Saskatoon, Canada. She is the coauthor, with HyeRan Kim-Cragg, of two volumes in this Wisdom Commentary series, *Hebrews* (2015) and *1–2 Thessalonians* (2016), and has written *What Does the Bible Say? A Critical Conversation with Popular Culture in a Biblically Illiterate World* (Eugene, OR: Cascade, 2017), and *The First Christian Slave: Onesimus in Context* (Eugene, OR: Cascade, 2021). Her current research interest is in the area of slave religiosity in early Christianity.

Series Editor

Barbara E. Reid, general editor of the Wisdom Commentary series, is a Dominican Sister of Grand Rapids, Michigan. She is the president of Catholic Theological Union and the first woman to hold the position. She has been a member of the CTU faculty since 1988 and also served as vice president and academic dean from 2009 to 2018. She holds a PhD in biblical studies from The Catholic University of America and was also president of the Catholic Biblical Association in 2014–2015. Her most recent publications are *Luke 1–9* and *Luke 10–24*, coauthored with Shelly Matthews, volumes 43A and 43B in Wisdom Commentary series, *Wisdom's Feast: An Invitation to Feminist Interpretation of the Scriptures* (Eerdmans, 2016), and *Abiding Word: Sunday Reflections on Year A, B, C* (3 vols.; Liturgical Press, 2011, 2012, 2013).